The Emancipation of Writing

STUDIES ON THE HISTORY OF SOCIETY AND CULTURE

Victoria E. Bonnell and Lynn Hunt, Editors

The Emancipation of Writing

German Civil Society in the Making, 1790s–1820s

IAN F. MCNEELY

University of California Press

BERKELEY   LOS ANGELES   LONDON

University of California Press
Berkeley and Los Angeles, California

University of California Press, Ltd.
London, England

Library of Congress Cataloging-in-Publication Data

McNeely, Ian F., 1971–
  The emancipation of writing : German civil society in the making,
1790s–1820s / Ian F. McNeely.
      p.   cm.
  Includes bibliographical references and index.
  ISBN 0–520-23330-1 (Cloth : alk. paper)
    1. Bureaucracy—Germany—History.   2. Written Communication—
Germany—History.   3. Civil society—Germany—History.   I. Title.

JN3221 .M37 2002
300'.943'09033—dc21   2002002314

Manufactured in the United States of America
10 09 08 07 06 05 04 03
12 11 10 9 8 7 6 5 4 3

The paper used in this publication is both acid-free and totally chlorine-
free (TCF). It meets the minimum requirements of ANSI/NISO Z39.48–
1992 (R 1997) (Permanence of Paper). ⊚

To my parents, G. F. and Sharon McNeely,
and my wife, Lisa Wolverton

Contents

Illustrations

Acknowledgments

This book was begun at the University of Michigan, researched in Stuttgart, Germany, and completed at the Harvard Society of Fellows and in Eugene, Oregon. I have incurred many debts in each of these places. My dissertation committee—Kathleen Canning, Geoff Eley, Margaret Somers, Laura Downs, and Helmut Puff—helped to make Michigan a uniquely exciting place to study history. Thanks to Andy Donson, Jordan Shapiro, Kathy Pence, Barb Ryan, Carolyn Comiskey, Sharmila Basu, Andrew Goss, and Pax Bobrow, Ann Arbor also became a community and a true home. Mary Wheeler, as I'm sure she already knows, is in a class by herself. In Stuttgart, I benefited from the collegiality and friendship of Scott Beard, Andreas Gestrich, Aimee Burant, Meike Grund, Mark Remshardt, Berthold Heusel, Kriszta Molnar, and Martin Kienzle. David Sabean, Hans Medick, and Dieter Langewiesche graciously offered their expertise at critical stages during my research. In Cambridge, Lisa Wolverton, Kevin Bolan, Adina Astor, Bernard Bailyn, Diana Morse, Jeff Dolven, and Jacob Hacker were among those who helped me through the arduous process of reconceptualization and revision. David Luebke, Richard Biernacki, Lynn Hunt, and Juliane Brand, my editor, offered crucial advice in the home stretch, as did two readers for the University of California Press, one of them David Sabean. Lisa and Wendy stood by me during the happiest as well as the most difficult times, and for that I remain enormously grateful.

Sam Welker, my ninth-grade World Civilizations teacher, taught me that the study of history is a philosophical, not an antiquarian, pursuit.

Funding for this project was provided by a number of institutions, including the Department of History and the Rackham School of Graduate Studies at the University of Michigan, the Council for European Studies in New York, the German Academic Exchange Service (DAAD), and the Social xii / *Acknowledgments*

Science Research Council (SSRC). I would also like to recognize, for their unstinting professionalism, the archivists and librarians at the Hauptstaat-sarchiv and the Württembergische Landesbibliothek in Stuttgart, as well as the Staatsarchiv in Ludwigsburg.

An earlier version of Chapter 8 appeared as "The Intelligence Gazette (*Intelligenzblatt*) as a Road Map to Civil Society: Information Networks and Local Dynamism in Germany, 1770s–1840s," in *Paradoxes of Civil Society: New Perspectives on Modern German and British History*, ed. Frank Trentmann (New York: Berghahn Books, 1999), 135–56.

Introduction

German history has long centered on the state. In its various incarnations, the German state has acted as an instrument of totalitarianism, an agent of national unification, and an architect of civil war, religious reform, and social discipline. Often depicted as the source of ultimate oppression, sometimes viewed as an "organic" entity with a life and purpose of its own, and always acknowledged as a decisive player in European geopolitics, the state in many ways figures as the prime mover of German historical development. Scholars from Max Weber onward have recognized the centrality of bureaucracy to the state's power. A country where every official encounter is subjected to a stamped form or a sealed certificate, Germany is both renowned and despised for its bureaucratic political culture. Little concrete attention has been paid, however, to the importance of writing as the handmaiden of bureaucracy and thus the medium of Germany's most potent apparatus of authority. The sheer abundance of written formalities in daily life has often seemed to reduce German citizens to passive creatures of an administrative monolith. Yet, as this book will argue, the German state's reliance upon writing could just as easily undercut its domination and disperse its influence.

This book situates the production and power of official texts amidst the strategies and assumptions governing the use of writing in German society as a whole. I want people who read it to think differently about the exercise of power, through official writing, at the interface between state and citizenry. "Bureaucracy" must be disaggregated into the specific texts and practices of writing conferring authority on state officials. Writing must, at the same time, be viewed as a means for ordinary people to practice their citizenship. Citizenship is often conceptualized as an identity, as an amalgam of legal rights and cultural statuses defining a body of citizens in its relation to the state. However, this book treats citizenship as a practice, unearthing

1

numerous instances when individuals and groups manipulated official texts to assert power within and against the state.[1] Even in its official, bureaucratic form, writing was a plastic medium susceptible to many readings and appropriations by those who encountered it. To follow the trails of paper circulating between officials and citizens reveals the German state as a community of political participation, not an apparatus of domination, and thereby restores the German citizenry to the making of their own history.

Germany's famed bureaucratic culture must in fact be understood as a profoundly civic culture as well: interactions between state and citizen through official writing lay the basis for modern civil society. Civil society, the realm where citizens interact independently of the state, is the outcome of the historical transformation described in this book. In Germany from the 1790s through the 1820s, civil society emerged as the product of countless decisions, deliberate and unselfconscious, by citizens and officials alike, to inscribe a space of free association where ideas and information could be exchanged and citizens could gather without the state's interference. Changes in writing practice promoted and simultaneously reflected civil society's disengagement from the state. A longstanding set of behaviors and beliefs centered on writing and predicated on the identity of state and society gave way to one in which these realms were viewed as distinct. Such changes in ordinary citizens' lived experience of authority and freedom coincided with higher-level intellectual debates and political reforms staking out the relation between state and citizen for the modern era. Yet the theory of civil society developed by G. W. F. Hegel and others only imperfectly captured changes in practice occurring beneath the level of discourse.[2] Likewise, the "reforms from above" marking Germany's path into civil society developed in a complex (and underappreciated) dialectic with citizen action.[3] The subject of this book is the subterranean, tectonic shifts, rather than the philosophical and political distinctions that later recognized and institutionalized them. They liberated writing from its source of power in the state and gave it a new role founding the freedoms of civil society.

Civil society encompasses more than the public sphere, the disembodied realm where ideas are exchanged in print, and more than the voluntary association, the institutional setting where citizens physically congregate in clubs and other organizations.[4] Instead it represents their fusion, in sites where free thought and free action reinforce one another to form a political community outside the state. This book concretizes the links between thought and action by focusing on writing practice, and in particular by treating the composition and uses of official texts in everyday settings. This leads inevitably onto specific local terrains where officials and citizens put claims to the test over the interpretation of documents and the actions they authorized. Such a method ensures that questions of power, centered on contests over material resources, social reputations, ideologies of community, symbols of authority, and access to justice, are not sidelined. Civil society is too often identified as a realm of radical freedom from power: the liberal vision. This view of civil society derives from philosophers' attempts to ground liberty in a regime of property rights or other "natural" freedoms in a mythical, prehistorical state of nature conceptually prior to the state. Restoring the state to its properly historical role, as the institution that sets the frame for social freedoms, reveals civil society as the outcome of a long learning process: the product of lessons that citizens take away from their encounters with state officials and documents and apply independently to their own political practices.

This conception of civil society allows us to overcome one-sided assumptions about the relations between communication and citizenship, knowledge and power, writing and emancipation. Jürgen Habermas, the most prominent theoretician of the public sphere as a vehicle for citizenship, subscribes to an unrealistic ideal of power-free communication precisely because he fails to consider the exercise of compulsion and persuasion in concrete, corporeal settings. His later work tends increasingly toward a model of pristine critical reason radically divorced from other faculties of human action and experience.[5] Michel Foucault remedies this idealism by treating knowledge as power; his work is in fact suffused with applications of knowledge for the control of human bodies—in armies, prisons, medical clinics, and practices of sexuality. Yet this method threatens to dissolve individuals in all-powerful "discourses," treating their resistance as a residual, often bodily, reflex: it renders the intellect, with its power to question and to critique, effectively mute.[6] Neither theorist offers a convincing account of how citizenship emerges from the matrix of domination: Habermas brackets off power from the life of the mind, Foucault sees the mind as itself colonized by power. A focus on writing, by contrast, promises to restore some balance to the interaction of mind and power in social life. *Pace* Habermas, writing only achieved its potency in a web of social interests and struggles for influence; and *pace* Foucault, it did, nonetheless, facilitate genuinely emancipatory communication transcending the dialectic of domination and resistance.

If writing provides access to the cognitive underpinnings of civil society, geography puts us in touch with its physical embodiment. Civil society is grounded in particular places, in the affiliations and networks people form within certain spaces and with the land itself.[7] This is nowhere clearer than in the local community of residence, the sphere of daily, face-to-face inter-action out of which citizenship grows. The living room, the neighborhood, the pub, the guild hall, the market, the fields, the town square: all these forums, rich in negotiations over power, are where civil society first coa-lesces.[8] But this is by no means the only way civil society feeds upon "pres-ence" for its flourishing. The territorial state and its administrative subdivi-sions also provide ready-made arenas for civil society to take root, and official texts, in particular, envelop citizens in wider webs of contact as they trace circuits over the state's terrain. In these and other ways, civil society transcends the physical, personal community.[9] Texts facilitate this process by providing surrogates for absent persons, recording their actions, utter-ances, knowledge, and commitments. Through print media, letters, and com-mercial contacts, for example, they stitch webs of relationships and allow civil society to span ever larger, more cosmopolitan, physically dispersed communities. Increasing territorial reach is in fact the hallmark of civil soci-ety in the modern world.

Within the state, however, the geographic growth of social networks comes up against an institution defined by its claim on monopolies of power over expanses of territory. Within the state, too, cognitive blueprints for new forms of human interaction challenge the existing social order that it is the state's function to uphold.[10] When this occurs, vibrant practices of citi-zenship, once nourished in fruitful interaction with the state, begin to out-grow its tutelage. Citizens transpose associational practices learned within the state to a realm outside its influence, whereupon the relation between state and citizen becomes subject to political renegotiation. Official texts are the written, archival residues of this contingent moment, and as such bear compelling witness to the making of civil society.

．　．　．　．　．

This book is set in the southwestern German duchy of Württemberg on the cusp of the nineteenth century. It traces the emancipation of writing from the tutelage of powerful, manipulative scribes who acted as political opera-tors in the duchy's towns and villages. These scribes, or *Schreiber*, were a hybrid species of half-private, half-official notaries public. On account of their intermediary position, they facilitated communication and exchange between government and citizenry. For the same reason, however, they straddled a fault line between state and civil society and experienced the dis-entanglement of the two especially acutely. Before the 1800s, the scribes presided over a civic culture binding citizens to the state, and to each other, through elaborate textual formalities. As certain scribes became enamored of the French Revolution in the late 1790s, they parlayed this underlying civic involvement into a truly political activism, manipulating the machinery of administrative communication and stretching the interpretation of official documents to its absolute limit. The scribes fell from power, though, when Napoleon's invasions led to the creation of a larger and more cosmopolitan state in Württemberg, unleashing a parliamentary and governmental campaign to strip them of their hegemony. Robbed of their mediating role, the scribes saw their tutelage replaced by an informational, entrepreneurial print culture designed to enlighten rather than patronize the citizenry. With these changes came a recognizably modern traffic in texts, stitching together the networks of communication and association undergirding civil society.

To weave the scribes' story together with that of civil society's formation, I have devised four concepts that frame the various tableaux narrated in the pages below within overarching historical dynamics. They are meant to highlight the deeper changes in social and cognitive practice that emerge from the details of the scribes' encounters with local citizens. The concepts are *formality, collegiality, sociography,* and *encyclopedism.* In various ways they concretize this book's focus on official writing. Methodologically, they accentuate practice over discourse, formative routines over formed institutions, strategies of communication over the materiality of the text, the plasticity of handwriting over the reification of print, and the archival record over published sources.[11]

Formality is the principal attribute of official texts: it codifies interpersonal bonds, and particularly relationships of power, by transcribing them onto the accessible, semipermanent form of a written page. Formality entails both a particular style of language and a way of arranging the layout of a text visually. Formal writing has a distinctly stilted sound, look, and feel; it invariably relies on time-tested, culturally specific conventions of expression standing behind and outside its author. By invoking a more impersonal authority in this way, formality helps to promote social trust and accountability. Formality is thus the aspect of citizenship most fully developed in situations where face-to-face agreement is not practicable and more stylized interactions are necessary to streamline and routinize political negotiation.[12] Such situations may be marked by physical separation, temporal distance (fading collective memory), anonymity and large scale, a multiplicity of participants, the absence of an existing sense of shared identity or community among participants, and potential distrust generated by opposing interests. Accommodating the complexity of developed societies is formality's virtue.

Formality can be mediated by a wide variety of texts. Examples discussed in this book include: contracts made between parents and children, offering property in exchange for care in old age; parliamentary mandates constraining delegates to parrot their constituents' opinions; and constitutional fragments reminding officials and citizens of ancient promises and obligations. By recording oral agreements, spelling out mutual obligations, providing scripts for conflict management, and serving as an official memory to which social actors have recourse in case of doubt or contestation, formality grounds an expectation of consistency and fairness in dealings with others, often founding trust and civic stability across generations. When they emanate from the state, such formalities connote not only fairness but justice, insofar as they then possess a legal and official character. Deciding which texts count as "official" and which do not, however, was a matter open to debate in those cases, frequent in this book, when citizens themselves improvised written formalities to regulate their own, private interactions. Citizens' insistence on formality frequently degenerated into fetish, the manifestation of rampant suspicion bred in times of civic disorder. Thus, while formality undergirds civic order, it is equally dependent on it for its functioning. In the best case, however, written formalities promote the smooth flow of social interaction, explicitly committing to paper those understandings that might be all too fluid and transient in informal oral discourse.

Collegiality, as a concept, sheds light on this gray area between informal oral discourse and formal written communication. It counts among the archetypical practices of citizenship, in which groups of people assemble to discuss matters of common interest, as in the classic *polis* or any other face-to-face community—although it need not occur in person. Collegiality refers to the sharing of perspectives for deliberation, whether orally or in writing. In this book, collegiality occurs in the town halls where scribes conferred with city councillors; in the bureaucratic chancelleries, where ministers and other officials met to draft written policies; in the Enlightenment public sphere, where ideas were discussed in print; and in the informal correspondence networks scribes used to share routine administrative information, as well as political news and ideological opinions. By bringing like-minded individuals together in forums such as these, collegiality becomes the crucial mediator of political, class, ideological, professional, and regional identities—an insight somewhat at odds with the current scholarly tendency to view the genesis of identity primarily in terms of difference, "othering," and hostility.

As a facilitator of common identities, collegiality also promotes political mobilization, both of formal corporative bodies (like city councils or bureaucratic agencies) and of more vaguely defined parties of opinion (in small-town factions or in the cosmopolitan public sphere). Collegiality may thus take place either within highly structured social environments, marked by rigid social or political roles and formal etiquette and rules of order; or spontaneously among social actors, so long as they have a common cultural basis for understanding and discussing the society around them. The resiliency of a civic culture can be measured by the number of interlocking and overlapping networks of collegiality that ramify through different levels and subdivisions of society. The practice of writing broadens these networks, even though it simultaneously renders them more abstract, impersonal, and sometimes unwieldy. Fortunately, writing also harbors the potential for reestablishing the trust that becomes attenuated in the absence of face-to-face contact.

The practice of *sociography* fulfills the craving for regularity and predictability in social interactions and the desire for a "map" of the social world. It is a means by which people actively come to know and understand the social networks in which they participate. Such knowledge informs both their conscious political logics and their unreflective background assumptions, though only the conscious rendering of social facts and observations in abstract written form counts as sociography. Sociography is intimately bound with a sense of place—a locality, a region, a nation—which furnishes the physical boundaries of a society, and therefore the realm in which people, places, and things become legible. Spatially, this book moves back and forth through concentric circles of locality, county, region, state, nation, and even continent, continually widening and constricting the sphere of social interaction in which sociography occurs. Each of these openings compounds the difficulties in achieving legibility while at the same time raising fascinating new possibilities and challenges for characterizing the social order—in writing—in order to understand and thus partially control it.

Two disparate examples suffice here to illustrate sociography: the "protocolled" report, a verbatim transcription of witness testimony in juridical contexts, allowing outside investigators to elicit truth from an otherwise closed community; and the statistical almanac, which attempts to survey comprehensively the physical and social topography of a given community. Here we see that sociography may be practiced through painstakingly precise reconstruction of social bonds: promises, exchanges, grudges, winks and nods, and other artifacts of face-to-face socialization. Or it may be developed through more panoramic but no less systematic processes of mapping, cataloging, and analysis. These latter, more macrosociological methods enhance the legibility of civil society, a social order in which citizenship must be practiced in conditions of increasing anonymity as social behaviors become less predictable and familiar. Sociography furnishes an expectation of what large groups of people will do without one's direct or even indirect knowledge. It is not only a primary instrument of state power but also a tool for citizenship.[13]

Encyclopedism refers to the vast panoply of natural and artificial objects (including human behaviors) consuming the interest of a large, complex, and increasingly cosmopolitan civil society. The systematic cataloging and arrangement of these objects—usually in print—promotes social literacy. Encyclopedism is a more historically specific term than the other concepts described here, inspired by the vast compendium of human knowledge that stands as the Enlightenment's central text, the *Encyclopédie* edited by Denis Diderot. Although this book does not address the famous encyclopedia's direct influence on Württemberg, I do mean to invoke its penchant for the free association of ideas, and in particular the promiscuous elaboration of imagined possibilities for social and political reform, which was utterly central to the Enlightenment project.[14] Encyclopedism denotes a faculty of imagination crucial to the practice of citizenship and to the likelihood of innovation within a civic culture: an ability to "think outside the box" by traversing the limitlessly ramifying objects of the Enlightenment's interest. In this book, encyclopedism is powerful as much by its absence as by its presence. For example, the chapter on constitutional fetishism emphasizes the difficulties in developing a political practice extending beyond a legalistic, hermetically sealed textual agency: a fixation upon written words to the exclusion of other metaphors of power and social order. Later on, a fascinating array of subjects treated in statistical topographies and intelligence gazettes engendered a more cosmopolitan civic discourse—together with important changes in the culture of citizenship.

Though convergent with the practice of sociography, these examples show how encyclopedism differs: whereas sociography is the science of the possible and the actually existing, encyclopedism belongs just as much to the realm of ideals and unrealized potentials. At the same time, encyclopedism is historically limited because the repertoire of human experience—the sum total of anthropological, scientific, and other knowledge available at a given moment—is always finite, subject to invention and new discovery. The limitations of the Enlightenment project are, however, relativized by the role that print plays in mediating the dissolution and recombination of intellectual edifices. Catchwords and evocative turns of phrase, peculiar phenomena and facts lifted out of context: all these become provocatively reordered through encyclopedism. By collecting information systematically, but organizing it arbitrarily (whether alphabetically or otherwise), encyclopedic print media do not so much codify knowledge as promote collective imagination and serendipitous connections. Encyclopedism generates the fodder for creative free association, while print facilitates the mass dissemination of new ideas.

· · · · ·

In formulating these concepts, I have adhered to a number of methodological strictures. None of the concepts is found in the utterances of historical actors, nor are they drawn from any one school of current social or political theory. They are meant purely heuristically and provisionally, rendering strange that which has become all too familiar in the present-day civil society, yet they remain intuitive enough to be accessible. Most importantly, they cross-cut the institutional landscape of their historical setting in fresh and surprising ways, blurring entrenched historiographical distinctions between officials and citizens, bureaucracies and parliaments, informal communication networks and highly structured decision-making settings. In particular, they possess the virtue of not presuming the very distinction—that between state and civil society—they purport to dissect. This is because they locate power indiscriminately among the various players in the narrative: scribes, other state officials, and everyday citizens. The behaviors and faculties which these concepts encompass were potentially available to anyone inhabiting the civic landscape I aim to describe.

The book's narrative falls naturally into two halves, corresponding to the evolution of civil society within, and then in opposition to, the state. Within each half, the sequence of chapters progressively leavens the argument with the concepts. Chapter 1 provides a baseline history of Württemberg without referring to any of them; then, in Chapter 2, we learn of the culture of formality—in many ways the master concept of the old regime—saturating official encounters with writing. Chapter 3 describes networks of collegiality underlying the duchy's politicization in the 1790s, which were in turn electrified by textual formality in the practices of popular constitutionalism detailed in Chapter 4. A synthesis emerges, in other words, between two of the concepts by the end of the book's first half. The second half proceeds to construct a different but entirely analogous tale around the other two. Chapter 5 explains how, after Napoleon's invasions, the synthesis of formality and collegiality collapsed under civil society's separation from the state. Chapter 6 then turns to institutional reforms in the relation between these newly distinct spheres, arguing that these relied on the practice of sociography for their success. State officials and local citizens drew, additionally, on a host of powerful Enlightenment ideas—encyclopedism—to portray and depict this new civic landscape in the statistical almanacs that are the subject of Chapter 7. With these almanacs and with the intelligence gazettes described in Chapter 8, we again reach a point of synthesis, in two sociographic print media, which catalyzed civil society through the encyclopedic assembly of information.

Civil society is an accretion of all the practices signified by the four concepts. While each one isolates a particular aspect of civic dynamism for analytical scrutiny, none should be taken, on its own, to refer to a cultural constellation with an independent historical unity or integrity. In principle, all the concepts are in play at any given time; particular chapters simply pluck from a seamless web of interactions those changes in practice and routine that signal the shift toward civil society. Far from being imposed upon the material to give it a particular plot or teleology, each concept is a synthetic creation encapsulating pregnant moments drawn from an independent narrative. Especially in my archival work, I have been at pains to construct this narrative without reproducing archivists' own categories and classifications, even as the end product aims precisely to trace the changing institutional contours of the Württemberg polity through the official written record. For all these reasons, the developments described below should not be taken as normative or representative of other societies' experiences: different civic cultures evolve along different paths and in different ways, and in Württemberg I have merely chosen one area sustaining an uncommonly vital network of written connections between state and citizenry.

The question of typicality is one that confronts all studies focused on specific regions: the concepts, as should now be clear, are designed to elicit general findings from the Württemberg case that apply, *mutatis mutandis*, to other parts of Germany and to other national settings as well. On a broader European level, the historical lessons of Württemberg's experience reveal a broad evolution in civic behavior that, in modern times, counts among the most salient characteristics of civil society everywhere. A close-knit provincial political community, united by a striking and unusual commitment to the written culture of the state, yielded to a more atomistic, cosmopolitan civil society. The new civic order favored citizens who could develop their own facility in mapping their social world and imagining fresh possibilities within it. The shift toward a more fluid and forward-looking civil society was at once a great gain of modern freedom and a great loss in civic interdependence. The emancipation of writing thus entailed significant ironies and tradeoffs, which I hope will become firmly lodged in the reader's mind by the end of this book.

PART I

Official Power and the Paper Trail

1   The Civic Landscape

Württemberg ranks among Germany's civic heartlands, as an area where constitutional government took root as early as the Protestant Reformation. By the nineteenth century, it furnished a home to the early liberal and democratic movements, and would play a prominent progressive role in the 1848 Revolution. The very entrenchment of its civic traditions, however, insulated Württemberg from the broader currents of dynamism sweeping Germany in the late 1700s. It failed to develop either a robust cameralism in the governmental sphere or a strong Enlightenment tradition in the cultural arena. The powerful burgher estates resolutely opposed any absolutist initiatives, and their isolationist brand of Protestantism cut off cultural life from the continental Enlightenment's mainstream.[1] Württemberg also lacked the voluntary associations and public sphere institutions commonly considered Germany's closest approximation to a modern civic culture before Napoleon. Newspapers, learned journals, essay contests, reading rooms, salons, masonic lodges, patriotic and scientific organizations, agricultural societies, and other cosmopolitan intellectual communities: all were rare in eighteenth-century Württemberg, save for a few elite circles in its capital cities.[2]

All this changed as a result of Napoleon's invasions. In the space of a generation Württemberg was transformed from an early modern duchy into a nineteenth-century kingdom, moving from corporative government via an absolutist interregnum to modern state power by the 1820s. It shed hometown provincialism for a cosmopolitan associational life, a Reformation-era constitution for parliamentary liberalism, burgher religiosity for bourgeois Enlightenment, administration by local notables for a disciplined bureaucracy, and, not least, networks of handwritten communication for a print-dominated public sphere. An archetypical Napoleonic state, Württemberg absorbed new territories and populations after 1803 and took part in the state-sponsored reform from above that marked Germany's experience as a whole. All the while, its citizenry preserved a deep connection to the civic culture of the Holy Roman Empire. Württembergers, at the moment when they were most embattled by French conquest, defended and renewed a distinctively German culture of formality, writing, and law, one centered on a profusion of edicts, police ordinances, and legal opinions emanating from the state and matched, on the citizen's part, by a reflexive recourse to supplication, petition, lawsuit, and improvised, extra-legal forms of remonstrance and protest.[3] In these ways, Württemberg's experience highlights civil society's growth within the German state generally. Compared to other regions, it was distinguished mainly by an impressive lack of violence: a true civility.[4]

Württemberg underwent a civic transformation that occurred more fitfully and unevenly, but no less decisively, in many parts of Germany in the decades surrounding Napoleon's reign. Its *Schreiber* epitomized the species of practical intellectuals who emerged as instigators of this change. Their activities shed much-needed light on how administrative power was woven into the fabric of daily life in Germany.[5] Scribes practiced the tutelary oversight of the mid-level official by uneasily straddling traditional distinctions of rank, class, and estate to construct a formally equal civil society. Their cultivation of civic practices among Württemberg citizens conformed to the self-image of officials all over Germany, struggling in imperfect homage to Immanuel Kant to emancipate subjects from their self-incurred tutelage. The scribes may be compared to a whole class of individuals practicing popular Enlightenment in the late eighteenth century; they shared, with civil servants, doctors, preachers, schoolteachers, and other unsung mediators of modernity dispersed throughout Germany's many small states, a potent liminal position between cosmopolitan intelligentsia and provincial society. Even more so than these well-defined (if often insecure) professionals, scribes experienced the anxieties plaguing many newly mobile groups in a postcorporate social order at the end of the Enlightenment. They bridged the categories of German society at large and thus combined many forms of social power in exercising their tutelage. Burgher, scholar, craftsman, official, gentleman, bumpkin—they were all these at once.

The purpose of this chapter is to introduce the scribes by examining their institutional power and demographic profile, but it unfolds at a measured pace, by first situating them in Württemberg's pre-Napoleonic civic landscape. It begins by describing the political culture and social geography of the old-regime duchy, and only then moves on to anatomize the institutions where scribes and citizens encountered each other before the French invasions. These were the sites of civic culture mediating between state and civil

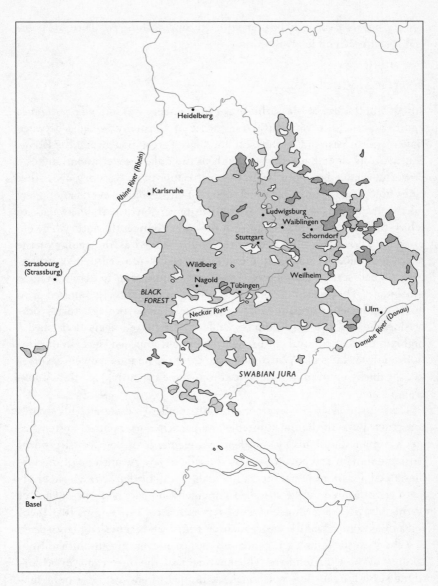

FIGURE 1. Map of the Duchy of Württemberg, ca. 1790

society, but they can only be understood by approaching populace and political system each on its own terms.

POLITICAL CULTURE

About half the size of Massachusetts, Württemberg was located near France and Switzerland in the southwest corner of Germany, wedged between Bavaria to the east and, to the west, the Black Forest, Baden, and the Rhine. Stuttgart, its capital and the seat both of the duke's government and of a powerful estates assembly, lay in the very center of its territory. Two other cities functioned as more informal capitals. Ludwigsburg, several kilometers north of Stuttgart, was the site of a miniature version of Versailles Palace, to which the duke relocated his court in the early eighteenth century. The old university town of Tübingen, to the south, served as the center of the duchy's intellectual life. By the end of the eighteenth century Württemberg's 9,000 square kilometers of territory were home to about 625,000 inhabitants. This made it a mid-sized polity among the three hundred or so kingdoms, lesser principalities, city-states, and ecclesiastical territories comprising the Holy Roman Empire. Under the Empire's aegis flourished a highly federalist political culture which, while it impeded German unification, allowed states like Württemberg to thrive as regional powers. In practice the duchy enjoyed considerable autonomy, constituting, in effect, a sovereign state.

During the early modern period, Württemberg's duke and his estates constructed one of the most durable and participatory political systems of any German state. This system featured elements of both constitutional parliamentarism and governance by the rule of law. As anchors of the former stood a class of nonaristocratic notables, the *Ehrbarkeit*, whose privileges were secured by the so-called Tübingen Compact with the duke. Out of this historic compromise evolved representative institutions that theoretically encompassed the entire male citizenry. The estates' vigilance acted as a check on the duke's arrogance and caprice, preventing absolutism from taking hold in Württemberg. This ensured that the duke came to be surrounded by bureaucratic policymakers, trained in law, who not only subscribed to a conception of the state transcending his personal rulership, but actively reconciled and adjudicated ducal and estates interests through their own official acts. These features of the duchy's political culture regulated and dispersed power, giving citizens a direct role in government. Contests for authority appealed not just to the duke's *Herrschaft*, to the assertion of lordly power or the invocation of lordly obligations, but also to the positive rights and responsibilities of his subjects. No ideology of the duke's power could hold sway over them, nor, conversely, could they question his ultimate sovereignty. Politics came to be seen in pragmatic, agonistic terms: as an ongoing and continually renewed struggle for influence within the same cohesive polity.

The history of old-regime Württemberg begins in 1514, the year of the Tübingen Compact *(Tübinger Vertrag)*, often referred to as the "Württemberg Magna Carta." At the end of the old regime, this was one of the few constitutions remaining in the German-speaking lands, prompting the English statesman Charles James Fox to claim that, besides England, Württemberg possessed the only constitution in Europe.[6] The origins of the Tübingen Compact are intimately bound to the history of the Reformation in Württemberg.[7] After the introduction of Protestantism in the early sixteenth century, the duchy's largely Catholic nobility balked at adopting the new creed. Having long agitated for independence from the duke for other reasons, the nobles seized the occasion to withdraw from the polity entirely. They became directly subject to the Holy Roman Emperor as imperial knights and effectively forfeited all seigneurial privileges as landholders within Württemberg. Their withdrawal left the Württemberg duke the sole remaining feudal overlord in the territory. It also elevated the urban burgher classes of the duchy's leading cities to a dominant position in the Württemberg estates assembly, or *Landtag*. This body, active since 1457, had assumed a commanding importance during the crisis of the early sixteenth century, when violent peasant unrest spread throughout southwestern Germany. Strapped for cash, the duke was forced to turn to the burgher-dominated *Landtag* for the funds necessary to quash these rebellions.

The Tübingen Compact was the nine-page document hammered out during their negotiations. It formed the cornerstone of the burghers' "Protestant civil piety"[8] and centerpiece of the duchy's political ritual: each new duke had to pledge to uphold the Tübingen Compact before formally ascending to the throne. Before his pledge was certified, the Württembergers owed their sovereign no particular allegiance, and even afterward the document technically granted all citizens the right of emigration. Most consequentially, the agreement vested the exclusive right of taxation in the *Landtag*, giving practical fiscal meaning to the duchy's vaunted "dualism" between duke and estates. The Compact was also construed to confer on the city councils the exclusive right to provide delegates to the *Landtag*. Collectively, the members of these councils, called magistracies, constituted the Württemberg *Ehrbarkeit*, the burgher "notability" functioning as a surrogate aristocracy founded on office rather than birth. Thus the nobility's withdrawal from the Württemberg polity facilitated the emergence of a formally egalitarian political order dominated by a single burgher estate.

In the decades after 1514, the *Ehrbarkeit*'s dominance in both society and politics continued to expand. The burgher notability came to comprise perhaps sixty extended families who often intermarried and who together set the tone for cultural life in the duchy. Generous estimates put them at no more than two or three percent of the population. Marked by a clannish provincialism, they spoke a Swabian dialect distinct from both High German and village patois, and developed a reputation for dourness, thrift, and sobriety still allegedly characteristic of the Swabian heartland.[9] Over the years they consolidated a strong hold over the ranks of the middle and lower officialdom and effectively colonized the ecclesiastical hierarchy as well, furnishing Württemberg's village pastors in addition to its powerful prelates. This elite homogenization had important political consequences for the complexion of the Württemberg estates assembly. Since the days of the Tübingen Compact, the *Landtag,* which met as a single house in Stuttgart, brought together fourteen religious prelates, sitting ex officio as heads of the Protestant cloisters, with about seventy representatives of the various territorial districts elected by the city councils. The notability's influence over both groups relativized their differences and undergirded the impressive unity of the Württemberg *Landtag* vis-à-vis the much less effectual estates assemblies of other German lands.

By the late eighteenth century, when this book's narrative opens, duke and estates had evolved in competitive symbiosis.[10] This constrained the Württemberg state to grow in a particularly law-bound way, in which the division of powers was respected and government, even when corrupt by modern standards, remained buffered against princely caprice and absolutism. This tendency affected domestic administration in two crucial ways. First, despite the impressive growth of the duke's bureaucracy, the two main bodies charged with policymaking and the adjudication of administrative and political conflicts never became simple creatures of his will. The bureaucrats[11] in the supreme Privy Council *(Geheimer Rat)* and the Governmental Council *(Regierungsrat or Oberrat)* standing just beneath it instead toed a strictly legalistic line under the estates' watchful eye. Their forbearance and refereeing shifted a great deal of initiative and agency from Stuttgart out to the provinces, which were thereby freer to develop their own institutions of self-government. Second, in his ever-increasing efforts to exploit his lands fiscally, the duke was compelled to work in an extremely roundabout fashion. Bound by the need to respect the Tübingen Compact's provisions, dukes found creative ways to play the village peasantry against the urban notability in order to undermine the *Ehrbarkeit*'s effective monopoly in the *Landtag*. Chiefly this meant enhancing, through ducal officials in the countryside, the villages' role in the election of deputies and the administration of taxes. Such a policy was patently Machiavellian but had the important byproduct of promoting the countryside's democratization.

The *Landtag*'s independence from the duke thus gave significant vitality to the sphere of burgher-dominated local administration, one which belied the conservatism of the estates representatives in Stuttgart. Conversely, local dynamism offset the oligarchic nature of the *Landtag*'s powerful Standing Committees *(Ausschüsse)*, meaning that at critical junctures in Württemberg history, localities would become able to make their voices heard in the capital. By the end of the old regime, the *Landtag* functioned less as an antiquated "estates assembly" than as a potentially viable forum for representing the political interests of the Württemberg citizenry as a whole.[12]

SOCIAL GEOGRAPHY

Highly stable and compact by the standards of the German southwest, which was otherwise blanketed by a mosaic of tiny jurisdictions, Württemberg's territorial cohesion accounts in large part for its strong civic, patriotic, and historical identity. Lacking natural borders, the duchy achieved its cohesion through the efforts of its dukes, the estates, and ordinary citizens to forge and maintain a unity grounded in close-knit village societies. The uniformity of its social geography gave rise to an uncommon equality of conditions among the duchy's inhabitants, reinforcing and reinforced by the formal equality of rights and the absence of legally inherited social distinction. This homogeneity also ensured a similarity of political and administrative institutions across regions, facilitating their integration into a unified territorial state.

Württemberg's borders and size remained largely unchanged in the century and a half between the Treaty of Westphalia in 1648, ending the Thirty Years' War, and the French invasions that began in the 1790s. Its heartland region is pleasantly hilly and temperate, graced by an undulating green landscape and winding river valleys dotted every kilometer or so with villages of red-tiled roofs and church spires. Centered on the Neckar river valley and its tributaries, the Fils, the Rems, and the Murr, this part of the duchy had the greatest concentration of people and the most fertile farmland. Roughly embracing what is today metropolitan Stuttgart, the Neckar heartland is bordered by two other regions located only partly within the old duchy. One of these, the Black Forest, separated Württemberg from

Baden and arced through a swath of dense, spiny evergreen woods in the heights south- and northwest of Tübingen. The other, the Swabian Jura, was a chain of high hills in the duchy's southeastern quadrant, less forested, rising just north of the Danube and following its northeasterly path toward Ulm. Both of these highland districts were colder, less fertile, and more sparsely peopled than the greater Neckar valley, and their inhabitants were regarded by the lowlanders as coarse, coal-burning hut-dwellers.

While both the Black Forest and the Swabian Jura boasted a robust proto-industry in timber and textiles, the duchy's heartland remained profoundly rural and agricultural and largely free from mercantile capitalist development.[13] As a whole, the eighteenth-century duchy lacked any significant urban settlements besides its capitals, and the larger towns of the countryside tended to serve administrative rather than commercial functions. The low degree of urbanization can be traced to the nearby presence of politically autonomous imperial free cities that fulfilled this need. Of these, Reutlingen, Esslingen, and Weil der Stadt stood as enclaves located entirely within the duchy's borders, while Heilbronn, Hall, Gmünd, Ulm, and Rottweil traced a clockwise semicircle along its eastern rim. The symbiosis between free cities and territorial state ensured that the duchy itself lacked strong internal distinctions between town and country, divisions which elsewhere in Germany came to be a defining aspect of civic and social life.

Though lacking urban centers, Württemberg counted among the most densely populated areas of Germany, particularly in its core Neckar region. Its landscape was spread thickly and evenly with village settlements, about 1,200 in total, which rose to greet the traveler with astonishing regularity every kilometer or two along the country roads. Coverage was uniform, contact easy, and isolation impossible. These villages, sometimes home to fewer than 200 people, each counted as its own tiny political jurisdiction. No one was simply resident "out in the country"; everyone belonged to a political community. A significant amount of administrative energy was in fact devoted to regulating the placement of boundary stones on account of the extreme density of settlement and the possibility of jurisdictional disputes among villages and individual property owners. The entire country was parcelled, fragmented, miniature, subsisting on a small scale. Besides the duke himself, there were few large landholders and no manorial complexes. Neither the vast Prussian latifundia nor even the prosperous Bavarian *Bauernhof* could find a home here. Small peasant farms managed by individual families, with at most a day laborer or two to help out, were everywhere the rule.

In Germany, both formal citizenship and the more cultural sense of local pride called *Heimat* have long been associated with the miniature urban communities Mack Walker dubs "home towns." Eighteenth-century Württemberg belies these notions, lacking the institution most important to Walker's ideal type: guilds. Guilds existed in Württemberg, to be sure, and in marginal highland areas even enjoyed considerable support from cameralist policymakers.[14] But they had no appreciable impact on political life, failing to perform the crucial function stressed by Walker: the conferral of citizenship rights, the *Bürgerrecht*. Adult male citizenship in Württemberg was instead all but universal. Founding a household entitled one to the full benefits of community membership, including suffrage and the right to stand in local elections, and obligated one to pay a tax (usually one gulden yearly) for the privilege. Married women, too, enjoyed the status of citizen (*Bürgerin*), though not the right to vote or hold office, and, in the case of widows, inherited the obligation to pay a (reduced) head tax. Each new *Bürger*, usually upon his marriage, planted and tended an apple or a pear tree in the village commons to mark his symbolic entry into the community.[15] His family's claim to its collective resources was cemented by the economically important right to use of the village pasture. Citizenship thus remained literally rooted in the *Heimat* while at the same time being replicated, in more or less identical form, in village after village. Married male Württembergers therefore met each other as formal equals within the web of spatial affiliations holding the duchy together.[16]

Citizens' legal freedom was complemented by the considerable latitude they enjoyed in managing their property and exercising their rights more tangibly. The system of land tenure in Württemberg was one of the freest in Germany. Since the Middle Ages, citizen-peasants in the duchy remained largely free from the petty service requirements, tenuous rights to property, and restrictions on marriage, occupation, and movement typical of full-blown feudalism.[17] Feudal obligations had been largely stripped of the personalized aspects of lordship and reduced to monetary contributions or payments in kind, much like modern taxes. Seigneurial encumbrances attached to the land and not the individual. The right of emigration was technically ensured by the Tübingen Compact, and no one was formally bound to the soil. Tenures were secure and heritable, and real estate did not legally revert to the landlord upon its holder's death. Property could be bought, sold, given, swapped, bequeathed, or subdivided more or less at will—by both men and women. Practically, and in most senses legally, those who worked the land owned it as well.[18]

Complementing free alienability was a second noteworthy aspect of land tenure in Württemberg, partible inheritance. In contrast to the system of primogeniture, this practice divided property equally among both sons and daughters in all of Württemberg except a few highland regions. Bequests came to consist of scattered holdings of real estate, houses, and movable goods, which would be jumbled up in every successive generation. No sentimentality was attached to particular bits of soil, and peasants adopted a purely calculating attitude toward their properties.[19] Far from turning them into atomized individualists, partible inheritance nurtured good citizenship and a strong civic community. A typical family might own strips of land distributed all over a village, being subject, with other citizens, to the various micro-climates and -ecologies within its borders. Partible inheritance also broke up large estates and retarded property accumulation, a fact which, for a long time, kept a prosperous peasantry from elevating itself above a landless rural proletariat.[20] It also anchored second and subsequent children to the community by giving them a tangible stake in it. Finally, it involved the state directly in private life through the devolution of family property. As the next chapter shows, the practice of partible inheritance entailed such a complex set of domestic family considerations that a well-developed arsenal of written legal instruments evolved to sort them out.

As in all of Germany before the Napoleonic peasant emancipation, land tenure in Württemberg remained inextricably connected to the practice of lordship. After the nobility's withdrawal, by far the largest landholder was a sole, remote individual living in the capital city: the Duke himself. Besides him, a host of other, corporative landlords in Württemberg, such as the university in Tübingen or the various monasteries and cloisters, hospitals, and charitable foundations, collected rents from the peasants who happened to come under their landlordship. The total value of these burdens constituted around 30% of the average peasant's gross agricultural yield, which put Württemberg on a par with neighboring German regions and made it broadly typical of western Germany as a whole.[21] In many places, lordship was territorially and functionally more fragmented, and by no means as conducive to civic culture. There was no sense of belonging to a state, but merely the obligation to render a host of discrete services and payments to a range of lordly authorities. In Württemberg, by contrast, all the forms of *Herrschaft* coincided in the duke and his administration, and the entire citizenry of any given village stood under the same judicial and administrative authority. Villages shared an analogous positioning with every other village in the duchy and enjoyed a natural political affinity across regions. The smallest peasant communities became seamlessly incorporated into a functionally and territorially unified political structure reaching from the village all the way to the duke.

An integrated territorial state provided a regular, institutionalized polit-ical framework for negotiating with lordly authority. Its center of gravity was a series of territorial districts, the cantons, in which comprehensive administrative powers came to be vested. Such districts became durable political communities defined by their common relation to a sovereign authority. Not only was this the most practical way to subdivide adminis-trative tasks, but it planted the seed for a civic community standing midway between state and village. As its hallmark, this arrangement invested local elites with comprehensive state functions without subsuming them into a centralized bureaucratic apparatus.[22] In a country whose aristocracy had withdrawn from social and political life, burgher notables filled this role, acquiring a collective consciousness rooted in their districts. The sole medi-ating authorities between citizens and duke, they replaced the personal, embodied component of his feudal lordship with a diffused, corporative, reflexive exercise in power. David Sabean, among others, has stressed the ways in which this system enlisted local officials in the domination of their own neighbors, and has eloquently depicted the burdens of their adminis-trative yoke on the peasant household.[23] Such relations applied throughout western Germany. But in Württemberg, it is possible to view these officials in a much more positive light, for the occupants of local office in the duchy were none other than the *Ehrbarkeit* responsible for the shape of Württemberg's constitutional order.

MEDIATING INSTITUTIONS

As a corps of notables, the *Ehrbarkeit* was quite unlike the middle-class groups lumped under the term *Bürgertum* in Germany. The nineteenth-century formula of "education and property" defining the bourgeoisie usu-ally connotes a more cosmopolitan and prosperous lifestyle than was possi-ble in the duchy, with its inward Protestant piety and laggard industry.[24] Württemberg's burgher class instead distinguished itself through its pursuit of, and passion for, local public office. Officeholding was, for them, the shortest route to both money and power—even more so than preaching, which admittedly commanded more prestige. It is no exaggeration to say that the saturation of daily life with administrative functions, entailing lucrative rewards for official appointment, hobbled the development of trade and industry in most parts of the duchy. Every post from cattle stall atten-dant up to county surgeon was ripe for the cronyism, family alliances, and *Vetterleswirtschaft* ("the husbandry of little cousins") that became the *Ehrbarkeit*'s stock in trade.[25] By the same token, the *Ehrbarkeit*, because it

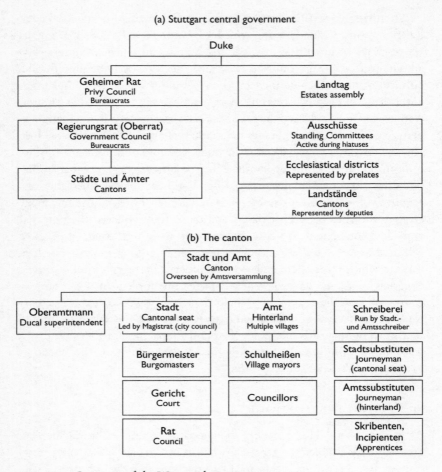

FIGURE 2.   Structure of the Württemberg state.

pursued power in institutions mediating between government and local community, sustained a dense web of connections between everyday citizens and the state.

The Canton

The canton was the central mediating institution between the state and the local community in old-regime Württemberg. My choice of the word "canton" is intended to evoke parallels with the famously independent alpine districts of the Swiss Federation. A hybrid cross between the republican city-state and the administrative district, the canton reconciled the exercise of ducal authority with the political interests of the burgher notability. The dynamic overlap of state exploitation and local self-government in these territorial units accounts in large part for the vitality of Württemberg civic culture. The duchy was divided into a number of cantons, called *Städte und Ämter* (singular: *Stadt und Amt*), each consisting of a cantonal seat *(Stadt)* surrounded by a number of villages comprising a cantonal hinterland *(Amt).*[26] In this book, the words "city" and "urban" normally refer to the cantonal seats and the terms "village" and "hinterland" to the countryside surrounding them. Though *Städte* tended to be larger than *Amt* villages, the difference in size was not always great, and both types of settlement tended to be very small-scale conurbations of anywhere between 200 and 4,000 people. In the eighteenth century there were approximately seventy cantons varying substantially in size from less than 1,000 to over 30,000 inhabitants, and comprising anywhere from one to seventy municipal units. A medium-sized canton had perhaps twelve villages and 15,000 souls. The boundaries of the state's districts for fiscal, judicial, military, police, and other administrative functions—everything but forestry—coincided within the canton. Cantons were also the districts of estates representation and can be looked upon as the atoms of self-government, dominated by the burgher notability sitting on the city councils of the cantonal seats (see figure 2a and b).

The highest-ranking state official in the canton, presiding over all aspects of administration, was the ducal superintendent or *Oberamtmann*. He was appointed and paid by the central bureaucratic authorities and, increasingly over the eighteenth century, foreign to the canton in which he served.[27] The superintendents' exclusion from deliberations to elect estates representatives in 1629 reflected their increasing re-identification with ducal interests, not those of the duke's subjects. By the 1700s superintendents had been largely co-opted by the ducal bureaucracy. Upward career mobility (often following frequent rotations among districts), centralized payment, university training, and increasingly cosmopolitan cultural attitudes all pulled them more into Stuttgart's orbit and weakened their bonds to particular cantons. One late-eighteenth-century apostle of good government called the superintendents "clumsy" in their dealings with their charges, many of whom now stood across a wide cultural divide.[28]

With the superintendents' co-optation, the burden of sustaining civic culture in the cantons fell upon the purely local officials gathered into the town council or magistracy *(Magistrat).*[29] The magistracies of the cantonal seats collectively constituted the core of the burgher *Ehrbarkeit* granted political privileges by the duke after the Tübingen Compact. Magistracies in cantonal seats were oligarchic, choosing their own replacements, and held their posts for life unless convicted of major crimes. Their activities centered on tax collection and municipal finance, but they also adjudicated civil and criminal offenses (in the first instance) and sat ex officio on committees with functions ranging from orphan placement to approving mortgages. Finally, they appointed a variety of local officials—from within their own ranks, for the more important jobs—for tasks like granary and common land administration, poor relief, fire protection, and night-watchman services. Structurally, the magistracies consisted of two burgomasters *(Bürgermeister)* plus two banks of councillors, called the *Gericht* and the *Rat*. The burgomasters did not act as mayors, as the modern usage of the term *Bürgermeister* suggests, but instead supervised town fiscal operations. The *Gericht* consisted of about twelve town elders who, together with the burgomasters, ran the town government; the *Rat* sometimes deliberated alongside the *Gericht* and acted as a holding pool for talented young councillors being groomed for later *Gericht* membership. For most purposes, the *Bürgermeister, Gericht,* and *Rat* will be treated as a single collective entity, the *Magistrat,* in the pages that follow.

The structure of village institutions reproduced in microcosm that of the cantonal seats, with notable exceptions. Magistracies there tended to be smaller and less internally differentiated by function and were elected by the collected citizens of each village instead of acting as self-selecting, self-perpetuating bodies. Though serving as civil courts, they lacked competence over criminal matters, which were automatically referred to the magistracies of the cantonal seat. Most importantly, they lacked *Ehrbarkeit* status. The village-level analogue to the *Oberamtmann* was the *Schultheiß,* also called the "village foreman" in this book, but his social and political position was again substantially different from that of his higher number in the canton. Though technically a ducal official, he was in practice elected (for life) by the adult male citizens of the village and merely confirmed in office by the ducal superintendent in most locales. Customarily, the village foremen belonged to one of the more powerful peasant families of the village elite. *Schultheißen* presided over the village councils and usually served ex officio as their representatives at cantonal assemblies. At such assemblies they served as focal points for efforts to redress the imbalance of power between *Stadt* and *Amt* during the eighteenth century.

The spread of cantonal assemblies, miniature representative parliaments called *Amtsversammlungen,* ranks among the most significant political innovations of the early modern period in Württemberg. Their appearance coincided with the Thirty Years' War, whose devastations forced the cities back on the resources of their hinterlands and awakened in the latter a desire for enhanced political participation. Though they possessed an ambiguous legal character and were governed by a mixture of improvisation and precedent, the duke heartily encouraged their development insofar as they undermined the monopolies of the urban magistracies.[30] The cantonal assemblies assessed canton-wide taxes to fund public works and local improvements, internally apportioned the canton's contribution to the statewide tax levy hammered out in the Stuttgart *Landtag,* and elected the canton's physician, scribe, and treasurer. Most importantly, they elected the canton's delegate to the estates assembly and outfitted him with written instructions. Early on, assemblies tended, not surprisingly, to be dominated by the magistracies of the cantonal seats. But *Amt* villages, represented by their foremen, still theoretically enjoyed the right to vote at the cantonal assemblies. Assisted by powerful scribes and other officials, many began in the 1700s to claim this right.

In the Stuttgart *Landtag,* each canton counted as its own estate, or *Stand.* Collectively, the cantons formed the "estates of the country," or *Landstände,* whose representatives sat alongside the ecclesiastical prelates in the *Landtag's* plenary assembly. An individual delegate to the assembly did not possess a free mandate but instead temporarily embodied his entire canton's will as a collectivity. Whereas the Stuttgart assembly may have only been convened ad hoc to vote new taxes and debate foreign policy, the cantons maintained political continuity in the countryside. As bases of civic action they uniquely combined day-to-day involvement in the application of state power with the durable rights and privileges to affect its use. This overlap of administrative function and political representation bred in them a highly unitary identity notwithstanding the deep-seated "dualism" between duke and estates. Two factors account for their solidarity. First, the failure of bureaucratic absolutism to reduce them to units of administrative convenience meant that the cantons remained the lowest level to which the systematic coordination of ducal power effectively penetrated. Second, the absence of legal social stratification in the duchy ensured that the cantons acted as the principal units into which Württemberg society as a whole was formally divided. Indeed, much of the classic status distinction and collective spirit enjoyed by occupational or social groups elsewhere in Europe (clergy, aristocracy, commoners, etc.) were instead vested in these communities, which cultivated the spirit of self-government in bounded, adjacent administrative districts within the duchy.

Socially and not just politically, then, the duchy emerged from the early modern period with a peculiarly modified form of a traditionally European social order, one which might be called territorial corporatism. In contrast to other, more overtly hierarchical estates societies, it managed to preserve not an occupational but a geographic segmentation of society down to the Napoleonic invasions. None of this meant is meant to deny the profound elitism embodied by the burgher notability. But it is important to stress that the corporative consciousness of the cantons' leading officials was based on a purely informal hegemony, lacking the sanction of overt caste privilege. It was instead cemented by the practice of officeholding, in particular the knowledge of and facility with writing. The *Schreiberei*—and especially its powerful scribes—furnished this cultural capital.

The Schreiberei

The office of the town scribe, the *Schreiberei*, was the nexus of administrative life in Württemberg. A lion's share of all the paperwork generated by eighteenth-century government in the duchy passed through this office. Clustered among the tightly packed, cross-timbered houses of every cantonal seat and a good number of outlying villages, the *Schreiberei* occupied either the first floor of the scribe's home or a room in the town hall. The scribe who worked and sometimes lived there was at once his town's notary, its archivist, its clerk, its secretary, its accountant, its court reporter, and its legal advisor. For local governments he prepared receipts for town revenues and expenditures, balanced and audited the books, and served as an official secretarial presence in matters like bankruptcies and orphan court hearings. Court records, tax ledgers, statute books, ducal ordinances, land surveys, and property deeds would all be found in his chambers. There, too, were housed reams of "protocols," the notes he took at city council meetings or on other official occasions, like depositions.

The scribes (*Schreiber*, singular or plural) maintained thriving private practices to complement these official functions. Paid on a fee-for-service basis or sometimes by the page, they were enlisted by private individuals and families to draw up mortgages and manage property sales, prepare wills and estates inventories, draft marriage contracts and birth certificates— anything, in short, needing to be put on paper with an official seal. These activities will receive individual attention in the next chapter as part of a broader culture of formality. The focus for now is less on the scribes' specific duties than on their general role within public administration.

Scribes served the various cantonal and municipal governments in two main capacities. *Stadtschreiber* were hired by the magistracies of the cantonal seats to oversee the routine administrative affairs of these towns. Convenience as well as official custom ensured that they did double duty by handling certain canton-wide matters as well. It was they who refereed access to the cantonal archives for precedents in resolving internal cantonal disputes, for example. One of their most politically influential functions was to protocol the full-scale cantonal assemblies where both city and village representatives convened to elect canton-wide officials. They enjoyed an enhanced role when these assemblies met to discuss estates matters as opposed to routine local business. Recall that on these solemn occasions the duke's superintendent was barred from what, in theory, was to remain a pristine and uncorrupted exercise of cantonal self-government. Effectively, this allowed scribes to direct the proceedings by preparing binding written instructions for the canton's *Landtag* deputy.

The second type of scribe was the *Amtsschreiber*, who saw to the business generated in each of the *Amt* villages surrounding the cantonal seats. Hinterland districts lacked the political influence of the cities but were more financially lucrative for the scribes who practiced in them. While the villages were long denied effective representation in the cantonal assemblies and thus in the *Landtag*, they had larger aggregate populations and generated more income from private and governmental sources alike. The *Amtsschreiber* was in a unique position to act as their advocate in return for political support. Aside from the ducal superintendent, he was the only prominent official resident in the cantonal seat to be in continuous contact with the countryside. As the superintendents themselves became co-opted by the duke, the *Amtsschreiber* emerged as the only significant local patrons the villages could expect to find in cantonal politics.[31]

In all but the very largest cantons, the city and country scribes were one and the same person, called the *Stadt- und Amtsschreiber*. The sixty or so inhabitants of these combined posts—one for every canton except Stuttgart, Ludwigsburg, and a few others large enough to partition responsibilities[32]—stood at the pinnacle of miniature administrative empires. All roads to power in the Württemberg canton led in one way or another through their offices, for, more than any other single official, they benefited the canton's hybrid status as both territorial unit *(Amt)* and municipality *(Stadt)*. On the one hand, the cantons' large hinterlands furnished an income base enabling them to maintain themselves in kingly fashion as self-sufficient, autonomous officials free from the blandishments of venality. This advantage, together with the cantons' constitutional insulation from ducal interference, set the Württemberg scribes above the more menial notaries found in other German states.[33] On the other hand, the cantons were dominated by a single administrative center, the *Stadt*, which provided a face-to-face community in which to cultivate power. The saturation of this one town with such a range of official functions, all traditionally dominated by the same burgher families from which the scribes came, provided powerful networks of friends and relations on which to draw. Trading favors in the conduct of official business was part of the local social economy, especially when the scribe combined so many functions in his own person.

The power of the *Stadt- und Amtsschreiber* derived from their simultaneous roles as notables *and* officials, active in both city *and* countryside. In contrast to ducal superintendents, who could also exploit such interlocking and mutually reinforcing practices of state power, *Stadt- und Amtsschreiber* had a deeper stake in the community. They almost invariably practiced in the same location throughout their professional lives, whereas superintendents could be rotated from district to district. They were also elected by their cantons—the ducal government's powers being limited to confirming the choices of cantonal assemblies—while the superintendents remained straightforward central appointees.[34]

Private businessmen with public functions, the *Stadt- und Amtsschreiber* thrived on a confusion between state and society that allowed local notables to participate in the apparatus of government power. They perfectly embodied the hegemony of small-town burghers exercised on the cantonal level. Not only did they come in almost all cases from *Ehrbarkeit* families, but they constituted an elite within this elite. In the larger cantons especially, they counted among the richest men in town. Income data from the old regime, though scattered, show that a *Schreiberei* practice could take in 4000–5000 fl. a year, over half of which was kept by the *Schreiber* himself as the profit left after deducting office and staff expenses. Many scribes accumulated personal fortunes running into the tens of thousands.[35]

Scribes were also quite privileged in terms of their social and geographic recruitment. As figure 3 shows, fully 87% were the sons of professionals: preachers, doctors, civil servants, or other scribes, all groups which could claim notable status ipso facto. Nearly 95% were born in the Duchy of Württemberg. As one might expect, these social and occupational ties were largely restricted to the cantonal seats, the redoubts of notable privilege: 76% were born in one of the *Städte* (34% serving in their hometowns, 42% in other cantons), while only about 19% hailed from the village hinterlands. Testifying to the difficulties of penetrating local *Ehrbarkeit* hegemony, a mere 2% came from the villages of their own cantons. In their pattern of dispersal, the scribes stitched networks of notable government together over the entire countryside. Totaling those from villages or *Städte* outside their canton of service (17% and 42%, respectively), nearly three-fifths had relo-

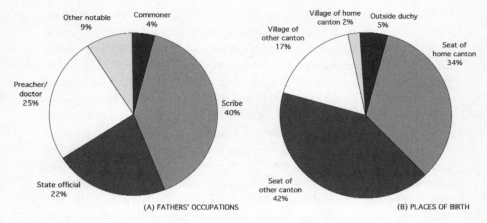

FIGURE 3.   The old-regime *Schreiber,* 1750–1800. Source: *NWD,* with father's occupation available for 136 and place of birth indicated for 149 out of a total of 222 scribes in service between 1750 and 1800. (*NWD* is simply a large compendium of biographical entries on all Württemberg government officials of the old regime.)

cated outside their home districts. All these factors gave the scribes a strong, statewide corporative identity: the scribes supplied the political voice of the provinces and stood as the guarantors of local civic culture during the old regime.

The scribes' countrywide influence was reinforced by the organization of their profession; the *Schreiberei* in fact resembled a guild in being anchored to the local community while also participating in a wider territorial network of exchange and reciprocality. It took on local boys as trainees, gave them a useful skill, and then farmed some of them out to other localities as apprentices. As in the guilds, domestic life and the rhythms of the craft overlapped in the *Schreiberei,* an office that doubled as a household. On entering the trade, at or before fourteen years of age, a so-called *Incipient* performed menial chores—setting the scribe's dinner table, grooming his horses—and took orders from his wife (usually depicted in the lore of the profession as a shrew, "a true copy of the hellish Furies"). Training at all levels was by repetition and routine, not theoretical introduction. Tales abound of abuse and neglect, of ceaseless busywork from dawn to dusk: copying receipts or simple inventories or, failing enough of these, passages from cookbooks.[36] The treatment of "incipients" was in keeping with a premodern conception of childhood. They were seen first as nuisances to be tolerated, and second as sources of income: scribes taking on trainees received a tuition or *Lehrgeld* from their families, creating a perverse incentive to increase staff size needlessly. Between the ages of seventeen and twenty, a budding scribe became a *Skribent,* a sort of apprentice, and not only began to acquire more official responsibilities, such as drafting simple estate inventories, but also gained release from the *Schreiberin's* tyranny. A 1739 ducal rescript criticized their disorderly, unsupervised lifestyle, calling them a "class of individuals which spends its idle time with shooting, working out, boozing, and carousing"—a classic depiction of a liminal life stage.[37]

Customarily, in his early twenties, the *Skribent* was sent to Stuttgart to be examined by ducal authorities. He then became a *Substitut,* capable of executing the full range of official instruments and comparable in status to a journeyman. A *Stadtsubstitut* acted as the scribe's chief deputy in the cantonal seat; supervising apprentices and managing routine business, he helped to free the *Stadt- und Amtsschreiber* for local political matters and could count as a weighty personage in his own right. By contrast, *Amtssubstituten,* numbering up to four or five in the larger cantons, led lonely, isolated, itinerant lives in the villages of the countryside. While they generated large sums of money for their employers and kept them in continuous contact with the hinterland, they themselves had become an increasingly restive and problematic element by the end of the eighteenth century. A good number of *Substituten*—perhaps a third—rotated into other *Schreibereien,* sometimes more than once, usually bearing letters of recommendation.[38] Finding a position on the other side of the duchy, on the strength of the profession's far-flung networks of communication, was just as common, however.

The scribes' decentralized system of placement helped secure their collective ability to operate as a profession almost completely independent of ducal influence. It was so successful and pervasive that the *Schreibereien,* informally referred to as "nurseries," became the preferred training grounds not just for future scribes but for the entire lower officialdom. Burgomasters, city councillors, ducal superintendents and their staffs, cantonal treasurers, charitable foundation administrators, granary supervisors, all manner of Stuttgart clerks and functionaries: all of these types of officials tended to have spent at least a part of their careers as trainees in the *Schreiberei.* Their ubiquity ensured that a craft spirit anchored in the provinces, not a bureaucratic ethos instilled in cosmopolitan universities, came to permeate all but the highest levels of government in the duchy. By the end of the eighteenth century, fully 1,300 individuals—one for every five hundred people in Württemberg—were trained scribes, about half of whom enjoyed employment in a variety of positions, with the other half still in training or going without official postings altogether.[39] A very few of these managed to secure high posts, in such bodies as the Government and Privy Councils, but as a rule the top echelons of the civil service were reserved for university-trained lawyers. The class divide between scribes and jurists served as a further obstacle to a unified bureaucratic spirit and procedure.

A fundamentally local operation replicated over the entire Württemberg territory, the *Schreiberei* cohered purely by virtue of the scribes' *esprit de corps*. The intensive but weakly bureaucratized nature of state power in Württemberg found its ideal expression in this highly developed but pervasively dispersed institution. The scribes came to power in the absence of intermediate noble authority on the one hand, and amidst the underdevelopment of a ducal bureaucracy penetrating down to the local level on the other. Unsupervised and largely unregulated, they trained their own replacements and thus propagated their influence throughout old-regime Württemberg at all levels. All this meant that the scribes who staffed the *Schreiberei* straddled the realms of state administration and local community to a greater degree than most other governing elites populating the historical literature. They stood much closer to their clients than, say, the Prussian Junker *Landräte,* and yet enjoyed a more elevated status than village *Schultheißen.* Neither bureaucratic civil servants subject to central discipline and education, nor independent operators in the manner of guild craftsmen, they combined aspects of both ideal types.

The only personage with a comparable mastery of the written word was the local pastor. Württemberg's clergy could boast membership in one of the best-run and most politically independent Protestant church hierarchies in Germany, and in many ways constituted an organic intelligentsia. Generation after generation of preachers were trained at the seminary and theological faculty at Tübingen, many of them studying on scholarships sponsored by a vast network of family foundations. They supervised grade schools (mandatory for all children since 1629) and convened morality courts *(Kirchenkonvente)* to discipline their flocks. While almost oppressively learned, however, the Württemberg clergy conformed in sphere after sphere to the narrower, rather than the more dynamic, currents in German intellectual culture. Central church authorities subjected them to stringent bureaucratic oversight and periodic visitations. Pietist theology alienated them from the more progressive deism found in much contemporary philosophy. And Tübingen, their preferred training ground, proved less an intellectual beehive than a hothouse of scholarly claustrophobia.[40]

The town preacher inhabited easily the highest-status and most comfortable occupation in old regime Württemberg. The scribe, by contrast, was difficult to label; he was a potent, enigmatic figure, unable to be pigeonholed in any of the traditional categories of eighteenth century German society: burgher, intellectual, bureaucrat, craftsman. The humble notarial status assigned even to the omnicompetent *Stadt- und Amtsschreiber* belied an enormous practical influence. In theory these scribes, like all other Württemberg scribes, were low-level functionaries, but in practice they often dominated their putative superiors and used them as their mouthpieces. They were formally subordinate not only to ducal superintendents but also to burgomasters and magistracies. Yet they were universally acknowledged as the most powerful officials in town for the sheer range of their activities. Though by the end of the 1700s, they had come to be resented for their hegemony, during most of the old regime the *Schreiber* acted as the true organic intellectuals, enjoying a unique rapport with local society. One of their apologists, the scribe Ferdinand Weckherlin, wrote of how they conducted their peers in the arts of citizenship:

> No other estate acquires a more precise understanding than he—none can—of the character and domestic constitution of the country man. He knows his character and understands his language . . . through attentive listening . . . through advice and confidences . . . in conversation as a good acquaintance and friend of the household, as an uninterested person, a teacher of truth. One day he may illuminate in this way a principle of morality, another he might explain this or that appearance out in the fields. . . . When the business of the day is over, he sits around for a while with the *Bürgermeister* [and] the town treasurer in the *Rathaus*. It does these people good to converse with him. He might fetch some appropriate book, read out excerpts from it, speak upon it, ask for their opinion and thus lead them to the truth.[41]

2   The Tutelage of the Scribes

The world of the scribes was a world saturated with formality. Official texts regulating all manner of social interactions proliferated in what, to modern expectations, seems wild disproportion to the size and complexity of the communities concerned. Scribes managed mortgages and liens for simple peasants remarkably conversant with the intricacies of credit and amortization. They drew up contracts between parents and their own children, using precise legal language to specify the nursing heirs had to provide their elderly parents in exchange for a share of the family bequest. And they crafted written petitions for citizens who knew how to exploit the legal system to pursue petty feuds and vendettas. The duke, for his part, proved equally assiduous in using writing to monitor and police his subjects. He required every newly married couple to have their household possessions meticulously inventoried for later probate settlements. He mandated that every property transaction be certified and tabulated with numerous redundancies and safeguards against tax evasion and malfeasance. And when allegations of local corruption came to his attention, he commissioned outside investigators to spend months, even years, deposing witnesses and redacting their testimonies into official "protocol" reports. The sheer abundance of official formalities meant that citizens saw their lives colonized by writing. Dealing in all these texts, scribes played a particularly influential role. They shepherded their clients through encounters with state authority while at the same time leading them in the arts of independent citizenship.

The scribes stood at the very nexus of Württemberg's civic culture. In the best of circumstances, they came to be regarded as trusted advisors, friends, and confidants in the conduct of justice, finance, politics, and household economy. Their tutelage over local communities was founded on thousands of daily assertions of influence, ranging from stern invocations of superior knowledge to gentler offers of practical advice and wisdom. Scribes lacked a formal standing commensurate with their vast informal authority, however: as clerks and accountants, secretaries and archivists, they had no independent voice and little official responsibility for actions of local government—which they influenced only from behind the scenes. Many of them chafed under the legal requirement that they speak only through the mouths of others. As one scribe put it, in the midst of a government investigation into his conduct of office, "The *Stadt- und Amtsschreiber* find themselves in the peculiar position that, on the one hand, everything is expected of them and, on the other, all that they do besides writing is called usurpation."[1]

In one interesting case, a community rebelled against its patronizing scribe, one Christian Gottlieb Schmid, handily enumerating his specific usurpations in a written "Instruction" to him.[2] Originating in 1780 in the canton of Schorndorf, the document was drafted by city councillors angered by Schmid's high-handed attempts to have a corrupt, adulterous, alcoholic crony elected to their ranks. Intended to curtail Schmid's "unrestrained lust for power" and "put him in restraints," the Schorndorf Instruction is interesting in its own right as a spontaneously improvised text, replete with German-style paragraph markers (§) and formal subsections, yet having absolutely no legal validity.[3] Here, as on many occasions recounted in this book, citizens simply fabricated quasi-official texts to conduct their disputes. In a culture so utterly dominated by written formality, this seemed an eminently logical way to discipline a scribe whose tutelage had crossed over into abuse.

The Schorndorf Instruction also shows how duties as simple as taking minutes at city council meetings enabled scribes to exert tutelage. Paragraph 4, section (a) alleged that when it befell him to transcribe opinions he found objectionable, the *Schreiber* Schmid literally "lays down the quill, and does not want to protocol what has been said." Section (b) added that the scribe "will not entertain contrary ideas until and unless he detours the city councillors and brings them around to his opinion." "Worst of all," section (c) claimed, he "forces them, as it were, through harsh speeches [made] under the pretense that he understands matters better than they and therefore must be responsible for them, to turn from their considered opinions and feel differently."

Schmid, like many Württemberg scribes, not only strained to exercise a more direct influence over local affairs but resented his official subordination. It proved especially difficult for him, as the Instruction's very first paragraph noted, to "respect the proper place" of the ducal superintendent. The Schorndorfer reminded him that scribes are "subordinate to the superintendent and the city council" and must show "respect," remain "loyal," and "refrain completely from all immodesty, impoliteness, improper threats, or harsh language" toward them (§2). At the same time, the city councillors found it impossible to dispense entirely with their scribe's superior understanding. When they overlooked or misinterpreted some duty arising in the course of council business, they insisted that "the scribe has to make a gentle reminder of this." But they wanted his knowledge without his patronizing interference: "The scribe is acquitted from all responsibility for that which the council does, acts, or resolves . . . with good knowledge, will, and conviction, and thereby the council will be made responsible for them" (§§24–25). Here, the councillors finessed the central contradiction in their relations with the scribe. They were dependent on his expertise, but unwilling to concede him the authority and responsibility that should naturally have accompanied it. They blithely upheld a quixotic ideal of the scribe's tutelage and expected Schmid to obey it: "The citizens of the town, who are ducal subjects, the scribe has to greet with love, both within and outside chambers: to listen to their desires with patience, to give them the proper information and direction, and in general to act toward them in such a way that they will not have cause to complain against him" (§43).

This chapter explores the tensions and frustrations inherent in the scribes' tutelage, and how they lent dynamism to Württemberg's culture of formality. Owing to the scribes' predicaments and ambitions as a class, official texts that might otherwise have proved static and inert were transformed into a potent, adaptable repertoire of strategies for asserting influence over local communities. Scribes exploited the plasticity that was part of formality's very nature, realizing that what made official writing "official," what gave it binding power, was neither historically given nor handed down from the state. Formality, per se, merely structured competition among individuals mobilizing various forms of influence—material wealth, emotional appeals, family connections, social prestige, and ideologies of community and authority—to assert their interests in and against the state. Tutelage arose naturally from scribes' handling of the many formalities dominating daily life in Württemberg. It was woven into community power struggles by scribes who manipulated formal texts to secure their positions. And, as we will see, it became overtly politicized by the end of the old regime, when critics in the public sphere held up the scribes to the standards of an Enlightened civil service.

THE FORMALITY OF DAILY LIFE

The scribes' tutelage, it must be said straight away, did not reflect an elite mastery over the written word. Literacy was, in fact, widespread among all classes and both genders of the Württemberg population, largely for religious reasons. Protestantism's emphasis on scripture and reverence for the Word and the Book, combined with the elementary schooling compulsory for the duchy's children, ensured that a clear majority of the population could read and at least sign their names in the early modern period.[4] Overwhelmingly, citizens signed the testaments, contracts, affidavits, and other documents placed before them in official settings, even if they did not always fully understand them.

Only women were formally excluded from the civic benefits of literacy, though many of them, too, could read and write. To conduct legal transactions or even sign her name, a woman had to be represented by a male guardian, called a *Kriegsvogt*, who acted as her legal advisor. The guardian's duty was to read aloud all official documents placed before his charge, explain their meanings to her, and obtain her consent before proceeding.[5] Women's formal incapacity to write meant that they were ineligible to vote or to hold any public office but that of midwife.[6] In a society where women enjoyed so many other legal and practical freedoms, owning property independently of their husbands and inheriting it in exactly the same quantities as their brothers, this is a striking exception to the rule of gender equality. To reserve writing, and writing alone, to men made it the definitive criterion of true civic standing in a patriarchal society. Gender tutelage was only abolished in 1828, and thus for nearly the entire period covered by this book, writing was officially the exclusive possession of an entire fraternity of male citizens. By the same token, however, it could not count as the monopoly of an official elite. From the scribes' perspective, writing functioned not as an instrument of domination but as the common currency of social expression and conflict resolution among male citizens.

It was not the scribe's literacy but his involvement in the formalities of daily life that endowed him with enormous practical influence. He tended to the town records and composed a large majority of them personally or through his staff; he also had access to everyone's public and private dealings and controlled how they would be represented textually. Most concretely, his office physically stored all the crucial documents bringing state and citizen in contact. Entering any *Schreiberei*, one would be struck by shelves of legal ordinances, property deeds, mortgage certificates, contracts, wills and testaments, receipts, city council minutes, renunciations of local citizenship, and many other official texts. Hospitals, charitable organizations, scholarship foundations, fire insurance funds, and other corporative entities often deposited their records there as well. Troves of miscellany on economic life, like records on grain, fruit, wood, and salt stores, and reports on guilds, markets, and fairs all found their way into the *Schreiberei*. Only that information pertaining to population statistics, such as census lists, baptismal records, and birth and death certificates, was stored at the pastor's office. The *Oberamtmann* also kept certain sensitive records in his possession. But the *Schreiberei* was where local, cantonal, and state governments stored and referred to important information affecting their lives, and the primary site where citizens practiced their freedoms.

Many of the records in the *Schreiberei* were compiled as large tomes *(Bücher)*.[7] Compendia of ducal orders called *Befehlbücher* preserved continuous official memory and reminded local citizens of their duties vis-à-vis the state. Protocol books *(Protocollbücher)* held the minutes of local and cantonal assembly meetings on how best to carry them out. Some communities had a *Stadt-* or *Dorfbuch* drawn up for their reference; this listed all the buildings, properties, marking stones, and public roadways found within their borders, together with information on communities' fiscal rights and obligations and any outstanding legal complaints.[8] All these volumes bear witness to the active, and not just pro forma, interest that Württemberg communities took in their fiscal and political self-government. A similar mix of civic freedom and governmental authority was embodied by a second set of books routinely found in the *Schreiberei*, comprising economic data, principally involving property rights and transactions. Land surveys or cadasters, called *Grund- und Lagerbücher*, established the boundaries, legal status, and tax assessments of each parcel of private property. Lists of property sales, called *Kaufbücher*, reflected an active market in real estate within and among extended families in even the smallest villages. And compendia of mortgages and liens *(Unterpfandsbücher)*, together with a variety of other interest-bearing securities, attest to the precocious development of complicated financial instruments in Württemberg society. Finally, tax ledgers *(Steuerbücher)* recorded all monies paid to the duke, the estates, cantons, and local governments. Collectively, these records documented the totality of a given community's material resources for the benefit of state and citizenry alike.

The scribes spent much of their time, and earned most of their money, compiling and revising these records. Tax ledgers had to be continually "renovated" to reflect changes in the ownership and value of various pieces of land; in them, the duke insisted that each property be listed alongside the four parcels physically abutting it and that their owners be indexed by both first and last names. Summaries were required of all tax contributors and their payments, along with summaries of these summaries.[9] Mortgage records likewise had to be periodically reviewed to unearth long-forgotten liens and encumbrances and prevent title disputes.[10] Finally, each year, the scribe participated, along with the burgomasters and other town officials, in a thorough auditing of local finances called a *Rechnungs-Abhör*. On these occasions, official receipts were checked for accuracy, read out publicly to the assembled citizenry, and formally submitted for correction and approval.[11]

An astounding amount of effort was devoted, through all these practices, to the "caretaking" *(Pflegen)* of local finance. The scribes organized masses of information from every possible perspective on all manner of financial transactions. The progress of textualization varied, of course, from locality to locality. Different scribes displayed different levels of commitment to such labor, and their ability to balance the books with fairness and efficiency, before officials and citizens alike, could make or break their local reputations. Even in well-administered communities, thorough documentation of financial obligations was not always complemented by systematic enforcement of tax compliance. Verbosity, redundancy, and inefficiency were ever-present. Scribes' bookkeeping methods, at their plodding best, were in fact less effective in intensifying the cameralist state's fiscal control than in satisfying the preindustrial community's profound concern for thrift, equity, and obsessive accountability in tending its hard-earned money. Thus many cameralists aimed to streamline and systematize the methods of *Pflegen*, and in their published handbooks for the scribes encouraged them to think of fiscal accounting in more dynamic, intrusive, active terms, as *Pflanzen* (planting): "Just like the beneficial light of the sun on our earth, a good cameralistic system operates on a state. Order . . . and activity bring forth blooms and fruits of the whole."[12]

The scribe's management of official texts enabled him to know everyone's business; he enjoyed access to privileged information in which both state authorities and local citizens had material interests. Above and beyond his mere possession of written records, this fact accounts for his pervasive influence. Every time a local citizen or corporative entity paid a tax to or collected a disbursement from local government, for example, the transaction generated a written receipt that passed through the *Schreiberei*. Although the scribe was legally barred from collecting the money or issuing receipts himself, he did record and index them systematically, which offered him the running opportunity to form impressions of individual citizens' financial dealings. This knowledge made the scribe an important repository of contacts for those seeking or offering credit.[13] People in fact came to him on all sorts of occasions. One scribe's office "resembled an audience hall where 20 or 30 people were always waiting for him"; townsfolk "had such a trust in him that they asked his advice on the smallest matters."[14] Copies, excerpts, and emendations of various contracts, property deeds, and birth certificates all provided a steady source of business from those needing the documents for ongoing legal transactions.[15] At such times, the scribe had ample opportunity to conceal important information as well as reveal it. He acted as gatekeeper to the town archives, for example, which he was often called upon to consult in the adjudication of property disputes and other legal matters. Providing commentary on these archival excerpts counted among his means of not-so-subtle influence: according to the Schorndorf Instruction, Schmid often "attached his own opinion when it was not demanded," "introduced irrelevant comments," and withheld important files not supporting his own interpretations.[16]

The scribe not only maintained a passive watch on local affairs from his perch in the *Schreiberei* but actively attended a host of official occasions out in the community. These gave him entrée into numerous situations where secrets and squabbles were aired, feuds and vendettas pursued, and misdeeds and improprieties exposed for the written record. Such occasions ranged from elections and city council meetings to church visitations, autopsies, orphan court hearings, boundary demarcations and disputes, and bankruptcy settlements. Scribes, especially *Substituten,* collected sizable fees for the large amount of time they spent on horseback, riding from village to village where their presence was required at these functions. They also attended tribunals *(Vogtruggerichte)* convened ad hoc by the *Oberamtmann,* in which the entire community of householders would gather to resolve nagging legal complaints and political disputes that had gotten out of hand. At all these affairs, scribes dispensed advice and rendered opinions on the application of various laws and precedents; just as importantly, they sounded out contacts and collected information extremely valuable in their local political machinations.

In the Schorndorf Instruction we have already seen how scribes' attendance and note-taking functions at city council meetings gave them a wide-open field for manipulation. Scribes' duties at local elections put them in a similar position of discretion and power. Elections took place at the town hall, where the ducal *Oberamtmann,* having consulted the record books in the *Schreiberei* for precedents and procedures observed at past elections, informed the assembled voters of "what has to be remembered," and admonished them against partisanship and violence.[17] Then, for the actual polling, the electors would first leave the room and then file back in, one by one, to cast their votes. Only the superintendent, the scribe, and perhaps one or two certifying witnesses *(Urkunds-Personen)* remained present the whole time. As each elector processed in, the scribe entered his vote into a special secret protocol drawn up for the occasion, which the elector would then sign. In some locales, voters had to a provide a reason for their choice, also written into the protocol. After the last vote was cast, the scribe physically sealed the election protocol, which was later stored in the town archives, and then entered only a summary version of it into the regular city council meeting minutes. Scribes often exploited the leeway this offered them to conceal or reveal important information that might be used as precedents in future elections. Scribes also knew how each person voted; if desired, they could hold their choice against them later, in public, or simply intimidate electors into voting a preferred way. Schmid at Schorndorf not only "interfered" at local elections but often demurred before recording undesirable votes; he was sternly admonished that when electors wanted their votes "entered into the protocol once and for all, [he] has to do so without hesitation."[18]

A final public duty requiring the scribe's attendance was his transcription of written "protocols" in legal cases and formal disputes. Protocols paraphrased the testimony of witnesses deposed for the purpose of state investigation or in civil or criminal lawsuits. In them, the scribe summarized the gist of their utterances without copying down each word, and also rendered Swabian dialect into High German. Witnesses could contest the protocol and have it revised, but this seems to have happened relatively infrequently. For particularly formal investigations, the protocol report's left column listed questions and the right listed answers, making it easy to skim for inconsistencies or specific facts, especially when, as was common, the same questions were asked of a series of protocollees. Witnesses could be "taken to protocol" individually or "in confrontation," with those who disputed them physically present. Alternatively, they could be confronted, alone with the scribe (or other investigator), with the *written* testimony of those who had gone before them. Such techniques reflected the extreme importance the state invested in pinning down precise meanings. This meant that the scribe's particular narrative rendition of citizens' words could either vindicate their claims or subject them to severe punishments for misrepresentation. Scribes again displayed varying degrees of aptitude for this task; many times, their protocol summaries failed to jibe with the substance of the utterances they themselves recorded. Schmid, for one, was notorious for protocolling sloppily, interjecting his own "provisional opinions too hastily," and refusing to allow his interlocutors to express themselves in more nuanced language.[19]

Scribes were as deeply involved in their clients' private lives as in their public encounters with official authority. Part of the reason the culture of formality had such an influence on the life of everyday citizens was that public and private were so weakly distinguished in the early modern community; very personal matters were continually subject to open negotiation among officials and other neighbors. In his daily routine, the scribe was often present at family situations freighted with high emotion, where his actions, competence, and professional wisdom could solidify bonds of trust and assuage conflicts, anxieties, and even pain. As he encountered private citizens, the scribe rendered judgments about people and things, moral character and material value. Contracts demonstrate this especially well. In preparing them, the scribe personally vouched for the parties' good character and put his own word of honor at stake, legally speaking, before bringing them "officially and formally to paper." He had to ensure that all parties had acted voluntarily, not under duress, with full knowledge and disclosure, and "signed with their own hand." The scribe also translated their wishes into proper legalese. Finally, he conducted them through very ritualized moments when they contemplated the future stability of the legal order, pledging to "bind our heirs and successors no less than ourselves."[20]

In the preparation of contracts, the scribe personally applied the methods of formality to the resolution of real-life dilemmas. Two standard contracts, drawn from a compendium of boilerplates for scribal trainees, are striking for their attempts to satisfy both the material and emotional needs of their signatories. Taken from actual cases yet representative by virtue of repetitive usage, these contracts employed formal legal language not just to specify transfers of resources or other financial obligations, but also to require that individuals adopt particular attitudes and feelings. In one "Contracta victalita," for example, the aging widow Susanne Magdalena Schreiner was given over to the care of the butcher Jörg Jacob Roller and his wife Maria Agnes.[21] This document specified the monetary compensation the Rollers were to receive and the specific times for Susanne to be fed and washed—but also, under penalty of official investigation "or even punishment," required that the Rollers "greet her with care and patience" and even "show her loyalty and love until her death." Here, the dry formality of a legal text reflects a deeper concern for the welfare of individuals whose contractual claims included emotional and not just material sustenance. And if morals and sentiments animate some contracts, then in others, a grim, legalistic pragmatism defused situations fraught with emotional

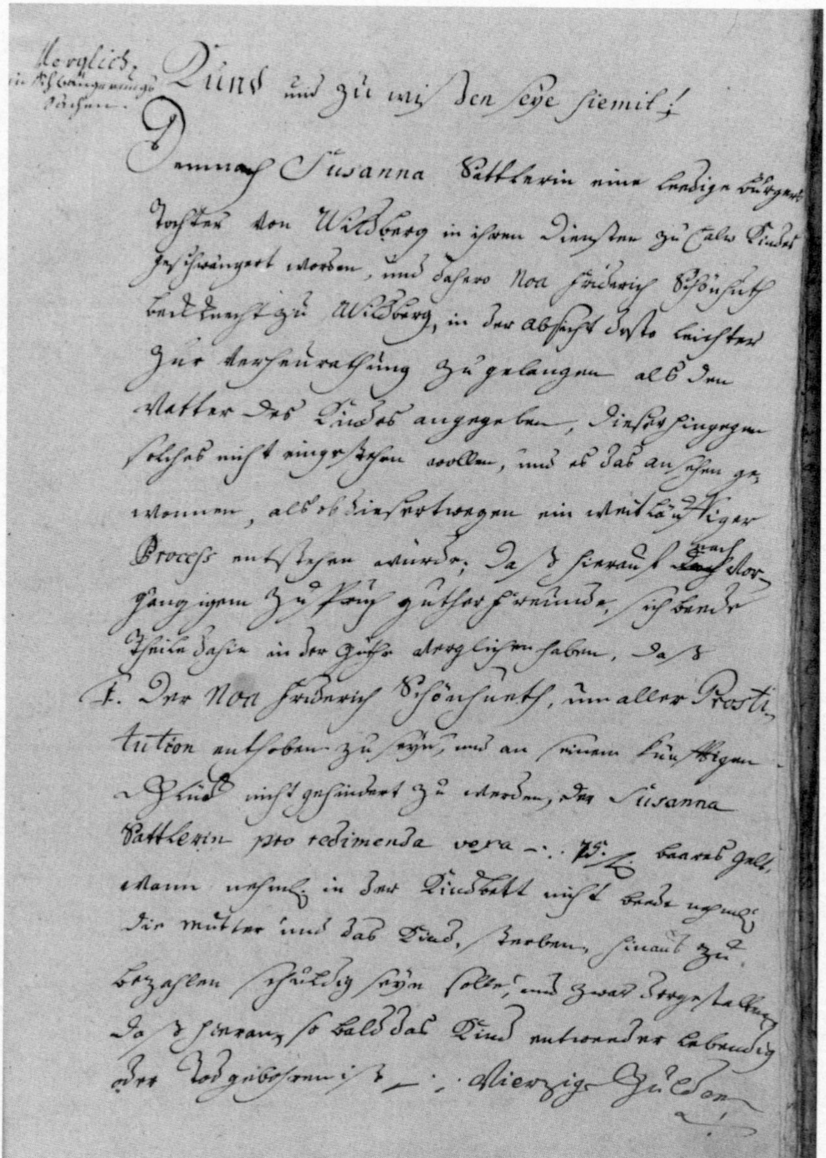

FIGURE 4. Front page of a "compact in matters of impregnation" between Susanna Sattler and Noah Friedrich Schönhuth. A copy of an actual agreement, it was used as a template by scribal trainees for similar cases. © Hauptstaatsarchiv Stuttgart, A 573 Bü 5214.

distress. "Alimentary contracts" enjoining unwed fathers to support their illegitimate children show this quite clearly. In one such "Compact in Matters of Impregnation," Susanne Sattler and Noah Friedrich Schönhuth, the man who had fathered her child, agreed on a detailed schedule of fees Noah would pay should Susanne and/or her baby die in childbirth.[22] Morbidly covering all four possible outcomes, the contract, when executed, formally "relieved" Noah of "all prostitution" and further responsibility for his actions. In this way, a transgression commonly atoned for in the community and the church found its resolution in the fulfillment of specific legal and monetary conditions.

In both these cases, contracts protected individuals cast outside conventional family structures, including widows, orphans, unwed mothers, and illegitimate children. The same device could also be applied within the nuclear family. As David Sabean notes, commenting on similar contracts between parents and their own children, "We get a sense from the documents of a group of people who exchanged resources and property for care, attention, and respect." The pervasive use of these texts for such purposes confirms Sabean's thesis that the "individual" in the modern sense, possessing superego, autonomous emotional makeup, and personal moral responsibility, was a creature largely absent from early modern village society.[23] Personal honor, guilt, and conscience indicated not one's internal mental condition but one's external standing among a web of peers. The scribes, as purveyors of formality, counted among those who dispensed such standing. In the contracts they prepared, they inscribed ethical obligations and states of grace upon the psyche, providing points of fixed written reference in negotiations among individuals who stood before them as official personages embodying the legal order.

A final genre of texts involved scribes even more deeply in citizens' personal affairs. These were the marital estate inventories mandatory in all Württemberg communities. Under the law code of 1567, all non-notable citizens in the duchy were required to have an inventory drawn up on each of three occasions. For a *Zubringens-Inventur*, drafted within three months of every new marriage, the scribe cataloged all the possessions each partner brought to the marital estate. The subsequent death of one of them occasioned a preliminary liquidation *(Eventualteilung)* cataloging the estate again and dividing its contents between a widow(er) and other heirs. Another complete reckoning occurred, finally, with the *Realteilung*, which ensued when the second partner died. These instruments originated in the ducal government's desire to promote an orderly transfer and taxation of estate property, as well as in ordinary citizens' wish to prevent conflicts from arising among heirs.[24] Inventories enabled all parties to keep track of marriage partners' respective contributions, as well as the assets gained or lost during the life of their union. Again, women held and bequeathed property separately from their husbands in Württemberg society, and daughters tended to inherit as much as sons. Thus a large number of parties, encompassing a range of in-laws and collateral lines of inheritance, had a claim on marital property. Such webs of affiliation multiplied steadily over the generations, and family trees grew even larger on account of the second and even third marriages made common by high mortality rates. All these complexities recommended an organized, written system for the devolution of estates. Inventories satisfied this need by disentangling the convoluted family lineages implicated in the practice of rigorously egalitarian, gender-blind partible inheritance.

The conduct of an estate inventory dramatized the encounter between official culture and daily life. Typically a *Substitut,* or journeyman scribe, would be sent to prepare the document. The need to step into an alien environment, quickly dispose of the case, and balance the wishes of the heirs, the interests of the state, and the defense of his own expertise and authority complicated his task. Customarily, one or two city councillors accompanied the scribe as official witnesses, and guardians *(Kriegsvögte)* attended on behalf on unmarried female heirs. Thus a small assembly of notable personages assembled in a peasant household, which, following a death in the family, was often in an especially disordered and confused condition. As his first duty, the scribe locked up and secured any cash, jewelry, or other valuables lying around so that greedy heirs could not abscond with them. He also issued written circulars to all cantonal offices to locate creditors with claims on the marital estate.

The scribe's principal task was then to list the possessions he found in the household, providing a precise description and estimated value for each. Scribes often relied on published handbooks to guide them through this duty. As an index of these handbooks' success in establishing common business routines statewide, the same categories and locutions crop up in inventory samples drawn from regions dispersed throughout the duchy.[25] Through them, a standardized set of rubrics and classifications emerged for cataloging the various types of estate property. A sort of homegrown encyclopedism is apparent in scribes' meticulous and comprehensive classifications of material life: their rubrics included land, houses, cattle-stalls, livestock, agricultural implements, furniture, silverware, dishes, pots and pans, linens, books, jewelry, heirlooms, clothes, and miscellaneous items, in addition to cash, securities, and outstanding debts.[26] Perversely, scribes were paid by the page, a source of incessant complaint by everyday citizens but a boon to present-day historians: for any given couple, living virtually anywhere in the eighteenth-century duchy, inventories make it possible to reconstruct the life cycle of their marriage in minute detail, assess the value accorded to different types of heirs and forms of kinship, and even venture conclusions on their material life and reading practices.[27]

As was the case with contracts, estate inventories required the scribe to show great emotional sensitivity while rendering judgments of monetary value. Of paramount importance was ensuring that each heir received his or her due. Family members displayed an almost fanatical insistence that estates be dispersed equally among all male and female siblings. Accordingly, the scribe often composed preliminary written allotments, called *Theil-* or *Loszettel,* dividing the estate in roughly equal portions. One slip might contain farm implements, say, and another a collection of kitchen-wares of similar worth.[28] Sometimes the scribe would be asked to shuffle these slips of paper and simply distribute them by lot to the various heirs; such a scrupulously impartial method of estate dispersal ensured that only at this moment did each beneficiary discover what he or she would inherit. In other cases, the scribe submitted the allotment slips to haggling and discussion before composing his final draft of the inventory. This process could last hours, during which time debates over inheritance became debates over the classification and worth of various, often incommensurable, objects. Great skill was required in shuttling between family negotiations and taxonomies of material culture, between the political and the technical. Here, the scribe's sense of monetary value and experience with mediation could either prolong or defuse family conflict. Recognizing the delicacy of this situation, the law enjoined scribes from taking sides or giving substantive advice to one party over another, although this might often have been violated in practice.[29]

Inventory preparations bring into focus many of the negotiations and practices of influence undergirding tutelage. In this duty, as in all his official tasks, the scribe controlled what went into, and came out of, the written record. It was this overarching prerogative that bestowed significance upon the scribe's other functions: tending the community's official memory, keeping and revealing its secrets, offering expert advice, enabling citizens to express themselves in proper language, vouching for their character, helping them through difficult personal situations, and determining the value of their property and possessions. Formality, in all these senses, constituted the ultimate source of the scribe's power. Scribes carried out their duties with varying degrees of competence, judgment, and probity in accordance with their individual interests and abilities. The room for corruption and error was great, as Schmid's case attests, but so too was the potential to command respect and, for some individuals, even awe. Tutelage was the sum total of those practices endowing them with power in Württemberg communities.

MANIPULATIONS OF AUTHORITY

Tutelage, because it relied so heavily on informal and not formal authority, inevitably attached to a particular man and not to the office he held. It was founded on daily assertions of influence, stamped by an individual style and personality, and repeated over years until it ultimately coalesced into a reputation enjoyed by one scribe alone. Whenever a long-serving scribe died or retired, the new incumbent of a *Schreiberei* was compelled, often with his predecessor's help, to reassert and rebuild tutelage from the ground up. Transfers of office therefore shed light on the pressures to which scribes were subject, and the machinations to which they were tempted, in negotiating transfers of actual authority. Quite often the scramble for power involved procedural irregularities that provoked the state to intervene. Scribes and other citizens sent written petitions and formal testimony to the central government, and Stuttgart authorities responded with expert opinions and ducal rescripts adjudicating local claims. A dynamic of appeal and decision, an exchange of local information in return for the state's power of enforcement, developed at these times. Transitions thus imparted dynamism to the culture of formality; they reveal scribes and other community members at work manipulating official texts to gain advantage and assert authority. This section takes up three such cases, drawn from the last half of the eighteenth century. Each relied on creative (and often illegal) textual improvisations, though, as time went on, each scribe was less successful than the last.

Wildberg, 1752.   Just under fifty percent of all scribes serving in the second half of the eighteenth century owed their posts to nepotism. The majority of these, at least before the 1770s, were the sons-in-law, rather than the actual sons, of their predecessors.[30] It was quite common, in fact, to marry the daughter of a *Schreiber* in order to take over his practice. As a rule the suitor was the scribe's own *Substitut*. Rudolf Magenau satirized this practice in his portrait of life in the old-Württemberg *Schreiberei*. Magenau, while a young trainee, endured a tense moment when the canton's head scribe confronted his chief *Substitut* over an intercepted love-letter to his daughter, Lotte. The missive was written in the notorious "chancellery style." Magenau watched the journeyman's fear melt as his superior began to read approvingly from its stilted protestations of love:

> The undersigned does not see himself in a position to contest any longer the devotion for you in which he perishes [and] the cause of which he ventures in the enclosed. [Evidently there were two attached affidavits].[31]

Though surely apocryphal, this anecdote illustrates how household reproduction and the culture of the craft overlapped in the ritual of succession from father to son-in-law. Scribes who married into the trade in this way tended to come from more diverse (though still notable) backgrounds than the normal lot in their profession, and only rarely from the canton of their service.[32] Transfers between fathers and sons-in-law thus maintained elite solidarity across regions and social classes. And in communities otherwise dominated by male officeholders, they put daughters in a position to transmit political alliances to the coming generation.

The case of Nikolaus Adam Wieland, *Stadt- und Amtsschreiber* at Wildberg, reveals the formal and informal machinations attending the transfer from father to son-in-law. In 1752, Wieland stepped down in favor of his daughter's fiancé, and, as scribes often did, formally conditioned his resignation on the election of his anointed successor. Wieland was facing death and had apprehensions about the future. Not only had chronic illness undermined his fitness for office, but his daughter, the widow of Wieland's own deceased *Substitut,* had been left without a husband to provide for her and her two small children. Kaspar Christoph Karl Grüb, a young scribe from the nearby canton of Altensteig, presented himself as an appropriate suitor and thus prevailed over a number of other candidates for the *Schreiberei.* To engineer Grüb's election and secure his daughter's well-being, Wieland called on allies in the cantonal assembly and appealed to the community's interest in family stability. Protocol extracts (minutes) from Wildberg's council meeting recorded the terms of their bargain. Grüb was to obtain the *Schreiberei* with all its traditional payments and perquisites, but, with cold instrumentality, council leaders reserved the "right and power to cancel everything and . . . nominate another capable individual" should Grüb renege on the "promised marriage."[33] Little concern was shown for his professional qualifications. Grüb's obligations to Wieland and to the broader community, obligations having nothing to do with his official duties, were thus cemented through the recourse to formal written agreement.

Standard procedure mandated that state bureaucrats ratify all new scribes' elections, and when called upon to do so in Grüb's case, they struck it down.[34] Tacitly acknowledging the nepotistic ways of local notables, they hardly took notice of Grüb's insider status as Wieland's future son-in-law. Ducal authorities instead objected to the way such status had been inscribed into the written council protocols. The fear was that extraneous provisions regarding Grüb's marriage and family duties might find their way into his *Capitulation*, his official service contract. Generally, *Capitulationen* spelled out a new scribe's formal rights and obligations, including his salary, and specified a substantial deposit, amortized against his future earnings, whose payment sufficed to anchor him in the local community. The deposit for a typical *Schreiberei* typically ran from 500 to 700 fl., which effectively excluded all but the wealthy notability from eligibility for office. Ducal policy on the scribes' *Capitulationen* explicitly sanctioned the use of such contracts to uphold community values and, more obliquely, notables' privileged status. Scribes must keep "good household," exhibit "good will [and] seriousness toward the fulfillment of their duties," and be "honorable people living with a family."[35] What the government could not approve in Grüb's case was such an overt linkage of his official competence to his officially unrelated family obligations. Ducal officials thus required that Grüb's election be repeated—and only after Wieland had resigned unconditionally.

When Wildberg's cantonal assembly met for a second time, ostensibly without the formal condition regarding Wieland's daughter, Grüb was again elected unanimously and duly confirmed by the state. In protocol excerpts forwarded for the government's approval, cantonal leaders now enthusiastically proclaimed their "voluntary" neutrality for the formal record, even as they clearly still linked the official with the familial in their hearts and with their votes.[36] They also congratulated themselves on having concluded a separate agreement whereby Grüb would support Wieland's widow and other children with a modest pension when he passed on.[37] In both these ways, the canton strove to ensure financial and emotional security for the various households involved in the transfer of a *Schreiberei*. Wieland, in a particularly revealing letter to the ducal authorities, personally thanked the canton for the "good affection" it had displayed, and remarked on the "grace" shown by all the parties to Grüb's election, including the rival candidates whose exclusion meant that his daughter could now enjoy her "daily bread."[38]

Wieland ultimately had to do without the certitudes of formality that, as an anxious retiree, he had initially sought to safeguard his family interests. His forty-six years of service to the "official interest" and the "public good" nonetheless bespoke a vast reserve of informal tutelage that powerful scribes could redeem in times of need. Wieland's ability to realize his scheme depended just as much, however, on the family-first policy of cantonal elites, a policy centered on household considerations to the chagrin of state authorities, who in practice were powerless to interfere with their decisions. Forty-two years later, an aging (and increasingly incompetent) Grüb himself bequeathed the *Schreiberei* to his stepson, Wieland's grandson.[39] The story thus ends as it began, in the cozy fraternity of notable male householders.

Weilheim, 1784.   Christian Ernst Salzer's election to the Weilheim *Schreiberei* in 1784 illustrates the near-total breakdown in tutelage that could occur when a new scribe lacked the close community ties enjoyed by a scribe like Grüb. Salzer came from Bretten, outside Württemberg; he was a doctor's son apprenticed in Weilheim who edged out five local favorites for his position.[40] One among only 5% of Württemberg scribes who did not hail from the duchy, Salzer lacked both the family connections and the official patronage on which most scribes relied. His former boss, the deceased scribe Finner, had been a poor mentor and an even worse professional, leaving his office in a shambles heaped with stacks of paper. Salzer had acquired his predecessor's "admittedly expansive business style" and proved incapable of straightening out the mess.[41] His lame attempt to pass himself off as Finner's daughter's fiancé misfired, too, when her mother publicly admitted that the thirteen-year-old was not yet marriageable. Soon afterward, the Finners packed up and moved to Stuttgart. This left Salzer alone to confront a "spoiled community" riven among litigious clans.[42] Finner's family had fought Johannes Sigel, a tanner, over debts he owed them, while Johanna Maria Wagner, a shepherd's wife, brought a complaint against Sigel's kin Hans Jörg to demand "alimentary support . . . on account of impregnation." The hotheaded Dürner family once invited an adversary to a pub for dinner and, in an act laden with Freudian symbolism, ended up whipping him across the face with a sausage.[43] Stranded in the crossfire, Salzer himself spent his entire term of office engaging in illegalities to secure his position in town.

Salzer's numerous improprieties provoked a "protocolled investigation" into his misconduct. Protocolled investigations revolved around acts of bribery, extortion, or other abuse of office. They were typically incited either by a local citizen's formal written complaint or by a report from the ducal *Oberamtmann* to his superiors in the central government. Inquiries were conducted by commissioned investigators of the Government Council, or *Regierungsrat*, also called the *Oberrat*, the bureaucratic body in Stuttgart overseeing matters of mid-level administration and justice.[44] Commissioners often took up semipermanent residence in the communities they investigated, interviewing not only the principal parties to corruption scandals, such as scribes, burgomasters, city councillors, and ducal superintendents, but also any ancillary characters who may have had evidence to offer. Cattle-stall attendants, servants, maids, pubkeepers, shepherd boys, and minor bystanders: all had keen ears and voluble testimony that often found its way into the official record. Obsessive commissioners used the methods of protocol, including written and oral "confrontation," to ferret out discrepancies in testimony. They then summarized their findings to the Government Council in official reports accompanied by sworn affidavits, raw protocol transcripts, petitions, and excerpts from the town archives. Expert opinions *(Gutachten)*, including determinations of punishment and review of government policy, if warranted, sometimes involved the participation of the Privy Council, the duchy's supreme policymaking organ. Many cases reached the duke himself. Owing to their scope and detail, the records of protocolled investigation form perhaps the richest vein of sources available on the daily life of early modern communities.[45]

Salzer's case generated six bundles of commission documents by the late 1790s, each containing over fifty testimonials, protocol extracts, interim summary reports, and expert opinions. His troubles began when he remained unmarried and without a household after his election. By staying single, he courted suspicions not just about his personal life but ipso facto about his very fitness for office. One local official, condescendingly and with feigned sympathy, later testified that he was "always in the hope that if [Salzer] would just get married, things would go better for him, but now it seems he just gets more irritable by the day."[46] The link between office and householding was not merely ideological but circumstantial and practical as well. Activities that could appear legitimate for a family man seemed inappropriate for a bachelor. For example, it was common for a new scribe to host a banquet for the city council at his home upon his election. Unable to offer this as a single man, Salzer instead had some wine and cheese brought to the *Rathaus* and passed out one *Reichsthaler* to each of the councillors. Finding this tasteless and hamfisted, many refused.[47] Unwilling to risk offense by foregoing the ritual entirely, Salzer had stripped the practice down to its bare, instrumental essence and exposed the ties of money and patronage lurking within the fraternity of upstanding householders.

Salzer had also bribed the ducal superintendent for help in securing his election. This act offended Salzer's chief rival, a local official named Gallus who had long wanted to combine the *Schreiberei* with his own practice. It was exposed when Gallus prevailed on his crony, a "restless, super-clever, and impudent" member of the Sigel clan, to accuse Salzer of having "greased" the superintendent.[48] Sigel's charge instigated the first protocolled investigation against Salzer, which revealed the accusation to be only partly accurate. In fact, being too poor to offer the *Oberamtmann* an actual bribe, Salzer had instead issued him an IOU worth 700–800 fl.; when the scandal erupted, Salzer asked for it back, which angered the superintendent but in no way diminished his own guilt. Poor Salzer often incriminated himself without going so far as to reap the benefits of his misdeeds. During the scandal he repeatedly denied any impropriety flatly and indignantly only to collapse instantly under protocolled interrogation. Salzer first called Gallus's accusation "the greatest lie," and then, unwilling to contradict direct testimony from the *Oberamtmann*, retreated to the position that he had not offered him "very much." Likewise, he labeled as a "rogue" that councillor who had exposed the *Rathaus* banquet fiasco, only to concede he was an "honest man" upon learning his identity, whereupon he caved in to the allegation.[49] Salzer eventually landed on secure footing in pronouncing his bribe an "honorarium," a quasi-legal gift customarily offered to an official at the New Year, after the birth of a son, or, as in this case, upon his performance of some important duty.[50] Provisionally at least, Salzer could thus argue in the protocol record that a ritual form of community corruption should not count as an actionable transgression in the state's eyes.

The war between Salzer and Gallus droned on for over a decade. Several outside commissioners were rotated in and out of Weilheim as the case dragged on, each one as tractable and suggestible as the last. Their protocolled investigations, ostensibly the Württemberg state's principal means of asserting authority, repeatedly foundered amidst concerted local interference. During one government commissioner's inquiry, Salzer charged, Gallus physically stationed himself at the *Rathaus* door and "instructed almost every citizen upon entering what to complain about me." For his part, Salzer, attempting to counteract these illegalities, drowned out Gallus with florid, ranting denunciations, practically admitting the distortions of truth that this entailed: "I would have to dip my feather in gall . . . if I wanted to expose the malevolent rancor and lies of *Amtmann* Gallus."[51] Local bias eventually proved so severe as to warrant an exasperated state's temporarily removing the case from Weilheim altogether. Frustrated by the volley of one-sided supplications, it determined "no longer to let the parties [campaign] against each other through writing." This was a revealing admission that citizens' manipulations of formality had put up an inscrutable veil before the state's methods of inquisition. Eventually, in a nearly unprecedented move, state officials had Gallus and Salzer travel to Stuttgart personally in order to be interviewed by a special deputation at the government chancellery. This still produced no resolution. The matter finally reached the Tübingen law faculty, Württemberg's highest judicial authority, which produced a 138-page expert opinion, very detailed but in no way conclusive about exactly what had happened.[52]

The chief reason the case became so confusing was that its principals polarized the community using the same textual instruments the state relied upon to uncover the truth. Both Gallus and Salzer led state investigators on a series of wild goose chases through writing. Gallus, openly confessing his desire to "drive out of office this poor lonely man without friend or patron," trumped up more than fifty formal petitions against Salzer, usually signed by familiar culprits among the Sigels, the Dürners, and the Wagners. Salzer, whose life had become a "burning hell," fought back by suborning a series of written accusations exploding around Gallus throughout the 1790s. Acting in his official capacity as notary for the nominal complainants he persuaded to serve as co-conspirators, he leveled all manner of new allegations against Gallus: that he seduced his own maid and wrecked her marriage; that he settled a payment dispute by telling the parties to brawl it out ("a nice theory in the mouth of an official who is supposed to look out for order and avoid conflict"); and that he jailed one Philipp Gentner for stealing some wine when it was Gallus's own crony, Christian Dürner, who was probably guilty.[53]

As a rule, Salzer made common cause with the humbler peasants in town, whereas Gallus counted the more influential families on the city council among his own allies. Salzer's exclusion from the town notability led him to impugn the rectitude of the legal order they supposedly upheld. By availing himself of protocols, petitions, and supplications to Stuttgart officials, Salzer invoked a higher, ducal authority as his best recourse against the combinations and conspiracies of local oligarchy. His efforts culminated in a complaint signed by seventy common (non-notable) citizens, alleging that Gallus had punished them severely and capriciously for grazing their cattle on lands to which, he claimed, they had no right.[54] Gallus and the council called this "insolent testimony," and, for once, the government agreed. In his commission report to the duke, the state's chief investigator determined that Salzer's appeals to ducal authority showed less interest in upholding the law than in waging community war by other means:

> Such collections of signatures, from people who do not know what they are doing, is the usual means by which the Weilheimer imagine they will be able to find access to Your Ducal Majesty, and to present as a general complaint of the citizenry that which is merely the exasperated hatred of an individual.[55]

Regardless of the state's position, community battles could still be won and lost over better or worse manipulations of texts, and by this standard, Salzer miraculously triumphed. Under his tutelage, the circle of those involved in the case became wider and wider, as ever humbler citizens were roped in for their signatures, given the opportunity to vent petty grievances through written petitions, and brought into participation, however staged and manipulated, in the affairs of government. The texts they produced completely overshadowed the original scandal giving rise to them. This eventually turned the tide against Gallus. Gallus said that the "people [had] actually gone wild," throwing stones through his windows while, on one terrifying night, he crouched with his wife and their sickly newborn in fear of an angry mob outside their house. He was eventually fined and transferred out of Weilheim.[56] Salzer got off with fines and a reprimand.

It is important to keep two lessons of the Salzer case in mind throughout this book. First, it is impossible to speak of official texts as instruments of state power in cases where local passions, partisanship, and competition for office and influence so completely undermined their formal intent. The sheer volume of sources shows how easily community factions were able to corrupt the state's protocol procedures and legal judgments with their own vendettas. At best, state and community shared a claim on the use of formality to assert authority. Second, local citizens' verbosity, here and in other protocolled investigations, offers no guarantee that the impressions they convey are in any way conclusive, accurate, or verifiable against one another. Quite the opposite: the willingness of local citizens, from everyday peasants to elevated officeholders, to seek recourse in writing is elegant testimony to their sophistication, and evidence that the culture of formality emphatically embraced a local conception of truth. Their testimonies must be treated with the maximum of reverence and circumspection. While their writings and utterances were undeniably elicited by the state's intimidation, they simultaneously counted as the very expression of communal autonomy.

Schorndorf, 1802.   The last and briefest case comes from the very end of the old regime, after several decades of significant expansion in the Württemberg state and its *Schreibereien.* The duchy's population boomed during this period, and each new citizen needed a certain number of inventories, contracts, property deeds, and other documents drawn up in the course of a lifetime.[57] Novel tasks the scribes acquired in the 1790s, including the oversight of conscription and special tax levies for the French Revolutionary wars, compounded the secular rise in business. Staff sizes burgeoned to keep pace with the demands of government, shattering the pretense that the *Schreiberei* functioned as a household operation. Junior scribes roved the

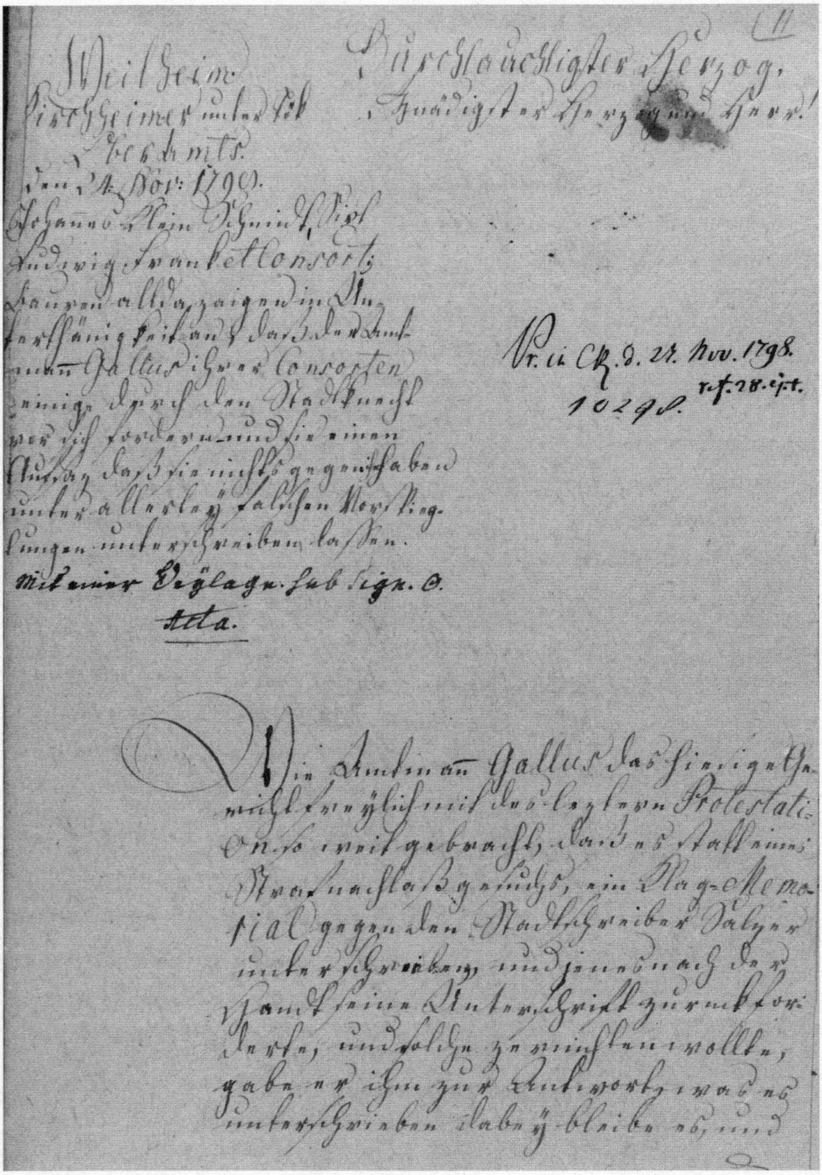

Weilheim

Durchlauchtigster Herzog,

Gnädigster Herzog und Herr!

Pr. d. 24. Nov. 1798.

Acta.

FIGURE 5. Front and back pages of a petition sent to the Duke of Württemberg by Weilheim citizens disgruntled with local official Gallus. As is typical, the text block in the upper left corner lists the location and date of composition, the names of the principal petitioners, and a brief summary of their complaint. Signed on the back by several citizens, each in their own hand, the petition was drawn up, and most probably suborned, by Stadtschreiber Salzer, whose name appears on the left margin. © Hauptstaatsarchiv Stuttgart, A 214 Bü 492 Nr. 11.

countryside, lonely, unsupervised, generating fortunes for their supervisors. Frequent rotations of *Amtssubstituten* unattached to fixed district offices diminished their connection to the cantonal seats and increased their resentment and isolation. Besides having to equip their own horses and drag them through the muddy hills of the Swabian landscape, they complained bitterly about the horrible food at village pubs in hamlet after monotonous hamlet. Journeyman ceased to view their supervisors as *Hausvater* and began to cultivate tutelage locally, on their own. Demographic growth created multiple, competing centers of tutelage in the traditional canton, and the traditional link between office and householding threatened to break. These factors complicated the ritual of succession within the *Schreiberei*.

Christian Gottlieb Schmid confronted exactly this problem when in 1800 he attempted to retire in favor of his son. Schmid was the senior scribe who, twenty years earlier, had survived his constituents' chastising Instruction. In the interim, he had watched his practice grow into one of the most lucrative in Württemberg. Schmid employed a staff of more than a dozen junior scribes, divided between the Schorndorf home office and several branches in the village hinterland. These served a cantonal population of 29,000, which had increased by over a third during Schmid's tenure and whose official business generated 4000–5000 fl. annually.[58] Managing all this growth had restored Schmid's tarnished reputation in Schorndorf's cantonal seat and expanded his influence over its hinterland. Owing to widespread support from all over the canton, Schmid had thus secured his son's election, provisionally at least, with nearly all of the votes cast.[59] The very circumstances attending this show of influence prevented him from completing the transfer of office, however. The size of Schmid's expanding empire distanced him from the personalized supervision on which tutelage was based and multiplied the number of competing players whose ambitions and conceptions of office, household, and self demanded appeasement. These problems led the state to invalidate the election of Schmid's son in 1802.

The collapse of Schmid's scheme was precipitated by two illegal manipulations of official texts uncovered by state investigators. The first of these hinged on the new *Capitulation* formalizing the transfer of power to his son, which Schmid *père* had hammered out in secret consultations with Schorndorf's village foremen. According to one report, he called the foremen into his office, offered them bribes for their votes at the election, and then had their understandings "fixed surely in writing."[60] Schmid agreed, in return, to sacrifice certain lucrative sources of *Schreiberei* business to various junior scribes in the foremen's home villages. These concessions were duly recorded in the preliminary *Capitulation*, revealing how the village foremen acted at the behest of the junior scribes who nominally served them, including some of Schmid's own *Substituten*.[61] The conspiracy was exposed by a protocolled investigation provoked by still other scribes, those left out of the deal. Investigations revealed that the village foremen had come to the election, as was routine, bearing written mandates *(Vollmachten)* from their home communities. But rather than reflecting the wishes of local populations, these mandates simply incorporated the demands of the various subaltern scribes vying for a piece of Schmid's practice. This was the second illegality: though the state's investigator could not prove that any *formal* violations had occurred in the drafting of electoral mandates, the texts clearly betrayed "the influence of those to whom an increase in their own incomes lies more at heart than . . . the common good."[62] Products of junior scribes' string-pulling, the *Vollmachten* illustrated how Schmid's former monopoly on tutelage had been dispersed among rival power bases.

The episode at Schorndorf revealed a new economy of tutelage ascendant in Württemberg's cantons at the end of the old regime, more vertical and hierarchical than the classic system found in places like Wildberg and Weilheim. Tutelage was less dependent on the perquisites of close-knit notable insiders—or even the machinations of outsiders craving admission to the community of householders—and more susceptible to pressures no longer contained within the cantonal seat. Such pressures came from below, from villages within the canton, as well as from above, in the form of an increased state interference. Schmid and his son, despite their exalted status, experienced them just as surely as their lowly counterparts in Schorndorf's villages. Because they could not supervise the local dealings between junior scribes and village communities nor, despite their best efforts, engineer to the state's satisfaction the textual formalities governing the junior Schmid's election, they found themselves beleaguered by challenges to their authority. After months of such challenges, the state eventually confirmed a credentialed lawyer from outside Schorndorf as its new scribe. Schmid's son found a lesser post in town.

CRISIS IN THE WRITING TRADES

No one in any of these cases—even Salzer's decades-long saga—ever thought to do away with the written texts enabling so many manipulations of authority. The old regime never witnessed any critique of formality, which in all its elaborateness and profusion remained the undisputed currency of power in Württemberg down to Napoleon's invasions. During the last quarter of the eighteenth century, however, the scribes' tutelage fell into crisis for very different reasons. Starting in the 1780s, the mounting excess of underemployed junior scribes began to undermine not only their local tutelage, as in Schmid's case, but also their occupational cohesion on a statewide level. Angry dissatisfaction was especially common among the younger generation, who felt that their *Stand*, their estate, could no longer provide for its own. Concurrently, the scribes were subjected to the vicious polemics of Enlightened intellectuals determined to uproot tutelage and expose what they regarded as corrupt influence. New expectations about the role of intellect and *Bildung* in guiding the citizenry, combined with standards of professional practice associated with the rise of modern bureaucracy, cast the scribes in an unflattering light. These twin threats, demographic and ideological, forced some ambitious and articulate scribes to refurbish their inherited claims to tutelage, and to justify their continued leadership in light of the new demands of a modern, Enlightened state.

The crisis besetting the scribes' younger generation had its origins in dynamics of state expansion familiar from the Schorndorf case. Junior scribes, despite considerable growth in their ranks, confronted a maddening stasis in the number of official appointments and were increasingly consigned to menial, underpaid posts. Between the 1770s and the 1790s, the proportion of examined journeymen going on to become *Stadt- und Amtsschreiber* dropped from a half to a quarter, while those suffering downward mobility into clerical positions climbed in almost equal measure.[63] Fully half the duchy's scribes languished without any stable employment. Balthasar Haug, author of a who's-who entitled *Educated Württemberg*, estimated it would take three full decades to draw down this backlog at then-current mortality levels.[64] Two corollary trends reinforce the impression that the path of ascent had become bottlenecked. Starting in the 1780s, a number of *Substituten* began petitioning the government for special permission to marry, and submitted evidence of moral character and fiscal solvency in order to do so.[65] These men, aging and with diminishing prospects, had jettisoned the classic narrative of their craft—working one's way up the ranks, marrying the boss's daughter, and inheriting his practice—preferring instead to establish their own households. Competition was further stiffened by a glut of university-educated lawyers seeking official appointment. One scribe accused "people hounded out of the universities" of slumming in the *Schreibereien;* others concurred that notable sons who were "too dumb or too poor" to attend universities sought refuge there. With an influx of outsiders, the number of scribes with legal backgrounds grew from a negligible percentage in the 1760s to over a quarter of the profession by the end of the old regime.[66]

As the glut of underemployed lawyers suggests, the problem of oversubscription was by no means specific to the scribes, but affected all of the writing trades. It also extended far beyond the duchy of Württemberg. Germany during the late Enlightenment was, almost everywhere, a society obsessed with academic learning and official appointment as a route to higher status and better economic prospects. Parents of all classes proved fanatical in having their children trained for the *Brodwissenschaften*, the professions— like law, preaching, teaching, the civil service, and, in Württemberg, the *Schreiberei*—offering "bread" for one's academic knowledge. Government offices all over Central Europe thus found themselves besieged with applicants in the 1780s and 1790s.[67]

Württemberg itself gained international notoriety as the "Empire of Teachers and *Schreiber*."[68] Its scribes symbolized a broader problem and inspired a wave of popular satires and philippics directed against the craft, some of which were widely disseminated across Germany. Critics in the public sphere were less concerned with the growing quantity than with the decreasing professional quality of the scribes. They found them woefully lacking in the cultural and intellectual attainments, the *Bildung*, expected of a modern civil servant. Friedrich Bernritter's well-known diatribe cited their "lack of cosmopolitanism, raw language, awkward manners, too little taste . . . an inclination to drink, emptiness of discourse, petty gaming, chasing girls in cattle-stalls and store-closets, lack of Enlightenment, and sloppiness."[69] With only slightly less acerbity, the travelogue of "Anselm Rabiosus" (a pseudonym for W. L. Wekhrlin) called the scribes "political quacks . . . who never travel outside the districts of their *Schreiberei* or their country [and who] do not combine the least foreign knowledge with their profession."[70] Both these critiques appealed to academic Germany's disdain for the provincial culture of the middling strata. They also reflected a widespread conviction that the longstanding divide in Württemberg between local, artisanal scribes and the university-educated jurists serving in the Stuttgart chancelleries was inappropriate to a truly Enlightened state. With competition so severe in the *Brodwissenschaften*, and particularly with the influx of so many lawyers into the *Schreibereien*, their previously unproblematic division of labor had flared into a full-blown clash of official cultures.[71]

Next to oversubscription, the scribes' lack of *Bildung* emerged as the paramount reform issue of the eighteenth century. The two were related insofar as the growth of the occupation and the attendant delegation of authority removed younger scribes from direct household supervision and made their training a concern of the state. The German Enlightenment's distinct preoccupation with pedagogy and childhood also prompted a heightened sensitivity to the problem of youth and early personality development. Critics told scandalous tales of "spirit-killing copying" among *Incipienten* taken on as "tuition corpses" and ill prepared for later, increasingly independent duties.[72] Once they became *Substituten* and were farmed out to the villages, scribes' morality declined even further. Gradually losing the feeling for "urbanity" and "fine thoughts," forced into "intercourse . . . with base and coarse-minded people," many succumbed to "love of companionship" and took over the styles of dress, speech, and drink typical of the peasants and craftsmen they served. Anti-scribe tracts accused them of drunkenness and stalking village maidens.[73] As remedies for these corrupting tendencies, advocates of better *Bildung* stressed the need for early inculcation of humanistic learning and abstract thought. They were eager to extract trainees from the routines of apprenticeship to produce a more competent and intellectually sophisticated *Schreiberstand*. A consolidated profession, elevated above the idiocy of rural life and fused with the culture-bearing stratum in general, was more in line with their thinking.[74]

Bildung was a universal ideal, a way of governing one's behavior by reason, utility, and culture, not by social convention, status, or hierarchy. Some scribes, if the critics are to be believed, adopted its outward trappings without its inner virtues. Lacking true moral centeredness, they found themselves adrift in a brave new world where the corporative system had ceased to provide fixed expectations for proper conduct. Their *Stand* was, after all, a liminal, anomalous group, with no clearly defined legal, social, and political privileges attaching to it. Scribes who attempted to overcome their coarse provincialism therefore exhibited a deep-seated—and quintessentially modern—status insecurity. They were branded as "affected," prone to "anxiety," marked by "a spirit of pettiness" and "a certain stiffness with which they appear in society." They showed a superficial tendency to judge others by their hairstyles and the quality of the buttons on their frocks. "They read not to extend their knowledge but rather read novels, comedies, almanacs, and fairy tales *[Siegfriede]*."[75] At the root of these behaviors lay the familiar frustrations of the scribe's lack of formal status and authority. As one commentator explained, his

> office itself brings him no greater honor than that of a simple *Bürger*; hence the scribe must attempt to cultivate a greater standing through his outward conduct. He therefore dresses according to fashion, he lives according to fashion, he marries according to fashion, he raises his chil-

dren according to fashion, in short: he and his family live in grand style. And for that his originally quite meager income does not go very far. It should and must, therefore, be supplemented . . . through subtle and unnoticed, and, for that reason, much more unwholesome, means.[76]

This passage, especially in its last two sentences, clearly connected scribes' anxieties about "standing" to the corruption and exploitation that, in places like Weilheim and Schorndorf, had always formed the flip side of their tutelage.

Eighteenth-century defenders of the scribes, who joined the public fray in their own pamphlets and commentaries, responded to these allegations by asserting the dignity and integrity of their *Stand*. Ferdinand Weckherlin (not to be confused with W. L. Wekhrlin), author of an influential *Apology* on their behalf, accepted the cultural differences exposed by educated critics and simply reversed the moral signs. To him, it may have been true that "the gleam of Enlightenment has forced itself only very lately into our circle," but by the same token, aristocratic "luxury, haughtiness, idleness, and flabbiness have not yet beset our *Stand* in the same measure as other estates." Critics of the scribes' crassness and unsophistication mistook their sometimes rambunctious, salt-of-the-earth rapport with the people for a deeper lack of seriousness and cultivation. "If [a scribe] appears . . . too careless and artless . . . people ascribe a total lack of inner *Bildung* to him." As for the contention that some scribes had become superficial, social-climbing trend-mongers, Weckherlin countered that if anything, scribes "trouble themselves too little with outward appearances, too little for gallantry and fashion."[77] Finally, the "theoretical knowledge" advocated by the enthusiasts of *Bildung* could never substitute for a keen eye in preparing an estate inventory or drawing up a receipt. Adult wisdom, not youthful book-learning, was what mattered. "The peculiar character, the peculiar advantage of the Württemberg *Schreiber* consists in a certain adeptness that can be imparted neither through oral nor written instruction, [but] in a certain practical sense" that only came from long experience.[78]

Defenders of the scribes' *Stand* dispensed with Enlightenment universalism and ascribed true ethical worth to the fulfillment of humbler aspirations varying by social station. While advocates of *Bildung* upheld a radically progressive standard of human conduct and cultivation, partisans of *Stand* emphasized the inherent limits of education and the essential imperfectability of human institutions. No general standards, they maintained, could ever be applied to the ethics of an entire estate. A *Stand* always encompassed a range of personality types with varying levels of morality. To Weckherlin, "there is good and evil, honorable and base, cultivated and uncultivated, just as it is everywhere." This mantra appears repeatedly in apologists' discourse: "Objections which have been made against individual *Schreiber* can never be applied to the whole *Stand*. . . . [H]ere, as everywhere, capable and incapable, honest men and villains are all mixed together."[79] Scribes' defenders smuggled their own brand of universalism into the political debate, asserting their shared fallibility and humanity. "Do we live in a different climate, under a different form of government? Is our education and upbringing as youths different, the society in which we live a different one?" They retained a clear commitment, however, to certain minimum expectations, the "moderate degree of spiritual energy [which] will be demanded" of any *Stand* member.[80] In short, the gentle restraints of occupational tradition, far from retarding general progress, offered attainable goals to fulfill, channeled human energies into constructive ends, framed one's morality and identity, and ultimately enhanced one's utility to the state.

On account of its ethical realism, the scribes' corporative rhetoric could, despite its fundamentally conservative bent, inspire a range of practical reform suggestions. At one extreme were proposals that entry into the *Stand* be legally restricted to notables, or even limited to strict hereditary succession; these ideas the government rejected as a ruse to institutionalize nepotism and privilege.[81] Other observers, less enamored of a neo-feudal reaction, recommended a bracing regimen of state-sponsored meritocracy such as was found among the clergy, whose *Stand* had, for centuries, been subjected to periodic, routine, and comprehensive administrative visitations and oversight.[82] The state itself considered a series of measures to encourage "the working classes of the population" to "select a *Stand*" outside the *Brodwissenschaften* and even published some edicts on this score. Typically for cameralist policymaking, however, it devoted no resources to rectifying the perceived imbalance between subjects and officials, the "producing" and "consuming" parts of the population. Reflecting the Duke's own preference for "indirect measures," state policy renounced any interference in parents' right to choose their children's careers, a "natural freedom" against which no "positive laws" should be set.[83]

The most interesting—and influential—responses came from those appropriating the notion of *Bildung* for incrementalist reform of the *Schreiberstand*. These authors produced new educational curricula, plans for the establishment of scribal training institutes, and a spate of reference handbooks on legal and administrative science.[84] Johann Bäuerlen, one of the most prolific of these, developed an ambitious educational plan stretching over ten semesters and including lessons in German, French, Latin, geometry, mathematics, fine arts, geography, history, law, philosophy, psychology, logic, and ethics. His *Handbook* for beginning scribes and especially his *Attempt at an Introduction for the Self-Cultivation of Württemberg Scribes* struggled to articulate what it would take to turn a battery of provincial notaries into a corps of Enlightened administrators. Taking his inspiration from the few mythic scribes who had burned the midnight oil reading law books while earning their bread as copyists, Bäuerlen advocated self-cultivation *(Selbstbildung)* for scribes along occupationally-specific *(standesmäßig)* lines: "Every person from every *Stand,* from every class of civil society *[bürgerliche Gesellschaft]* must have, along with the general moral *Bildung* that every person undergoes, an individual education appropriate to his *Stand* and class."[85]

Bäuerlen's invocation of "civil society" here conflated two meanings of the term, corporative and universalistic, that competed for supremacy in the discourse of eighteenth-century reformers. His use of the words *Stand* and *Bildung* side-by-side illustrates, in particular, how the concept of civil society was still being assembled from the many individual tools at hand for thinking about social status, identity, and progress. Their dialectical opposition framed a political language still drawing upon the civic pride and political privilege of the estates order, but straining beyond its particularism toward a more universal standard of ethics. The two concepts were again strikingly imbricated in a petition drawn up by about thirty *Substituten* in the summer of 1798. Convening at the Waldhorn pub in Böblingen and representing over half the duchy's cantons, the cream of the duchy's junior scribes addressed their petition to the Württemberg estates assembly. In it they combined practical suggestions for improving their *Stand,* in both its material and moral constitution, with a clear sensitivity to the need to justify their continued "political existence" in modern, Enlightened terms evoking the rhetoric of *Bildung:*

> A common spirit that was foreign to our *Stand* and whose absence
> clearly hindered us from refinement but now spurs us to perfection . . .
> has finally brought together the scattered members of our *Stand.* . . . If
> every human institution . . . is allowed a further perfection, why should
> our *Stand* lack the same sensibility for refinement?[86]

Formulations such as this illustrate how, in the eighteenth century, the lines dividing the *Schreiber* from their opponents remained fluid and indistinct. Participants in public discourse groped for a vocabulary to express their concerns, and operated in a situation of uncertainty created by the shortcomings of cameralist policymaking amidst the continued indispensability of the scribes. On the surface, political stasis reigned. Even the more extreme quarters shied away from calling for the complete abolition of the *Stand,* whereas defenders conceded many of their critics' points about the depravity of the profession. What emerged was a subtly differentiated use of political keywords accenting different approaches toward reform: the one, *Stand,* based on defensive occupationalism and gradualist improvement; the other, *Bildung,* offering a bracingly radical standard of Enlightenment applicable to society as a whole. Both sides of the debate converged, however, in addressing themselves exclusively to scribes' personality and professional ethics; very little attention was paid to their functions in the state. Missing from the entire discourse on the scribes' crisis is any real concern with the culture of formality and its excesses. The critique of *Vielschreiberei,* of the verbiage and red tape the scribes purveyed in such overwhelming quantities, would have to wait until after Napoleon. Among all the vituperations hurled in their direction, and all the resentments harbored by the scribes' younger generation, this remains a striking omission. It meant that the scribes, as long as they maintained ultimate control over the official texts suffusing daily life, would not see their tutelage fundamentally undercut.

The public campaign did succeed in awakening many scribes to the need for reform, however. It put issues of official morality and the common good on the political agenda. And it led many to adopt a more articulated, self-conscious position on the nature of their tutelage in its connection to ideals of the Enlightenment. At the end of the eighteenth century, a few activist scribes living through the crisis of their *Stand* would parlay crisis into opportunity and redeem the historic virtues of the craft against its detractors. The next chapter describes one such attempt, showing how tutelage acquired an explicitly progressive cast among one group of scribes inspired by the ideas of the French Revolution.

3   The Black Forest Cahier

Among the most important texts produced during the French Revolution were the *cahiers des doléances* prepared in the various districts of the realm, notebooks listing the particular grievances each wanted to present before the Estates General. Alexis de Tocqueville called them "the swan song of the old regime, the ultimate expression of its ambitions, its last will and testament."[1] As a rule, the cahiers shied away from calling for an end to the monarchy, much less a bloody overthrow of the entire political system. Textually, they are more interesting as residues of collegiality than as portents of violence. A great many bore the mark of coordinated regional campaigns by notaries, lawyers, and other ambitious practical intellectuals. Because they often took their cues from circulated models, one often finds verbatim language in separate cahiers drawn up in neighboring districts. Cahiers from small villages were passed up the chain to larger assemblies, which sifted and recombined their contents before sending them with each district's deputy to Paris. The results hardly provide a transparent, unmediated picture of French political sentiment. But when mediation and manipulation are themselves made the objects of scrutiny, the cahiers reveal how political power was formed and transmitted during the pre-Revolutionary period.

In the archives of an obscure, remote highland canton in Württemberg there is a document very similar to the French cahiers. It dates from 1796, seven years after the Revolution began in France and four years after that country invaded Germany. A small handwritten notebook about seventy pages long, its title page bears the inscription "Cahier / Stadt und Amt ~~Wildberg~~ Nagold / Mit Instruktionen für seinen Landtagsdeputierten."[2] The document survives not in the Nagold but in the Wildberg *Schreiberei*, whose holdings were transferred to the ducal administration in Stuttgart when the canton was dissolved after the Napoleonic invasions.[3] Other, similar copies may survive in collections dispersed elsewhere, such as community archives. Whatever their fate, the original document owes its inception to meetings and communications among many politically active cantons in the Black Forest region of Württemberg. Of these, Nagold was by far the most important, and this certainly accounts for the substitution of its name for Wildberg's on the Cahier's title page. For this reason, the document is often called the "Nagold Cahier."[4] Because the Cahier is better regarded as a regional, not a municipal, product, it will instead be referred to below as the "Black Forest Cahier."

The Black Forest Cahier spearheaded the most ambitious campaign to reform the duchy's political system between the Tübingen Compact and the Napoleonic wars. This mobilization catapulted a number of Jacobin sympathizers to leadership of the Württemberg *Landtag* and awakened demands for a substantive democratization of the duchy's cantonal system of political representation. Under the tutelage of Nagold scribe Ludwig Hofacker, republican reform programs arose in surprising fusion with traditional corporatism in politically potent hybrid forms. And though Hofacker ultimately failed, his crusade for political Enlightenment—conducted alongside many other scribes—fleetingly radicalized the so-called Reform *Landtag* of 1798 and left an enduring legacy in the process. The energies the Cahier unleashed, though they lay dormant in the decade of absolutist rule after the Napoleonic invasions, resurfaced during the 1810s, enabling Württemberg's parliamentarians to reconstruct civil society on much more advantageous terms than the new king was originally willing to concede.

The Cahier and its effects are no less important for what they reveal about collegiality. The Black Forest mobilization showed how scribes cultivated written and unwritten contacts in a number of settings: out in the cantons, among each other, in the Stuttgart *Landtag,* and in the Enlightenment public sphere. Corporative representation placed a premium on collective expression and consensus politics, and relied heavily on written formality to ensure "collegial deliberation." Beneath this façade, however, the scribes' coalition-building actually occurred in separate and more informal networks of information exchange and debate. These networks gave rise to the Cahier's specific ideological concern with the exclusion of provincials from cosmopolitan society in the capital. Ludwig Hofacker's attempt to open the Stuttgart *Landtag* to dynamic men of merit and ability, including scribes like himself, aimed to remedy the Black Forest's marginalization. His campaign called into question the old regime's ability to modernize its means of political representation, showing how corporative collegiality fused, yet also clashed, with a freer and more individualistic style of deliberation pioneered during the Enlightenment. The limited plasticity of corporative formalities in fact contributed to Hofacker's downfall back in Nagold. The chapter thus ends, having shown how formal texts acted to facilitate, and then thwart, a collegiality underlying the entire Black Forest campaign.

All these insights derive from the Cahier's uniqueness as a written text. In both its content and manner of composition, it traced a web of linkages between the high and low, cosmopolitan and provincial, political cultures of late Enlightenment Germany. Following these pathways of politicization unearths a host of other texts—formal and informal, public and private, individual and collective, oral and written—generated during the Black Forest mobilization. Evidence of collegiality in its polymorphous forms, such texts sustained the solidarity this remote, provincial region mustered, and help us to account for the sudden and surprising appearance of a cahier there, in 1796.

POLITICAL VENTRILOQUISM

To follow the drafting and early impact of the Black Forest Cahier is to witness the acts of mediation—and manipulation—involved in translating inchoate local aspirations into the language and practice of a coherent coalition, one with designs on statewide, even international, political influence. Württemberg's civic culture placed a much higher value on "collegial deliberation" in "patriotic community" than on personal initiative, compelling ambitious individuals to express their opinions creatively and surreptitiously. Scribes therefore relied on the ruses of political ventriloquism to project their voices from the provinces into the chambers of the Stuttgart *Landtag*. Using cantonal assemblies as their mouthpieces, they influenced the election and formal instruction of parliamentary delegates to enunciate the Cahier's reformist principles, all the while concealing their own hand in authorship. Later sections will turn to the source of their ambition and to the ideas they drew from the Enlightenment public sphere. The focus for now is on the mechanics of representation: on the institutions of corporative politics the scribes commandeered to produce the Black Forest Cahier.

The Cahier originated at a secret conference called by the Nagold city council, which in the late summer of 1796 sent out invitations to about a dozen neighboring cantons scattered around the Black Forest highland. Delegates convened in the picturesque river-valley town at eight in the morning on September 15.[5] Roughly one scribe and one city councillor attended from each of several districts: Nagold, Sindelfingen, Böblingen,

Wildberg, Reichenbach, Freudenstadt, Dornstetten, Liebenzell, Wildbad, Neuenbürg, and Ebingen.[6] Geographically, these cantons stretched from the suburbs of present-day Stuttgart to the duchy's forested borderland regions in the west and northwest. Ludwig Hofacker, the Nagold *Stadt- und Amtsschreiber*, acted as conference host; his meteoric rise to parliamentary leadership, followed by an equally precipitous fall, began at this time. Hofacker had served as a journeyman scribe in the Nagold *Schreiberei* under his father, who in 1785 transferred the office to his son through an act of contractually-sanctioned nepotism still typical in communities of unchallenged notable dominance.[7] A certified lawyer who had studied at Tübingen, he embodied the higher ambitions and proclivities toward Enlightenment of a new generation. Although it was rumored that Hofacker personally composed the Cahier, and we may assume that the document owes more to his guiding hand than anyone else's, it is important to stress that as a piece of writing, it retains the appearance of collaborative effort and collective authorship. No individual voice, in the records that descend to us, is allowed to corrupt what appears to have been a pristine exercise in unanimous collegiality. In any case, there were many others present, besides Hofacker, equally capable of contributing to the Cahier's fashioning.

The purpose of what came to be known as the "Nagold pre-parliament" was to coordinate responses to the duke's convocation of the Württemberg *Landtag* for the first time since 1770. A burdensome war indemnity levied by the victorious French armies had put an end to its long hiatus, the Tübingen Compact having compelled the duke to ask the estates for the needed funds. Judging by the agenda items mentioned in its conference invitation, the Nagold city council saw the *Landtag*'s convocation as an opportunity to force a thorough reform of parliamentary powers in the duchy. In this spirit, the council floated the idea of drafting a "general cahier" emphasizing suffrage and institutional reform, but its specific content otherwise remained unclear.[8] Only the deliberations themselves—or so we must infer, given the absence of protocols—produced the list of particular grievances appearing in the final version of the Black Forest Cahier housed in the Wildberg *Schreiberei*.

As was the case with the French Revolutionary *cahiers des doléances*, the final document was envisioned for the limited purpose of instructing parliamentary deputies. Its inscription, "with instructions for [Nagold's] *Landtag* deputy," identifies its intent as such, and a separate formal "Instruktion" from the canton of Wildberg to its deputy, also preserved in the Wildberg *Schreiberei*, mimics the text of the Cahier on almost every point.[9] The much longer *Instruktion* is far from an exact copy, however, suggesting that the Cahier simply provided talking points for cantonal assemblies sympathetic to its reformist program, as they prepared to elect their *Landtag* deputies. Divergences between the Cahier and the *Instruktion* apparently arose when assemblies met separately to draft their instructions immediately after their delegates' return from Nagold.

It is possible to read the Cahier, at least on the first pass, as a straightforward imitation of its French predecessors. Invocations of citizen rights, patriotism, and the rhetoric of progress abound alongside tirades against dead traditions, feudal anachronisms, and religious superstition. In twenty-four separate sections (expanded to forty-three in the Wildberg *Instruktion*), the document rails against privilege, wealth, and undue influence, whether on the part of entrenched municipal and parliamentary oligarchies, capricious ducal officials, or even exploitative "capitalists" (articles 5 and 20 and *passim*). In a region with a precocious development of cottage industry, this flicker of modern class consciousness is especially suggestive. No doubt it refers to the dependent economic relationship in which many of the highland cantons, Nagold and Wildberg included, stood in relation to nearby Calw, seat of a large textile manufactory. In the main, however, the Cahier comprehended more traditional and less modern forms of exploitation under the rubric of privilege. A litany of complaint against various feudal dues and burdens, like those on wood, wine, and real estate, evokes the *doléances* of the French Revolution (11–18, 22–23). Classic peasant grievances concerning the use of the duke's forests and the depredations of his hunting expeditions complete this picture. And a list of wealthy institutions from which to extract monies for the French war indemnity, including charitable foundations, the Church endowment, and the University of Tübingen, spoke to a grinding dissatisfaction with the countryside's disproportionate tax burden (1).

While appropriating a French Revolutionary device and its attendant rhetoric, the Cahier stood squarely within indigenous traditions of writing practice. As was the case in many Western and Central European polities, the Württemberg estates relied on a system of written mandate and instruction to empower their deputies. Besides the French cahiers, vestiges of a similar practice also continued in England down to the nineteenth century and informally served as the object of intense political agitation even after the forms themselves had lost their legal validity.[10] "Mandates" were sealed certificates bestowing powers on a deputy to act on behalf of the corporation electing him, in this case, the cantonal assembly. Called *mandats imperatifs* in France, these documents went by the name *Vollmachten* in Württemberg. They had the legal character of powers of attorney, which could be drawn up for same types of mundane civil and property matters we associate with them today. A deputy who bore such a certificate in a political context was said to possess his corporation's "power," or *Gewalt*—a term also referring, tellingly, to the document itself.[11] His papers were checked for accuracy and illegalities before he was allowed to take his seat in Stuttgart.[12]

The Wildberg deputy's formal *Instruktion* was, to be precise, the analogue of the French cahier proper. Instructions detailed in more specific, written terms the provisions of a mandate, itself merely a formal transfer of powers and responsibilities. Their obligations were binding as a matter of civil law in Württemberg. A deputy could theoretically be punished for failing to obey his written instructions, though in practice disgruntled cantons relied on exhortations and appeals to supervisory parliamentary and ducal authorities to bring wayward delegates to task. In addition to instructions, a mandate might include grievances *(Gravamina)*. Every community, including the meanest village, had the legal right to tuck such complaints into its deputy's papers; alternatively, they might be sent directly to parliament itself.[13] Most of the Black Forest Cahier's grander points take the form of grievances, the more technical provisions being consigned to a much shorter official *Instruktion* at the end of the document. This heightened its appearance as a direct, straightforward expression of the people's wishes, its force undiluted by the need to phrase them in the form of specific directives for a designated representative.

Mandates and instructions prevented the accumulation of power in the capital and preserved it for the cantons. The framers of the Cahier no doubt knew that they rendered the *Landtag* representative himself virtually impotent by severely curtailing his freedom of action. Historically in Württemberg, the length and detail, and therefore the restrictiveness, of the combined mandate, instruction, and grievance list tended to increase with the severity of the political climate, ironically just when freedom and decisiveness in parliamentary action were most needed. When the turn of events warranted, deputies had to solicit new instructions from their constituents and either await their arrival in Stuttgart or travel back to their home districts for face-to-face consultations.[14] Cantons exercised a "right of communication" with their deputies, who were required to inform their districts of their activities and often made to keep diaries. An overzealous assembly at Markgröningen went so far as to demand weekly written reports from their deputy, with whom they had become extremely dissatisfied.[15]

All these constraints made it possible for the scribes to orchestrate political action from their posts in the countryside, where they counted as the most knowledgeable and capable officials at meetings where delegates were elected and instructed. When cantonal assemblies met to discuss political matters, the ducal superintendents who normally led them were required to withdraw. At the *Landtag*'s insistence, these officials lost any role in estates affairs once they became agents of the ducal bureaucracy. *Oberamtmänner* were also barred from breaking the seals of any letters addressed to the urban magistracies from parliament or its staff.[16] All this left scribes unchaperoned. They took protocols and managed paperwork and occupied a position of discretion and trust, ducal officials pragmatically acknowledging that cantons kept "secrets" to which their scribes, as "advisors of the citizenry," could and should remain privy.[17] Scribes also composed first drafts *(Concepte)* of mandates and instructions, read them aloud, and submitted them for revision. This act was often a mere formality: Fritz Benzing, in a 1924 dissertation, compared such drafts with their final versions and as a rule discerned only minor differences.[18] Mandates and instructions thus provided a perfect device to amplify the local scribe's voice and simultaneously deflect responsibility away from him. Where a degree of comity existed between a canton and its scribe, his ambition, knowledge, and political entrepreneurship could make themselves felt as the voice of an entire corporation.

Viewed in this light, the Black Forest Cahier was almost certainly produced by scribes wishing to manipulate the system of mandate and instruction and control the Stuttgart *Landtag* anonymously from afar. By design, the document relied exclusively on a block of existing cantonal assemblies as its mouthpiece in the *Landtag*, and on a network of scribes to rework its points into written instructions. It does not seem to have circulated outside the rather small circle of scribes and other leaders active in the cantons concerned. Knowledge of its production was extremely limited, and even the state long remained ignorant of its origins and influence. The Cahier would not even have entered the state's possession had it not been for the fortuitous dissolution of the Wildberg *Schreiberei* much later.[19] Public provocation never counted among the drafters' aims. Although it was commented upon in the contemporary press, the Cahier was never published. This is striking, given the sudden appearance in the late 1790s of a vigorous public-sphere pamphlet literature reacting to (and influencing) the happenings in parliament and skirting the bounds of censorship. A "By-Instruction for the Cantonal Assembly at X in Württemberg, Issued to Its *Landtag* Deputy" took this form, for example. Its author, the Göttingen professor and later Württemberg Privy Councillor, Ludwig Timotheus Spittler, evidently intended to make it widely available as a generic template for use by upstart cantons drafting their own instructions.[20]

By contrast, the Cahier's framers believed they commanded more power as political ventriloquists, speaking through others, than as agitators stepping directly into the public limelight. Their predilection for corporative subterfuge was already manifest in the Nagold pre-parliament's invitations, which had stressed that cantonal delegates should appear with written powers of attorney enabling them to draft "collective resolutions" on behalf of their districts. Conspirators relied on such *Vollmachten* on at least two later occasions, including a meeting in Calw on 9 June 1797, again dominated by scribes, to discuss the sharp rise in wood prices.[21] In Calw, as in Nagold, the powers of attorney clearly mimicked the procedures of mandate and instruction attending the *Landtag*'s own convocation. They were, however, a completely extralegal improvisation. The Württemberg constitution recognized no right of spontaneous association, much less the gathering of citizens under such specious, extralegal formalities. Still, the *Vollmachten* gave a convincing façade of legality to an otherwise irregular mock parliament. They made it appear to be authorized by corporative decision, not individual caprice. Furthermore, they preserved on paper and for the written record the fiction that those attending spoke simply and plainly on behalf of the cantons sending them as delegates. This is precisely the powerful rhetorical effect produced by the Black Forest Cahier. The reality of the situation, as we will now see, was somewhat different.

NETWORKS OF COLLEGIALITY

The delegates who convened at the Nagold pre-parliament occupied a place of such privilege in the regional information economy that to pretend they acted at the behest of their districts, and not the other way around, mistakes formal for effective power. The scribes in attendance presided over a thriving information network that underlay the very functioning of the cantons as corporative estates. Extensive, longstanding, and covert, their collegiality sustained the cohesion of districts dispersed over the Black Forest and under constant threat of having their communications exposed by a hostile ducal government. The pattern of their interaction also ensured that while the region's scribes enjoyed a tight solidarity among themselves, they suffered an alienating detachment from the rest of the duchy. Their marginalization accounts for both the regionally specific nature and the particular ideological content of the Black Forest Cahier. On a second and closer reading, the document's superficially generic invocations of Enlightened reform yield to a distinct litany of injustices plaguing the infrastructure of collegiality in

Württemberg politics. Before probing further into its pages, we must therefore reconstruct this link between collegiality and ideology.

If simple ambition and a knowledge of law had been sufficient to generate a document such as the Cahier, it would be possible to regard it, as most historians have done, as the product of a broad mobilization among the provincial elite.[22] Aside from the scribes, however, it is difficult to locate any body of notables who could have staged such a feat. To be sure, many city councillors exhibited a high degree of independence and sophistication. Papers from cantonal leaders in Wildberg, who emerged as junior partners alongside their Nagold counterparts, include lists of paginated constitutional citations regarding issues as diverse as forest rights and the occupation of public offices.[23] Phrasing grievances in the correct legal form counted for far less, however, than the ability to share perspectives with like-minded neighbors. At a time of massive French threats to the Württemberg polity, the Nagold delegates' stress on "communal deliberation" and "unity" made it clear that establishing group cohesion was at least as important as marshalling effective constitutional argumentation.[24] In the remoteness of the Black Forest, connections, not competence, bestowed political power.

The scribes provided these connections and came to identify with the cantons where they served, acting as nodes in the exchange of information among cantonal councils, and between them and the *Landtag* and its committees. The *Landtag* archives are filled with letters, reports, and memoranda processed by a well-developed staff of copyists maintaining a steady stream of contacts with virtually all the Württemberg territories.[25] Whereas parliament coordinated this network and served as its institutional center, the scribes produced and thereby controlled the supply of raw information constituting its vital content. The archive of the Wildberg *Schreiberei*, for example, preserves receipts on levies collected, grievances sent to the parliament's Standing Committees, questionnaires these committees sent back to the cantons, and ducal rescripts on parliamentary matters.[26] As often as not, scribes corresponded among themselves rather than through central parliamentary officials. They relayed messages from canton to canton, adding their own observations and commentaries along the way. Particularly in times of war or stress, this sharing of perspectives helped districts mobilize against excessive fiscal exactions and develop a unified front on what could be extremely divisive matters. Between 1796 and 1805, in particular, debates on military appropriations, rising wood and other commodity prices, and other subjects speak to a climate of vigilance and solidarity among cantons and their scribes.[27] The duke tried repeatedly to infiltrate these communications but was generally unsuccessful in discovering what his subjects discussed in secret.[28]

A 1799 meeting at Herrenberg, following up on the Nagold convention, illustrates how the scribes' control over important cantonal information preserved the balance of ducal and estates powers. The Herrenberg meeting's secret protocol was signed by a number of Black Forest scribes, as well as the Nagold *Oberamtmann*.[29] Their gathering had been necessitated by an onerous military requisition that threatened to overextend the cantons' "physical abilities." At issue was whether to turn the matter over to the General Commando and avoid the unpleasant and unpopular business of collecting the monies themselves, or to render the funds voluntarily, in the hopes that through cooperation and self-administration a more equitable apportionment of funds could be arranged. The question, in short, was whether military and logistical imperatives or political and social negotiation would prevail. As a matter of law the decision fell to the cantonal assemblies, whose constitutional responsibilities included distributing the burden of payments among their towns and villages.[30] Their ability to do so equitably and justly again depended on the scribes' knowledge. Through their staffs of *Amtssubstituten* in the countryside, the scribes gathered information from the villages and kept an ear to the ground for their moods. In an era whose leading doctrine of state practice, cameralism, emphasized the need for scientific fiscal exploitation, they had in their hands the raw data for assessing their cantons' strength.[31] Snapshots of the *Land*'s productivity and resources formed the heart of the estates' effective leverage against the duke and enhanced the very perception of their power. Scribes' access and knowledge reinforced their pivotal position in the economy of political information.

As information referees, the Herrenberg scribes walked a characteristic tightrope between cantonal advocacy and service to their duke. Their memoranda demonstrated a conscientious concern to pursue "a golden mean between the interests of *Herrschaft* and what is best for the subjects" by keeping the channels of "unprejudiced" communication open.[32] The scribes found this to be surprisingly difficult. Having dismissed, as hopelessly naïve, the opening of each canton's finances to scrutiny by state military officials, they wondered if they could expect any more forthrightness in their dealings with each other. Here they faced a classic prisoner's dilemma, whereby the "honorably inclined" cantons who truthfully represented their ability to pay ran the risk of being made "sacrifices by the unfaithful." By deciding to undergo this risk, the scribes evinced an unusual degree of solidarity among themselves. They proved willing to countenance the possibility that "frugal" and "better organized" cantons might bear disproportionate burdens relative to poorer, badly managed ones, as long as the latter did not conceal their fiscal shortcomings. In this way, the scribes upheld the fundamental distinction between state and estates power, *Herrschaft* and *Landschaft:* the one exerted domination individually and hierarchically, as by a lord or sovereign, the other reflexively and collectively, as by a corporation.[33] Discretion being the handmaiden of their secretive collegiality, the scribes' indispensable and delicate role remained concealed, as a secret prerogative of their tutelage. This further explains why the scribes relied for so long on corporative subterfuges, here and in documents like the Black Forest Cahier.

There remains the question of how the delegates in Nagold and Herrenberg (and several scribes attended both meetings) came to see their interests and identities as rooted in a particular region, the Black Forest. A deeper look into the history of their collegiality reveals a group spirit arising from rhythms of daily practice molding their image of the outside world, literally over centuries. Records from the early 1600s attest to regular and official exchanges of information among the *Schreibereien* of such places as Neuenbürg, Calw, Nagold, Dornstetten, and Böblingen.[34] Called "circulars" and meant to save duplication effort, these documents rounded the *Schreibereien* of a given region and were copied into the relevant logbooks by apprentices. Overwhelmingly, they concerned routine business having no intrinsic political interest, principally property transactions, announcements of liquidations, notices of bankruptcies, and searches for creditors and debtors. Still, the scribes' role in assisting their colleagues in such transactions could not fail to envelop them in webs of reciprocality and daily familiarity with a latently political potential. A folder dated 1615–1686 already speaks of the circulars' effects in this way, as promoting an "exchange of experiences" on "matters that extend over several cantons."

Benedict Anderson, tracing the origin of the various Latin American nationalisms, has suggested that the rather arbitrary territorial distinctions carved out by the pathways of officials and information in administrative settings can lead to the formation of durable political identities.[35] Exactly this dynamic was at work in the Black Forest cantons. Although its composition varied slightly over time, this network, clustered in Württemberg's western highlands, had a core membership in the cantons of the Nagold river valley, extending outward to the border regions near Baden and also embracing those located west-southwest of Stuttgart. These were precisely the areas represented at the Nagold pre-parliament. Only by the early nineteenth century does one find, on a regular basis, evidence of communication

networks spanning the whole duchy. By then, memoranda appear from far-
flung places like Spaichingen, Göppingen, and Ulm, such as an Ulm wool
merchant's demand that the Wildberg towelmaker Widmaier pay him his
due.[36] Still later, the state's determination to replace scribal monopolies and
streamline regional communication led it to support the intelligence
gazettes described in Chapter 8. These gazettes established information networks tracing out new, statewide circuits of what Anderson calls "imagined
community." Until the new medium arrived, though, the Black Forest network retained the territorially closed composition it had had for at least two
centuries. By the late eighteenth century, a robust sense of regional identity
with unmistakable political valences had emerged purely as a by-product of
the way administrative practice intertwined with technological constraint
through writing.

The Black Forest's collegiality undergirded its traditionally "refractory"
politics in the *Landtag* and sharpened the region's sense of alienation from
the rest of the duchy.[37] An index of its marginalization is offered by the
membership lists of the two Standing Committees that oversaw the estates'
interests during the long hiatuses of the plenary *Landtag*.[38] With the exceptions of Freudenstadt, which probably owed its inclusion to its status as a
ducal fortress town, and Calw, seat of a textile manufacture under economic
protection by the duke (and only a sporadic participant in the Nagold network anyway), the northwestern highland is conspicuously underrepre-
sented. Large, prosperous cantons, like Urach and Nürtingen, and the three
capitals, Stuttgart, Tübingen, and Ludwigsburg, all with an ex officio right
to seats, tended to predominate on the Committees. By the end of the eighteenth century, there was universal agreement that such cantons had
become almost permanently entrenched, and many critical intellectuals
came to view their power in the Standing Committees as an illegitimate
"dictatorship."[39]

The same pattern holds true for the rank-listings of cantons found in the
so-called "location slips" in the parliamentary archives, which established
their seating and polling order and general precedence.[40] The highland cantons cluster in the middle of a list headed by the same privileged group
mentioned above, plus other rich cantons located in the Neckar valley heartland, such as Kirchheim, Göppingen, Marbach, Schorndorf, and Leonberg.
At the bottom stand the numerous smaller *Ämter* lacking the full corporative privileges of a canton, most of which routinely transferred their parliamentary mandates to more prosperous neighbors.[41] In contrast to these
extremely disadvantaged territories, the Black Forest cantons possessed the
political wherewithal—but only as a group—to mount a bid for higher sta-

tus and influence. This information refines our portrait of the highland mobilization, not as a revolt by the radically dispossessed, but as a clamor by second-tier estates for inclusion in an oligarchy that had long dominated parliamentary affairs at the top.

Returning with more detailed attention to the points of the Cahier bears out this interpretation. A distinct constellation of socially very specific grievances lurked behind its reformist fulminations. For example, it criticized the stipend system that granted Tübingen fellowships to the sons of patrician families, provoking the outrage of the "so-called middle class *[mittler Stand]*" unable to enjoy such hereditary benefits (4). In the ossification of the *Schreiberstand* and the bureaucracy and the increasing haughtiness of the clergy, the document found two parallel manifestations of elitism (19, 7–8). The government's tendency to pass over native Württembergers in selecting new officials came under harsh criticism, as did the influence of the foreign aristocracy in the upper echelons of the state administration (3). The Nagold delegates reserved special condemnation, however, for commoners who seemed to have sold out to these cosmopolitan social circles. "It has begun to appear," the Wildberg *Instruktion* explained, "that the long privileged families believe themselves to possess exclusive right to the best positions, although every citizen *[Staats Bürger]* of knowledge and merit has equal rights to them."[42] In its class dynamics, then, the Cahier portrays a struggle of the virtuous and capable against an unjust oligarchy, one mirroring that between provincial burghers and Stuttgart patricians associated with a sham cosmopolitanism.

To these social resentments, which the highland scribes experienced especially acutely, were added political grievances of general interest to the Black Forest cantons. The two proposals most germane to later reform efforts aimed to make the *Landtag* more representative by introducing regular and periodic meetings every nine years and breaking up the oligarchies dominating the Standing Committees (2, "Instruction" at end). These demands obliquely indicted parliament's increasing isolation from the people and its dominance by an elite centered in the rich cities near Stuttgart. But the Cahier trod lightly here lest it betray its drafters' true aspirations, omitting the key demand intended to benefit the scribes: extending the so-called "passive franchise," the right to *be* elected, from members of the magistracies to all competent, solvent male Württemberg subjects. The absence of this demand in the Cahier is striking, for it figured prominently not only in the original invitation to the Nagold pre-parliament but in two petitions drafted on the day it met. Sent to the duke himself, these petitions underscored the need for men of "knowledge" and "character" to shepherd complex constitutional reforms through the *Landtag.* Only two days later, the duke responded by upholding the existing law of passive franchise, indicating that scribes' maneuvers were already the subject of intense concern.[43]

The Cahier itself, however, concealed all traces of the scribes' personal ambition and, conforming to the model of an *Instruktion,* preserved the rhetorical integrity of corporative will. An ideological alchemy is apparent in its pages, a striving to articulate general principles transcending particular interests. Here the document drew liberally from a language of classic republicanism associated with the Aristotelian polis and Machiavelli's Italy and then being revived in England, France, and America.[44] This discourse centered on ineluctable cycles of corruption and decay followed by virtuous regeneration and the rediscovery of ancient liberties. In this spirit, the Cahier repeatedly evoked "civic *[städtische]* freedoms" undermined over time by capricious dukes, the officials they had co-opted, and the institutions, such as the standing army (10), which threatened civic virtue and autonomy. At the heart of this republican vision stood not the classical polis but the Württemberg canton, the *Stadt und Amt,* which the Cahier spoke of in the grammatical singular, as a self-evident unity—for better or for worse. For all their class consciousness, the Cahier's framers left the preeminence of *Stadt* over *Amt,* municipal oligarchy over village hinterland, utterly unquestioned (4–5), an omission that later haunted Ludwig Hofacker and would drive him from power. For the time being, though, the notion of ancient civic liberties had such an appeal that the elision of corporative and universal freedoms either went unnoticed by the Nagold delegates or remained a conscious suppression.

In a general sense, the document spoke the vocabulary of the European Enlightenment and was prone to its flights of idealistic progressivism. Glimmers of encyclopedism, of an immersion in the Enlightenment's pedagogical imagination, are apparent in demands reflecting deep affinities between literacy and citizenship in the drafters' minds. These included a proposal that civics *(Bürgerkunde)* be taught to every schoolchild in the duchy, including patriotic history, constitutional law, and the "rights and duties of future citizens"; that a new law code or *Codex* summarize all the constitutional, legal, and police ordinances in "excerpts intelligible in the language of the people"; and that the clergy's monopoly on schooling be broken in favor of more competent and "honorable" instructors (8–9). These excerpts, however brief, point to the existence of concerns largely divorced from the immediate interests of their authors. Collectively, they brought highlanders' grievances to a higher level of rhetorical appeal, framing problems peculiar to Württemberg's musty institutions, from the

Tübingen stipends to the *Landtag* itself, in a general, forward-looking language shared by reformers all over the continent. Hofacker and his collaborators worked, in short, from an intoxicating condition of "Enlightenment" back toward that which needed renewal in the corporative order, a mindset that bespoke more than merely an instrumental or piecemeal appropriation of new dressings for reactionary principles.

Such idealism is especially significant given the Cahier's conception amidst extremely old, even humdrum, networks of political communication, in the hands of officials ostensibly more removed from the currents of cosmopolitanism than any other politically active social group. In this important sense, the work of imagining, of vaulting over the liabilities of political and cultural isolation, was also the work of forgetting. The Black Forest Cahier built upon inherited practices of corporative collegiality, while jettisoning their underlying assumptions in ways barely apparent to participants at the time. Hofacker and his collaborators substituted their own expertise, connections, and interests for corporatism's carefully formalized procedures, but they behaved as if their actions merely rediscovered a political will long thwarted but still palpable in the virtuous cantons of the provinces. Their political theater came complete with the trappings of parliamentary legitimacy, like *Vollmachten* and *Instruktionen,* while in fact they carefully choreographed exercises in political ventriloquism to construct and represent this will in writing. Such corporative encumbrances clearly subverted the Black Forest scribes' own wish for Enlightened transparency. The next section focuses, then, on the effort to convert their tutelage into a more publicly negotiable currency of influence.

PROVINCIALS AND COSMOPOLITANS

For all their creativity, the scribes, with their reliance on ideological elan, secret communications, and the ruses of political ventriloquism, were still deprived of a direct and unmediated voice in the duchy's political system. They operated in a world burdened by formality and lacking the resiliency and openness, the deliberative spontaneity that is the sine qua non of a more Enlightened collegiality. Hofacker and his co-conspirators realized this and drew on their international contacts to agitate for open debate among representatives of the people freely elected on the basis of merit and expertise. A republic of letters in microcosm, they lived dispersed over the countryside and corresponded with their peers from a distance. It was only natural that they would attempt to universalize the collegiality they possessed so strongly among themselves. The progress of their campaign allows us to compare and contrast the Enlightened and corporative modes of political representation, alternative ways of gathering and projecting political power, each with its own degree of responsiveness, forcefulness, and social equity. To frame this discussion, we need first to situate the Cahier's demands within the broader context of reform agitation in the duchy.

The path by which the ideas of the French Revolution entered the world of the cantons inevitably remains obscure, but any explanation must begin with Ludwig Hofacker. Hofacker belonged to a small but active circle of south German Jacobins who sympathized with the ideals of the Revolution and sometimes even wore tricolor cocards.[45] Its epicenter in Württemberg was a moderate and eminently reformist "Society" of well-heeled independent reformers who enjoyed contacts with Swiss and Rhenish Jacobin clubs and formed links to Republican France through its secret agent, Théremin. Besides Hofacker, these included Christian Baz, a Ludwigsburg burgomaster and Enlightened constitutionalist; Elias Steeb, a Tübingen law professor; and a few other burgomasters and local officials. Together, these men formed the cell of a "Reform Party" that commandeered the *Landtag*'s agenda and proposed sweeping constitutional revisions, including reforms of the Standing Committees and the passive franchise, and publication of parliamentary debates. Just as important, the Reform *Landtag* of 1797–98 catalyzed an intense and wide-ranging constitutional debate in the public sphere, spawning a flurry of pamphlets collected and reprinted in a twelve-volume series.[46]

In its scope, ambitions, and political vocabulary, the pamphlet campaign was a true novelty in Württemberg politics, and bespoke an expansive vision of the power an Enlightened public could wield. Participants came mostly from a tight-knit elite of lawyers, scribes, professors, and independent public intellectuals, such as J. G. Pahl. A small group, they nonetheless tended to conduct themselves anonymously and in the style of disinterested critical debate. Satires (especially Pahl's), legal exegeses, opinion pieces, political essays, review articles, printed cantonal petitions (otherwise normally unpublished), and edited collections of legal source materials (including the *Landtag* debates themselves) all counted among their forms of critique and presentation. Much like intellectuals elsewhere in Europe and America, pamphlet authors groped for a mode of collegiality divorced from personal status and tied exclusively to the merits of one's public writing.

Collectively, the pamphleteers argued that political society and public society should coincide: that Württemberg's secretive corporate estates be opened to bracing encounters with Enlightened critique. Thus an anonymous tract entitled "The Friend of the Constitution" contended that political information acquired a greater power before a vigilant public than in the hermetically sealed channels of communication between cantons and *Landtag*. The traditional rationales for discretion, leading the scribes to conceal their knowledge, yielded to an Enlightened urge to destroy a formality breeding "mistrust":

> The word of the master no longer holds simply because it is the word of the master. The time has passed when people, even those from the lowest class *[Klasse]*, can be diverted and pacified by formulas that used to possess a sort of magical power.

Now that the average "lawyer, physician, preacher, administrator, [and] schoolteacher" had an interest in politics, the "judgment of the public" could make itself felt. But this could only happen if the "common man," who had "begun to deliberate about laws and the constitution . . . about the rights of the *Volk* and the sovereign," gained the right to have his opinions represented.[47] The Habermasian ideal of rational-critical debate, as it was then practiced all over Europe, could not have been expressed better.

A volley of pamphlets on suffrage reform showed this ideal in operation, so self-consciously that new contributions to the debate began to accumulate strings of references to previous works in their own titles.[48] One in particular, authored by Waiblingen *Amtsschreiber* Heinrich Bolley, summed up the issues at stake. Introduced by a page-long quotation from Immanuel Kant's "An Answer to the Question: What is Enlightenment?" it substituted the question "Who Can be Elected to the Württemberg *Landtag?*"[49] Bolley's model parliamentarian jettisoned Kant's famous injunction to argue freely while obeying political authority and decisively promoted political change. At the same time, he acted with Kantian universalism in the name "of the entire people" and was not "confined to matters of a particular estate." Bolley's ideal thus dispensed with the formality of imperative mandates as expressions of a canton's collective will and proposed a vaguely specified public aristocracy of merit in its place. He saw parliament not as a corporative institution but as the "unification point of all the intellectual powers of the country," bringing together the "best and most capable heads from all estates."[50] Besides reflecting the influence of political Enlightenment on reformers' notions of political collegiality, Bolley's pamphlet betrayed their strategy for overhauling Württemberg's parliamentary institutions. In it, the personal ambitions provoking the Black Forest Cahier, yet concealed for rhetorical purposes both by its form and content, finally came into their own.

Efforts to bring representatives of the public into the political realm naturally devolved on those straddling both worlds, and Hofacker, the provincial political operator with international contacts, presented himself as the most obvious candidate. Only an occasional contributor to the whole public debate,[51] he focused his energies on developing his cantonal power base into a springboard to parliament. Hofacker soon emerged as the most influential and controversial figure in the Reform *Landtag*. At the height of his power he secured the position of *Konsulent,* once occupied by the famous jurist Johann Jakob Moser, by muscling out Eberhard Georgii, known as the "last Old Württemberger." Georgii, sympathetic to reform but lacking Hofacker's drive and ambition, himself succeeded the arch-conservative Stockmayer, who had come to symbolize the decadence and oligarchism of the Standing Committees.[52] Hofacker would also gain a seat for Nagold, and thus himself, on the Smaller Committee, for the first time in centuries. First, however, he needed to step from behind the scenes and cease practicing political ventriloquism.

In 1797 Hofacker had himself elected as Nagold's parliamentary deputy. Both the ducal government and the Standing Committees promptly disqualified him on the grounds that deputies must legally be drawn only "from the midst" of the city councils. On 27 March Hofacker duly submitted evidence that he had been formally accepted onto the Nagold *Magistrat.*[53] He also produced a string of exceptions to this restriction, including several scribes and one Urach cantonal treasurer who had been allowed to sit in the last parliament without *Magistrat* membership.[54] This satisfied parliament, which urged the duke to ratify the election in pragmatic recognition of the need for capable men "who are acquainted with the constitution of the country." This failed to elicit any ducal concessions.[55] A temporary compromise was found in the decision to make Hofacker a special "private counselor" to the *Landtag*. A number of small Black Forest cantons also transferred their official mandates to him, giving him a somewhat more direct role in parliamentary debates.[56] This was a cumbersome arrangement, however, one that undermined the very thrust of Hofacker's agitation, to inject more openness and entrepreneurialism into parliamentary activities. Besides, it too met with ducal disfavor.

Before being allowed his place as a full, participating, speaking member, Hofacker was compelled to resign from his *Schreiberei* and renounce any claim to his previous office, the source of his material sustenance and political base. No longer a scribe, he became a regular Nagold city councillor. The reasons for his exclusion before resigning remain clouded behind a mixture of legalism and politics, and nowhere was it spelled out as a matter of principle why a practicing scribe could not simultaneously occupy a *Landtag* seat. This situation of legal indeterminacy frustrated contemporaries as well.[57]

Most obviously, to elect a scribe, or any delegate, on the basis of individual merit would have affronted the deep-seated collectivism at the heart of the cantonal system. As the representative of a corporation, a deputy acted merely as the mouthpiece of the body instructing him. His responsibility may be likened to the mix of legal and personal liability borne by the members of a business partnership. He did not sign his mandate, as a contract, since politically he had no individual will to exchange in the transaction.[58] "A parliamentary deputy," as one ducal official pointed out in repulsing Heinrich Bolley's election, "does not act in accord with the general provisions of an official's contract but must adhere literally to the given instruction." His obligations instead rested on literal identification with the corporation, the canton, that empowered him. Thus "it is a matter of indifference who is named to be a deputy."[59] A deputy's bond, his mandate, derived from membership alone. The oft-repeated provision that "none other than a voting member of a *Magistrat*" could himself be voted into office confirms that the election of a parliamentary deputy merely delegated a first among equals to represent the corporation's will, and the deputy partook of this will solely by virtue of his office.[60] Because scribes did not possess *Magistrat* membership, they enjoyed no formal stake in political representation, and for that reason could not be trusted to act as delegates despite their knowledge and competence.

Amending this condition would have entailed the more sweeping admission that, beneath the pretense of collective will, individual skill and action had always kept the institutions of corporative representation running. Parliament had long been dominated by burgomasters with special fiscal responsibilities and expertise, and not simple city councillors. In 1797, for example, the *Landtag* included 53 of the former and only nine of the latter.[61] A large number of these officials owed their training to the scribes themselves, having apprenticed in the *Schreiberei* before leaving the profession. An 1800 report for the Duke on *Landtag* deputies listed 19 trained as scribes (23 if one counts those with extra legal training), alongside 13 craftsmen, 11 merchants, 11 peasants/farmers, 5 jurists, and 3 of no stated occupation. Importantly, most of the larger, more influential cantons tended to be represented by trained scribes.[62] To the extent that parliamentary deputies made any impact at all, it was despite and not because of their *Magistrat* membership; J. G. Pahl's sketch of the fictional Ypsilon burgomaster Wurstsak, who knew nothing but to ape the positions of the powerful

Konsulent Stockmayer, satirized the ignorance of the typical *Landtag* back-bencher.[63] Real influence came from skills acquired in the *Schreiberei*, in "using archives," "critical investigation" of documents, and "the capability for judgment," whereas corporative mandates proved elegant in theory but impotent in practice.[64] Recognizing acting *Stadt- und Amtsschreiber* as qualified deputies would plainly have validated an informal predominance of skill their profession had long enjoyed.

The conservatives' mantra, that deputies must come "aus dem Mittel des Magistrats," offers a clue to the specifically political motivations for excluding the scribes. A phrase normally used to establish appointment "from the midst of the *Magistrat*" as the criterion of eligibility, it can also be construed to refer to the deputy's financial support, as in "out of the means of the *Magistrat*." The ability to support a deputy in Stuttgart correlated directly with the wealth and proximity of the canton itself, making a mockery of the corporative system's pretense to represent every *Stand*. Historically, this had been an abiding and overwhelming concern behind the vast majority of mandate transfers from smaller cantons to more capable and influential designates. Most of these cited the absence of a dispensable communal official or a simple inability to fund his travel, lodging, and board. Some offered elaborate and plaintive excuses and even named figures in *Gulden* to prove their need, but by the eighteenth century, such substitutions had become so routine that protestations of patriotism and regret fell away.[65]

By law, cantons could transfer their powers, and issue explicit instructions, to one of three substitutes: a deputy from another canton, a prelate, or the Standing Committees or one of their officials.[66] This procedure offered at least some hope that cash-strapped cantons could see their interests represented, but there is little evidence, on a regular basis, of durable regional constellations of the sort found around Hofacker. Rather, the more established cantons, like Stuttgart or Urach, simply accreted even more power by collecting substitutions, and more commonly, the Standing Committees would use them to augment their already considerable institutional power. Nothing, in other words, suggested that the system of *Gewalt* transfers, which in principle only extended the procedures of imperative mandate to qualified deputies from the outside, made the effective representation of cantonal interests any more equitable.

The linkage of a canton's overall fiscal solvency to its specific ability to support a *Landtag* deputy, and by extension to the very quality of its political representation, was more than coincidental. In the corporative system, representatives stood for their communities metonymically, as parts symbolizing the whole. They literally embodied their corporation's powers, which under the estate system were essentially fiscal, expressions of their control over the purse. The delegate's simple ability to "get away,"—what Weber called *Abkömmlichkeit*—was a tangible expression of his corporation's influence, especially when cumbersome mandates and instructions systematically devalued the more active, rhetorical, deliberative aspects of representation. Frequently cantons were not allowed to transfer their mandates and recall their own deputies until they had physically appeared at least once, in Stuttgart, for the *Landtag* opening ceremonies. Parliamentary officials made it clear that a bodily show of influence, embracing as many individual *Landstände* as possible, was indispensable for gaining leverage against the duke. Even this overextended some communities' means.[67]

To have allowed poor and remote cantons simply to turn their mandates over to rich, ambitious, and independent individuals would have meant that the assembled parliamentary delegates in Stuttgart no longer appeared as a living portrait of their respective cantons' strength. Widening the right to be elected and granting the freedom from mandate would have instantly unburdened cantons of the need to support their delegates and engage in laborious and dilatory communications with them. Conceding passive franchise to the scribes, or any official not directly implicated in his own empowerment and sustenance, would have disrupted a delicate ecology working to the more powerful cantons' advantage over those forming Hofacker's core constituency. In this way, the criterion of *Magistrat* membership obliquely delivered power into the hands of the Standing Committees and the wealthier cantons clustered around Stuttgart—the very group against which the Black Forest Cahier explicitly protested.

In a system whose main failures were a certain lumbering institutional conservatism and a concomitant denigration of free thought and action, the scribes possessed all the compensatory advantages necessary to exercise an advocacy role for their cantons: knowledge, independence, and wealth. Previous precedents for scribes' elections had all sprung from anti-oligarchic attempts by smaller and less effectual cantons to overcome the problems of *Abkömmlichkeit*. Among the districts which had attempted to send their scribes to the *Landtag* were Dornstetten in 1651, Liebenzell in 1698, and Gartach, Stetten, and Niederhofen in 1737.[68] All were poorer, obscure, and rather remote cantons which probably had no other knowledgeable candidates available and a tendency to abrogate their powers to more prosperous substitutes.[69] This pattern held for many other *Schreiber* elections until the end of the eighteenth century. "Under the pressure of poverty," Liebenzell, for example, renewed efforts to designate its *Stadtschreiber*, Cuhorst, for the 1800 *Landtag*.[70] It failed.

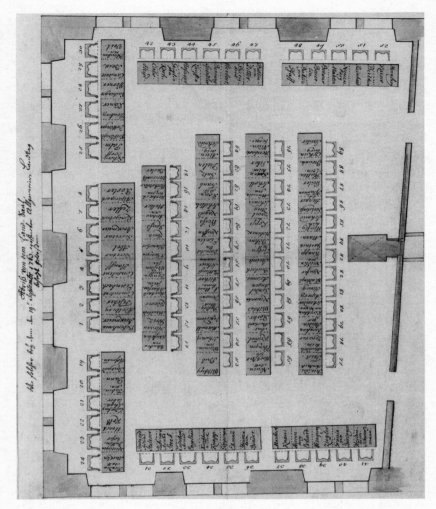

FIGURE 6. Seating chart for the 1763 *Landtag*. Supervisory officials and ecclesiastical prelates sat in the front two rows. Cantonal deputies sat along the sides, and then in the center of the room, in order of precedence (indicated by seat numbers). Deputies from cantons later represented at Nagold pre-parliament in 1796 sat in positions 24, 47, 50, 53, 59, 61, 66, 68, 69, 71, and 77. The provincial Black Forest cantons thus clustered in the "back benches" in the center of the chamber, while, ironically, the more powerful, centrally-located cantons physically occupied the margins of the room. © Hauptstaatsarchiv Stuttgart, A 203 Bü 142.

In other cases drawn from 1796, the year of Hofacker's election, the impetus again came from constituencies that saw in the scribes their only hope for effective representation. *Stadtschreiber* Wolf at Großbottwar twice declined the attempt of the cantonal council there to name him their *Landtag* deputy, on the grounds that this would violate precedent.[71] Lang in Maulbronn showed a similar coyness after being elected by a group of village foremen, who "themselves admitted that no qualified candidate was available save the *Amtsschreiber*."[72] Maulbronn was a religious territory normally represented by a prelate, who served ex officio and without imperative mandate. Its deputies, clamoring for separate representation, stemmed from the Maulbronn villages and were likely of peasant background. They saw in Lang literally the only possibility to express their political interests. Acknowledged in all quarters as an exceptionally capable official, Lang resisted his clients' entreaties for as long as possible before undertaking a scrupulously impartial election at which he received all but one of the votes cast. His actions still provoked controversy when he had himself installed on a village *Magistrat*, after the fact, to bring the election into conformity with the law.

The results illustrate just how bottlenecked the system had become owing to the conservatism of the government and the Standing Committee. Asked to adjudicate the case, the latter issued an unpopular ruling declaring Lang's maneuver a "conscious circumvention of procedure . . . fraudulent in law and precedent." Several publicists and privy councillors, and the *Landtag*'s councillor himself, found this to be excessively stringent. Yet the same reasoning was applied in denying *Stadtschreiber* Wagner the right to represent Sindelfingen, whose *Magistrat* had also agreed to take him on and designate him their deputy.[73] A similar fate almost befell Hofacker's collaborator in the Reform Party, Elias Steeb (not a scribe), whom the *Magistrat* at Reichenbach had co-opted in preparation for electing him their deputy. Steeb, like Hofacker, had to renounce his professorship before entering the *Landtag*, forgoing his means of sustenance to rely on personal savings and meager, if not nonexistent, constituent support. These two exceptions only prove the general rule that the political oligarchy was determined to thwart both the less powerful cantons and their Enlightened (and simultaneously self-interested) advocates, exacting a heavy personal price for any maneuver venturing beyond the bounds of the strictest formality.[74]

Viewed in this historical perspective, Hofacker's innovation consisted in raising the struggle against oligarchy above scattershot incursions into privilege and up to the level of a regional mobilization. The real novelty in this attempt, though, lay in the use of his Black Forest political base as a platform for launching explicitly ideological claims. To the material fact of greater *Abkömmlichkeit* he added personal and political ambitions increasingly typical of the scribes generally. The *Schreiber* by no means monopolized the traits of independence, Enlightenment, and material security typical of the modern representative.[75] Still, the qualities of *Abkömmlichkeit* in a more general sense, a predisposition founded on both material and ideological factors to make oneself available to represent the people, favored the scribes more than any other group.

The scribes held an effective monopoly founded not on the exclusive prerogatives of a particular *Stand*—it was the closed, restrictive conception of this term that progressives were fighting—but on the nature of their office, both in its essential and incidental, officially established and historically evolved, senses. Their knowledge of constitution and administration bridged the realms of *Landschaft* and *Herrschaft*. This pulled them into networks of political communication that instilled a sense of responsibility and provided them with crucial resources in the struggle over information. Their competence also manifested itself more formally, in their mastery of written instruments allowing them to commandeer the modes of political collegiality without abandoning the corporative system as a whole. And their status as a dispersed, exclusively provincial elite led them to identify with the structural exclusion of their cantons that this system had promoted. To this was added the prevailing sense of professional identity among the German officialdom, combining Enlightened idealism with corporative solidarity, commitment to *Bildung* with the pride of *Stand*, to use the terminology of Chapter 2. In the intensely politicized climate of 1797, all this accounts for the richly paradoxical role played by Hofacker and his associates, provincial ambassadors of a cosmopolitan culture exploiting the hinterland's vitality to reform a sleepy, un-Enlightened capital.

A BREACH OF PROTOCOL

Modern representation, as we have traced its evolution from and conflict with an older corporative system, entailed a certain collective amnesia, as external, Enlightened modes of thought surreptitiously dissolved the rationales behind long-existing practices of collegiality. Notionally at least, collectivism yielded to individual will, solidarity to political entrepreneurship, secrecy to publicity, and formal statuses to capability and merit as qualifications for office. Hofacker, at least for the duration of the Reform *Landtag*, managed to pull off a series of political manipulations that exploited the antinomies of old and new without bringing them into contradiction or jeopardizing his still-traditional political base in the pursuit of progressive ideals. These were less the products of compromise than the manifestations of dynamism and energy: the attempt, centered on scribes, to rejuvenate what appeared outdated and oppressive with what seemed novel and forward-looking. But it is important to keep in mind the fragility of this synthesis. As corporative practices lost their connections within a logical system, they began to appear discretely, as the naked remnants of privilege and oppression.

One corporative fiction Hofacker never jettisoned was the pretense that the canton, whatever the nature of its representation, remained the indivisible unit of politics. Events subsequent to Hofacker's *Schreiberei* resignation proved the fragility of the political base he cobbled together on this assumption, as the village hinterland in Nagold rebelled against the political tutelage of the cantonal seat. A breach of formality in internal cantonal politics left Hofacker crucially exposed in what should have been the very stronghold of his power. His circumventions of written procedure caused a breakdown in the canton-wide collegiality upon which the scribes had traditionally relied. Village mutiny need not have been fatal to his career, and the next chapter examines the ways scribes could reconcile formality and collegiality to promote the cantons' internal democratization. But in Nagold, Hofacker's failures met up against a state eager to exploit any cracks in the wall of cantonal solidarity. Perched as a sort of bystander during the entire parliamentary controversy, the duke's government now came into its own, clamping down on the stirrings of reformist, seditious political activity in the Black Forest. By treating Nagold not as a parliamentary district (over which it had no jurisdiction) but as a unit of the state's own administration, government investigators drew out the paradoxes inherent in Hofacker's view of the canton as an ideal republican polis.

The focal point for the state's intervention was Hofacker's attempt, immediately after quitting his *Schreiberei* to take a seat in parliament, to have the office transferred to his brother. In a patriotic speech to Nagold's cantonal assembly, he requested this small recompense for his "sacrifice for the fatherland." Thereafter, he resorted to less public, less virtuous, and more oblique methods to cushion his loss.[76] In a scene evoking the corruption of smoke-filled back rooms, Hofacker met over dinner with friends on the city council, with the *Gasthaus zur Sonne* the locale, and wine, not cigars, the social lubricant. There he revealed a plan to rig the election in favor of Viktor Immanuel, his younger brother. A protocolled investigation launched by ducal superintendent Lang revealed that Hofacker had secretly prevailed on the city council to name two of his allies as witnesses *(Urkunds-Personen)* to the election of his successor.[77] The mere presence of such witnesses was often sufficient to intimidate voters and swing an election in the desired direction. Normally the *Oberamtmann* himself performed this role, but Hofacker led the councillors to believe that Lang had sanctioned the change and thus overcame their objections. His devious maneuver appears to have offended Lang as a manifestation of Hofacker's duplicity and "mistrust." Together with another instance when the city council *(Magistrat)* had acted behind his back, it was a slight all the more wounding in view of his historically close relations with Hofacker.[78] And Lang's superiors in the state government were only too willing to help him exact revenge.

If the historically amicable collegiality of ducal and cantonal officials seemed compromised, the latter's solidarity remained intact, at least for a time. When interrogated, Hofacker's cronies resorted to that evasive cunning so familiar from other protocolled investigations, greeting any suggestions of impropriety on their part or by others as completely novel revelations.[79] Asked whether it did not seem especially convenient for Hofacker to name the witnesses to the new election "in order to intimidate the electors," the forty-year-old bookbinder Johann Friedrich Eberhard replied, "No, it had not occurred to him, but it would well be possible." Confronted with such cheerful disingenuousness, Lang indignantly clarified that, indeed, burgomaster Schmid was "well known *in publico*" as a "follower" of Hofacker. To a man, the other signers also professed ignorance of any undue influence. Johann Friedrich Fuchßstatt, a saddle master, gave practically the same response as Eberhard's, as did the merchant Gottfried Adam Sautter, who however let it slip, somewhat damningly, that the *Stadtschreiberei* was always drawing up documents in the city council's name. *Magistrat* members who had not signed professed shock and horror when told of Hofacker's manipulations, emotions that may actually have been sincere, since up to this point they had been left out of his conspiracy. But whether they claimed total ignorance or merely expressed a blind trust in Hofacker and his methods, the Nagolders failed to buckle under procedures of protocolling meant to pit them against each other. Thus, even after the election was turned over to a disinterested outsider, *Stadtschreiber* Krafft at Herrenberg, Viktor Immanuel Hofacker still prevailed with a clear majority of votes over several well-qualified competitors, three of whom came from Nagold. On 2 August 1797, the *Schwäbische Chronik*, an official organ, published the confirmation of his election.[80]

Between 1797 and 1804, Ludwig Hofacker clung tenaciously to his Nagold base even as he lost influence on the national stage. Evidence of coordinated communications in his defense among Nagold, Tübingen, Wildberg, Altensteig, and Dornstetten, as well as on general political matters, speaks to the continuing vitality of the Black Forest network.[81] But in the upper echelons of the Württemberg state, a coordinated campaign was growing against him. This culminated in 1800 in his expulsion, by the duke, from the Standing Committee on trumped-up political charges, followed by an investigation of his contacts with the French government.[82] By 1801 the ducal *Kabinett* had assembled a dossier on Hofacker's "revolutionary machinations" and intercepted some of his correspondence with Christian Baz in Vienna.[83] A campaign of reprisal against his reformist agitation and illegal maneuvering was mounting in the government. Biding its time, however, it continued to observe the most legalistic scruples possible.

The decisive breakdown came only in 1804, when the Nagold canton suffered a sudden rebellion by its village hinterland, the *Amt*, heretofore silent. There is no direct evidence of meddling or subornment either by the ducal superintendent Lang or any other authority of the central administration. Rather, the state investigation pursuant to the revolt simply capitalized on latent fractures between *Stadt* and *Amt* endemic to all cantons. The catalyst was a complaint dated 20 November 1804, from the collected village foremen and other deputies of the "common *Amt*."[84] These protested the attempt of the Nagold city council to stack a new *Landtag* election by sending its entire number (sixteen members) to vote, individually and with free mandate, and thereby crowding out their thirteen electors. They alleged the *Magistrat* had the right only to send four deputies from its ranks, although Lang, consulting precedents reaching back to the sixteenth century, could not verify this claim conclusively.[85] The earliest elections had proceeded "collegially," with no signatures to the protocols or any other evidence pointing to the participation of particular individuals. Other, more recent excerpts, from 1737, 1763, and 1796 (Ludwig Hofacker's election) pointed to the repeated presence of village delegates, strengthening the *Amt*'s claim without thereby denying the Nagold council's own prerogatives. In 1800, during Viktor Hofacker's tenure, the record had contracted so sharply in detail as to indicate merely the deputy's name. Frustrated by this situation, Lang clearly inclined to support the *Amt* in light of its heavier tax burden and the presence of what he called "capable men" among their number. Still, he could do nothing to compel the recognition of their claim.

The situation was, as the next chapter will show, a typical one of ambiguous written precedent and incomplete official memory newly subjected to political struggle. A flurry of protocol excerpts, snippets from debates and decisions at past elections, was unearthed from the town records by the two battling sides, with the Hofackers and the Nagold *Stadtmagistrat* ranged against Lang and the Nagold *Amt*. Viktor Hofacker came under attack for three maneuvers, one impolitic and undisputed, and two illegal and merely alleged. First, he arrived at the 1804 parliamentary election having drawn up a complete *Instruktion* for the new deputy, which was approved "unanimously."[86] In the interests of harmony, the *Amt* never questioned this, in itself a common procedure, but had insisted that a "protestation" be entered into the record in defense of their voting rights. Hofacker's purported failure to do so was his second and more serious misstep. Third and finally, Lang, in his report, wondered suspiciously what had gone on at the sparsely documented 1800 election, having been excluded himself as a ducal official. He knew of separate, supplementary protocols with more detailed information. These, however, had remained in the possession of none other than the *Stadtschreiber* himself, who had sealed and closed them without witnesses. All this amounted to an unmistakable accusation of corruption against Viktor Hofacker for withholding politically disadvantageous precedents. The whole debacle seems to have resulted from the latter's hamfisted management of the scribe's tutelary role and an inability to conceal, as his brother had done so successfully before him, the traces of his manipulation without overt obfuscation. In fairness, however, never were the pressures coming from the state and its officials so intense.

A government expert opinion dated 20 June 1805 adjudicated the matter of conflicting precedents, marking the decisive interference of a state heretofore constrained to preserve its evenhandedness in parliamentary affairs.[87] The opinion revealed both the limits and the potentials of the state's strictly legalistic approach to subverting cantonal oligarchy. On all the substantive points of the Nagold complaint it was forced to rule in favor of the Hofacker brothers and the *Magistrat.* It conceded that no general ordinance prescribed the proportion of *Amt* deputies at cantonal council meetings; validated a string of precedents upholding the *Magistrat* electors' right to vote with free mandates; and repulsed as unproven the *Amt* allegations that Viktor Hofacker had concealed important precedents in favor of their case. As to their claim that he had also refused to enter their protest into the protocolled record, the very absence of any such written document made the disagreement a matter of hearsay. They could have avoided this double bind only by refusing to sign the election protocol altogether. State Councillor Wächter duly reported the official rejection of the *Amt*'s petition by the government.[88]

Losing the battle against municipal oligarchy did not preclude winning the war, however. Here the report's tone changed from dutiful resignation to sly calculation, and what came next betrayed a Machiavellian attitude toward the potential usage of legal and administrative instruments.

Bemoaning the "fragmentary" nature of information on voting practices in the various cantons, the expert opinion suggested the collection of more systematic data from every *Stadt und Amt.* Ostensibly advocating the mere compilation of a general table and report, the opinion "could not leave unremarked" the likely failure of this procedure to generate unitary results, and the political opportunity lurking within this state of indeterminacy. Winking to his superiors, the opinion's author added that "the solicitation of this report" would itself "give rise to . . . struggles" in the cantons "which would not have come into being without this external occasion." The strategy here was to exploit the ambiguity of traditional observance as only partially documented, and to foment local conflict and disarray through the very act of written codification. The effort to introduce system and rationality, a hallmark of state practice everywhere, threatened to rob scribes of their ability either to produce or to withhold legal citations as their interests and caprice dictated. The novelty lay in the use of complementary and opposed techniques of writing practice to press their respective interests. Hofacker wanted to muddle the written record, the government to bring its contradictions and gaps into glaring written form, as a catalyst for broader political change.

The next chapter pursues in depth the tension between written formality and "collegial deliberation," as well as the pouncing opportunism of a state eager to undermine cantonal harmony. For now, this epilogue suffices to illustrate the limits of evolution in a corporative system Hofacker and his allies had pushed to the limit in the Black Forest Cahier and the Reform *Landtag* it helped to inaugurate. Similarities between the scribes' reformism and the general struggle against parliamentary stasis may best be described as elective affinities, alliances borne of historical contingency and acquiring a temporary durability from the cement of ideas. Doctrines of republican citizenship covered certain blind spots in the cantonal constitution where the rhetoric of universalism overlay practices of real inequality and oligarchy. This remained true even if, in the scribes' hands, such ideas founded a perception of common interest with powerful political effects. The source of these effects lay in the networks of collegiality ascendant in the Württemberg cantons, combined with the peculiar feats of identity- and coalition-building that writing made possible within this system. Knitting together groups publicly and in secret, whether for corporative assemblies in meeting rooms or publishing individuals flung wide over European borders, written networks of collegiality ramified throughout Württemberg society during the agitations of 1796–1798 and were subverted only by rival uses of writing exposing their weaknesses.

4 Constitutional Fetishism

In September 1805 near Ulm, on Württemberg's eastern frontier, 200,000 French soldiers met and subsequently defeated 73,000 men from Austria. This battle and the ones that followed brought an end to the Holy Roman Empire in Germany. Napoleon himself traveled to the Ludwigsburg palace on 2 October, met Duke Friedrich, and offered to convert his duchy either into a conquered French province or, if Friedrich cooperated with him, into a richer, larger, and still autonomous land. Friedrich, acceding, was made King of Württemberg by Napoleon late that year and his kingdom included, under French auspices, in the new Confederation of the Rhine.

When Friedrich dissolved his Privy Council and abrogated the Tübingen Compact on 27 December 1805, only the canton of Waiblingen raised its voice in protest. All the other cantons took an oath of allegiance to Friedrich, whereupon the estates in Stuttgart also acquiesced, the *Landtag* was shut down, and its treasury was seized by Friedrich's men. "Such a despotism has never been heard of," Ludwig Hofacker, the former Reform Party leader now retired from politics, wrote in his diary soon thereafter; "We are letting ourselves be defeated without resistance."[1] Down to the end of 1805, rumors spread of a coordinated petition drive in the countryside to protect the constitution, and some cantons, including Bietigheim and Besigheim, may have made abortive attempts to mount legal resistance.[2] Yet the only tangible evidence of local protest to find its way into the state archives remains a petition from Waiblingen, a prosperous canton in the duchy's heartland, signed by both the city council and the village foremen there. Dated 4 January 1806, it had been drawn up at the behest of one Heinrich Bolley, the renegade son of a well-known family of Württemberg scribes. With florid language the Waiblingen petition spoke in mock bewilderment at Friedrich's coup d'état and pleaded with him, respectfully but firmly, to restore the Württembergers' Magna Carta.

Amidst violence of continental proportions, and as war raged all around them, Bolley and the leading citizens of Waiblingen chose a written text to brand the king's actions illegal. They made legal instruments their weapons and invoked constitutional formalities to oppose gross violations against a political order that, to everyone else, had already ceased to exist. This "constitutional fetishism," another instance of that dogged propensity to resolve conflict through writing, may seem quaint, naïve, and myopically ineffectual. Indeed, like the Black Forest Cahier, the Waiblingen petition utterly failed in its stated aims. Another extralegal textual improvisation, it was summarily annulled by the state as Friedrich, unperturbed, inaugurated a decade of absolutist dictatorship. Still, a crucial difference sets this document apart from the one drawn up nearly a decade earlier in Nagold. Whereas the Cahier relied on elaborately staged exercises in political ventriloquism and cannot be viewed as the product of a true grassroots mobilization, Bolley's petition drew upon the active participation, agency, and moral responsibility of those who signed the document. To appreciate this requires devoting most of our attention, in this chapter, to the document's prehistory.

In the world the Waiblinger inhabited, merely to commit one's signature to such a text was at once deliriously provocative and a logical extension of daily political practice. For over a decade, Heinrich Bolley and his fellow citizens had pursued their own local feuds and disagreements through similar written instruments. Starting with his campaign to win the Waiblingen *Schreiberei* in 1794, Bolley had become embroiled in petty factions and vendettas of a type that plagued many early modern communities. Yet almost despite themselves, Bolley, his allies, and his enemies always converged around constitutional texts as talismans of political legitimacy. Such texts included not only the Tübingen Compact but especially the local documents—election protocols, legal precedents, ducal memoranda, and administrative decrees—making up the so-called "communal constitution." Bolley's gift consisted in playing these genres against each other for broader political ends. By subjecting texts to creative reinterpretations, he reconciled local factions and ultimately instilled in them a sincere respect for law and proper procedure. Consistently, he put himself at the vanguard of larger trends in administration, demography, and constitutional interpretation to bring ever wider circles of the Waiblingen population into exercise of their rights as citizens. Yet while Bolley furnished his peers with the words to express their sentiments, he always remained the good ventriloquist and never signed his written creations, least of all his 1806 petition. His silence before the official record increased the risk, but also the responsibility, incurred by those practicing their citizenship under his tutelage.

Bolley, in exercising this tutelage, exploited the potent blend of collegiality and formality sustaining constitutional fetishism. Citizen action of this kind required, first, an open community for deliberation and debate, the natural seedbed of a democratic collegiality; but it also demanded, second, the formality of ground rules, protocols of etiquette, and procedural constraints to provide scripts for participation. The same persons may converge in different communities, so defined, to stage different types of civic activism. Three such communities, professional, political, and popular, may be identified among the officeholders of Waiblingen canton. Treated successively in this chapter, these included, respectively, the professional domain of electoral contest mastered by Bolley in obtaining the Waiblingen *Schreiberei;* the political institutions of cantonal and village corporative representation he manipulated (unsuccessfully) in campaigning for election to the Reform *Landtag* in 1796; and a final, popular community comprised of taverns, private houses, and street-corner conversations manifest throughout the pages below but only truly mobilized during the drafting of the 1806 petition. These communities operated more as infrastructures of communication than as unstructured arenas for free, critical debate and discussion. They alternately amplified and muted individual actors' ideas, grievances, and claims, and translated prepolitical ambitions and anxieties into overtly political practices with a claim on state power. Their flourishing as arenas for collegiality owed less to the reality, or even the presumption, of participants' rationality or equality than to the political sociology of the early modern community, the culture and institutions of the old Württemberg canton, and, above all, the fetish for textual formality shared by members of society at all levels.[3]

LITIGATING LOCAL CONFLICT

Heinrich Bolley's agitation in Waiblingen was not the fruit of an abiding commitment to political reform, nor even the product, so far as we can tell, of a consistently held political ideology. Lacking the firebrand commitment of a Jacobin like Ludwig Hofacker, he remained remarkably pliant and adaptable throughout his career. In later life, for example, Bolley proved capable both of a stinging opposition to the prevailing political order and of an utter submission to working within the system. With regard to democracy—a burning issue in wake of the French Revolution—he would manifest an early sympathy for Württemberg's village population. Yet in his

1796 commissioned investigation into the ritual sacrifice of a live bull in Beutelsbach, he could write that "the common man has . . . little receptivity for purer notions."[4] What Bolley exhibited consistently from the beginning of his career was a relentless instinct for politicking combined with a profound aptitude for complex legal argument. These skills served him well in Waiblingen's professional community, which he entered in 1793 as an aspirant to become *Stadt- und Amtsschreiber*. He began this campaign as a solitary careerist but soon found himself allied with disenfranchised elements of the canton's population. By the end of the campaign, Bolley and his cocombatants had learned to pursue collective aims through legal instruments. In the process, they internalized the recourse to written formality almost as a reflex action, acquiring skills that would serve them well in the years to come.

Heinrich Bolley enjoyed the best the eighteenth century had to offer. He came from an affluent, though not exalted, background, rooted in the provinces but with connections to the cosmopolitan elite. His mother was a Wächter from Stuttgart, daughter of a well-positioned bureaucratic official from a family esteemed for both state service and activism in culture and the arts. His father had been *Stadtschreiber* at Neuenbürg, on the northeastern tip of the Black Forest, the site where Bolley and his two older brothers learned the craft.[5] Of the three, Karl inherited the *Schreiberei* from his father and went on to participate alongside Ludwig Hofacker at the Nagold pre-parliament. Christian enjoyed an itinerant career as an *Oberamtmann* in at least five cantonal seats and earned a somewhat bawdy reputation as a heavy drinker. Heinrich, by contrast, was more of a straight arrow, an overachiever prematurely gray around the temples. After apprenticing under his father, he served three years, until age twenty, as a junior notary and receipt auditor under the Waiblingen superintendent Pistorius—in a civil service post, in other words, and not in a *Schreiberei* proper. He then spent another three years studying law at Tübingen, after which he could call himself *Kanzlei Advokat*.[6] The combination of legal and practical training was reserved for the most privileged young scribes, and Bolley excelled even among this elite group. After law school, five Tübingen professors commended his academic virtues, two state finance officials praised his "facility" and "good judgment," and his law board referee wrote glowingly of his extraordinary knowledge of Roman and canon law, volunteering in his report to recommend Bolley again "at his request."[7]

Bolley makes his first appearance in Waiblingen's archival record in November 1793. In that month he submitted an application to be elected *Stadt- und Amtsschreiber*, a bold move, considering his relative lack of on-the-job experience, and one that offended the provincial notability. The Waiblingen *Magistrat,* proud, conservative, and a vigorous practitioner of nepotism—one report listed all the cousins, nephews, in-laws, and stepsons packing the court and council—immediately pressed for his disqualification. Its campaign against Bolley, waged in Waiblingen's taverns, living rooms, and town offices, spawned a series of written denunciations directed to the ducal government. Drafted in the hope that the duke might disallow Bolley's candidacy, these texts showcase the manipulation of legal formality to vent cultural prejudices and pursue local feuds properly belonging outside the legal sphere.

In its petitions, the city councillors assimilated news of Bolley's candidacy to their own distrustful ways of viewing the outside world, interpreting his character, qualifications, and handicaps in the idiom of small-town partisanship.[8] Youth was his greatest liability; the *Magistrat* used it to justify fears of his alleged proclivity for reckless independence and, paradoxically, to argue that he would become the tool of elder, more powerful colleagues. Youth also effectively prevented him from contributing to community solidarity by marrying the previous *Schreiber*'s widow and adopting her two orphaned children.[9] His education they regarded with the insincere admiration of the ignorant and proud. They feared, with absolute justification as it turned out, that Bolley's "pride in his legal knowledge" might tempt him to overstep the bounds of office with political projects and neglect his more mundane duties. Their more conservative outlook revolved around humbler qualities of "probity," "insight," and "character," subjective criteria only measurable by the "most convincing testimonials" from the outside, or found in someone "known to the *Magistrat* itself as an individual endowed with such qualities."

Bolley's close relations with his former boss, the Waiblingen *Oberamtmann* Pistorius, did not provide the city council with the reassurance it sought. The *Magistrat* had been at odds with Pistorius ever since he successfully thwarted the burgomaster's pet candidate at a cantonal treasurer election back in 1792. Not only did Pistorius and his wife act as informal godparents to Bolley's fiancée, but his purely professional connection to Bolley they could only comprehend as a partisan friendship. Such "politically intimate allegiances," their petitions claimed, entailed "understandings [that] can result in more trust than one would expect from a blood relation."[10] In these petitions, the terms "blood relation" and "blood friendship" were used interchangeably, signifying the fluid boundaries between relatives and friends in small-town discourse. This confusion also gave the *Magistrat* its legal pretext for opposing Bolley's candidacy, founded on its dubious (and hypocritical) attempt to construe his friendship with Pistorius as a form of nepotism disallowed by law. These objections, despite lacking legal validity, led Pistorius to recuse himself from conducting the election.[11]

To commit these allegations to writing, alas, did not imply any consistency of logic or conviction on the part of the city councillors; their petitions often aired self-contradictory rumors. Betraying the righteous provincial's *ressentiment*, the councillors sometimes depicted Bolley's social set as a group of snickering, elitist cosmopolitans. They said that behind closed doors, Bolley was known to have called them "sheep's heads" *(Schafsköpfe)* while his fiancée, Elisabetha Jäger, ridiculed them as "rogues" *(Spitzbuben).*[12] Blatantly hedging their bets, the *Magistrat* simultaneously reproached Bolley with the coarse traits of the hometown ruffian, citing domestic quarrels with Elisabetha, heavy drinking and a "hotheaded temperament," and an incident in which Bolley allegedly ripped a colleague (his later political collaborator, Theuß) from his horse and pummeled him in "a large public gathering."[13] These charges may have constituted a deliberate attempt to mislead ducal officials into confusing Bolley with his more boisterous brother, Christian. The government curtly dismissed them as excessively "partisan" and "irrelevant" to Bolley's fitness for office; Pistorius testified that if anything, Bolley was of "phlegmatic temperament," a characterization which certainly squares with the plodding, pedantic style of his later legal tracts. Weapons in a semi-public smear campaign, rumors were less the source than the expression of the councillors' unwillingness to "extend him our trust." To gain such trust required an identification with their interests, a willingness to exchange personal independence for the perquisites of community honor, and a submission to the more collectivist dynamics of local partisanship, nepotism, and solidarity—all of which Bolley was clearly unprepared to offer.[14]

Had these denunciations merely reflected the cultural narrowness of a small-town society, Bolley's election would hardly deserve extended comment. But what they produced, more deeply, was an actual formalization of social conflict, whose rigors straitjacketed free politicking and refracted social tensions through the medium of textuality. From this point forward, the recourse to legal texts brought new groups into the struggle, submerged individual voices beneath corporatively generated appeals, and progressively robbed the state of its ability to sort out competing versions of local "truth." On account of Pistorius's illness and recusal, the election date was postponed numerous times and its direction transferred to an outside commissioned investigator. This allowed the conflict to fester and the various parties to consolidate their political bases. It was said that in the pubs of

Waiblingen, wagers were being made that the election would drag out half a year or more.[15] The battle reached its peak in the formal procedures of mandate, instruction, and (hardly) collegial deliberation preceding the election itself, which, typically, was never envisioned as a democratic contest but as validation of "intrigues" and "cabals" before the fact. While the state, embodied in its commissioned investigator, acted as a referee to the unfolding conflict, participants turned to corrupting the electoral process and shoring up their respective factions. Their efforts focused on two technical but extremely important matters concerning the cantonal assembly where the new scribe would be elected: first, the apportionment of electors between *Stadt* and *Amt;* and second, the manner by which these would be mandated by their constituents through *Vollmachten.*[16]

The procedural requirement of *Amt* representation gave Waiblingen's village foremen their first chance to weigh in on Bolley's candidacy. Though traditionally excluded from influence in the cantonal seat, the *Schutlheißen* were entitled by law to participate in all elections bearing on the canton's general well-being, and the choice of a new scribe certainly qualified. Offering the first formal riposte to the *Magistrat,* their petitions of 8 and 14 November 1793 accused the Waiblingen burgomaster, Franck, of attacking Bolley for selfish political reasons.[17] Signed by all nine village foremen and composed by one Carl Gottlieb Keller, the petitions alleged that Franck wanted to "make the future *Stadt- und Amtsschreiber* into the instrument of his will" in order to enhance his influence over the *Magistrat,* a faction of whose elder members had begun to oppose him. Franck had indeed attempted to have Heinrich Knaus, a "senile" 78-year-old, and J. G. Bunz, aged 82, both supporters of Bolley, disqualified on the grounds of age.[18] This was highly ironic given the correlation he had previously drawn between seniority and probity to attack Bolley's youth.

The villagers enumerated a series of corrupt, ventriloquistic deceits that Franck had perpetrated within the written record. Among his specific methods they cited the suborning of signatures to the various city council petitions slandering Bolley. This was compounded by an act of bald-faced deception. According to an affidavit from Knaus and Bunz, again composed by Keller, Franck had *spoken* highly of Bolley in the same moment that he lay documents before them to be signed, expressing precisely the opposite sentiment.[19] Finally, Franck had allegedly attempted to stack the election against Bolley by having the councillors choose their electors to the cantonal assembly from among his own, younger cronies.[20] The *Schultheißen* did not fail to point out that such "conspiracies" to set up voting blocs compelled them to either acquiesce in the *Magistrat's* decisions or resort to illegal "confederations" of their own.

Protocolled investigation soon revealed that such a confederation already existed among the village foremen, who were in cahoots with Bolley. The state's commissioner focused on Bolley's suspect relationship with Keller, the man who had composed the village petitions. According to his report, Keller stood in the "tightest bonds of friendship" with Bolley, although it is unclear when and how Bolley acquired this selfless ally, Keller being identified only as the son of a minor official in Unterweißach. Whatever their connection, Bolley proved remarkably deft at evading responsibility for their written and verbal communications. Protocolled on 14–15 February 1794, Keller admitted that Bolley may have "furnished him material in the course of their conversations" but it was "by no means written." This left Keller to take full responsibility for the "form and composition" of the village petitions. As to their content, Keller insisted that he had merely "led the feather"—transcribed, in other words—"according to the will of the *Schultheißen*," and had no role in tarting up those passages the state investigator construed as "insulting" for their partisanship and harsh language.[21]

Emboldened by these findings of impropriety, the *Magistrat* moved to cast doubt on the validity of the written mandates the *Schultheißen* had solicited from their constituents to draw up the petitions. Suspecting the *Schultheißen* were reluctant to make themselves pawns in the whole affair, the city councillors alleged that Keller and Bolley had cajoled them into signing the various complaints drawn up in their names.[22] Then, in the hopes that their façade of unanimous opposition to Franck's party would fracture under pressure, the *Magistrat* insisted that the village foremen resolicit their mandates before the election of a new scribe could take place. This argument was given new force by several documents attesting to irregularities in the mandating process and to doubts among village leaders as to Bolley's suitability for office. Specifically, in the Waiblingen village of Bittenfeld, a potential dissenter had been duped into leaving town on unrelated business before the communal *Vollmacht* was drafted. This deception was exposed when the dupe, a shepherd named Jacob Luithard, came forward with several kin to reclaim their rights to mandate and instruct their deputy.[23] Owing to its suspiciously sophisticated legal language, Luithard's protest was found by a provisional government report to be the "work of the [Waiblingen] *Magistrat*." This finding was overruled, however, by even higher authorities who took an agnostic position on the question of subornment. These ordered the *Schultheißen* to refresh their mandates on the more general grounds that they had acted "for themselves, rather than merely in the name of and after empowerment by their communities."[24] This solution reflected the state's misplaced belief that the procedures of collegial deliberation could somehow naturally circumvent partisanship and enmity, if "foreign influence" could only be removed from communal decisions.

Since it refused to adjudicate between competing versions of the truth in the written record, the state found itself once again confronted with extralegal, cultural arguments about the honor and integrity of various combatants. Reveling in disgust and *Schadenfreude,* the city council argued that the villagers' chicanery only reinforced their own claim to represent the interests of the entire canton more dispassionately and wisely than these country bumpkins. Such an assertion was entirely in keeping with the historical privileges and social esteem that accompanied notable status in the Württemberg cantons. Speaking the language of unvarnished oligarchism, they consistently portrayed themselves as "righteous, impartial electors unswayed by private advantage" and marked by "solid character"—all of which they used to ground claims for more favorable representation, at the villagers' expense, at the new scribe's election.[25] Unmoved, the state again applied a strictly impartial remedy in ruling that the *Magistrat* electors be chosen by lot, not in accord with Franck's wishes. This occasioned appeals, which stalled the matter long enough that the government began to suspect it was being stonewalled.[26] Yet the state possessed few other options to break communal logjams; exercising an evenhanded approach, policing the observance of law, and requiring that election procedures be repeated until they produced a harmonious result—these measures were as much interference as the government allowed itself.

If, in all these machinations, the intricacies of formality and proper procedure distorted the truth, confused the state, and prolonged social conflict, they also led actors, sometimes unwittingly, into a closer engagement with texts as resources of citizenship. The more the Waiblinger manipulated legal texts, the more concerned they became with the niceties of legal argument, and this concern, however disingenuous at first, would deepen over the following decade. This is illustrated by a separate but entirely related battle, which raged even as the exchange of petitions and denunications droned on in the fall of 1793, and which concerned the written legal "observances" *(Observanzen)* governing the conduct of cantonal elections. State arbiters recognized these precedents alone as decisive in controversial elections such as Bolley's. In a 1797 dispute between municipal and village representatives in the huge canton of Urach, for example, the government instructed its

Oberamtmann to ransack the "statute books . . . election proceedings, [parliamentary] convocation orders, and powers of attorney" for all previous communal and *Landtag* elections so that the duke could "judge the matter according to its fullest extent."[27] *Oberamtmänner* refereed the exchange of such materials between central officials and local parties. A certain power lay in the ability to extract, both locally and in the Stuttgart chancelleries, only the most relevant information from the politically charged context attending the production of documents in daily life. Even as this procedure enhanced the state's claim to disinterested superiority, it just as surely distorted its perspective and compromised its desire to be informed of all pertinent facts. This left local actors considerable leeway to affect the interpretation of texts.

The need for close, conscientious reading of texts was especially great in cases where legal objectivity was in practice impossible, and local knowledge all the more necessary. Far from a routine search, interrogating the written record involved making political judgments and staking professional reputations. First, protocol excerpts establishing the procedures for past elections had to be researched in the town archives by the local scribe. Missing, damaged, illegible, inaccurate, and poorly annotated records were quite common, a frustrating situation that compelled diligence and probity in tense circumstances. These fragmentary protocols then had to be redacted and compiled into a meaningful, coherent account of past political practice on the basis of guesswork and logical inference. In a nearly identical case twenty-five years earlier, a scribe in Tübingen, faced with "completely summary" reports on events "lost in darkness," resorted to the highly controversial method of reconstructing what "must . . . have transpired at the last alleged election." He then suffered rebuke for his "vehemence" in twisting his interpretations to the benefit of *Amt* deputies.[28] For similar reasons, back in Waiblingen, a minor scandal erupted between Pistorius and the "saucy" acting scribe, August Schuster. Pistorius had accused Schuster of withholding protocol excerpts and siding with the Franck party. This caused Schuster to demand "satisfaction" for his reputation having been "publicly prostituted."[29]

Record searches in an acrimoniously divided community held up a mirror of its own past, a past which, given the way official memory was preserved, usually appeared deceptively harmonious, pristine, and unspoiled. Typically, protocol excerpts recorded practically nothing on the internal conduct of old debates, an expression of that cherished corporative solidarity, which brooked no outward dissent and no trace of factionalism outside the chambers of the *Rathaus*. Such was the case in Waiblingen for a 1740 "compromise" *(Vergleich)* between *Stadt* and *Amt* that proved the focal point for competing legal interpretations, centered on both its textual ambiguities and its apparent contradiction in postelectoral practice.[30] Corollary to this problem was whether the testimony of living witnesses, taken to oral protocol, could substitute for the silences of official memory, or whether these would appear hopelessly partisan. Usually it took a "concurrence of circumstances"—i.e., mutually reinforcing testimonies from several presumptively partisan witnesses—and an absolutely intractable deficit of the "certificates" themselves to warrant the introduction of new (and still carefully protocolled) personal recollections.[31] Finally, participants argued over the relevance of more recent precedents gathered from other cantons. Whereas native precedents tended to confirm municipal oligarchies' claims to act as custodians of a bygone golden age, contemporary examples drawn from elsewhere favored village upstarts, by establishing a comparative benchmark of progress and evolution. Invoking these comparisons, the *Schultheißen* wished to submit the cantonal suffrage procedure to the most thorough documentary review possible: a sort of democratization by codification familiar from the denouement of the Hofacker case.[32]

The recourse to written *Observanz* produced no conclusive results in the realm of law but had a decisive impact in bidding up the stakes in this internecine cantonal conflict. As the layers of uninterrogated tradition, of urban prerogative and village apathy, were stripped away in a search for the truest protocols, the rights of the "citizenry" *(Bürgerschaft)* and "community" on which these ultimately rested came increasingly under political scrutiny.[33] It was in this climate that the *Magistrat* parried the painstaking legalism of Bolley and the village foremen. Staging an end run around his populist machinations, it orchestrated its own demands for popular citizenship. Its first attempt in this regard, a signature drive among the common Waiblingen *Bürger* to stir up opposition against Bolley, was admittedly heavy-handed. Mounted by Franck's cronies in late 1793, the trumped-up petition produced a meager number of signatures, which the city councillors nonetheless used to "prophesy a revolt of the citizenry" and "convert their voice into the voice of the people." These, at least, were the words of the village foremen who successfully exposed the drive as an attempt to "draw the citizenry into parties" and offend the "harmony and order" all were rhetorically committed to upholding.[34]

A later effort was at once more sophisticated and more radical, pushing the interpretation of law to its logical conclusion. This was a petition, dated 18 February 1794 from Bittenfeld, citing an old ducal rescript from 1725 according to which, it claimed, the instruction of its deputy must occur by polling "the entire citizenry man for man."[35] This is the first argument, anywhere in the case, for extending political rights to the lowest rung of Württemberg citizen: the village *Bürger*. It was only when Pistorius produced documents alleging that an ally of Franck's had stirred up the Bittenfelders' complaints that this too was revealed as the handiwork of the *Magistrat*.[36] The papers he turned over to the state investigation also betray an extremely shaky penmanship, casting heavy suspicion on the Bittenfelders' contention to have dreamed up such a sophisticated legal argument all by themselves. References to the 1725 rescript in particular had by then become a sort of signature for the Franck party. Still, the effort proved convincing enough to provoke government admonitions to "calm"—directed at the Bittenfelder—and the following reminder, intended for all participants and showing just how far things had spun out of control in Waiblingen: now completely unmoored from legal guidelines, the state argued, "the petitioners labor under the misperception that the election of a *Stadt- und Amtsschreiber* is actually a popular vote." There could be no clearer evidence of the spontaneous innovations in legal culture and citizenship practice that textual recourse could call forth.

The outcome remained undecided. Through February 1794 the city and its countryside battled interminably over their respective suffrage rights and the "observances" upon which their cases rested. A third outside election supervisor had replaced the official who took over after Pistorius's recusal, but his efforts to bring the parties together proved "fruitless." Eventually the government conceded the intractability of the problem and accepted a proposal from one Friedrich Ludwig Wilhelm Theuß, a well-credentialed lawyer, that the Waiblingen *Schreiberei* be divided in two, at least temporarily. Theuß was slightly older than Bolley but otherwise quite similar in terms of background and qualifications, as the village foremen pointed out in exasperation.[37] A Tübingen graduate, he was well known in Waiblingen but not in Franck's thrall, and his main advantage lay simply in not being allied with Pistorius.[38] Under the terms of his proposal, Bolley would acquire the substantial *Amt* business and Theuß, possessed of independent financial means, would oversee the less lucrative affairs of the *Stadt*.[39] On matters of general importance, such as cantonal assemblies, they would alternate in their secretarial and consultative functions. The expedient ended the immediate legal struggle but could not resolve the deep schisms with Waiblingen's professional community, between oligarchic local councillors and cosmopolitan officials such as Bolley, and now also between *Stadt* and *Amt*. As long as the canton, as the sole constitutional forum for legitimate citizen action, had to contain these rivalries, the armistice declared among these rival and intersecting factions would be an uneasy peace.

DEMOCRATIZATION BY CODIFICATION

In the course of Bolley's campaign for the *Schreiberei*, various factions in Waiblingen canton mastered a range of textual formalities to pursue their interests. Conflicts in the professional community were, in the first instance, waged by self-serving individuals manipulating corporative collegiality for their own ends. Yet such manipulations also harbored the potential, more positively, to widen the sphere of participation in Waiblingen's *political* community. Viewed in political terms, the petty factionalism Waiblingen suffered in 1793–94 betokened a deeper constitutional conflict affecting all parts of the duchy. Far from an isolated occurrence, the fracturing of corporative unity, in the form of discord between *Stadt* and *Amt*, reflected pervasive and longstanding pressures for the democratization of cantonal institutions. These pressures dated to the Thirty Years' War, whose urban devastations forced the cities back on the resources of the countryside, whereupon villages demanded a say in cantonal affairs commensurate with their ever-growing tax burden.[40] This shift, promising to fulfill the canton's pretense to represent the entire male citizenry, was as much a secular trend as a sudden development, neither evenly spread nor fully complete by Bolley's time. It depended on isolated, sporadic crises to jar local institutions into reform. Heinrich Bolley seized upon such a crisis to further his ambitions soon after obtaining the Waiblingen *Amtsschreiberei*. While standing for the *Landtag* elections of 1796, Bolley, newly politicized by the activities of the Reform Party, began to cultivate the more active participation of village foremen whom he had merely exploited in his initial rise to power.

To track this evolution in Waiblingen's political community, this section follows competing interpretations of what contemporaries referred to as the canton's "communal constitution" *(Kommun-Verfassung)*, essentially its official memory: the collection of written observances, protocol excerpts, compacts and agreements, and other legal precedents establishing its procedures of collegial deliberation and its rights and obligations vis-à-vis the duke and the estates. The situation in Waiblingen was utterly typical in that its constitution was riddled, as we have seen, with gaps and textual inconsistencies historically operating to the advantage of those persons and groups who knew how to exploit them. Throughout most cantons' histories, these had remained the city councillors. Their culture of collegiality had rested on the presumption of greater honor and probity that they enjoyed as town notables, in addition to the more practical advantages of what the last chapter, following Max Weber, called *Abkömmlichkeit*—simply being available, in the loop. Yet such privilege had always had a shaky legal foundation. The handbook on cantonal self-government, Johann Jakob Moser's *Communal Ordinance* of 1758, guaranteed a role for both cantonal seats and village delegates in cantonal assemblies, as did a number of other legal precedents, notably the 1725 ducal rescript that has already been mentioned.[41] Such positive laws stood in relation to local customs as theme and variation in the cantonal constitutions, each of which contained vestigial privileges and peculiarities and therefore differed in detail but not in kind from every variant elsewhere.[42] As a Waiblingen *Amt* petition correctly observed, however, no mere *"Observanz* can exist where it stands in conflict with . . . an explicit law."[43]

All that was needed to activate latent constitutional formalities and widen the sphere of democratic collegiality was a catalyst, an advocate having the knowledge, influence, and interest to do so. On 13 September 1796, Bolley assumed this role when the Waiblingen cantonal assembly elected him as its representative to what would become known as the Württemberg "Reform Parliament." He had the votes of nine assembled village foremen from the *Amt* and one city councillor. The remaining city councillors voted unanimously for burgomaster Franck, but since several among their number were mysteriously absent (this was never explained), Bolley triumphed, provisionally, with a majority.[44] Two petitions drafted that day and the next, one from the village foremen to the duke and one from the city councillors to parliament, declared their respective candidates the winners and their respective electors the bearers of right and justice.[45]

Of the two, the *Amt* villagers' petition clearly possessed the weaker legal argument, riddled as it was with extraneous claims about citizenship reflecting Bolley's newfound political passions. The petition deemed it illogical and perverse that "for [the villagers] alone there is no political freedom in Württemberg," wondering "how much their patriotism must thereby be impaired." Here it strained to add that the "right of peasants does not base itself solely on the presumption of equal rights among all estates." This protested too much, however, since evidently no concrete precedents could be produced to support repeated invocations of an "unbroken practice" of village participation. As practical evidence, it duly invoked the countryside's disproportionate fiscal burden to prove that the "villages are not laggards behind the cities," but again proffered no textual exegesis to support this claim. The *Stadt* petition, by contrast, combined constitutional citations from 1514, 1520, 1607, and 1629 with a now-familiar ideological appeal to "harmony." In addition to the language requiring deputies to come "from the midst of the magistracies," watertight evidence against Bolley's election that derived from the Tübingen Compact, this petition called attention to Bolley's illegal and disruptive influence over the village foremen, alleging for the record that they followed the "lead of the *Amtsschreiber* blindly in all cases where one could speak against the *Stadt.*"

Bolley's desire to avoid drawing attention to himself at the very moment he prepared to enter a wider, more public forum offers a possible reason for the *Amt* petition's lapses. A window into his motivations around this time is provided by the anonymous "Contribution" he published in "Answer to the Question: Who Can Be Elected to the Württemberg *Landtag?*" This pamphlet was dated only nine days after the *Amt* petition, on 22 September 1796, and yet in its first sentence Bolley made the outrageous claim that he had "for himself not the least interest in the answer to the question posed."[46] His obvious desire to claim a rhetorically neutral position before a public audience explains the technical shortcomings of the petition: had he filled it with the same legal arguments contained in the pamphlet, a well-informed investigator, putting two and two together, might have been able to link the two documents and expose Bolley's ulterior motives. His preferred method, reflected J. G. Pahl in 1840, was to parade telltale "mottos" which, while legally untraceable, still "betrayed his whole bag of tricks." These mottos had had been taken from "the writings of the famous Immanuel Kant" and, as Pahl somewhat crudely editorialized, "meant nothing more and nothing less than that everyone should have the freedom to do and to write what he wants."[47]

Viewed in this perspective, the *Amt* petition was a stopgap measure meant to furnish a pretext for struggle rather than procure immediate gains for the villagers. It was a provocative first salvo in a campaign Bolley intended to prosecute further through much subtler tactics. His pamphlet disclosed the broader strategy. In it, Bolley expounded the Enlightened view, discussed in the previous chapter, that politics should be open to all men of merit—a view that he clearly applied to himself. On behalf of his constituents, he also dispatched the magistracies' legal claim to patronize cantonal assemblies. Bolley's characteristically meticulous and convoluted justification of this argument make the methods of sophistry seem blandly commonsensical by comparison. Essentially, he took the stock legal phrase "Burgomaster, Court & Council," for which the term *Magistrat* functioned as an unofficial shorthand, and dissected it, showing that each element had a competing claim to representation. This analysis proved that, even at its apparent core, the cantonal constitution had no unimpeachable unity beneath its variant historical incarnations and that its textual ambiguities were therefore subject to political renegotiation. Clearing away the cobwebs of corporative privileges now voided of their original rationales, Bolley added in a Tocquevillean twist, was the only way to avert "revolutionary evils" such as had just been witnessed in France.[48]

This, a fundamentally political and not a legal insight, also harmonized with the state's own desire to reform the cantonal constitutions in a gradualist manner; here, at least, Bolley's arguments did carry the sanction of official policy. Since the beginning of the eighteenth century, Württemberg's dukes had consistently favored the villages in conflicts with the city councils, hoping to undermine the latter as standard-bearers of a recalcitrant estates assembly. The dukes' motivations were also pragmatic, borne of the conviction that a closer correspondence between taxation and representation in the cantons would lubricate the machinery of fiscal exploitation.[49] Constrained by the estates' vigilance, the ducal government necessarily relied on the cantons themselves to generate occasions for reform. In its two great "communal ordinances" of 1702 and 1758 codifying the right of *Amt* participation, it had set a yardstick in positive law and could afford to wait for its provisions to be attained over time, through the efforts of long-suffering villages and their ambitious advocates. These included not only scribes but other officials possessing a broad cantonal mandate, such as treasurers and superintendents. With their help, the ducal government managed to arbitrate conflicts and negotiations, leading a string of cantons to revise their constitutions in favor of village representation: Tübingen in 1771, Schorndorf in 1780, Backnang in 1786, Leonberg in 1792.[50]

The government's response to Bolley's petition proved to be the decisive catalyst enabling Waiblingen to join this list of reformed cantons. Its decision was a blow for him personally but poured new fuel on the struggle he had unleashed. On the one hand, it decisively rejected Bolley's election, applying in a judgment issued 15 September 1796 the same logic that had driven Hofacker to lay down his position as *Schreiber* at Nagold: no scribe had, by virtue of office alone, a stake in corporative representation comparable to a *Magistrat* member. On the other hand, the state explicitly invited the *Amt* to press its claims for greater representation at the cantonal assemblies. It instructed *Oberamtmann* Pistorius to advise the villagers of their "rights" in order to "fix a proper relation of *Stadt* and *Amt* votes," in writing if possible.[51] The involvement of Pistorius at this point signaled a much more direct role for the state than had previously been the case. It styled him a competitor to Bolley, his former protégé, and forced both men to pursue strategies that would enhance the rights of the villagers. The dispute that would soon erupt between the two men also shows how Bolley, in his political thinking, had begun to evolve beyond the strictly bureaucratic approach to reform represented by Pistorius and the state.

Professionally embarrassed at the conflict festering under his watch, Pistorius, for his part, favored a course offering the quickest possible restoration of "peace and order." He may have had his eye on a post as Government Councillor, a position to which he in fact ascended in 1804, and therefore felt a desire to please his superiors.[52] A new election that he called for 19 September came out in favor of burgomaster Franck, the village foremen having thrown him their support after Pistorius assured them, somewhat quixotically, that through a properly crafted *Instruktion* Franck was honor-bound to do their bidding despite their personal animosities.[53] The reversal also reflected the *Oberamtmann's* success in negotiating a "Compact" signed by the village foremen and city councillors alike. In three provisions amending the cantonal constitution, this Compact pointed a way out of the impasse.[54] First, at cantonal assemblies concerning strictly financial matters, the *Stadt* would send two delegates, the *Amt* four. This stood in direct proportion to the hinterland's fiscal burden in the cantonal tax levy. Second, to fill vacancies in cantonal posts for scribes, treasurers, and other local officials, equal numbers of formally mandated village deputies would meet alongside *Magistrat* members instead deliberating "according to their best will and conscience." A paradox of this arrangement was that, while it conferred greater honor upon the urban delegates, presumed to possess more reliable "conscience" and thus enjoy free mandate, it worked institutionally to prevent the kind of monolithic municipal voting blocs Franck had tried to put together through binding instructions. The final provision held that parliamentary deputies be elected "in patriotic community," with all sixteen city councillors present along with nine *Schultheißen,* whom they could easily overrule. This provision later struck both Bolley and the government as particularly naïve.

By contemporary standards, the compromise Pistorius hammered out was a fair, if not especially decisive, victory for the villages of the Waiblingen *Amt.* Many other cantons had completed an even more thorough devolution of institutional control to the countryside. The villages of Nürtingen, for example, sent fully 56% of the delegates present at the 1737 parliamentary election, a proportion which grew to 70% in 1763 and an impressive 84% in 1796—including all but five of the 32 in attendance. In Urach, an enormous rural canton, assemblies grew to include upwards of eighty delegates, resembling miniature parliaments with heavy peasant representation.

Stuttgart's *Amt* assembly met as often as seven times a year in the first decade of the eighteenth century and remained institutionally independent from the capital city's magistracy. In these places and in many of the duchy's other large cantons—Leonberg, Cannstatt, Schorndorf, Backnang, Göppingen—villages had achieved at least a parity with, if not a numerical majority over, the urban oligarchies that had traditionally dominated cantonal politics.[55] Each of the reformed districts lay, like Waiblingen itself, in Württemberg's rich, conservative heartland, even as the more politically "Enlightened" cantons of the Black Forest retained oligarchic constitutions, as in Hofacker's Nagold. The dynamic of reform was thus immanent to the duchy's cantonal system, more developed precisely where it was more ensconced, and not the product of either external (French) influence or haphazard deviations on the periphery. On this basis, it is reasonable to expect that, had the Württemberg old regime not been cut short by the Napoleonic invasions, its venerable cantonal structure would have evolved into a formally, and to some extent substantively, democratic political system.

To Bolley, Pistorius's timidity foreclosed upon this promise of further democratic evolution, frittering away the vitality of the Württemberg constitution. Despite his disqualification, he felt moved to "save his own honor and redeem the rights of the *Amt* against this extremely disadvantageous contract." The problem was that in assenting to the Compact, the village foremen had in one stroke deprived Bolley of any pretext for further grievance. Thus, in a striking illustration of the use of legal texts as proxies in a broader personal and political struggle, the conduct of disagreements thenceforward consisted entirely in a duel of officially recorded notes. Reading "at home" sometime after 19 September, Bolley first discovered the Pistorius Compact in the protocol book containing cantonal assembly minutes, and on the 26th entered into the same a "Protestation" against it. Having absented himself from the actual drafting of the Compact to avoid appearing partisan, he could only voice his objections after the fact.[56] Pistorius in turn learned of Bolley's Protestation at the next cantonal assembly meeting, when a reading of its previous minutes turned up his unorthodox interpellation. The breach that had been opening between the two flared into public confrontation, as nearly as the documents allow, at this precise moment on 14 October 1796. Attempting to squelch the allegations Bolley had leveled, Pistorius undertook to allay the concerns of the village foremen. The latter denied giving Bolley "the slightest mission" to draw up the Protestation. Still, Bolley's "totally unexpected move" compelled Pistorius to request that the Privy Council ratify his Compact, giving Bolley crucial room for maneuver.[57]

Much more was at stake here than the personal crusade of a constitutional gadfly against a complacent bureaucrat. Bolley believed that in an age of "revolutionary evils," reconciling the ancient cantonal constitution with the universalistic ideals of the Enlightenment was the only way to keep its traditions alive. And what made the constitution a living tradition was its ability to trump the present opinions or actions of any of those it temporarily authorized, in the flesh and blood, to carry out its provisions.[58] This conviction lay at the heart of Bolley's Protestation, which insisted upon the limited malleability of the cantonal constitution under shifting human caprice. Referring to the Pistorius Compact, he denied that the village delegates possessed the competence, in the here and now, to found "abiding bonds and rights . . . for the future" through their own actions and agreements. Only the political alchemy of mandate and instruction, converting individual voices into the will of corporations, had a purchase on subsequent generations. Pistorius's failure to solicit such mandates made his hastily signed Compact both legally invalid and manipulative—an opinion the government endorsed.[59]

Bolley's invocation of the village mandate dispensed with the ideological arguments of his original *Amt* petition and instead stood on the much firmer legal basis provided by the 1725 General Rescript so beloved by the Franck party. This state ordinance extended the procedures of mandate and instruction customarily reserved for urban parliamentary deputies downward to the villages and their delegates to cantonal assemblies.[60] In a striking display of protodemocratic reasoning, it prescribed that, prior to attending such assemblies, *Amt* delegates should consult a host of village elders, if not "include . . . the entire community," before being "reliably" (i.e., textually) mandated through formal instructions. Such mandates, and the deliberations on which they rested, would be physically appended to the village protocols *(Dorfprotokolle)* and assume the same importance in the written record reserved for all other precedents within the cantonal constitution. Not only did this invalidate Pistorius's Compact as a circumvention of formal procedure, but it cast doubt on the specific formulas he worked out regarding *Amt* participation. As the government elaborated in its response to Bolley's Protestation, "the size of the [villages'] population [is] the most convenient measure for the participation of *Stadt* and *Amt*." This shed a previous emphasis on corporative rights and legally documented privileges in favor of a more fiscally and demographically pragmatic approach, thus prying open a space for reform.[61]

In the village mandate, traditional constitutionalism and Enlightened universalism came full circle. This textual device harbored the potential to bring every Württemberger's voice, not just the will of the urban notabilities, to bear on politics. Through corporative channels, it formally extended networks of collegiality to those citizens whom scribes like Bolley had always manipulated for their own purposes.[62] And while apparently intended to restrict the villagers' competence, Bolley's insistence that they be formally mandated actually ascribed to them the fullest form of citizenship known to the old regime: however counterintuitive it may seem to modern sensibilities, one found one's voice not in the exercise of individual responsibility or conscience, but in being tied to, and seeking identity within, a corporation. This move styled the village community not as an ad hoc participant in the affairs of its canton but as a durable representative institution with its own collective voice and will, deriving from *all* of its members across *all* of its generations. This implicitly put village delegates on an equal footing with *Magistrat* members, who had long used the rhetoric of corporative solidarity, ancient tradition, and probity as a ruse for their own machinations. It inducted them into the mysteries of collegial deliberation, elegantly conceived as a progression of successively narrower circles of representation extending from the villages up through the cantons and into parliament itself, like nested Russian dolls.

Casting off the legal, practical, and cultural predominance of notable honor as a basis for citizenship was a radical innovation, one whose trial in practice would have to await a more auspicious moment. By December, the state authorities had finally responded to Pistorius on the matter of Bolley's Protestation, and for the second time in four years the civil conflict in Waiblingen remained unresolved.[63] The government admonished Bolley for his "self-interested" behavior while voicing strong doubts that Pistorius's compromise would work. The only novelty in the state's response was its willingness to allow the conflict between *Stadt* and *Amt* to fester. Traditionally, the duke's Machiavellian desire to cultivate challenges to cantonal oligarchies had been blunted by the bureaucracy's scrupulous wish to uphold order and restore harmony. By the time Napoleon arrived, however, a more aggressive state had become bent on rooting up the cantonal constitutions themselves. The last section in this chapter explains how Bolley rose to this unprecedented challenge, drawing upon the wider forms of collegiality he had introduced to Waiblingen in an act of patriotic resistance.

HEINRICH BOLLEY *v.* THE KING

Duke Friedrich's sudden revocation of the Württemberg constitution in December 1805 necessitated an equally rapid circling of the wagons in the canton of Waiblingen. On New Year's Eve, one day after formally ascending to the kingship, Friedrich promulgated a rescript curtailing the powers of the cantonal assemblies and robbing them of their status as constitutive elements of a now-defunct *Landtag*. He thereby extended his coup d'état from Stuttgart into the countryside. This move found Waiblingen still politically riven, and Bolley scrambling to reassert constitutional rights and restore cantonal harmony in one and the same effort. Several developments made it easier for him, acting in haste, to engineer such a feat. First, a new "compact" between *Stadt* and *Amt*, signed in April 1800 and apparently mediated by *Stadtschreiber* Theuß, had resolved the nagging question of representation at cantonal assemblies and laid the matter to rest, at least temporarily.[64] Perhaps more decisive was burgomaster Franck's steady decline in health, which effectively removed him as an adversary to Bolley. Franck's physical incapacity had been an issue ever since 1793, when a bout of vomiting had torn him away from a crucially-timed city council meeting and required him to redouble his efforts to subvert Bolley's election as scribe.[65] As for Pistorius, he had received his promotion, and took with him to Stuttgart any lingering embers of that old enmity with Franck, as well as any newer resentments occasioned by his conflict with Bolley. With his departure, Bolley finally emerged indisputably as Waiblingen's most powerful political operator.

As a means for mustering a formal resistance against the king, Bolley and his collaborators chose the instrument of petition. Many eighteenth-century German politicians saw in the right of petition the best hope for renewing a constitutional order chronically under siege by monarchs with absolutist pretensions. Expressing the will of the people and the spirit of "progress," petitions bypassed unwieldy corporative channels of grievance (*viz.* the Black Forest Cahier) and appealed directly to the grace and generosity of the prince. They embodied a centuries-old tradition, sanctioned by the law courts of Holy Roman Empire, at the same time as they provided an opportunity, textually, to incorporate the latest in Enlightenment political rhetoric.[66]

In drafting his petition, Bolley took the lead of Christian Friedrich Baz, the former Ludwigburg burgomaster and Hofacker ally in the 1797 Reform Parliament. Political pressure had led Baz to flee to Vienna in 1800 and then return to Württemberg under Bolley's aegis, living in Waiblingen as an internal exile. Baz's influential pamphlet, "On the Right of Petition," assimilated constitutional reform to the Enlightenment's overall faith in universal human progress. Constitutions, he wrote, furnish standards for achievement among the various groups in society, ruler and ruled alike: "Most of them set a goal for the human being," specifying "what he may think, believe, and hold true or false." Where they go awry is in presuming that these standards will last for all time, since "it is in the nature of all human things to degenerate or be degenerated." To this problem of cyclic decay, an abiding concern of eighteenth-century civic republicanism, Baz counterposed the more hopeful belief that "everything . . . concerning the education, sustenance, and happiness of the human race . . . can change and must be improved and transcended." The role of petitions in this process, he explained, was to arrest an otherwise inevitable decline, stepping outside the imperfections of existing "institutions of civil society" and submitting suggestions for improvement to a beneficent sovereign.[67]

By virtue of his physical presence in Waiblingen, Baz's pamphlet had at least an indirect influence on Bolley's 1806 petition, if not directly inspiring it. Their affinities ran deep. Both men envisioned the constitution's universal applicability to every Württemberg subject—Baz even speaking of "the will of the people"—yet neither suggested that actual sovereignty ever inhered in anyone but the ruler, to whom fealty continued to be owed as to a father. "A *Volk* is that which speaks to the prince," Baz wrote, and not the source of political power in itself. In Bolley's case, a conservative attachment to the monarchy was not incompatible with a deep and often insolently oppositional commitment to political reform and activism. Baz also invoked the 1725 General Rescript to argue for the same "mission" and "duty" to enhance villagers' political participation that Bolley himself had undertook to realize in practice. Finally, in a way that directly anticipated the 1806 petition, Baz's pamphlet contrasted progress to violence, seeing in gradualist, Enlightened development the only sure prophylactic against "violent changes." Besides resonating with Bolley's outspoken aversion to "revolutionary evils," this capitalized on classic historical associations in old-regime political culture between the state and war, estates vitality and a policy of peace. Such associations derived from the estates' reluctance to finance standing armies and costly military expeditions.[68] Baz's and Bolley's insistent desire to avoid Jacobin excesses also reflected Germany's experience of the French Revolution more generally.

The petition of 4 January 1806, signed by the entire Waiblingen *Magistrat* and all of the village foremen, was the 36-year-old Bolley's masterpiece. Even as its author figuratively kowtowed before the new Majesty, he gazed upward with a cocky, grimacing righteousness. More than any other of his anonymous writings, the document also conveys the yawning gap between what he wrote and how he actually behaved, taking the submissive language of old-regime constitutionalism to new heights of insincerity and cant. Formally, the petition was cast as a "Congratulation" to Friedrich for his attainment of the kingship at Napoleon's hands.[69] Such an august sovereign, the petition "flattered" the king in the "sweetest hope," would naturally see fit to uphold the existing constitution, "for three hundred years the happiness of the people and their rulers." One can only imagine the priggish glee Bolley felt upon penning passages of such overwrought ornateness as these:

I.

Die Nachricht von der Wiederherstellung des so sehnlichst gewünschten Friedens und die höchsterfreuliche Kunde von dem neuen Glanz der in Gefolge desselben Euer Könglichen Majestät und allerhöchstdero höchstes Fürstenhaus umstrahlt müßen in dem Herzen eines jeden getreuen Unterthanen die reinsten Empfindungn von Freude hervorbringen.	News of the restoration of a peace so longingly wished for and the most celebrated announcement of the new radiance that in consequence thereupon bathes Your Royal Majesty and His All-Highest princely house with light, must call forth the purest feelings of joy in the heart of every loyal subject.

II.

O! gewiss ein Volk, das sich ohne Wehmuth von seiner, durch so viele Aufopferungen errungenen Verfassung, die seit Jahrhunderten sein Glück und das Glück seiner Regenten gründete, trennen kann, müßte selbst in Allerhöchstdero Augen als ein leichtsinniges, höchstverächtliches Volk erscheinen.	Oh! Certainly a people that can separate itself without wistfulness from its constitution, acquired through so many sacrifices, which has for centuries grounded its happiness and the happiness of its rulers, must itself in your all-highest eyes appear as a frivolous and most contemptible people.

III.

Mögen die Zeitumstände immerhin einige Modificationen in der Constitution erheischen, gewiß mit hingebender Bereitwilligkeit würden wir und die übrigen Stände die Hände dazu bieten, wann nur das wesentliche einer Verfassung erhalten bleibt, die nur einem eroberten Lande durch den Drang der Umstände, oder einem undenkbaren Lande, in welchem Empörung oder Bürgerkrieg gewüthet haben, zur Strafe entrissen werden kann.	If the circumstances of the time nonetheless demand some modifications in the constitution, certainly we and the rest of the estates would offer our hand with devoted readiness, if only that which is essential to a constitution remains, which can only be ripped as punishment from a conquered land through the force of circumstances, or from an inconceivable country in which rebellion or civil war has raged.

IV.

Wir ersterben in tiefster Erniedrigung.	We perish in deepest abasement.

Although it is difficult for contemporary sensibilities to grasp, these passages constituted a clear affront to a sovereign in no need of congratulations from his subjects. Royal inquisitors, on receiving the document, set upon passage 3 in particular as uppity and disrespectful: the canton's claim to offer an olive branch that was no longer theirs to give. This passage also came close to suggesting, as Baz had intimated, that the possibility of violence lurked behind the king's failure to keep constitutional rights in step with politics generally. Despite its exquisitely oblique phrasing here and throughout the text, the petition implicated Bolley and his co-conspirators in a potentially seditious act of rebellion and invited state retribution.

To appreciate the dangers incurred by the Waiblinger, one need only look at the fate suffered a year earlier by a similar group of petitioners in the neighboring canton of Winnenden. Their "Protestation," though drafted with "the most abject respect" to oppose an illegal tax levied in 1805, brought down swift justice from the state. Signed by the Winnenden *Magistrat* in the name of a "citizenry become alarmed" by rumors of a constitutional upheaval, the document conjured up a threat with no existence outside its author's linguistic flourish.[70] Protocolled investigation revealed that Winnenden's scribe, one Friedrich Carl Schmid, had secretly authored the document, while *Magistrat* members "had simply relied on its composer and his knowledge," having signed "everything put before them, blind and without consideration." Skillfully exploiting discrepancies between Schmid's testimony and that of the Winnenden city councillors, the state's investigator had placed their respective utterances *"in confrontatione,"* literally reading their transcribed depositions alongside one another. Then, by leading Schmid through close readings of textual excerpts from the Protestation, the commissioner determined the origins of particular provocations and infelicities that had crept into the document, only to discover that most were the products of "haste," "excess," and Schmid's own "human weakness"—not genuine popular outrage. Schmid was reduced to a "torrent of tears" by cross-examination and sentenced to four weeks in prison; members of the *Magistrat* were assessed heavy fines and/or received severe demerits.[71] The entire episode revealed a culpable disjunction between a text's representation of dissent and the palpable limits of political will among its author and signatories.

Bolley's "Congratulation," by contrast, relied on a much more responsible, activist, and sophisticated citizenry. This was a community no longer constrained by professional, or political, rules of play but driven by a genuinely popular activism. Having been schooled for a decade in the use of constitutional formality—and its evasion—the Waiblinger now showed themselves fully capable of improvising an effective collegiality in a series of much more informal situations.

This coalescence of popular collegiality, as reconstructed by commissioners' protocols, occurred as follows.[72] On Saturday, 4 January, the cantonal treasurer and burgomaster, a certain Johann Christoph Weisser, had met Bolley after dinner at Lamb's Pub and there "they discussed the events of the day." "There has been talk," Weisser replied to Bolley's query about what to do about the "present crisis," of drafting a petition to the king. The recourse here to rumor, talk, or "*Rede,*" in an evasion of personal responsibility was but one of a number of instances in which participants winked at one another, unwilling to commit even to oral expression where they could rely upon implicit understandings. Bolley promised Weisser that if the "cooperation of the *Amt* was demanded, it would certainly take part without hesitation," whereupon Weisser sought out the *Stadtschreiber* Theuß, who likewise spoke cryptically, pledging that "what[ever] the *Magistrat* and *Amt* representatives decide," he would "fulfill his official duties" and "draw up an essay" if called upon to do so. It was later determined that Weisser played the "most active role in the whole story," while paradoxically remaining "merely the tool of others," specifically Bolley and Theuß. Through him, both scribes carefully preserved an official neutrality in keeping with their limited notarial functions, which at the same time shielded them from direct responsibility for the canton's collective actions.

The conspirators' circumvention of individual accountability meant that the paper trail was an exceptionally lengthy and tortuous one. Irritated inquisitors had to interrupt Bolley's lengthy, florid tirades in an attempt to elicit crisper answers to their questions concerning the petition's origins.[73] What they finally determined was that Bolley had prepared a first draft of the "Congratulation," which he turned over to Theuß for further elaboration; after receiving it back, Bolley either lost or destroyed it, thereby insulating himself all the more from official reproach. Theuß, alarmed at some of Bolley's language, evidently toned the draft down. After that, an unofficial, illegal meeting of the Waiblingen *Magistrat* was convened at 8 a.m. on Sunday 5 January 1806 at Weisser's house, where a new version of the petition, approved by Bolley based on Theuß's second draft and sent to Weisser's house late the previous night, was read to the assembled councillors. The so-called *Mundum,* a final draft bearing their signatures, was thereupon prepared by Theuß himself, and not by a copyist or *Substitut,* "in order to observe discretion." It then made its way to Bolley, who held a separate informal meeting at his house among the *Amt* elders, who duly affixed their signatures. There were thus two separate meetings, a fact that reflected the historical animosity of *Stadt* and *Amt* but also a devious political calculation. Neither constituted a formal cantonal assembly and thus neither was formally disallowed by the king's New Year's Eve rescript, which itself only arrived in Waiblingen on Monday the sixth—one day too late to have effectively forbidden the meetings. Relying on this fact, Bolley was able to erect yet another wall of legal protection when he explained his actions for the state's protocols.[74]

The clandestine circulation of drafts not only diluted the scribes' legal responsibility but, in equal measure, parceled out moral accountability and even political agency among Weisser and the various delegates from *Stadt* and *Amt*. Though correct as a first approximation, to regard Bolley as the prime mover behind the 1806 petition underestimates the success of his efforts at civic education, practiced since his arrival in Waiblingen over thirteen years earlier. Weisser in particular bore the brunt of many of Bolley's initiatives while making no attempt to dodge responsibility for what he maintained, under protocolled investigation, was a "devoted and modestly phrased supplication."[75] "There was no encouragement needed," Weisser proclaimed, "to cause the *Magistrat* to sign the petition draft." In this he spoke for his colleagues, and "perhaps all Württembergers," who wished for the "protection of the constitution." As a sole exception he singled out burgomaster Franck, whose "exaggerated nervousness" led him to "tergiversate" as soon as the last man had signed and laid down his quill. "Because he wanted to slip out of any responsibility," Franck sought refuge behind legal "precedents" and avoided doing, in Weisser's words, "what was good in itself." This last statement proves that to act in accord with one's political conscience required stepping outside the realm of strict formality and making determinations of justice for oneself, and this demanded a great deal of civic courage.

It would be wrong to perceive the stirrings of modern, individualist citizenship here. The bulk of the petitioners certainly did not operate under the guidance of their own wills and cognition. As with the Winnenden Protestation, some of the signatories later admitted they had "not understood most of the draft" and had "perhaps given [a] signature without thinking."[76] A standard evasiveness before the hostile procedure of protocol may have prompted these excuses, yet many had clearly been pressured by their patrons to act, given that time was of the essence. Thus some councillors conceived "regrets" upon "arriving back home." Seizing on such admissions, the state's investigation concentrated on the disparity between the signatories' clear possession of at least minimal literacy and their decision to acquiesce in signing the petition. By investing signature with the property of individual will, and not mere identification with the corporate body of which one was a member, as was the case with compacts, mandates, protocol excerpts, and other legal documents treated in this chapter, the state penetrated the veil of community defensiveness. This was the real reason behind its obsession with the forms and proprieties of cantonal assemblies. It held up a standard of individual conscience and judgment where most citizens tended to act only in concert with their peers. Such a notion was not completely alien to the petitioners, accustomed as they were, like all citizens, to signing their names to all manner of official documents, but they rarely had occasion consciously to consider the precise implications of staking their reputations on documents laid before them by official personages.

These circumstances do not mitigate what has been said about the local culture of constitutional fetishism, but rather point precisely to its vitality. Constitutional fetishism consisted in a kind of active acquiescence produced less by external manipulation than by an internal sense of being caught up in the moment, in the spirit that infected corporative entities as a spontaneous manifestation of collective will. More than mere stooges brought in to commit their signatures to paper, participants in such collective action burst the confines of dry legal provision through their writing practice. Indeed, the more formal procedures of collegial deliberation, which Bolley and his co-conspirators circumvented, were intended precisely to brake this kind of enthusiasm. In this spirit, the state's investigator prescribed a series of seven steps that would have stalled the avalanche of protest and brought the two disallowed meetings into conformity with the law on cantonal assemblies.[77] He emphasized the specific burdens of office attaching to each participant, as well as the need for comprehensive written records: protocols transcribing, "where not every individual utterance" at least the "sense of the whole." Together with signature, the practice of protocol held state witnesses up to a standard of accountability founded on the capacity to extract oneself, through the analysis of motive and fact, from the webs of allegiance obscuring the "truth" and sustaining a collectivist esprit de corps.

Precisely where such accountability was missing, and the procedural firewalls to collective enthusiasm omitted, one witnesses the power of constitutional fetishism in its naked, autonomous, unconstrained form: the flourishing of a popular community, stripped of hindrances to collegial deliberation yet *still* dominated by written formalities, whose development this chapter has tried to trace. True, without the institutions of corporatism and their attendant textual forms, there would have been no forum in which political agency, so weak on an individual level, could be effectual. But without the experiences of the previous thirteen years, of Bolley's relentless agitation, this dynamic imbrication of textuality and civic activism would never have been sustainable, and the written documents it generated would have remained dry and lifeless formalities. It is this circumstance, finally, that distinguishes Bolley's manipulative practices from Ludwig Hofacker's breaches of protocol in the aftermath of the Black Forest Cahier. It allowed him to put up a deeper, fuller, and longer-lasting resistance than the Nagold scribe had ever managed to do. In the conclusion to this chapter, we turn to appraise the legacy of Bolley's efforts—and the entire nexus of formality and collegiality on which they relied.

EPILOGUE

The society of late eighteenth-century Württemberg was one bounded by the rule of law at both foundation and apex: by the formality of daily life on the one hand, and the officious jurisprudence of the Stuttgart chancelleries on the other. In the middle stood men like Bolley, his opponents, and his fellow travelers, along with the arsenal of legal forms and written instruments granting them a purchase on power. The cultural and political conflicts narrated in this chapter all took place within rooms filled with shelves of protocol books, albums of ducal orders headed by florid cursive invocations of majesty, files with musty contracts bearing the scrawled signatures of long-deceased councillors, and binders of legal citations on papers yellowed and crumbling at the edges—even at that time. Constitutional fetishism inscribed a hermeneutic circle around citizen action and human agency, preventing more radical currents of political Enlightenment, such as republicanism and popular sovereignty, from being embraced in an otherwise so proudly civic-minded polity. The appearance of radical ideologies would have presumed a source for power and progress, discursive practice and rhetorical appeal, outside laws and constitutions, which remained limited as political resources, no matter how creatively they were reinterpreted.

Was this nonetheless evidence of "civil society"? The book's introduction defined this term as a realm where citizens interact independently of the state, emphasizing the cognitive and social practices that enable free association to emerge. The intervening chapters have endeavored to locate these practices in the modes of written discourse and conflict specific to the Württemberg canton. Contracts, protocols, powers of attorney, supplications, and legal certificates, textual formalities that appear repeatedly in the pages above, made up an integral part of average citizens' routine involvement with the state in ways that would have seemed second nature to them. These texts furnished scripts for civic collegiality embodying received values of corporate collectivism, social equity, notable honor, generational solidarity, and community cohesion. The current chapter forms a natural epilogue to this treatment, showing these instruments of writing at work, still in daily life, but now with an unmistakably political valence. None of their usages, however, suggests the presence of "free association" in the dual sense of both cognitive and social practice: of a promiscuity of ideas and rhetorics to match an equally diverse assembly of social groups with various identities and interests. The stricturing of imagination by a deeply habitual resort to formality foreclosed on civil society just as surely as the state's procedural restrictions on the practice of collegiality outside the bounds of codified, corporate institutions.

Even without a vigilant state, in other words, the purely local culture of constitutional fetishism remained limited in its capacity for innovation. Conspicuously absent from all of the texts discussed above, and from the broader political culture they helped constitute, are discourses of gender, historical time, and the natural world, indeed all those cultural objects populating a realm of imagination beyond law: icons of Hercules and Marianne, wheels of fortune and Greco-Roman ruins symbolizing ancient virtue, liberty trees and primeval forest gatherings. This panoply—the stock-in-trade of late-Enlightenment encyclopedism—helped to make French Jacobinism, Atlantic civic republicanism, and later, Central European Romantic nationalism such colorful and resourceful political traditions, not to mention mediate their affinities with an equally vital realm of popular culture: of charivaris, carnivals, and festivals.[78] Especially the ancient constitutionalism so powerfully analyzed by J. G. A. Pocock, and for which Laurence Dickey has uncovered, on the level of *high* politics, a native Württemberg tradition of comparable color, vigor, and vitality, did not find an echo on the level of the cantons and their scribes and the practices of everyday citizenship.[79] This should temper any premature celebrations of an "Enlightened" politics either in the Black Forest Cahier or in the constitutional fetishism the Waiblinger exhibited.

The manifestations of Enlightenment glimpsed in the chapters above— tracts on official meritocracy, appeals to civic republicanism, invocations of universal rights and progress—were indeed relatively limited in impact, confined in influence to certain pressure points on the old regime's civic culture. Bolley's was one of the most fecund attempts to bring all these reformist currents, professional, political, and popular, to bear on the formulation of a progressive constitutionalism. His petitions and published writings and the secrets he betrayed in protocolled investigations all reveal a sensitivity to the invention of patriotism and the importance of freedom, the promise of social contracts and the power of the people. However, his legal mindset prescribed application of these precepts in limited ways entirely coterminous with the culture and practice of classic corporatism. His sympathy for the plight of peasants and villagers, his invocation of their rights, and his inclusion of them under the banner of constitutional renewal never took him outside the political culture of Old Württemberg, constraining him to pour his energies, and his limitless verbosity, into flourishes of the quill, even as Napoleon's armies poured across the frontier.

In short, neither the values nor the practices, the new visions nor the concrete actions, were at hand to enable free association to flourish. This in no way denigrates the activism and vitality of the old regime's civic culture. Constitutional fetishism, in the form Bolley mediated, was the culmination of a long tradition of citizen action in Germany resonating far beyond Württemberg, a tradition that drew its strength from the interpenetration of state and local community.[80] But it could only inspire the construction of civil society once the state disengaged from its intrusive involvement in community life. This story occupies the book's second half. Beginning with the scribes' fortunes during the period of violence and statemaking ushered in by Napoleon, it then turns to the institutional reforms robbing them of their historic mediating role. These reforms reshaped the civic landscape and promoted entirely new types of citizenship practice far less dependent on the cognitive and institutional moorings provided by constitutional texts. First, they compelled citizens to map out their position and possibilities for action in a more anonymous social order through the practice of sociography. Second, they forged new channels for Enlightenment to enter the cantons, enabling everyday citizens to imagine new possibilities through encyclopedic print media. Writing thus acquired a wider social utility and a less constricted range of applications for promoting change than existed in Bolley's hermetically sealed universe. The new reality made free association both real and ideal, and with this achievement, civil society would finally come to fruition.

PART II

Inscribing a Space of Freedom

5   Transcending "Textual Serfdom"

The formal emancipation of civil society from the state in Germany culminated under Napoleon's rule. During a decade of continental wars and occupations, from 1803 to 1815, Napoleon redrew the political boundaries of the Holy Roman Empire. Partly in response, partly in reaction, and both before and after his fall, German states created a new civic order through modernizing reforms in government, law, the military, economics, and infrastructure. Though the process was highly uneven from region to region, and though many progressive measures were later rolled back or eviscerated, the reform epoch ushered Central Europe into the modern world. For the first time, a substantial portion of the German population was legally recognized as state citizens, *Staatsbürger*, members not merely of a locality but of a much larger and more dynamic civil society. After reform from above, states—not tiny principalities, not far-flung empires, but solid, territorially bounded, socially integrated polities—formed the dominant organizing principle for German society as a whole. This story is often told from the perspective of states themselves, with little attention given to mediation between officials and citizens.[1] The purpose of this chapter—and of the remainder of this book—is to show how, in a quintessential Napoleonic state, civil society's emancipation was in fact a highly negotiated, contested process.

In Württemberg, Napoleon's inundation of the civic landscape caused a sea change in the scribes' relation to the citizenry. The vibrant, if excessively formal, civic culture over which they had presided finally reached a point of textual saturation. A powerful realization that Württemberg had become burdened with excessive writing—*Vielschreiberei*—took root among the people. The scribes, it was argued, bore a unique responsibility for this lamentable state of affairs. The issue burst upon the public scene in 1815, the

129

year of Napoleon's defeat at Waterloo, when King Friedrich moved to restore constitutional rule in his realm. Writing in response to the parliamentary debates published after the restoration, the philosopher G. W. F. Hegel offered the most viciously eloquent of the many tirades penned against the Württemberg *Schreiber* at this time. Hegel accused the scribes of keeping the kingdom's citizens in a state of "textual serfdom," one way of translating what he termed, in an evocative and typically German concatenation, "*Schreibhörigkeit* or *Schreibleibeigenschaft.*" A native Stuttgarter, Hegel grew up with an intimate knowledge of the scribes. Now that the old duchy was no more, he faulted them for blocking the creation of a new civic order:

> As long as Württemberg's peculiar bourgeois aristocracy existed, collected a bishop's income through writing, exercised a general domination over communities, their leaders, and private citizens, as long as these communities were not ripped from the claws of this privileged class, and this element of moral and intellectual degradation ensnaring the mass of the people not destroyed, no true concept of law, freedom, and constitution could take root.[2]

Hegel's criticisms arose out of an undeniable deterioration in the scribes' relationship to their clients. Napoleon's invasions had transformed a small, provincial duchy into a larger and more cosmopolitan kingdom, one in which the scribes inevitably seemed outmoded and oppressive. Scribes appointed in the kingdom's newly annexed territories practiced a particularly oppressive *Vielschreiberei* over their new clients. To view this situation simply as a perversion of the classic tutelary relationship, however, neglects their crucial positive role in Württemberg's civic regeneration after Napoleon. The scribes themselves became a more diverse and robust profession after the annexations, combining the old craft's solidarity with an openness to new members. With parliament's restoration, they drew upon far-flung occupational networks to enlist new notables in politics and help the citizenry to reassert its political interests after a decade of absolutist rule. Only after grassroots complaints against *Vielschreiberei* challenged their hegemony in a series of localities did the weakness of these alliances become clear. Capitalizing on the greater openness and diversity of post-Napoleonic society, crusading parliamentarians and journalistic critics exploited new modes of political communication to challenge the scribes for leadership in the public sphere. Under their pressure, the constitutional fetishism that the scribes revived in the 1810s yielded to a more ideological style of politics better suited to the demands of a dynamic, cosmopolitan polity.

The scribes, then, far from holding citizens in "textual serfdom," pre-

FIGURE 7. Map of the Kingdom of Württemberg, 1806

served their link to Württemberg's civic culture; they simply failed, despite this, to keep pace with a world that transcended them. Problems in refurbishing the culture of formality and extending networks of collegiality into the nineteenth century drew increasing attention to their anachronism. *Vielschreiberei* showed that the cumbersome textual interactions already plaguing a small, old-regime polity could not easily be applied to a state of greater proportions and more intensive governmental demands. Similarly, the connections among notables, the common bonds once provided by constitutional traditions and the rhythms of professional communication, could not sustain the influx of new elites, with different cultural backgrounds, streaming into Württemberg society after Napoleon. Practices of formality and collegiality once united under the scribes' tutelage were thus divided and recombined during their fall from influence. While the scribes co-opted new elites to muster collective action against the abuses of a dictatorial monarch, their departure allowed civil society to develop in a novel independence from the state. The self-consciousness of a new leadership class in turn registered the significant expansion and diversification of Württemberg's civic landscape after Napoleon.

ADMINISTRATIVE COLONIZATION

Napoleon was a force sui generis in Germany's political development. After his invasions, power politics, *Macht,* the imperatives of armies, occupiers, and reformers—all these assumed a commanding new importance relative to the macropolitical stalemate enforced under the Holy Roman Empire. Dissolving old polities and cobbling together new ones, Napoleon reduced the over three hundred political entities comprising the Empire to about forty. Ecclesiastical enclaves were "secularized" and petty nobles were "mediatized" on being assimilated into territorial states like Württemberg, Baden, and Bavaria. At the stroke of a pen, populations were thrown together with little regard for administrative difficulties and political consequences. Batteries of new officials were installed in new districts, with new titles and new duties. All these disruptions opened an enormous gulf between state and society, particularly in Württemberg. Starting with its first new acquisitions in 1803, the Württemberg state imposed its vast textual formalities on local communities, while at the same time closing the avenues of written communication that the old regime's civic culture had long made possible. The scribes ceased to function as a mediating class and instead became the agents of administrative colonization. This fed the perception that Württemberg society had become burdened by too much formality: by *Vielschreiberei.*

Vielschreiberei

King Friedrich of Württemberg, who became known as the "Swabian Czar," typified the pretensions of a Napoleonic ruler emboldened by the heady gift of full domestic sovereignty at the hands of the European conqueror. To a degree unmatched in nearby states, the new king lay claim to an untrammeled, arbitrary authority centered on his own person and theoretically absolute in nature.[3] He treated his officials as pawns on a chessboard and, with agnostic complacency, expected them to discharge their duties as faithful instruments of his personal will. Since 1803 the royal government had been appointing new *Schreiber* in the annexed lands, and in 1807 it usurped control over their appointment in the old duchy as well. Thereafter, the king's deputies located appointees for new positions and rotated existing scribes into further assignments. Coursing over the kingdom's territories, scribes encountered alien legal and administrative customs, unfamiliar social practices, and the hostility of foreigners. The shock troops of an aggressive occupying regime, they embodied the clash of political cultures between the Napoleonic state and its local citizens.

The *Schreiberei* was an unknown institution in the new territories, at least in the elaborate form indigenous to the old duchy. "New Württemberg" in fact lacked any common political institutions whatsoever; it was a hodgepodge of formerly independent city-states, small principalities, and ecclesiastical territories ruled, until 1815, as a separate state abutting Old Württemberg. The king's government, only partly respecting existing political divisions, created seventy-eight new cantons in these territories as a prelude to installing a scribe in each.[4] While a number of regional officials and administrative sectors *(Landvogteien)* were also established to coordinate the occupation, the *Schreibereien* themselves were left totally unsupervised on the ground. It remained for each scribe to establish a new practice, hire new staff, and wend his way through the complicated process of acclimating new subjects to the old duchy's laws and customs of governance.

The sheer novelty and uncertainty of the situation must have spawned a series of tense encounters between scribes and their new clienteles. Unfortunately, very little can be known about them. The decade following the annexations was a period of disorganization in which the rich archival record of the scribes' manipulations trails off almost entirely. The few investigations to have been conducted into corrupt activity are striking for their archival thinness, summary judgments, and utter lack of concern with scribes' lives in society.[5] The majority revolved around squabbles among scribes over the right to collect fees for certain forms of business in a situation where administrative boundaries were ill-defined and a matter of continual dispute. Some were downright petty, as evidenced by one complaint against "*Schreiber* Laux's biting dog." Such cases remained matters generated and handled by officials, for officials. Allegations of impropriety were resolved by central or regional authorities in a much more cursory fashion than before, with citizens rarely brought in to give their testimonies. Punishments were meted out and fines levied after the briefest internal review.[6]

Higher officials' lack of interest in the scribes' activities was symptomatic of a more pervasive tendency in Napoleonic government. Far from reveling in its newfound sovereignty, the Württemberg state was flummoxed by what contemporaries called "organizationitis."[7] It responded to the exigencies of territorial occupation with a mixture of improvisation, economization, and temporization, abrogating its commitment to monitor local communities with the same righteous fervor it had previously shown. Not only were protocolled investigations no longer conducted, but a flood of petitions sent to the king by disgruntled citizens in the new lands provoked only a series of admonitions that they seek recourse with their local *Oberamt-männer*. Mandates and instructions, the only other means of written communication between state and society, had also become obsolete with the *Landtag*'s suspension. In short, the written bond between state and citizen previously mediated by formality had been severed.

Although for these reasons, detailed information on the Napoleonic *Schreibereien* is lost to history, one brute fact about the scribes' fortunes after the annexations remains abundantly clear: most scribes managed to enrich themselves substantially through *Vielschreiberei*. Income data collected from the scribes by the government attest to an across-the-board increase in the scribes' revenues between 1808 and 1818, the two years when the government made its surveys.[8] The average scribe's income shot up by over one half (56%) throughout the kingdom during the Napoleonic interlude, from 901 fl. in 1808 to 1402 fl. by 1818. This upward trend was most pronounced in New Württemberg, where the rise totaled 91% — nearly doubling original incomes—and where the average scribe's net take, having markedly lagged behind that of his Old-Württemberg counterpart in the early years, in fact overtook it before the decade was out. While in 1808 the average New Württemberg scribe made only 765 fl., compared with 1000 fl. in the old duchy, ten years later his income had risen to 1460 fl., with his counterpart in Old Württemberg now making only 1370 fl.

The impressive jump in the incomes of New Württemberg *Schreiber* can be attributed to the massive adjustments inherent in a change of regime: *Vielschreiberei* resulted when the scribes applied a battery of new textual formalities to localities previously unaccustomed to them. Among the most hated impositions were the taking of mandatory estates inventories in regions where primogeniture or other, less formalized inheritance customs rendered them superfluous, and the byzantine systems of accounting that gave the scribes a formal and practical monopoly on receipt preparation and other aspects of local fiscal management.[9] The scribes' usurpation of such powers from city councillors and other local officials was especially grating in the proudly civic, formerly independent Free Cities, whose fiscal autonomy had long undergirded the practice of self-government. On top of the sheer waste and inefficiency involved in establishing new practices, these novel forms of official business generated substantial revenues for the *Schreibereien*. Systematic corruption surely played a role as well, since many scribes no doubt took advantage of their clients' ignorance of the new laws to extort money from them. Hegel tells the tale of a wealthy nobleman, legally exempt from the estates inventories mandatory for non-noble citizens, who was nonetheless cajoled by the local scribe to pay him for what the inventory would have cost: a sum well over 200 fl.[10] Given the moral hazard that service in new Württemberg offered, it is not unreasonable to believe that a good portion of the scribes' financial windfall derived from extortion and bribery. By the same token, however, bribes and other illegal monies are unlikely to have been reported as official income on the government's surveys. Even without added corruption, in other words, the scribes' aboveboard, reported revenues increased dramatically in New Württemberg.

The finding that New Württemberg incomes started low and ended up high is especially revealing. It suggests that the *original* foundation of a *Schreiberei* was an enterprise fraught with little reward and much inconvenience. Scribes often had to set up new households, relocate their families, and hang their shingles before an unwelcoming populace; later apologists used such cases to claim that these difficulties had in fact impoverished, rather than enriched, many in the profession.[11] In cantons where the government was not able to appoint a *Schreiber* from old Württemberg, for reasons described in the next section, new appointees may have been as ignorant of Württemberg's laws and textual formalities as their clients. All this made it extremely difficult to run an efficient, lucrative practice. Such appointees were all too successful in parlaying their initial disadvantage into the source of great wealth later, however, since traditional community restraints on scribal extortion were absent in the new lands. While in the closed, nepotistic cantons of the old duchy, scribes would have been reluctant to extort money from their own friends and relatives, these qualms did not apply to communities composed entirely of strangers. In New Württemberg, there were no standards on what constituted "acceptable" graft and what forms of extortion crossed the line: *every* imposition of a new textual formality brought over from the old duchy counted as an affront, and as these became routinized, there was no theoretical limit to how high the scribes' incomes might climb. Scribes often simply inflated the amount of time and paper they used in preparing perfectly legal instruments. Inexperience in new situations also meant that many new scribes were poor supervisors, and many of their *Substituten,* as later critics would attest, took advantage of their laxity to extract bribes from clients and illegally inflate the fees they charged.

Württemberg's reorganization under Napoleon by no means distributed its financial rewards exclusively to New Württemberg scribes. Even for the old duchy, where they were long ensconced, one finds a hefty 37% increase in the scribes' incomes. Since such a significant rise occurred in regions altogether accustomed to the *Schreiberei,* the scribes' Napoleonic windfall could not have derived exclusively from new impositions of formality. Rather, the increased financial demands of government as a whole generated higher routine revenues. Military levies and troop quarterings, combined with heavier taxes and other duties imposed by the central government associated with war-making and statecraft: all required massive increases in paperwork, from which the scribes profited as middlemen. Such impositions originated in the central government and were applied uniformly, irrespective of region. Thus, by 1818, the average incomes of scribes in Old and New Württemberg had roughly converged at the hefty sum of around 1400 fl. a year.

This fact had two very important implications for the scribes' fortunes in the years ahead. First, the palpable increase in government's fiscal burden across the kingdom helped deflect criticism away from the *Schreiber* and steer it toward Friedrich's absolutist regime: all citizens shared a common hatred of the Swabian Czar. Politically, this helped forestall any mobilization against the scribes until well after the king relented in his arbitrariness, attained a greater popularity, and above all, restored a parliamentary and constitutional regime where the people could air their grievances against both him and the *Schreiber.* Second, the leveling of scribes' incomes across regions promoted their cohesion as an occupation. New fortunes, common to Old and New Württemberg scribes alike, gave appointees recently coopted into the *Schreiberstand* a reason to identify with their colleagues in the old duchy. Whether a native son of the old duchy steeped in the musty traditions of the classic *Schreiberei,* or a university-educated civil servant commandeered by the royal government and encumbered with new duties and a new office, the typical Napoleonic scribe was at one with his counterparts elsewhere in the kingdom. Both had acquired a profound financial interest in the *Schreiberei* system. This solidarity, as we will now see, was cemented by the scribes' professionalization in the late 1810s.

The Scribes as a Profession

Besides the income reports, only one other complete body of sources on the scribes is preserved for the Napoleonic era. At this time, the state needed a pliable, professional corps of administrators who could be deployed rapidly to assume their new duties. Each scribe had to be matched to a suitable *Schreiberei* in the new lands, and yet the bureaucratic personnel officers who made these appointments had little time to evaluate individual candidates, much less engage in any systematic vetting of their professional credentials, political reliability, or personal merit. As artifacts of this need stand a series of personnel dossiers on the *Schreiber* that, following the state's assertion of control over their appointment, were collected as a matter of course.[12] Intended to summarize each scribe's new qualifications for office in a standardized, easily accessible, tabular format, the dossiers appealed to central administrators requiring quick snapshots of the human resources at their disposal. Called *Nationallisten*, these texts not only enabled the state to design and deploy a mobile phalanx of interchangeable officials to staff the kingdom's *Schreibereien*, but also provide a comprehensive demographic portrait of the profession in this period.

A typical dossier included the scribe's age, birthplace, religion, father's name and occupation, mother's name with *her* father's occupation, children's names and occupations, university training (if any), previous employment (if any), net worth, and the names of any relatives in state service. All these data were entered by the scribe himself on a preprinted template sheet, then sent to the county superintendents, who relayed them to higher, regional officials. At each level, remarks on each scribe's penmanship, fitness for duty, and general moral character were added. Personal recommendation letters and cronyism, key factors at old-regime scribes' elections, had no formal role in this process. Thus were the *Nationallisten* largely cleansed of the nepotism, patronage, and local bias plaguing the decentralized electoral system of the old duchy. They allowed placement officials to make rapid decisions that nonetheless embodied a consistent practical philosophy. The *Nationallisten* reflected a style of government more detached from local conditions after Napoleon. By their very nature, the dossiers instilled a new occupational culture in the scribes, binding their careers to the state bureaucracy instead of the communities that had once elected them. Reconstructing the rules of thumb used to select appointees helps show how the scribes' submission to the imperatives of professionalization affected their mediating function between state and society.[13]

The first compilation of *Nationallisten* occurred in 1809, six years after the first annexations and two years after the government arrogated the right to appoint scribes in the old duchy. By this time, the government had appointed 75 new scribes, most of whom served, not surprisingly, in New Württemberg districts. The new appointees were drawn from a very diverse

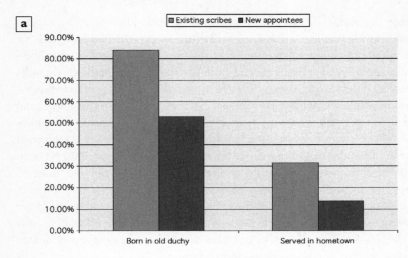

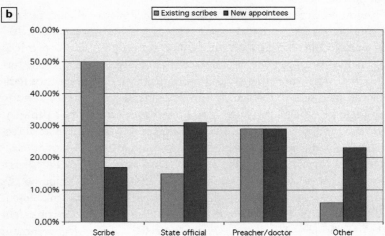

FIGURE 8.   The Napoleonic *Schreiber,* 1809. (a) Geographic origin (places of
birth); (b) Social origin (fathers' occupations); (c) Education and training; (d)
Career background

pool of candidates, allowing the state personnel authority significant latitude—with key exceptions—in its choice of officials.[14] Since these comprised just over half of the 148 scribes then in service, the 1809 cohort
allows us to examine how the state refashioned the profession's image by
comparing new appointees with the almost equally large cadre of existing
scribes held over from pre-Napoleonic times. Summarized in figures 8a
though 8d, the results of this comparison illustrate the scribes' transforma-

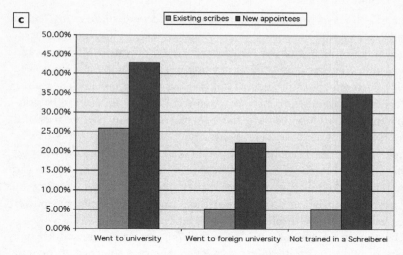

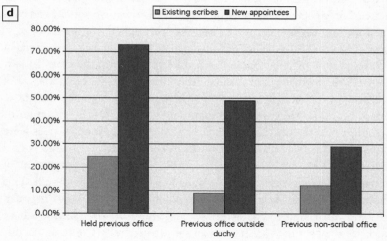

tion into a surprisingly diverse, cosmopolitan, and professional battery of officials.

As figure 8a shows, new appointees were significantly less likely than existing scribes to have been born in the old duchy. Central administrators in fact complained that it was extremely difficult to locate native Württemberg scribes willing to assume posts in the annexed territories. Instead, a combination of "family connections, [considerations of] comfort, and also perhaps feelings of personal weakness" conspired to dissuade many native sons from applying for posts in New Württemberg.[15] This finding contradicts a common image of the Napoleonic scribes, prevalent in Hegel's and other public diatribes against the profession, as an occupying force mustered in old Württemberg and then sent out into the new acquisitions. In reality, the agents of administrative colonization were almost as likely to be non-Württembergers co-opted into the *Schreiberei*. These new scribes still appeared as foreigners in their clients' eyes, however, with a mere 14%, compared with nearly a third of existing scribes, serving in their home-town. Thus a substantial majority lacked the intimate connection to, and knowledge of, their district of service that local birth conferred. This important trend, dissociating scribes from their traditional hometown power bases, would continue throughout the Napoleonic period.

Owing to the influx of outsiders, a fraternity rooted in the culture and society of Old Württemberg lost its insular character. Analysis of the new appointees' social origins in figure 8b reveals how the government had constructed a more diverse corps of *Schreiber* through the infusion of new members. Whereas fully half of existing scribes were themselves the sons of scribes, only 17% of new appointees had been born into the craft. In part this reflects their greater recruitment from the families of other classes of state official in regions outside the old duchy, where *Schreiber* were not to be found. Yet it also suggests the government's willingness to induct humble outsiders into the officialdom. Nearly a quarter of new appointees were the sons of minor local officials or outright commoners, compared with a minuscule 6% among existing scribes. Interestingly, the proportion of preachers and doctors was exactly the same in both groups, about 29%. This similarity may reflect the long-established networks of exchange between clergy and officialdom characteristic not just of the Württemberg *Ehrbarkeit* but of southwestern German society generally. Confessional differences did add a novel dimension to this familiar pattern of occupational circulation. Five Catholics joined what had been an exclusively Protestant profession, all in New Württemberg, and a host of colorful given names—an Anton, a Johann Nepomuk, and even an Ignatz—appeared alongside the Friedrichs, Heinrichs, Christians, and other, more sober monikers favored by the Old Württemberg *Ehrbarkeit*.

Not simply more diverse, new appointees were also more cosmopolitan than existing scribes in their education and training, as charted in figure 8c. A higher proportion had studied at universities, especially foreign ones, while at the same time, fewer had trained in the *Schreiberei*. Whereas a mere 5% of existing scribes had never "learned the *Schreiberei*," in the government's words, more than one third of new appointees came from outside the craft; these men embodied the state's clear willingness to break the guild-like closure of the old *Schreiberei* system. The state particularly favored men with formal education in law or cameralistic science, a credential that had become all but mandatory for higher-level civil servants in the eighteenth century. The increasing salience of university education probably derived less from a deliberate policy of professionalization than from the chronic surplus of educated men clamoring for employment in early nineteenth-century Germany. Whatever the reason, many new scribes had indisputably gained valuable, enlightening contact with academic cultures elsewhere in Germany. Whereas existing scribes, if they had visited any university, tended to have attended Tübingen or the short-lived *Karlsschule* in Stuttgart, Napoleonic appointees included alumni of regional centers of higher learning in Freiburg, Erlangen, Marburg, and Rottweil. The Austrian universities of Vienna and Ingolstadt trained a few scribes in Württemberg's Upper Swabian acquisitions, formerly in Habsburg possession, and Göttingen and Cologne, both far to the north, each furnished a new appointee, illustrating the wide range of new scribes' affiliations.

In many ways, the narrow provincialism of what had long seemed an artisanal guild yielded to more flexible career pathways increasingly typical of bureaucratic elites elsewhere in Germany. Above all, rotation among different districts and types of office had accustomed many Napoleonic scribes to dealings outside their home communities and even their home states. The tendency to have occupied at least one previous office was a true novelty of the Napoleonic period. Whereas it was unusual for an existing scribe to have changed positions once installed in office, nearly three quarters of new appointees in 1809, as figure 8d shows, had already held at least one other scribal or civil service position. Just under half of them had served outside of the old duchy, where administrative styles, courses of training, career paths, and networks of favoritism were all much looser, less tradition-bound, and more diverse. In the small, fragmented principalities of New Württemberg, an indigenous, autonomous, self-reproducing officialdom like the Old Württemberg *Schreiberstand* was an utter impossibility. Circulation had long been the norm, not the exception. Nearly a third of newly appointed scribes could thus boast some career experience outside the *Schreiberei*, having served as jurists, foresters, archivists, parliamentary secretaries, tax collectors, diplomatic attachés, military field adjuncts, customs officials, administrators for small patrimonial territories, or senators in Imperial Free Cities. Others had subsisted as freelance lawyers with no prior experience as scribes. Such multifarious career pathways were virtually unheard-of among old-regime scribes like Hofacker and Bolley, who had cultivated dense networks of patronage within their local communities and exploited their rootedness in the *Schreiberei* for political ends. With rotations increasingly the rule, such machinations became more difficult.

The emergence of a new type of scribe, experienced, educated, cosmopolitan, but with shallow local roots, was not the product of some grand social experiment to refashion the profession into the Hegelian ideal of an Enlightened civil service elite. Where it could, the state continued to favor competent, humble, reliable practitioners born and trained in the old duchy.[16] Indeed, after 1809, some of the trends promoting the scribes' professionalization reversed themselves. Among the 84 new *Schreiber* appointed between 1809 and the end of the Napoleonic period, the proportion of those educated at universities dropped to one-half its previous level, from 40% to 20%. Fully 80%, by contrast, had learned the *Schreiberei*, a trend that restored a great deal of the scribes' old-style occupational cohesion. Finally, this second wave of appointees was, once again, more likely than not to hail from the old duchy.[17] In their education and geographic recruitment, then, the scribes had largely returned to their former eighteenth-century profile.

Other, more telling trends, continued unabated, however, as the state promoted the careers of men with no qualms about relocating and little attachment to the provincialism of old Württemberg hometowns. Rotations held constant as placement officials cultivated scribes' allegiance to a state that now prescribed career paths upward and outward from their communities of increasingly temporary service. Three quarters of appointees after 1809, as the *Nationallisten* for these years show, had already served in at least one other official post, and half had done so outside the old duchy. Betraying the same logic, the government also decreased the scribes' ability to draw on hometown connections to maintain themselves in positions of dominance over particular communities. Only a single appointee after 1809 served in his town of birth, a clear sign that the state was absolutely bent on eradicating the types of *Schreiber* dynasties founded on hereditary succession that had been entrenched in powerful cities like Stuttgart and Schorndorf during the old regime. The government's determination to uproot patronage was broad-based and not limited to overt practices of local favoritism. Reinforcing a trend already apparent before 1809, the proportion of scribes descended from scribes or other state officials, and thus presumptively able to draw upon family connections within the bureaucracy for help in securing official appointment, continued to drop. Over half of the scribes appointed during the absolutist period were the sons of preachers, teachers, doctors, merchants, local officials, and simple commoners. Co-opting unconnected outsiders into the profession had evidently become a guiding maxim of government policy during the years of absolutist rule.

In the dossiers one thus sees, in tentative outline, a distancing of bureaucracy from community that foreshadows the scribes' later loss of hegemony as intermediaries between state and civil society. Placement officials, in using the dossiers, had never intended to create such a distance, but by rotating scribes through new appointments, they ultimately subverted their local authority. Moreover, because the dossiers shed no light on local circumstances and conditions—unlike the protocol reports used in different contexts—these officials could not anticipate that local citizens would eventually rise up in opposition to their "textual serfdom." Still, these observations take us much too far ahead of the story: at no point was it a foregone conclusion that the state's ability to place and re-place the scribes at its whim naturally entailed a weakening of their power. On the contrary, the scribes' high mobility and cosmopolitanism only seem to have enhanced their classic occupational collegiality. Their professional networks revitalized themselves after the constitution's restoration in 1815, when the scribes participated in a statewide political mobilization against the king.

TUTELAGE ON A NEW TERRAIN

In the year of Waterloo, King Friedrich put a sudden end to nearly a decade of unconstitutional rule. With his patron and protector headed toward exile, Friedrich, suddenly sympathetic to his people's wishes, unilaterally promulgated a new constitution and convened a new parliament to ratify it. In this act, he joined a wave of law-giving that swept southwestern Germany between 1808 and 1820. Yet while the rulers of nearby Baden, Bavaria, Hesse-Darmstadt, and Nassau witnessed no significant protest against their state-imposed constitutions, Württemberg's king alone suffered bitter and highly orchestrated popular opposition. Crystallizing around the so-called "Good Old Law" *(gutes altes Recht)* faction in parliament, the Württembergers rejected his draft constitution and demanded that the Tübingen Compact simply be reinstated and extended to New Württemberg. Debating, somewhat hypocritically, within the parliamentary institutions provided by Friedrich's draft, the *Altrechtler* remained locked in stalemate with the king until a final compromise was reached four years later, in 1819. Such a unique and sustained resistance derived, among other factors, from the scribes' vigorous mobilization in defense of the old constitutional order, which they rightly perceived as the wellspring of their historic influence.

Having become more cosmopolitan and dynamic in ways that paralleled the kingdom's own transformation, scribes readily agitated alongside other notables and won them over to their cause. While the networks of collegiality they once monopolized were thus extended over new terrains, underlying disagreements remained about the evils of *Vielschreiberei,* and whether the constitution's restoration would alleviate or exacerbate them.

Countrywide Agitation

Friedrich's restoration caught Württemberg in a completely novel and uncertain political situation; it was not immediately apparent that the scribes would still be able to manipulate parliamentary affairs from their posts in the countryside as they had in the 1790s. The revised procedures for parliamentary election erected an entirely new grid of political institutions untested for the purposes of deliberation and resistance.[18] Gone was the cumbersome apparatus of mandate and instruction previously binding *Landtag* delegates to their constituents, which scribes had once used to project their will from afar. Gone, too, was the exclusion of royal *Oberamtmänner* from election chambers. Royal superintendents now personally supervised election proceedings, where voters signed written slips opened and tallied under watchful eyes. Most importantly, parliamentary delegates ceased to be selected by the cantonal assemblies—the old corporative bodies comprising from twenty to at most seventy electors—and, for the first vote at least, received free mandates through direct elections. A much-widened suffrage meant that new voters were far less acquainted with, and beholden to, the scribes than cantonal assemblymen.[19] With all these changes, one interior ministry report boasted that "the *Stadt- und Amts-schreiber* no longer have anything at all to do with parliamentary affairs."[20]

Politicking became looser and more open once it emerged from the scribes' direct influence. Nepotism, back-room deals, and intimidation continued to run rampant but now had to operate more publicly, with less assured outcomes. The *Stadtschreiber* at Oberndorf, for instance, plied electors with free beer in an unsuccessful bid to win their support for his candidacy. Georg Weckherlin, the Cannstatt burgomaster and a trained *Schreiber,* had to engineer a series of election postponements while he frantically assembled a political base. And in Geislingen, the electoral crossfire between *Stadtschreiber* Häberle and the local *Oberamtmann,* pushing his stepson's candidacy, secured the triumph of a third aspirant, an unknown peasant/hotelier. In the absence of party platforms or even vague ideological inclinations, elections had essentially become popularity contests among local notables.[21] Together with the abolition of formal *Instruktionen,* this meant that as delegates traveled to Stuttgart, their political tendencies were, more than ever before, an open question.

The new parliament brought together a more diverse class of politicians than had ever been found in the old Württemberg *Landtag*. Academically educated burgomasters from former Imperial Free Cities, patrimonial tax collectors, ex-military officers, a large number of Catholics, and a battery of freelance lawyers—hungry and presumptively radical because deprived of bureaucratic office—injected new blood into the assembly.[22] The number of trained scribes, whether actually serving as *Schreiber,* acting as *Bürgermeister,* or employed in other capacities, dropped proportionally by one half, from nearly 31% of assembly members in 1800 to just under 16% in 1815. At the same time, the lifting of formal restrictions on who could stand for office enabled five practicing *Schreiber*—Frey from Ludwigsbronn, Lang from Maulbronn, the *Substitut* Löw from Nürtingen, Sandberger from Albeck, and Heinrich Bolley, representing Marbach—to gain seats in the new body. Bolley, still resident in Waiblingen, profited from the absence of residence requirements in the new suffrage law. His election in Marbach, engineered by the *Stadtschreiber* there, attests to the tight networks of political patronage and communication still active in Old Württemberg. Bolley himself typified a strong correlation between far-flung connections and conservative political ideology. Of the fourteen delegates elected in districts where they were not resident, twelve still opposed the royal draft constitution as late as 1817, earning them distinction as hard-core *Altrechtler.*[23] Thus, if the vagaries of local politics determined the fates of individual delegates, the salience of interregional contacts, especially in the lands of the old duchy, accounted for parliament's rapid coalescence around the Good Old Law platform.

The *altes Recht* party proved able to unify new parliamentarians while at the same time promoting the scribes' interests. Its platform was spelled out in the *Grievances of the Land,* a published compendium edited by Heinrich Bolley and collected by a special parliamentary committee empowered in July 1815. This work was one of the first attempts to style the various complaints against Friedrich's absolutism as a truly national rebellion embracing both New and Old Württemberg.[24] The *Grievances* foregrounded the cardinal argument of the *Altrechtler:* that the king's promulgation of a new constitution violated a series of written contracts, starting with the 1514 Tübingen Compact, from which no party had the right to withdraw unilaterally. Legally speaking, the *Altrechtler* refused to recognize any other document as a valid basis for negotiation. Such a principled constitutional fetishism marginalized and subordinated many of the more mundane complaints generated by

Vielschreiberei. To attribute the problems of administrative colonization to a single act of illegality on Friedrich's part served a powerfully integrative rhetorical function, however. By ascribing official abuse to a breach of moral covenant by which the king had taken hold of the new lands, parliamentarians focused discontent on the personage who threatened their freedoms. Nowhere were the striking similarities between the *altes Recht*'s dogmatic constitutionalism and the scribes' costly fetish for formality remarked upon; the profound affinities between the two groups' political styles as yet remained subterranean and lacked ideological articulation.

The *Altrechtler* in fact thrived in the face of mounting discontent with *Vielschreiberei* by accommodating diverse social groups within forms of political collegiality the scribes had once dominated. The prowess of the party's leaders mobilized those who found its attachment to contractual scruple irrelevant, impolitic, or even bizarre, and thus forestalled internal dissent. The true potency of the *altes Recht* political machine was revealed after the king, frustrated by his subjects' intransigent rejection of his constitutional offering, dissolved the parliamentary assembly in August 1815. From then until the next October, supporters of the Good Old Law agitated in protest against the suspension of negotiations, summoning local notables from across the countryside to demand that parliament be reconvened. Representatives, on returning home, had reported personally before their constituents, sometimes at formal council meetings (the old *Amtsversammlungen*), sometimes in surreptitious private settings.[25] Then they began to plan meetings, exchange written communications, and gather in groups, usually at inns and pubs, with delegates from other districts.

A series of reports on their deliberations, solicited from local *Oberamtmänner* by an anxious government, reveals a much higher degree of open cooperation and contact among regions than had been possible under the old regime.[26] While such communication was still overwhelmingly concentrated in Old Württemberg, scribes now conferred alongside a more occupationally diverse class of notables than the old *Ehrbarkeit*. Meetings in early fall 1815, in Kornwestheim, Besigheim, Metzingen, and Nagold, mixed scribes together promiscuously with doctors, tradesmen, treasurers, pharmacists, and even noblemen. In Nagold, where scribes and other officials from the Black Forest had drafted a Cahier in 1798, there assembled a group of area representatives, drawn from the same core regions as before, but now in association with their counterparts from the Rems and Murr river valleys, in the east of the old duchy. The Nagold meeting also included a group of noblemen from the parliament's upper house and five professionals from Reutlingen and Stuttgart.

Textually as well as socially, the forms of political mobilization in Old Württemberg showed a fascinating mix of innovation and tradition. Where handwritten communications among cantonal assemblies had previously flourished, printed broadsides now circulated in great numbers. Yet, in a bow to custom, electors in Leonberg issued a mandate and instruction for their deputy even though such texts had lost all formal legal validity. Cantonal assemblies continued to act informally as political flash points, drafting supplications in the classic style of disingenuous humility familiar from Bolley's 1806 Waiblingen petition. At the same time, however, bluntly phrased petitions for the maintenance of the constitution also made their way around the "common people." Drawn up in ad hoc assemblages or "carried around from house to house," these petitions embodied, in a subtle shift, collective, not corporative resolution. They were produced informally and popularly, rather than through formal channels and by elites only. Representative Cammerer, from Reutlingen, thought "it would be good if the people itself spoke its will" through such texts. While not yet challenging the scribes, he and many other representatives styled themselves conduits of a popular opinion on which they themselves had a "direct and indirect influence," according to government surveillance reports.[27]

The meagerness of similar agitation in New Württemberg can be ascribed to the lack of such networks and the absence of an existing constitution to provide political bearings. Reports from the *Oberamtmänner* in these districts reveal disorganization and despair rather than apathy and ignorance per se.[28] Though there was overwhelming support for the idea of wresting a better constitution from Friedrich, and palpable "dissatisfaction" with the existing order, citizens in New Württemberg harbored little expectation of successful resistance against the King. The absence of grassroots political activism reflected not an underlying ideological unsophistication but a simple lack of information, depriving actors of the sense of shared grievance and solidarity necessary to sustain opposition. This meant that, down to early 1816 at least, delegates from these areas largely remained fellow-travelers of the old Württemberg *Altrechtler*, unable collectively to question their hegemony. It also ensured that resistance to King Friedrich in New Württemberg was spotty, random, and uncoordinated: in Öhringen, local notables demanded that the old constitution be applied to the new lands, while in the neighboring canton of Mergentheim, confusion and defeatism were the rule.[29] In former Free Cities like Heilbronn and Reutlingen, both with strong ties to the old duchy rooted in elite intermarriage and geographic proximity, banquets and open-air festivals were held and altars erected to congratulate their delegates and strengthen their political resolve. In Rottweil, Gmünd, and Hall, by contrast, the mood was quiet, and no demonstrations were reported.[30]

Owing to the prevailing political disarray in New Württemberg, scribes emerged more conspicuously there as the switchposts of interregional political networks. Two assemblies of Danube-area *Stadtschreiber*, in particular, meeting first at Ulm and then in the "miserable village" of Gamerschwang, evoked those of the Black Forest network two decades earlier. Having been convened to oppose the controversial imposition of an annual tax during parliament's suspension, these two meetings brought together municipal leaders from Ulm and scribes from districts in Upper Swabia, easily the kingdom's most politically remote region. In a telling concession to the New Württembergers, the scribes' program emphasized "uniting . . . the old Württemberg constitution with modifications appropriate to the *Zeitgeist*."[31]

All over the kingdom, scribes plied their influence in the same traditional ways, but now in much broader circles: if not actually in public, then in an atmosphere bestowing political influence in proportion to notability. Attempting to counter their influence, the government distributed pamphlets arguing against the election of scribes and warning of the dangerous consequences of their influence.[32] In several localities, it found that "*Stadtschreiber* convened so-called notables *(Honoratioren)* in order to get their wishes to the representatives." Such meetings gathered a "mass of citizens giving signatures" into "arbitrary political associations" with no legal, corporative basis.[33] Additionally, after parliament was reconvened, the scribes received representatives' communications and saw to their distribution among constituents. Drawing on the corporative pride of the old Württemberg *Schreiberstand*, scribes in the new annexations thus formed the only group of officials with the regional dispersion and habitual commitment to *altes Recht* ideology sufficient to sustain political opposition. As long as they retained this practical influence—even though they had lost so much direct power over parliamentary proceedings—the scribes formed the great hidden buttress of Good Old Law sentiment and helped prevent heterodox opinions from emerging.[34]

Grassroots Resistance

The palpable resistance spearheaded by scribes and other notables during the suspension of deliberations convinced Friedrich to reconvene parliament in October 1815 and resume negotiations over the shape of the new constitution. This period witnessed a loosening of the bonds between communicative networks and Good Old Law ideology that had given the deliberations of 1815 their peculiarly conservative and oppositional character. The torch of political activism passed imperceptibly, because entirely locally, into New Württemberg, and in that environment, a fatal ideological connection between the *altes Recht* party and the scribes' *Vielschreiberei* would finally be made. From this point forward, their fortunes, together with those of the old constitution itself, declined, as scribes began to feel the effects of a grass-roots movement to drive them from power in 1816–17.

The new districts' emergence from the shadow of political marginalization was intimately bound with local struggles against the *Schreiber.* Starting in February 1816, a parade of representatives from the new lands began to present parliament with petitions, gathered from constituents in the various communities of their districts and leveling accusations against the scribes.[35] Petitions from different parts of Württemberg often followed formulaic models and cast their complaints in identical language, showing the marks of well-orchestrated protest campaigns on the regional level.[36] Their content revolved around the injustices of *Schreiber* "oppression" and scornfully denied that these problems derived solely from "the novelty of the institution" in New Württemberg, as one *Altrechtler* had argued, or from circumstantial factors like poor training or indeterminate laws. Parliamentarians in the assembly emerged as the new spokesmen for their communities, undertaking their roles with an independent, often antagonistic stance toward both the state and the *Altrechtler.* Publicly and politically, they narrated constituent grievances to style themselves "trustees of the people," as one delegate put it. These representatives rekindled complaints long neglected by a state disengaged from local communities: they possessed firsthand knowledge of precisely those official abuses about which the archives remain so silent. Moreover, in an entirely novel way, such representatives cast their local advocacy in emphatically statewide terms. As Representative Haakh, from Besigheim, put it, delegates had the "same duties [before] the inhabitants of all provinces," not just their own constituents, and therefore a mandate to uproot *Schreiber* influence in both New and Old Württemberg.[37]

Such statements reflect the first inklings of a collective consciousness among reform-minded parliamentarians to counter the formidable esprit de corps of the scribes themselves. One case from Horb, read before parliament on 9 February 1816, reveals how this parliamentary collegiality arose amidst local contests against the scribes' influence.[38] At issue in Horb was *Amtsschreiber* von Olnhausen's attack against Representative Kurz, who was attempting to solicit complaints against him at village council meetings. Village councillors emerged as pawns in the struggle, having put their names to a series of Kurz's petitions, thereby incurring the scribe's wrath.

Directing "all possible accusations" against the councillors, the scribe used his administrative muscle to intimidate them and slander Representative Kurz as a manipulator. This prompted Kurz to charge von Olnhausen with "undermining the trust of his constituents in their representatives," provoking the scribe to submit a formal defense and counter-charges to parliament. Kurz in turn pleaded for parliament to assert its "honor" as a corporation against the offender. Not only did he demand personal "satisfaction" for the injury to his reputation, but he held that "when a member of a collegium or another corporation is insulted, the entire collegium or the entire corporation is also so [insulted], and both have an equal right of complaint." Kurz's plea is striking because it illustrates how sanctions from the assembly in Stuttgart were believed to exert a decisive influence over struggles in the countryside—a very modern conception of parliamentary power.

Similar dramas were played out all over New Württemberg, with representatives and scribes trading accusations both locally and in parliamentary petitions. Representative Seybold from Gmünd charged the scribe Nast with making the burgomaster his "slave," forcing him to commit illegalities that disrupted the poor man's sleep at night. Nast countered that Seybold himself was not above cultivating patronage, expressing surprise that the seventeen influential petitioners he had managed to round up could speak for all 21,000 inhabitants of Gmünd canton.[39] In making this accusation, the scribe failed to grasp any distinction between his own corrupt patronage and the more open and publicly negotiated stewardship to which the representative aspired. Practically speaking, he may have been correct to assert that, in staging petition drives among their own friends and cronies, representatives like Seybold were attempting to substitute one form of tutelage for another. Rhetorically, however, representatives voiced more convincing claims to having emancipated the broader mass of citizens in the process. As one petition from Schörzingen declared, "We now longer have the old times where sometimes not a single man in a whole village could be found who could read and write."[40]

Introducing public scrutiny and accountability into the workings of local government emerged as the ideological cornerstone of representatives' efforts. This ideal was contrasted with the hidden, secretive, ventriloquistic ways of the scribes. In an address delivered in October 1816, Geislingen representative Reiter boasted of breaking up a conspiracy in the village of Hohenrechberg. There, a "pernicious confederation" of *Schreiber* and town officials had privately falsified communal receipts to finance their "reveling" at the local tavern, then practiced "arbitrariness, violations, and deceptions" to hide their misdeeds. Reiter told how he had discovered the conspiracy after being approached by a group of disgruntled citizens, and then examined the village's records personally. He found that the yearly auditing of communal receipts—theoretically an entirely open and public proceeding—had become an empty formality conducted in haste, one at which no ordinary citizen felt comfortable voicing complaints and pointing out errors. That these assemblies were marked by "secrecy amidst the outward appearance of publicity" he found to be particularly disturbing, for it discredited not secrecy, which everyone knew to breed corruption, but publicity, which ought to have been supported and encouraged. "If true publicity had been introduced," Reiter claimed, not only would local corruption be reduced, but, more positively, "the conscientious [official] would be secured against any dishonoring suspicions" about his conduct of office. The speech occasioned enough outrage that a somnolent parliamentary committee investigating problems with the *Schreiberei*, described in the next section, swung decisively into action in response.[41]

Like Kurz, Reiter was concerned primarily with issues of honor and probity, a currency of influence negotiated—publicly—among peers, both locally and in parliament. Their campaigns, together with others in such places as Ellwangen, Mergentheim, and Tuttlingen, represented an attempt to parlay the political advantages conferred by parliament, as a public, statewide forum, into a practical stewardship of local affairs.[42] Such stewardship was still cultivated primarily through local struggles and daily encounters, but now drew as well upon publicity's broader, ideological appeal on the national level. Delegates' exposés before the assembly indeed relied, for their persuasive force, on parliament's public image and its reputation as an organ of the people.

Several broad lessons emerge from these encounters between representatives and scribes. Politics had traveled a considerable distance since the days when scribes ventriloquized cantonal assemblies electing delegates to the old *Landtag*. Their informal hegemony no longer translated directly into formal political power, not because the *Schreiber* had dropped out of sight, but because politicking now occurred in multiple sites and among actors officially and unofficially separate from government—in short, in civil society. In civil society, scribes' traditional and highly formalized culture of collegiality no longer carried the sanction and aura of the state, despite being revived for one last burst of activism in the rekindled constitutional fetishism of the *Altrechtler*. The Good Old Law movement embodied the scribes' legalistic way of thinking, and proved able to accommodate a variety of groups with a variety of grievances. Yet its success was based more on practical resilience than on a convincing constitutional platform. This made possible a gradual dissociation of communicative practice from conservative ideology, medium from message, in the newly public struggles for local hegemony by parliamentary representatives. In the space thus created, other political styles could emerge. Bypassing the *altes Recht* machine and taking their grievances directly to parliament, oppositional delegates groped toward a new synthesis of constituent pressure and the power of public activity. Only the ideological implications of this synthesis yet remained to be spelled out.

THE RECONSTITUTION OF POLITICS

If *altes Recht* politics coalesced within private communication networks, the opposition to it gained strength in the crucible of publicity. Local struggles against the *Schreiber* would never have been perceived as indictments against the Good Old Law itself had public debate not tied *Vielschreiberei* to the very constitution they defended. The modern parliament, in contrast to the old *Landtag*, was a forum in which such debate could take place openly. In parliament, delegates articulated grievances specific to regional and social constituencies in universal, ideological terms, invoking the good of the state rather than the privileges and prerogatives of corporative constitutions. Through their speeches—published for the first time in Württemberg history—as well as in books and pamphlets widely disseminated throughout Germany, parliamentary leaders transmuted constituent pressure into the pressure of public opinion. Their efforts not only paved the way for a new, more progressive constitution to replace the Tübingen Compact, but, more significantly, pioneered a new style of representation giving civil society its political voice. Ideologies of the common good assumed a novel importance at this time; arguments about the public interest, practical and direct and unstrictured by constitutional tradition and legal formality, enabled a new generation of parliamentarians to challenge the *Altrechter* for leadership and reconstitute the culture of politics for the modern age.

Parliament and the Public

The impetus for *Schreiber* reform in parliament came from Gerabronn representative Georg Forstner von Dambenoy, scion of a prominent Swabian family. In a series of motions beginning in May 1815 and continuing through the next year, Forstner attacked the scribes as a "general plague on the country" and took issue with conservatives' attempts to localize abuse to New Württemberg.[43] Striking at the sacred core of *altes Recht* ideology, Forstner claimed that "*Vielschreiberei* is at home in the Württemberg constitution," not somehow linked to King Friedrich's period of unconstitutional rule. The scribes' faults lay "not in the immorality and decadence of the current generation of scribes so much as in the constitution that permits this mischief." As evidence, Forstner cited the waves of emigrants from the old-regime duchy who, he contended, had left their homeland to escape the scribes' excessive financial burden. The irony of this contention surely was not lost on the *Altrechtler,* for one pillar of Good Old Law ideology—the very basis for its legitimacy—was that membership in the state was voluntary. This belief reflected a contractual view of the polity, in which the citizen's obligations toward the state were strictly limited by the provisions of the Tübingen Compact, one of whose clauses guaranteed the right to withdraw completely through emigration. By their own logic, the frequency of emigration constituted an "enlightening indicator of the people's welfare," as a prominent *Altrechtler* himself put it.[44] That so many Württembergers had chosen to emigate, rather than pay tribute to the *Schreiber,* proved to Forstner that the old constitution was beyond repair.

For the first time, with such arguments, Forstner forged a damning ideological connection between the scribes and the *altes Recht.* To be sure, his association of *Vielschreiberei* with the Tübingen Compact was at best indirect, since the document did not even mention the scribes, merely placing local fiscal administration in the hands of the cantons. But Forstner viewed the old constitution less in terms of its legal stipulations than as the anchor and symbol of an entire political culture overburdened by writing. This fact alone set him apart from the *Altrechtler,* for whom the appeal of formality and contractual precedent was so deeply ingrained as to exclude any self-awareness about their own political traditions. Forstner deployed freer modes of argumentation, drawing on metaphors of natural, organic, rational development. Breaking away during an otherwise mundane speech about the *Schreiber,* he waxed philosophical about the need to revamp the kingdom's political institutions:

> Nothing in all of nature remains forever in undisturbed form. Everything higher changes through different forms and is rejuvenated, is reworked into new compositions. Nature wants it that way! That is the model of every human spiritual beginning. . . . And reason, which is free, becomes, according to its nature—not a creed, but a free Credo—It knows no other categorical imperative than the results of . . . its own view and conviction.

Such language—imaginative, ideological, unmoored from legal hermeneutics—staked out a new style in Württemberg politics. Ideally suited for public consumption, this style thrived on the free association of ideas, precisely the faculty that old constitutionalists lacked.

In response to Forstner's criticisms, parliament empanelled a five-member commission, chaired by one Gottfried Knapp and generally conservative in membership, to investigate the allegations against the *Schreiber*. Forstner was not himself an original member. The commission undertook a cursory investigation of receipts, inventories, and fee structures in a range of communities. Its methods were admittedly unsystematic and impressionistic, rendering it susceptible to external political influences and manipulation.[45] The committee's productivity waxed and waned with the fortunes of the Good Old Law's opponents in parliament. Debates in the larger body evinced a general deadlock in opinions, with attitudes toward the scribes split more or less evenly between proreform New Württemberg delegates and conservative *Altrechtler* from the old lands. Delays in the production of the committee's final report prompted an exasperated Forstner to repeat his criticisms no fewer than five times. Meanwhile, the assembly remained preoccupied with highly rarefied debates over the juridical validity of the new constitutional draft.

This stalling had ideological and not just narrowly political roots in committee chairman Knapp's nostalgic, even reactionary, view of the scribes' role in the polity. Knapp believed that the constitution's restoration would naturally redeem the inherent, historic virtue of the *Schreiberei* system. The traditions symbolized by the Tübingen Compact simply needed to be extended to the latest generation of practitioners. Knapp, in his published treatise on the subject, showed a special concern for the alleged moral decline of the *Substituten*. Whatever abuses may have occurred at their hands in New Württemberg had less to do with the *Schreiberei* system per se than with the general decline in "religion, morality, and ethics" among Germany's wayward youth and their addiction to "luxury and search for distraction and enjoyment" during a period of social upheaval.[46] Now that the rule of law had been restored, however, it followed that young scribes' corruption would end naturally if only they could "be shown [their] proper place in *civil society* and relation to others according to the proper measure."[47]

Knapp was one of the few figures to use the term "civil society" during the parliamentary debates of 1815–16, illustrating how the term still carried older connotations of corporative privilege. State officials, in his view, bore no special mandate to supervise and stand over civil society at large, but were themselves subject to its ethical limitations as a set of occupational estates, or *Stände*, with discrete, bounded functions in the polity. Other conservatives in the public sphere revived this eighteenth-century conception of *Stand* to argue for the same kind of moral relativism. One petition sent to parliament in 1817, from a group of scribes in northeastern Württemberg, argued that the scribes' *Stand* was being judged too harshly:

> Whether deficits and defects in the entire *Schreiberstand* distinguish it to any considerable degree from the other estates . . . can well be doubted. In which *Stand* and in which state are there not to be found more or less ignorant individuals, who bring [their estate] no honor?[48]

A *Need and Assistance Handbook for the Württemberg Schreiberstand*, published the same year, defended the scribes in much the same terms:

> Everyone, installed in his proper place, fulfills a need. . . . Every *Stand* in life, as long as it is directed at a useful purpose at all, therefore has a most rightful claim to our sincerest respect.[49]

Both these quotations almost exactly match those of *Schreiber* apologists twenty-five years earlier.[50] They shared with their predecessors a constrained notion of political morality and applied a fatalistic vision of politics to the problem of *Vielschreiberei*. Unwilling to engage the public interest or the good of society, conservatives again acted with a narrowly contractual understanding of duty, one that ascribed particular tasks to particular occupational *Stände* and compartmentalizing tasks among them. Having long subscribed to a constitutional "dualism" between duke and estates institutionalized by the Tübingen Compact, *Altrechtler* foisted concern for the common good upon the ruler himself, sparing his subjects any role save obedience and vigilance toward their corporative prerogatives.[51]

It was Hegel who expressed the educated public's view that this ideology was morally bankrupt and fundamentally anachronistic to the task of statebuilding. Monitoring the published constitutional deliberations from his professor's perch in nearby Heidelberg, Hegel applauded "the tireless efforts of Herr von Forstner for having lifted this matter out of a melancholy litany of grievances . . . to make the public acquainted with this institution, the *Schreiberei*, entirely peculiar to Württemberg."[52] Writing for this wider audience, Hegel articulated a more organic, ethically progressive vision of the state/society dualism. To him, the traditionalists' segmented view of the polity, mechanically constructed from various privileged corporations like the *Schreiber*, obeyed no overarching, rational, organic principle.[53] He thus supported Friedrich's effort to create a unitary state based on rational law and the equality of citizens, faulting the *Altrechtler* for obstructing this goal through their adherence to the contractually enshrined particularism of the estates system:

> In the Middle Ages, when state power had sunk and everything had dis-
> solved into atoms, [people] formed fraternities and corporations . . . that
> achieved a passable coexistence alongside each other. Now, though, it is
> high time . . . to bring these lower spheres again into a political order . . .
> and, cleansed of privileges and injustices, *incorporate them into the*
> *state as an organic creation.* A living connection is only possible in
> a structured whole.[54]

Such recommendations anticipated Durkheim's opposition between mechanical and organic solidarity: premodern division of labor and modern unity
of norm and purpose.[55] The crucial difference concerned whether the state
could or could not exceed the sum of its parts existing as separate occupations, or *Stände*, in civil society. Hegel thought that it could. To him, the
constitutional discourse of the Good Old Law hindered a greater political
unity by poisoning the mutual relationships binding government and people with defensiveness and suspicion.

Hegel naturally singled out the scribes as primary culprits in this state of
affairs and envisioned a new order led by more enlightened and selfless
advocates:

> It has been shown in most cases of great political movement that ruler
> and people had been of one mind and will, but that only too often an
> intermediate estate *[Mittelstand]*, as in France the nobility and the
> clergy, so in Württemberg [the nobility] and the bourgeois aristocracy
> of the *Schreiberei*, instead of forming a bond between the two as is its
> function, hardened in privilege and monopoly and prevented—even
> destroyed—the realization of the foundations of rational law and the
> general welfare.[56]

This offered a radical alternative to the Good Old Law party's notion of state
citizenship: to universalize the constitution did not mean submitting all citizens to a dead written document, the Tübingen Compact, but integrating
them into a living entity managed by a benevolent elite in fulfillment of
rational principles. He called for a new leadership of civil society, an "intermediate *Stand* . . . forming the intelligentsia of a people and directly managing its rights and duties" that would transcend moral particularism and
instead cultivate a universal, panoramic perspective. This rhetoric subscribed
to a distinction between state and civil society binding officials to the morality of the former, not the latter. What the intermediate estate provided was
an alternative to the increasingly conservative tutelage of the scribes, anticipating the dynamism of a "universal estate" of enlightened bureaucrats
Hegel would soon propose in the *Philosophy of Right*.

Ludwig Griesinger, the Stuttgart representative and a trained lawyer, typified the new species of statist progressive who emerged to promote this ideological project. Griesinger sat on Knapp's *Schreiber* reform committee, where he penned a lengthy expert opinion on the scribes. This work was published in 1816 in three places: as an addendum to the parliamentary minutes, as a contribution to the *Württembergisches Archiv*, and as a stand-alone monograph.[57] It soon achieved a canonical status as the most balanced and historically sensitive treatment of the *Schreiber*. More importantly, it reflected the emergence of an entirely new political climate after Friedrich's death and succession by his son Wilhelm. With the Tübingen publisher Johann Friedrich Cotta, Griesinger helped break the early hegemony of the Good Old Law party in parliament by allying with the reformist government minister Wangenheim. From this kernel developed the coalition among early liberals, ex-*Altrechtler,* and government advocates that surmounted the resistance of the traditionalists, put an end to discussions about the restoration of the Tübingen Compact, and gave Württemberg a thoroughly revised constitution in 1819.[58]

Griesinger sympathized with Hegel's objective of establishing an enlightened bureaucracy and bestowing on it the leadership functions held by the scribes. Attacking the venality endemic to the old-regime craft, he argued that "public offices do not exist on behalf of the officials but rather for the state." He advocated fixed salaries, better education, and civil-service status for the scribes and favored sharp reductions in the size of their districts to bring clients/citizens in closer contact with benevolent authority. Smaller districts, Griesinger observed, suffered fewer tax revolts, lawsuits, and payment defaults due to the possibility of an "orderly supervision over every family." In them, cameralist officials could tend to the "culture *(Kultur)* of men and fields"—a telling elision.[59] Griesinger further articulated an idea of the universal estate, disciplined and abstracted from the Hegelian system of needs and yet watching over it, that would become a staple of bureaucrats' occupational culture in the nineteenth century:

> The decision to dedicate oneself to state service is at the same time a
> public renunciation of the ease and freedom to move in the circles of
> civil affairs [and] a formal declaration of withdrawal from all the estates
> of society and of entrance into a sphere from which the effective regula-
> tion of society proceeds.[60]

Even before the distinction had been drawn explicitly in political rhetoric, these policy recommendations posited the existence of a civil society apart from the state, one for which new instruments of regulation and authority must be developed from above. The philosophically inchoate, ad hoc nature of the distinction meant that the political relation between state and civil society remained somewhat unclear in Griesinger's conception. In particular, Griesinger evidently saw no conflict between bureaucratic paternalism and parliamentarians' own advocacy role for the people. But to progressive constitutionalists, the two forms of stewardship were part and parcel of the same process of state formation.

It is worth lingering for a moment over this homology between bureaucratic and parliamentary stewardship, barely recognized or commented upon by Griesinger. That such a conflation could go unnoticed reflected the culture of the southwest German parliamentary class, whose members came disproportionately from the officialdom even as they articulated the interests of society against the state when wearing the politician's hat.[61] Yet one would expect statist progressives like Griesinger to *oppose* any individuals' possessing dual competence in both politics and administration, the very advantage the *Schreiber* had long exploited. Fears that a failure to separate these spheres would only benefit the scribes were well grounded. Bolley, to take just one prominent example, traded his parliamentary seat in 1817 for a position as an *Oberamtsrichter* (similar to an *Oberamtmann*) and ended his career as a high judicial official. In the interim he wielded an enormous influence in stalling *Schreiber* reform. Given this, to account for what made the universal estate a unitary and progressive class in the eyes of reform advocates like Griesinger requires an explanation of what distinguished it, ideologically and occupationally, from the scribes.

The difference hinges on the medium of publicity. Publicity made parliament a forum where delegates—especially if they held concurrent official postings—could represent civil society's interests in a style entirely divorced from the provincialism and secrecy of the *Schreiberei*. Public debate compelled a nimbler and more imaginative approach to politics than the scribes or the *Altrechtler*, with a lofty rhetoric of contract masking behind-the-scenes manipulations, had ever mustered. This was a politics dominated by ideologies of the common good, following what in Germany went variously by the names *Gemeinwohl, Gemeinwesen,* and *Gemeinnützigkeit.* Owing to their position in society and their self-image as a universal estate, officials in parliament developed a natural feel for the common good, whether they toiled in the chambers of the provincial town halls or in the bureaucratic chancelleries in Stuttgart. What parliaments offered to these government servants, local and national, was a radically new opportunity to apply their hard-won knowledge to the ideological construction of what was best for the state—knowledge that had had a particularly contorted means of expression in the political ventriloquism of the old regime.

Friedrich List on the Common Good

A powerful illustration of the way publicity enabled administrators to articulate their knowledge of the common good is offered by the career of
Friedrich List, the famous political economist. List's arguments took many
of the criticisms leveled against the scribes to their logical conclusion. In
both their substance and their manner of public presentation, List's writings
defined the new role formality should play in modern civic culture.

Friedrich List was a native of Reutlingen, a New Württemberg city with
close ties to the old duchy, and had himself trained as a *Schreiber* in several
districts in the annexed territories. Author of the *National System of
Political Economy,* he is the only Württemberg scribe ever to have gained a
lasting reputation outside his home country. List can be credited with two
important interventions in the campaign against his own profession, in 1816
and 1817. In the middle of the debates following Forstner's motions, he
penned an attack against an apologia submitted to parliament by his former
supervisor, the *Stadtschreiber* in Ulm. Written from the perspective of a
Substitut who had witnessed his supervisor's corruption firsthand, List's
report was read before the assembly by Reutlingen Representative Clemens
Cammerer.[62] Together with Forstner and Cammerer, List co-edited the
Württembergisches Archiv, a prominent reformist organ that, as has been
mentioned, published Griesinger's treatise. List also contributed an unsigned prologue to the parliamentary Expert Opinion on the scribes when it
was republished in Johann Friedrich Cotta's renowned Augsburg newspaper,
the *Allgemeine Zeitung.* This piece of writing provoked several angry
replies, and only Cotta's willingness to protect List's confidentiality prevented his exposure.[63] Despite being widely influential on account of his
personal connections in politics and the publishing world, both of List's
works thus remained anonymous, perfectly illustrating the power that
administrative experience, divorced from the identity of its possessor, could
exert on public opinion.

Public agitation, it should be emphasized, was never List's original inten-
tion; his early years were spent working within the bureaucracy, not outside
it. List had become a low-level civil servant after a dispiriting apprenticeship
in the *Schreiberei* dominated by menial chores like setting his boss's dinner
table (or rather paying off a subordinate *Incipient* to do the job). Rising
quickly through the bureaucratic ranks thanks to his brilliance and ambition, List authored several important expert opinions on local fiscal administration, managed for a time the revision of Johann Jakob Moser's
Communal Ordinance for New Württemberg, and eventually gained an

appointment, through the patronage of senior government minister Karl August von Wangenheim, as secretary to a government commission investigating the *Schreiber*.[64] In this capacity, List barely escaped stiff censure for inscribing his own opinions into commission protocols and correcting what he viewed as his superiors' mistakes when his duty as a scribe was simply to take notes. This maverick act inaugurated a career of insubordination, leading ultimately to his arrest on trumped-up political charges and his subsequent emigration to America in 1821, and feeding a lifelong "persecution complex" culminating in his suicide in 1846.[65] In 1816, only his wide-ranging connections seem to have saved his early civil service career. List was one of the most forceful advocates of *Schreiber* reform within the Württemberg bureaucracy, but chafing under its hierarchy and burned by its internal politicking, he instead chose public campaigning to promote his ideals.

List had firsthand acquaintance with the administrative issues and personalities surrounding *Schreiber* reform. This enabled him to gather the various suggestions to emerge from the parliamentary debate and project them into a vision of the common good that mingled local freedom with bureaucratic stewardship. His contributions mark a critical advance in the process of intellectual abstraction whereby the narrow issue of *Schreiber* reform was integrated into emerging discussions on the broader shape of post-Napoleonic civil society. His pamphlets on the scribes thus stand naturally alongside his other writings on government from this time. In these writings, List placed the idea of "community" on a footing rooted more in natural rights than in constitutional tradition. Mixing Rousseauian republicanism with a classical liberal vision of prepolitical autonomy in the state of nature, he viewed the community as the first and most important site of human socialization, a happy medium between natural freedoms and the restrictions on individual conduct necessary to promote general welfare and common defense. To List, "the community [is] a picture of a rational civil society in miniature."[66] In Württemberg, however, the *Schreiber* had disturbed the community's pristine harmony and undermined civic virtue. Their corruption fostered distrust by the citizenry; their partisanship and favoritism, suspicion; their decadence and luxury, the general decline of conscience and morality and a "brutal rawness among the people." Young *Substituten* with "peach fuzz" (*Milchbärten*), grown arrogant with power and wealth, led around "men of reputation and knowledge," subverting self-government and filial respect in one stroke. Unable to "despotize" from a lack of formal power, the scribes had instead to "patronize" their putative superiors through indirect means, creating communities full of "yes-men (*Ja-Männer*) . . . in the patronage of the scribes."[67]

All this suggested that the regeneration of the state's custodial authority over society, long subverted by the scribes, would reinstill ethical behavior in a corrupted people. As bearers of this task, List idealized the virtuous official described by Hegel and Griesinger. Bearing a striking resemblance to himself, this official was a civil servant rooted in the community, whose experience straddled theory and practice, rational law and local knowledge. Such a figure embodied all the best qualities of the scribes in his practical sensitivities and connections with the people and, at the same time, belonged to the upper stratum in his cultivation *(Bildung)* and righteousness. Far from reflecting an empty idealism, List's suggestions for improving the scribes' training led directly to the formation of a political science faculty at Tübingen, which later achieved an international reputation.[68] Otherwise, however, List's confidence in state officials remained problematically undertheorized: if List feared purchasing civil freedom at the price of administrative oppression, he specified no practical or theoretical limits on the state's trusteeship of the community. He simply believed that the state's "breeding" *(Erziehung)* of the people from above could release them from bondage and enable them to assert self-determination.

To be sure, List buttressed this somewhat naïve political theory with insights from political economy. With many contemporaries, List participated in the transition from cameralism to "national economy," attempting to reformulate the role of bureaucracy in the liberalized economic order of civil society.[69] In this context, List's views on the scribes confound the widespread image of him as a protectionist alternative to Adam Smith: rather than striving to submit the doctrine of laissez-faire to the higher demands of the nation, as is commonly thought, List worked in the opposite direction, to liberalize an existing, highly intrusive doctrine of government, cameralism, by leavening it with insights from classical economic theory.[70] List saw the *Schreiber* as frontline obstacles in this crusade to rationalize administration and streamline its textually mediated power to emancipate the community. The scribes' stultifying tyranny of paperwork, in his view, "had brought about a lethargy . . . from which a progressive paralysis of national energy must inevitably result."[71]

This diagnosis fully partook of the postcameralist move to unfetter civil society as an autonomous economic unit. It also anticipates his later concern with "national" productivity. Finally, it brought the ethical and legal traditions of republican civic virtue into dialogue with a dynamic modernism of productive forces: decentralized "communal resources," not the "centralized resources of the state," were the true fount of "national powers."[72] Despite these qualifications on state power, however, List's equation of

Schreiber reform with both political restoration and economic liberalization papered over the sharp differences between the two. In fact and in theory, this vision of communal liberty required a sovereign state authority to force these goals into alignment by eliminating the scribes as a political class. List's political philosophy has been called a "monarchical republicanism" for precisely this reason: his beliefs vacillated paradoxically between endorsing bureaucracy and defending the community against its incursions. While the scribes had acted to channel conflict between the two realms under the old regime, List's attempt to eliminate mediating authorities between bureaucracy and community begged the question of their new relationship. The oppression of "dead forms" he associated with the *Schreiber* was, after all, equally characteristic of the state servants who were to replace them, and the burdens of their tutelage (what he called *Vormundschaft*) upon civic freedoms equally heavy.[73]

List's tirades against "official despotism" found greater resonance as commentaries on the written word's debasement of political culture than as maxims for practical policy reform. He was hardly original in using the term *Vielschreiberei* as Württemberg's mark of dubious distinction, but, more than other commentators, he grasped intuitively how it corrupted public discourse. He accused the *Schreiber* of overcomplicating their business with meaningless phraseology and "bombast," obstructing the clarity, rationality, and openness of state business. Especially irksome was their outmoded, affected style of discourse, peppering mundane bureaucratic language with sycophantic flourishes like *allerunterthänigst* and *allergnädigst*.[74] List advocated radical openness within the state to rid its bureaucracy of such outmoded and obfuscatory formality. When officials could write and speak directly and honestly to both superiors and inferiors, their "clumsy and stilted" style of communication would yield to a more direct "effusion of opinions" up and down the ranks, free and unhindered, and "cleansed" of superficiality and pomp. To stimulate debate about *Schreiber* reform both within and outside the state, he demanded "*publicity before all things*" and proposed essay competitions and prizes to "consist only in honor" and conferring new forms of public reputation.[75]

Although most of these suggestions were confined to matters of *Schreiber* reform, they betokened a radically new approach toward the formation of political will and the legitimation of state power, stripped of formality and demanding that bureaucratic officials negotiate their power, openly, in the public sphere. Whereas the scribes, and later the *Altrechtler*, had brokered influence in secretive networks of collegiality in Old Württemberg's cantons, List recognized only the tribunal of reason, harmonizing form and content, claim and justification, before what he called a "critical public." His Habermasian idealism applied indiscriminately to the intra- and extra-bureaucratic realms, state and civil society alike. List realized, of course, that his was an as yet unrealized ideal. In a small country where personal connections sufficed for the discussion of issues, and the public sphere was itself largely populated by bureaucrats and officials, power still flowed through channels of favoritism, patronage, and friendship. List himself personally knew, trained under, owed favors to, or had run-ins with practically all the principals in the campaign against the scribes—including none other than Heinrich Bolley himself, who played an instrumental role in hounding him out of parliament in 1821.[76] Fearing the covert machinations of such powerful politicians, List chose to express himself anonymously. In his publications, he adopted a style calculated to arouse public passions, which progressively harmed his reputation, since, as a practical matter, he could not forever conceal his identity.

Nonetheless, List had staked out an arena for newer, more open practices of stewardship over civil society, less constrained by formality and radically independent from the traditional mechanisms for articulating society's interests: the secretive cantons and the powerful corps of political ventriloquists who retained their influence over this body long into the post-Napoleonic period. Through his public activity, List recast and updated an earlier practice of politics associated with the scribes' highly formalized collegiality. He developed new arguments for replacing them with a post-Napoleonic elite, a universal estate of newly mobile, knowledgeable and rhetorically selfless bureaucrats and parliamentarians. And where List's theoretical and practical political acumen was left wanting, his agitational enthusiasm illuminated the possibilities for legitimating civil society's leadership based on reason, not tradition; right, not privilege; public community, not private corporations; Enlightenment morality, not *Altes Recht* cynicism; civic utility, not constitutional formality.

List's writings, a testament to the power of writing to steer public debates, were the culmination of a new political style pioneered by reformist parliamentarians in 1815–17. They articulated criticisms against *Vielschreiberei* brewing ever since Napoleon's invasions but temporarily squelched by the scribes' surge in power just after parliament's restoration. List, of course, was himself a *Schreiber;* his background gave him not only the knowledge, but also the personal connections, to develop critiques of his colleagues and publicize them before a civil society straining to rid itself of their tutelage. List's methods of cultivating influence, however, placed him squarely outside the traditions of old Württemberg. His writings did not rely for their effectiveness on constitutional exegesis or behind-the-scenes maneuvers, but stood on their own terms as purely ideological tracts intended for broad popular consumption. In short, List's publications represented the emancipation of writing from all aspects of the scribes' influence; they gave a voice to a civil society now fully liberated from textual serfdom. The next chapter examines the other side of civil society's separation from the state. It turns to the reforms undertaken by the Württemberg government in response to the campaign against the scribes, and to the very different ways civil society was conceptualized in the bureaucratic arena List had left behind.

6   Reading, Writing, and Reform

The true measure of any civil society's coalescence is its ability to compel governmental action on its behalf. In Württemberg, the public and parliamentary agitation against the scribes strikingly illustrated the potential for citizen action to focus the state on problems of official corruption. In direct response to this campaign, the government, having dawdled for a decade and temporized with piecemeal measures, acted decisively and systematically to dismantle the scribes' profession. Between 1817 and 1826, it handed down a wave of edicts converting the scribes into menial notaries public salaried and appointed by the state, and dispersed their monopoly over writing among a host of new and old officials. Concurrently, it empowered a series of *Schreiber* reform commissions to enforce these policy enactments. In light of their predecessors' neglect, these commissioners confronted maddening absences in the previous decade's archival record. This made it impossible to document and punish specific acts of malfeasance for the period since 1806. Unable to recover such cases individually, however, they determined to ferret out the historic patterns of administrative exploitation and address their underlying demographic and economic causes.

Reformers' efforts had significant repercussions outside the domain of intra-administrative practice. Their comprehensive accounting of local officials was one of the first instances in which the state successfully applied procedures of statistical and demographic measurement to subclasses of its own population and acted upon the data to produced nuanced, effective reform. With mountains of data in hand, *Schreiber* reform commissioners practiced a rough-and-ready sociography, acquiring a new perspective on the civil society they studied and surveyed. This was especially true in contrast to their eighteenth-century predecessors, those commissioned investigators who had often found themselves embroiled in the very communal conflicts they protocolled. In the nineteenth century, the state derived power from its detached sovereignty over local affairs, not its interference with them. Civil society had called reform into being; now the reformers would act, reciprocally, to define and demarcate this realm from the state bureaucracy—on their own terms.

The very notion of "reform from above" evokes a rarefied domain of law and policy prescription as the source of the state's power. Civil society's emancipation is thus classically understood as a legal and administrative framework erected by the state, protecting property rights, conferring freedom from feudal obligations, curtailing bureaucratic high-handedness, establishing civil equality, and (in some areas) expanding the sphere of local self-government. Certainly the state's ability to formulate such policies experienced a substantial boost in the Napoleonic period. The number and quality of expert opinions on the minutest problems of administration, taxation, and economics skyrocketed during this period, and the bureaucrats who authored them were in many ways the most knowledgeable and experienced statesmen Germany had ever known.[1] But the state's increasing control over law, edict, and ordinance was not novel to the post-Napoleonic period, and instead continued a secular trend dating from early modern times.[2] Indeed, with the empowerment of deliberative parliaments in many southern German states, governments' room for policy maneuver arguably declined relative to the absolutist prerogatives of eighteenth-century states. This was certainly true of Württemberg, with its active and vigilant parliament.

Needed, then, is an explanation of how the state asserted its external power, over civil society, at the same time as it consolidated its own regulatory apparatus and capacity for policy implementation, internally, through bureaucratization. Any such explanation must include treatment of a messier and more contingent domain than abstract policy or rational law: the epistemology of civil society itself. In the scribes' case, the simple legal demarcation of a realm of civic freedom through administrative edict was insufficient to deprive them of their social power. Only the precise calibration of the scribes' incomes to the sociological conditions of their districts could establish a proper standing for them in local communities, one befitting membership in the new bureaucratic class. Effective reform thus depended on sociography: on enhancing the government's ability to "read" society by training its apparatus of surveillance on a specific social problem. In the pages below, our aim is to track reformers' evolution from edict to enforcement, for their sociographic efforts provide the best account possible of why the *Schreiberei* had become such a detested institution. The method of this chapter in turn gives a clue to its argument: state power in the post-Napoleonic period had been refounded on a new epistemological base, the ability to construe civil society, and produce knowledge of it, as an object of government regulation separate from the state. Such knowledge, originally a monopoly of the state, soon became the faculty by which citizens made their own way in civil society.

EDICTS: THE LETTER OF THE LAW

Starting in 1816, the Württemberg central government promulgated a series of edicts bringing an end, at least institutionally, to the influence of the *Schreiber.* The enactments, while obviously crucial for understanding the scribes' fall from power, are equally significant as printed artifacts of a growing state. Policymakers read and sorted through a mass of legal opinions, ducal memoranda, and reports from the countryside before condensing their findings into textually coherent, streamlined edicts. Their policies balanced interest groups within and outside government, coordinated various forms of administrative expertise for the solution of a very complex problem, and, above all, simultaneously constructed and adhered to a modern notion of law. These pioneering innovations over old-regime as well as Napoleonic policymaking gave new form and system to the conduct of governance. Through such efforts, state policy architects took recognition of a new civil society taking shape around them and, at the same time, gave it clearer lineaments through an administrative infrastructure they themselves erected. Reform refurbished state power for the post-Napoleonic era and established new standards for nineteenth-century bureaucracy centered on the production of policy writing.

On 22 November 1816, the Württemberg parliament forwarded its *Schreiber* reform committee's expert opinion to the king, who in turn empowered his government to investigate "which flaws in this institution, both in the new as well as in the old lands, can be remedied." The king also directed his officials to draw on the examples of other German states, stressing that a complete eradication of the *Schreiberei* should not be ruled out. Over the next three years, the government established a series of three commissions: one to discover the sources of scribal abuse, one to develop appropriate policy instruments to root it out, and one to administer the technicalities of their promulgation.[3] The first commission, active between November 1816 and August 1817, included some of the most knowledgeable officials in the kingdom, including the elite *Karlsschule* alumnus and Privy Councillor Albrecht von Lempp as president and a young Friedrich

List as recording secretary. The commission rejected parliamentary proposals that their respective committees work in tandem, finding the parliamentary committee's brief, twenty-page opinion on the *Schreiber* problem irritatingly incomplete and impressionistic.[4] Instead, it produced its own, more extensive (352-page) expert opinion, the *Main Report on the Schreiberei System*, which sparked discussion in the highest circles of government.[5]

The Lempp commission's assertion of independence from parliament reflects the state's growing policymaking confidence and a newly systematic approach to the *Schreiber* problem. Its *Main Report,* both exhaustive and exhausting in its attention to the mechanics of local government, generated a series of reform edicts in 1817. These freed key areas of communal business from the scribes' control while subjecting them to more stringent oversight from higher state authorities.[6] First, extending a simplification of official procedure begun in piecemeal fashion during the absolutist period, the measures streamlined inheritance procedures for uncontested wills and testaments. This reform, which also simplified the drafting of estates inventories and the probate process generally, addressed perhaps the most hated aspect of the scribes' hegemony in New Württemberg, where extreme variations in inheritance customs had sparked persistent clashes of legal culture and complaints of abuse. Second, the 1817 edicts allowed "capable, honest citizens" to audit local finances and keep tax logs without any cooperation from the *Schreiber.* The simple ability to avoid routing every governmental receipt and expenditure through the scribes' offices for certification—until then the single greatest source of their incomes—presaged a general liberalization of communal self-government expanded in subsequent policy pronouncements. Complementing this liberalization was a third and final requirement, that originals (and not copies) of official documents now be forwarded to county-level *(Oberamt)* authorities. This reflected an ongoing move to reconfigure the *Oberamt* as a supervisory organ monitoring communities' new powers of self-administration from a greater distance.[7] The 1817 measures thus combined liberalization with centralization, sharply curtailing the scribes' mediating role between state and society.

By acting directly on the findings of the *Main Report* through these edicts, the Württemberg state tested its power to control the scribes' profession through simple administrative fiat. Having emerged from the Napoleonic trial by fire and the growing pains of "organizationitis," the state had greatly enhanced its policymaking ability by marshaling the energies of trained bureaucratic experts. The critical innovation, adopted not just in Württemberg but in many post-Napoleonic governments, was the "collegial system" in which such experts participated collectively, without hierarchy, almost as equals, in the drafting of government policy. Expert opinions *(Gutachten)* shuttled within and between various reform bodies, accumulating layers of marginalia and memoranda in the process of collegial review. Policymakers often plagiarized each other unself-consciously, and final drafts of commission reports in turn cribbed passages from previous opinions before being signed by all their authors. They thus projected not just the façade, but the reality, of collective, unanimous decision. Reinhart Koselleck, in his account of similar developments in Prussia, argues that this "intra-administrative public sphere" formed the basis of an "ersatz constitutionalism" in which officials transposed quasi-parliamentary practices, complete with rules of order, to the bureaucratic chancelleries.[8] The same dynamic was at work in the circulation of expert opinions like the *Main Report:* continually reread and rewritten, such opinions became the vehicles of bureaucratic collegiality: they were the primary means by which knowledge was produced and collective will was mustered for policy action in the upper reaches of the German state.

The Lempp commission's handling of its cocky young secretary, Friedrich List, showed both the limits and the strengths of the collegial system in Württemberg. Recall from the previous chapter that List had cavalierly injected his own opinions into commission protocols when his duty was merely to transcribe. He went on to argue for a radical openness within the bureaucracy, analogous in his mind to parliamentary debate, but conflicting with the more hierarchical practices of intra-administrative discourse favored by his superiors. List's punishment—he was formally rebuked in 1817—reveals the pitfalls in regarding bureaucratic collegiality as a form of freewheeling constitutional government. Nonetheless, what remains striking about the List case is the willingness of senior commission members to stall the production of their *Main Report,* distract themselves from the work of *Schreiber* reform, and generate a stack of formal recriminations against List, simply to discipline him and keep him from overstepping his secretarial role. List was even given the formal opportunity to submit written defenses of his behavior in which he insolently denied any wrongdoing.[9] This extreme insistence on formal procedure in collegial deliberations— striking, even bizarre, given that they usually encompassed only a few men who already knew each other casually—was entirely in keeping with bureaucrats' self-image as stewards of society. If they were to live up to their self-appointed tasks as rigorously impartial agents of the state, they had to conduct themselves according to the strictest possible formality.

The List episode demonstrates how the classic culture of formality, having been subjected to greater openness and ideological flexibility in the parliamentary campaign, underwent precisely the opposite transformation within the bureaucracy: a further elaboration and refinement. A new commitment to the rule of law, habitually reinforced by a stylized collegiality, lent post-Napoleonic state policy a purity, a thoroughness, a Weberian rationality lacking in the ad hoc enactments of the capricious, improvisational Napoleonic state under Friedrich. The rigors of law promised not only to routinize bureaucracy's internal dealings, but also to revamp its external power over civil society. While it constrained officials to act in accord with fixed principles, the recourse to law focused their energies on constructing uniform rules of governance for which they themselves served as guarantors. Such impulses came to fruition in the *Rechtsstaat*, a state based on law and formally separate from a civil society that was now to be protected from arbitrary governmental incursions.

The doctrine of the *Rechtsstaat* found its clearest application to *Schreiber* reform in the activities of a second reform body, called the Office Organization Commission. Its Organizational Edict enacted a key corollary to the doctrine of rule by law—the division of institutional powers—by distinguishing justice from administration for the first time.[10] In practice this meant parceling out the scribes' business among various local officials, including both *Oberamtmänner* and new officials called *Oberamtsrichter* (in charge of county-level justice), local town councils, county councils, and a special new official, the so-called Court Notary *(Gerichtsnotar)*. Court Notaries were to oversee noncontentious litigation (property matters, inventories, testaments, bankruptcies, and other routine legal transactions) and were envisioned as eventual replacements for the *Stadt- und Amtsschreiber*. This redistribution of competencies extended an earlier strategy, begun in the Napoleonic era, to erode the scribes' monopolies piecemeal and from below. At that time, a series of new communal positions—actuaries, notaries, auditors, tax collectors—had been created ad hoc to manage local finances, perform routine notarial functions, draw up simple petitions, and transcribe town council minutes.[11] By 1818, the assault had become much more systematic, having integrated previous, improvisational reforms under a general legal framework.

The 1818 Organizational Edict illustrated an elegant convergence of bureaucratic rationalization with the (partial) unfettering of civil society, two complementary ways in which the bond between state and citizen was reshaped under the *Rechtsstaat*. It not only explicitly envisioned the future dissolution of the *Schreiberei* as an intermediary authority, but already destroyed the functional monopolies from which the scribes had always profited. Together with four other edicts also promulgated on the last day of

1818, the edict on the scribes reformed both communal self-government and the lowest level of state bureaucracy and drew new divisions between them. Terminologically, the old Württemberg "canton" *(Stadt und Amt)* yielded to the bureaucratic "county" *(Oberamt)* on the one hand and the individual *Gemeinde,* or community, on the other. Upholding the community, not the canton, as the atom of civil society and the locus of citizenship was an ideal made explicit in the edict's language:

> The communal unit as the natural foundation of the state *[Staats-Verbandes],* in consideration of the community of residence, of a sufficient population for the functioning of civic ends [and] for the coherence and compactness of territory, is to be maintained and perfected everywhere.

The decision to extend the institutions of local self-government to the smallest possible community and not locate them, as before, on the cantonal or district level, completed the democratization of the old Württemberg canton described in Chapter 4.[12] It also betokened a new concern with the political sociology of good government rooted in considerations of population size and territorial reach.

In all these ways, the rule of law formed a potent instrument facilitating the enactment of more systematic administrative decrees and insinuating the state into local power relations. This heralded a significant improvement on the old duchy's higher policy organs, specifically the Privy and Government Councils, which had traditionally vacillated between apathy and high-handedness and whose policy armamentarium had been notoriously ineffective during the old regime.[13] At the same time, however, the rule of law subjected the post-Napoleonic state's room for policy maneuver to important structural constraints. The autonomy symbolized by its issuing of edicts belied deeper struggles among various interest groups within and outside the bureaucracy. These factions exploited the natural openness of the collegial system, knowing that the workup of new edicts required the most comprehensive and doctrinally informed expert opinions possible. Here it should come as no surprise that the figure who first capitalized on this cumbersome requirement to assert the scribes' interests was Heinrich Bolley, who truly deserves to be regarded as the Württemberg Talleyrand for his ability to survive regime changes and shifting ideological winds. Bolley had managed to gain a seat on the Office Organization Commission, where he authored or co-authored at least seven expert opinions on all aspects of communal administration. In them, one sees in perhaps the most extreme form yet his ability to couch the naked pursuit of occupational self-interest in the most long-winded, obscure, and pedantic modes of argumentation imaginable.[14] Bolley never availed himself of rhetorical flourishes when citing a precise legal authority would suffice, and in the system of collegial deliberation he found the perfect milieu for practical action.

Unlike many parliamentary conservatives who had dug in their heels against any sort of change, Bolley played the pragmatist and preferred to work the back channels of government. He was willing to concede the scribes' replacement by the Court Notaries envisioned in the 1818 edict as long as their functional range of competence remained as wide as possible and former scribes were favored for these new positions. Bolley wished to win for the Court Notaries the right to be elected as secretaries to the refashioned county assemblies *(Amtsversammlungen)*, for he believed that the scribes' advisory role there was an indispensable counterweight to the arbitrariness of the royal *Oberamtmänner*.[15] Here and elsewhere, Bolley joined fellow conservatives in opposing the *functional* separation of powers in the modern *Rechtsstaat*, instead endorsing their old-regime division along *political* lines, that is, between state and local authorities acting as mutual watchdogs with overlapping competence. Additionally, he correctly saw that the scribes' hegemony had long derived from their ability to trade one form of official practice for another. Proposals to divide justice from administration were of particular concern, because the dispensing of justice cultivated respect and admiration among the citizenry, whereas administrative power only inspired fear and resentment.[16] Bolley therefore pressed to restore the scribes' advisory and tutelary roles, particularly in the conduct of noncontentious justice, to their administrative and fiscal duties, like tax auditing.[17] These concessions were incorporated into the Notarial Edict of 1819, spelling out the competence of the new Court Notaries. Under certain conditions, the edict duly allowed these officials to perform administrative duties while at the same time acting as formally recognized legal experts in advising local city councils.[18]

Despite this rear-guard success, Bolley's machinations had their limits, since the intra-administrative public sphere in which he acted was subject to many countervailing pressures. Specifically, in contrast to Koselleck's Prussia, where the collegial system formed an "ersatz" constitutionalism in the absence of parliamentary authority, post-Napoleonic Württemberg additionally benefited from a newly flourishing and fully functional constitution. Especially after its ratification in 1819, parliament could influence the formulation of government policy through formal legal channels. Early parliamentary liberals aimed to prevent official despotism and insisted that the boundaries between state and civil society be upheld by the most precise possible delineation of bureaucratic powers. Bolley's scramble to preserve as much competence as he could for the scribes proved the necessity of just such safeguards. More pertinently, his determination to maintain a wide administrative and judicial competence for his peers led him to touch upon the sphere of civil law and thus legislation in his expert opinions, a matter that constitutionally required parliament's participation.[19] This fact, together with the government's commitment to preserve a still very young and fragile constitutional settlement, gave parliamentarians the standing to intervene in what had so far been a purely internal administrative discussion.

Consultations with parliament not only reasserted the division of powers but rendered it even more comprehensive than would otherwise have been the case. The so-called Parliamentary Agreement of 1821 vindicated the very principle Bolley had attempted to undermine: the separation of judicial from administrative functions at the lowest level of government.[20] As its only exceptions, the agreement allowed acting *Stadt- und Amtsschreiber* to combine these duties temporarily, but only after negotiating with their local communities and then petitioning the government for approval. Many civically precocious localities seized on this opportunity to subcontract their business to other officials.[21] The 1821 compromise also led directly to the promulgation of a far-reaching Administrative Edict the next year.[22] According to its stipulations, a newly created official called an Administrative Actuary *(Verwaltungsaktuar)* would acquire control of precisely those administrative functions the scribes had been temporarily allowed to continue exercising.[23] These actuaries would be employed on an exclusively provisional basis and could be dismissed at any time. The creation of such posts eliminated the possibility that through the mere lack of any capable alternatives, former scribes would continue to control local finance willy-nilly. Finally, both acting *Schreiber* and Court Notaries yet to be named would be subjected to salary regulations applying to all state officials. The size of their districts—and indirectly, of their incomes as well— would remain unchanged for the time being, but the government reserved the right to shrink or enlarge them later and "to set their incomes in a proper relation" to the actual amount of work they performed.

This last provision signaled a new determination to revamp the scribes' income structure, calibrate their standing in civil society, and combat the economic roots of corruption. Before enacting such fundamental changes, however, the state would have to contend with one final structural constraint: the protests of the scribes themselves. Between 1821 and 1826, a veritable flood of formal complaints against the loss of income brought about by the reform edicts poured in from scribes all across Württemberg. Bolley, acting in his capacity as Waiblingen *Amtsschreiber*, even fabricated legal rights deriving from a dubious "official contract" which, he claimed, had been violated by the very edicts he had participated in drafting.[24] His protests were dismissed with irritation, but those of his colleagues were taken quite seriously. Here, the state's power of administrative fiat conflicted with its commitment to apply the principles and procedures of law most conscientiously to its own officials. The law on officials *(Beamtenrecht)*, which concerned their appointment, payment, examination, and dismissal, made up a central element of the nineteenth-century *Rechtsstaat* all over Germany.[25] Formulating a robust set of rights and privileges for state servants loomed surprisingly large in the policy debates and decisions attending the advent of civil society. In Württemberg it was clear that if scribes were to be made the guarantors of a rational, legal order animated by the rights of individuals and the limitations of the state, they themselves had to be rigorously protected from arbitrary authority. Because payment reform bore on their very livelihood, it would require even more policy wrangling than the reassignment of official duties.[26]

The scribes' concerted reaction reflected their coalescence into an independent professional interest group, one poised to dilute the implementation of the state's policy enactments. It was thus highly ironic that such a sophisticated assertion of privilege should have rested on the very measures the state undertook to cultivate their allegiance. As the last chapter showed, the government's rotation of scribes through new districts instilled an identification with the bureaucracy and diminished the contacts they enjoyed with local communities. During the 1810s, the state had also begun, more formally, to treat scribes as civil servants. First it subjected *Substituten* and lower clerks to oaths and service contracts, and then gradually extended the requirement until all of those performing clerical functions in the bureaucracy, including the *Stadt- und Amtsschreiber*, were officially employed by the state.[27] Finally, it overhauled the system of examinations so that, starting in 1813, these formerly ad hoc affairs gave way to routine sittings approximately three times a year, for which *Substituten* from all over the kingdom had to travel to Stuttgart. Examinees were presented a battery of problems ranging from calculating the square root of 1,728 to defining the rights women held to their husbands' property.[28] Indications of official merit and recommendations based on examination results became part and parcel of the state's mechanism for placing new scribes, adding yet another layer of professionalism to their training and identity.

By 1826 the scribes' co-optation into the civil service was complete, the *Schreibereien* formally dissolved, and a number of new Court Notaries (some scribes, some not) appointed.[29] The shift from *Schreiber* to mere

Notar marked a painful decline in status, as one pamphleteer ruefully noted.[30] But it would also entail a compensatory benefit deriving from the symbolic capital that state service offered. While scribes' demands for monetary compensation reflected the long-standing power of their office, the corrupt proceeds of official "honor" enjoyed by old Württemberg *Ehrbarkeit* had yielded to the legally recognized right to severance pay from the state bureaucracy. The scribes' historic ability to trade symbolic for material capital no longer took place locally, in other words, but within a state whose entire officialdom, top to bottom, was now animated by the rule of law.[31] The next section explores the methods by which the state met the scribes' material needs while remaining true to this principle. It picks up where many administrative histories leave off: after the promulgation of edicts and the reorganization of official powers. In Germany especially, with its proud traditions of civil service, it is often assumed that state officials possessed a reflexive commitment to the rule of law that naturally led them to obey the pronouncements of their superiors.[32] The entire previous history of the *Schreiber* suggests otherwise, however, making it all the more important to explain how the state could compel their submission to the reforms of 1817–21.

SOCIOGRAPHY AND ENFORCEMENT

Reforms of the scribes' appointment, examination, and official duties enabled bureaucrats of the early 1820s to turn squarely to the knotty question of their payment. Using income surveys solicited from each scribe in state service, they established new salaries and pensions, assumed responsibility for paying them, and thus definitively elevated the scribes from the temptation to exploit their clients. To accomplish this, reform commissioners combined raw income data from the surveys with the results of rudimentary sociological surveys indexing patterns of land tenure and inheritance practice. This produced a comprehensive administrative geography of Württemberg's old and new territories, enabling reformers to map out the varying intensity of official exploitation county by county. Commissioners isolated distinct variables for statistical analysis and incorporated them into a complex formula used to calculate the scribes' future compensation. This in turn rested on a careful consideration of what business a scribe could generate in a "typical" community defined in terms of these variables. The results proved remarkably successful: efficient, just, fiscally sound, and politically astute. Sociography thus functioned as the very instrument of the state's power.

Practically speaking, these findings cemented previous reform efforts by allowing the government, in effect, to buy off the scribes for their political quiescence. Scribes nearing retirement age would be eased out of service with pensions; younger ones kept on as new *Gerichtsnotare* would receive an income supplement to maintain them at the standard of living to which they had become accustomed.[33] The manner of the scribes' compensation determined whether they would remain a disaffected, disenchanted, and perhaps politically dangerous element, or whether they could be coaxed as a profession to cede their power and retreat quietly into the obscurity of mere local notoriety. Pensions had to be calculated with hairline precision, in a way that would neither offend the scribes nor drain the state's coffers. Additionally, the supplemental incomes of new *Gerichtsnotare* had be regulated so that they would neither command disproportionately large sums of wealth nor be tempted by poverty to exploit their clients. All these were the duties of the government's third reform body, the Organization Implementation Commission, or OVK by its German initials.[34] Active between 1821 and 1826, its calculation of compensation schedules was substantially complete by 1823. During this time, the OVK produced a wealth of knowledge on the sociology of local administration in Württemberg. This research led them—as it will lead us—into a deeper understanding of official power in civil society, based no longer on case studies but on systematic sociography.

As its first order of business, the OVK generated a baseline for compensation by making an exact appraisal of the scribes' existing earnings. This was the purpose of the income surveys *(Einkommens-Fassionen)*, covering the scribes' practices during 1817–20, the very period of government reform.[35] Surveys consisted of template sheets that the scribes were required to fill out in detail; this tabular format not only promoted a standardization of responses but drew attention, visually, to any gaps respondents might have left on the page. The surveys relied entirely on information reported by the scribes themselves, and the OVK later found creative ways to circumvent their built-in incentive to exaggerate income figures. Provisionally, it encouraged accuracy and honesty through the minute specificity of its questions. Surveys included individual entries on everything from communal receipts and estates inventories to the costs of writing supplies and heating the scribes' offices. Scribes were also required to report on the size of their staffs and the manner of their compensation. "Perks"—payments in kind (wine, firewood, foodstuffs, etc.), the value of free apartments owned by municipalities that some scribes occupied, income derived from side duties in addition to core *Schreiber* business, and quasi-

	County			
Criterion	*Bietigheim*	*Herrenberg*	*Künzelsau*	*Tettnang*
Geographic				
Old/New Württemberg	old	old	new	new
Region	Neckar	Black Forest	Jagst	Danube
Sociological				
Population	6,552	14,044	13,081	13,843
No. of communities	5	18	58	14
Marital property	separate	separate	mixed	joint
Land tenure	partible	partible	partible	closed, feudal
Economic				
Total 1822 revenue	2,058	5,660	4,702	5,497
Public business	51%	59%	66%	43%
Estate inventories	33%	28%	18%	29%
Other private	16%	13%	16%	28%
	100%	100%	100%	100%
Administrative				
No. of Amtssubstituten	2	4	2	2
Other staff	2	5	4	3
Office overhead	19%	23%	16%	25%
Expenses for staff	35%	39%	33%	34%
Scribe's take-home pay	47%	38%	51%	41%
	100%	100%	100%	100%

FIGURE 9.   Operation of sample *Schreibereien,* 1821. Source: HStAS E 301 Bü 107–118, Dienst-Einkommens-Berechnungen of 1821. Percentages were calculated from raw figures in these income surveys; figures do not add exactly to 100% due to rounding. All income statistics, here and elsewhere, are in Gulden (fl.).

legal "honoraria"—were also included. Finally, scribes indicated the nature of land tenure and inheritance practice in their districts. This information included whether marital property was held jointly or separately by husband and wife and whether parcels of land were divided up among heirs, bequeathed intact, or held only provisionally, in feudal relationships renewed each generation. All these data bespeak the tremendous variety in the Württemberg kingdom's rural sociology and would become extremely important to the OVK in its efforts to document the varying intensity of the economic burden placed by scribes on the kingdom's citizens.

To provide a feel for the income surveys' content, four sample *Schreibereien* have been analyzed and their operations summarized in figure 9. Considerable simplification has been necessary to render the data comprehensible, but otherwise the diagram includes roughly the types of information OVK commissioners would have pored over as they skimmed through the income surveys. Geographically, the counties sampled represent both New and Old Württemberg as well as each of the four *Kreise*, or political regions, into which the kingdom had been divided: those of the Neckar, Jagst, and Danube river system, plus that of the Black Forest.[36] The sample also incorporates the full diversity of sociological conditions prevalent in the kingdom. A marked variety is apparent, finally, in the economic structure of the scribes' revenues, as broken down by source of business. Public duties, chiefly the management of communal funds and the keeping of receipts, predominated uniformly, though they could account for anywhere from 43% to 66% of total revenues. Estates inventories weighed in somewhere between a fifth and a third. Other private matters, consisting mainly of contracts, testaments, and miscellaneous property transactions, comprised the smallest portion in each of the sample districts, yet showed the widest variation proportionally: 13–28%. These figures reflect regional variation, not just in governmental practice but in local citizens' propensity to seek out the scribes' private services; collectively, they illustrate the lack of a consistent structure to the scribes' incomes over the countryside, which made it harder for the OVK to calculate standard compensation for them.

The "administrative" criteria in figure 9 reveal that the *Schreiberei* was a complex administrative operation in which more money passed through the scribe's hands than actually remained in his purse. About a fifth of gross income went to office overhead, including rent for office space, heating and lighting costs, writing supplies, travel expenses, and petty cash disbursements to copyists hired on a part-time basis. Compensation for full-time staffs ranging from four to nine employees accounted for a further third. Memoranda appended to the income tables give a sense of how these staff expenditures were themselves broken down. A typical *Amtssubstitut*, overseeing business in county hinterlands, kept anywhere from one- to two-thirds of the income he generated, and paid for horses, lodging, and writing materials from his own pocket. The rest of his revenue went to the *Schreiberei* itself. A *Stadtsubstitut* working in the scribe's office, by contrast, was typically salaried at a rate of 200–400 fl. and might be given a room there in which to sleep; an apprentice *Skribent* made about half this sum. Generally, these amounts were sufficient to secure a comfortable existence for trainees. The pecuniary benefits of the Napoleonic period had not failed to trickle down to them, in other words. These facts soften the image of the stereotypical *Stadt- und Amtsschreiber* as a rapacious, tribute-collecting overlord. In fact, his outlays put the scribe's personal take-home income at only 38–51% of gross revenues.

The impression that not all scribes were wealthy is confirmed by a glimpse at the range of incomes documented by the surveys. These numbers exhibited an extremely wide variation depending on the size of the districts in which the scribes served. Indeed, they show how difficult it was to make generalizations about the *Schreiberei* as an economic enterprise and about the scribes as a profession. To be sure, the "average" scribe in 1822 possessed an income, 1226 fl., well in line with his official standing and certainly not excessive by comparative standards. It was far less than that of the average *Oberamtmann*, for example, who made 1835 fl. and who could be expected to have made more money, given his higher official status. Still, a considerable number of scribes presided over truly enormous offices, with revenues over 5000 fl., and the richest scribes made more than the richest *Oberamtmänner.*[37] At the other extreme, there was a high percentage of scribes with incomes under 500 fl.—one made as little as 83 fl. in 1822—who tended to be employed on an exclusively adjunct basis. By contrast, no *Oberamtmann* made less than 1775 fl.

Confronted with this mass of disparate information yielding no unified picture of the model *Schreiberei,* the OVK focused on tabulating and summarizing the data. It produced a plethora of charts cross-indexing a broad set of variables relevant to the compensation effort—old income versus new, staff size versus county population, the costs of probate instruments in relation to geographic location, and so on. Juxtaposing discrete strands of data rendered them progressively more distant from the original income surveys, and by transcribing information from old charts to create new ones, as was sometimes done repeatedly, OVK commissioners attained an ever greater level of abstraction from the flesh-and-blood operation of a *Schreiberei* practice (see figure 10). A standard set of figures emerged and circulated among these charts, so that it was tempting to forget that they ultimately relied upon the scribes' honesty in reporting their own incomes. Insofar as they derived from calculations idiosyncratic to each individual scribe, moreover, they had to be heavily manipulated in order that apples might be compared with apples. Difficulties in assessing the value of such

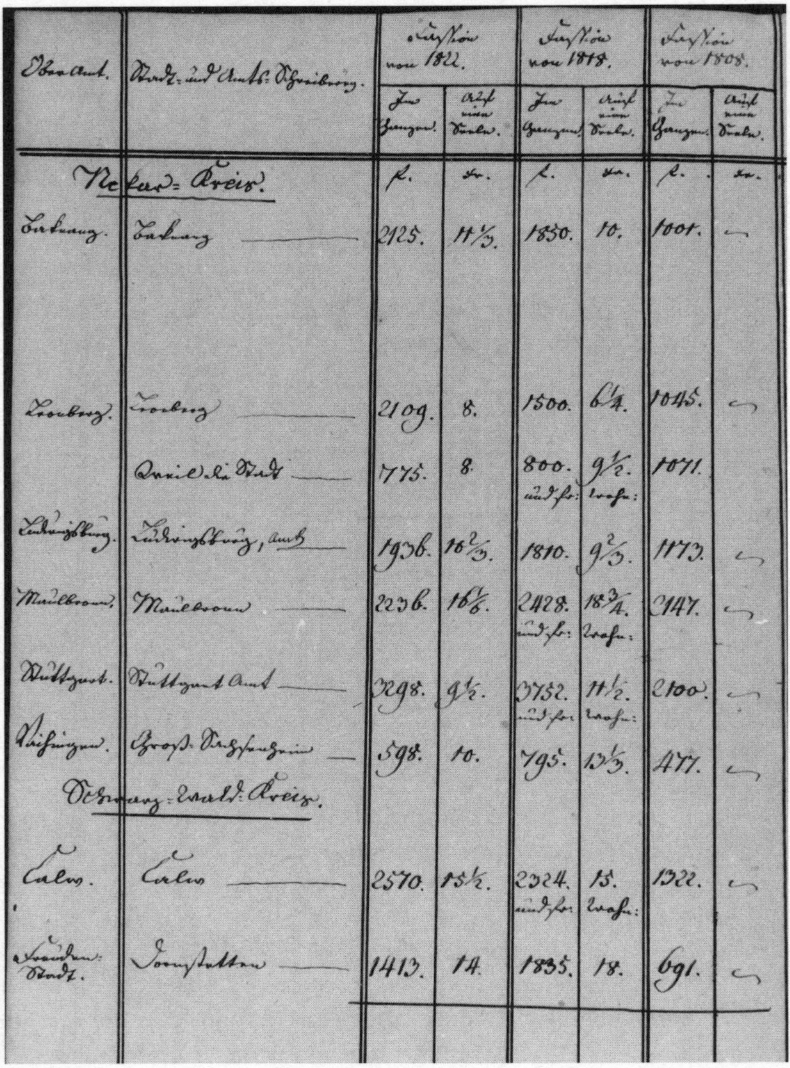

FIGURE 10. OVK chart comparing scribes' reported incomes in 1808, 1818, and 1822, in absolute terms and per capita. The marked increase in scribes' fortunes between 1808 and 1818 is visually apparent as one scans each row from right to left. The trend between 1818 and 1822, the period of government reform, is more equivocal, reflecting the uneven impact of reform legislation on scribes' practices. Per capita indices eventually became a central part of the OVK's compensation scheme. © Hauptstaatsarchiv Stuttgart, E 301 Bü 106.

perquisites as free apartments, for example, made standardization arduous, not to mention error-prone.

The charts nonetheless allowed OVK commissioners to cultivate a socio-graphic perspective by rapidly scanning and manipulating tables of numbers to arrive at ever simpler and more schematic representations of the *Schreiberei* system. This process culminated in the OVK's most ambitious computational effort, measuring the aggregate financial burden placed on the kingdom of Württemberg by the scribes. Undertaking what must have been a very tedious computation, the OVK condensed revenue figures from no fewer than thirty-two subdivisions on the original income surveys into eight master categories and then added them up for the entire kingdom. This calculation revealed that the sum total of all transaction fees collected by the scribes for their private as well as official services in 1821 amounted to 454,155 fl. and 30 kr. Such an absurdly precise number no doubt gratified the OVK's pretensions to statistical rigor. But there was method in its mad-ness: this figure provided the simplest, most compelling snapshot of the scribes' burden on society ever produced. Given that the total population of the scribes' districts (and therefore Württemberg as a whole) was 1,413,382 souls, a simple division computation shows that the aggregate per capita income from all revenue sources was 32.13 fl. per 100 inhabitants. To put it in everyday terms, this meant that every man, woman, and child in the kingdom rendered one day of hard manual labor each year for his or her local scribe.[38]

For a time, the OVK toyed with a compensation scheme based on just such a per capita index. Many of its charts and internal memoranda bandied about figures in "kroners per soul" as a convenient rule of thumb for assess-ing the economic burden of a given *Schreiberei*. It was logical to think that such figures might converge around some norm or average in an ideal scribe's practice. Statistical analysis confirms that the reform legislation of 1817–21 not only decreased scribes' incomes overall, but, in regularizing administrative procedures across the kingdom, all but eliminated the income differential once dividing New Württemberg from Old Württemberg.[39] Apparently, this convergence suggested to OVK members that it was theo-retically possible to tally up the amount a typical scribe ought to have derived from each revenue source, and then compensate him on a per-person basis according to the population size of his district. Such a procedure had long been advocated by parliamentary and other public commentators on the *Schreiber* problem, who saw in capitation schemes a compelling alternative to the existing fee-for-service arrangement, which had enabled scribes to multiply business and inflate their incomes. Per capita figures had also featured prominently in the policy discourse of the old-regime duchy, where, on account of uniform administrative routines hammered out over centuries, district population sizes had correlated very well with total revenues.[40]

The problem was that in New Württemberg, by contrast, investigators could discover no mythical fixed quantum of business each citizen could be expected to generate. Divergent social customs and administrative histories in the new lands made it unfeasible simply to reckon the average yearly revenue a scribe should have derived from each client. These difficulties are visually apparent in an enormous chart the government drew up, which tabulated prescribed payments for various duties ranging from the taking of witness protocols to the drafting of final wills and testaments (see figure 11).[41] The chart's rows listed these various forms of business, and its columns sampled several territories scattered around Württemberg's post-Napoleonic acquisitions. The old duchy was also included as a benchmark. If this format was intended to render the variation in methods of governance among the kingdom's regions easily readable, it was a miserable failure. The grid of categories it laid out did such violence to the diversity of administrative practices in Württemberg that individual entries had as many clarifications and exceptions as straightforward, numeric data. Column entries were filled with elaborate formulas for calculating official payments. A deposition in Ulm might be charged by the page, and one in Rottweil by the hour. A property sale might be certified by a moonlighting schoolteacher in New Württemberg, whereas in the old lands a scribe's expertise would be required. Since this made one-to-one comparison among regions extremely awkward, developing a uniform fee schedule became difficult, if not impossible. As a result, the OVK could never work out a compensation scheme based on such computations alone.

Such inconclusive findings were themselves instructive, however, for they compelled the OVK to plunge still deeper into the everyday lives of the communities the scribes served. If administrative practices could not be standardized as the irreducible elements of a scribe's income, then perhaps a pattern could yet be discerned in the geographic variation of certain economic behaviors requiring the scribe's official participation: the partition of inheritances, the creation of marital estates, the production of different crops and commodities. The Gordian knot produced by comparing abstract legal and administrative codes could, in other words, be severed by devoting more empirical attention to the underlying social practices giving local administration its varying contours.

These problems were addressed in a government report of 1823, comparing fee schedules in a series of New and Old Württemberg regions—but

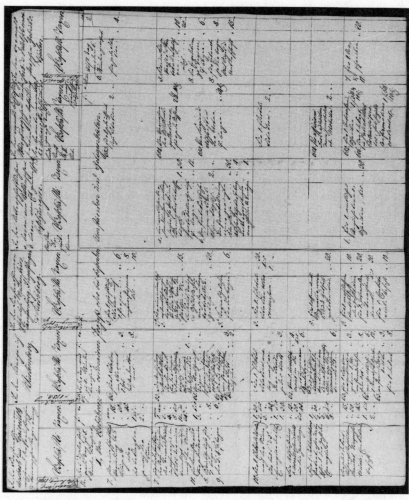

FIGURE 11. An almost illegible chart attempting to compare administrative practices in Württemberg's new acquisitions. Columns correspond to different regions in the kingdom, and rows to different written business formalities. Numbers indicate payments for various scribal services. Owing to the awkwardness of tabulation and comparison at the level of administrative routine, the OVK instead based its research into the scribes' income structures on deeper sociological variables. © Hauptstaatsarchiv Stuttgart, E 31 Bü 283.

this time narratively.[42] The report's findings were compiled from raw archival materials the government had more or less stumbled upon when taking possession of its new acquisitions. What it unearthed were insights into the multifarious individual choices and family strategies around which administrative routines had sedimented over the years. To take one example: in regions where marital property tended to be held jointly between husband and wife instead of separately, marriage contracts functioned as a sort of practical substitute for the estates inventories used for centuries in the old duchy. Contracts could be drawn up to regulate the devolution of marital property in the same way as inventories did, and were simply a different legal instrument adapted to different social practices but accomplishing the same end. With modern computerized spreadsheets, the correlation between joint marital property-holding and increased reliance on marriage contracts can be verified statistically, based on the OVK's own figures.[43] The point, however, is that in the early nineteenth century, such knowledge was generated intuitively. Qualitative, more than quantitative, inquiry conditioned bureaucrats' instincts about the way administration was run in a variety of social settings; this form of sociography cultivated in them an experiential sense for the rhythms of official power that they would have otherwise had no occasion to develop.

This social research facilitated the final breakthrough in formulating the actual compensation scheme in 1823. Armed with its rough-and-ready local knowledge and dissatisfied with the straight per capita index, the OVK devised a series of four classes based on sociological criteria, into which each *Schreiberei* would be placed.[44] Numbered I to IV, these classes were arranged by decreasing intensity of administrative exploitation. Four sub-classes were created for those districts whose populations were insufficiently large to merit inclusion in the scheme. This reflects an awareness among state officials that only with economies of scale do statistical regularities become apparent above and beyond the fixed costs associated with administrative overhead. For the purposes of compensation the OVK devised a simple formula based on the four-class system. A preliminary figure was obtained by multiplying the population size in a scribe's district (divided by one hundred) by a "tariff" ranging from 18 fl. in class I down to 12 fl. in class IV. It was thus a modified per capita system taking into account the varying administrative burden in each type of district. Ten percent was then deducted, since a fixed income was thought to be inherently preferable to a variable one. Finally, this formula would not apply to scribes already making less than what the tariff for their class granted them; these individuals would simply be offered their existing incomes, again, minus ten percent.

The key variables within the four-class system were the raw extent of land parcellization and the specific type of agriculture predominating in a given district. The practice of parcelling out property among heirs naturally generated more business for the scribes—more estates inventories, testaments, contracts, and the like. Additionally, certain crops, in particular, lent themselves to partible inheritance more than others and/or simply generated more income, which again helped to line the scribes' pockets. A vineyard (corresponding to class I) was worth more than twice the same area of arable cropland (class II), which was in turn almost four times as valuable as a forested plot of equal size (class III).[45] While thus ultimately dependent on local ecology, the scribes' incomes were also subject to intervening social factors concerning how the land was cultivated: how it was arranged in plots, managed as an economic operation, and above all, transferred to the next generation. For these reasons, the assignment of counties to classes could not be made on the basis of wealth alone, because "poorer districts with an extensive division of land tend to be more profitable [to the scribes] than richer ones."[46]

Class I consisted of districts with a high parcellization of land in which viniculture formed a significant part of the local economy. Wine production, as a highly lucrative form of cultivation, was an operation suitable for division among one's sons; requiring far more labor than land, it could take place on very small plots.[47] This class was filled with many Old Württemberg counties whose vineyards still line the banks of the Neckar. Class II covered all other regions of high property division in which traditional cultivation (arable fields and hay meadows) was more the rule. Most of the rest of Old Württemberg, with the exception of certain pockets of the Black Forest, came under this designation, as did a number of New Württemberg *Schreibereien* located in former city-states and other absorbed enclaves of the old duchy. Classes III and IV were reserved for those districts with a low parcellization of territory (closed inheritance, principally primogeniture). The former included regions where forestry coexisted with field cultivation, and swept over many New Württemberg counties ringing the Swabian Jura, as well as the northeast plains of the Hohenlohe regions. In these regions, the relatively large size of property holdings—especially in woodland districts requiring extensive cultivation techniques, offering low profit, and thus unsuited to partible inheritance—made for less need to enlist the scribes' services.[48] For those areas where closed inheritance was not only socially practiced but mandated by law, class IV was created. Here, in the southeastern counties between the Danube and Lake Constance, not only were parcels of land kept intact over the generations, but they were held in

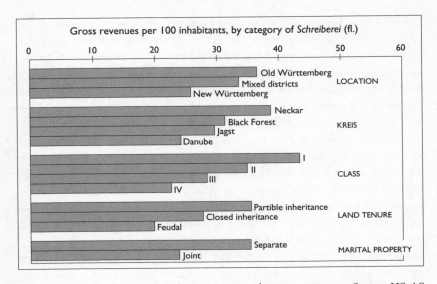

Gross revenues per 100 inhabitants, by category of *Schreiberei* (fl.)

FIGURE 12. Social geography of administrative exploitation, 1821–23. Source: HStAS E 301 Bü 106, Übersicht der Stadt- und Amtsschreibereien mit Notizen über ihren bisherigen Umfang und ihren Ertrag, 1821–1823. These data were calculated as follows: for each district, a per capita exploitation figure was arrived at by dividing total *Schreiberei* revenues by district population size; then, to figure the values charted above, individual figures from the districts in each category were averaged on an unweighted basis. Note that all figures reflect exploitation per *100* inhabitants.

a sort of feudal tenure. Due to the inalienability of property, these districts tended to generate the least amount of business for the scribes.

With these classes in place we are now in a position to appreciate the variability of administrative exploitation according to sociographic indices the OVK devised. By "administrative exploitation" is meant the total economic burden placed by the state on local communities through various compulsory and noncompulsory transaction fees for the scribes' services. Figure 12 is a social geography of exploitation showing the scribes' gross revenues per 100 inhabitants for different types of *Schreiberei,* and is complemented by a color-shaded map graphically illustrating these same figures county by county (see figure 13). The table (not an original OVK source but a computerized assessment of its results) is laid out according to a series of political and social criteria. The average exploitation for all districts whose scribes were eligible for compensation was 32.37, remarkably close to the overall figure (32.13) that results when one also includes provisionally occupied *Schreibereien* whose scribes were not so entitled.[49] Not surprisingly,

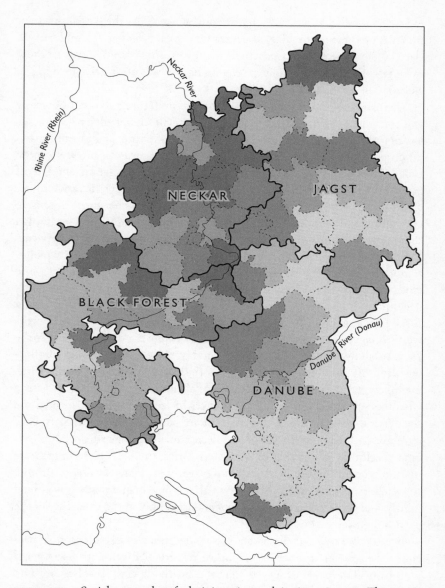

FIGURE 13.   Social geography of administrative exploitation, 1821–23. This map's five hues correspond to the five quintiles of the kingdom's *Schreibereien* when ranked by per capita income: the darker the color, the more intensive the scribes' financial exactions. Note that only the principal *Schreiberei* of each county was considered in determining its color; a substantial number of smaller district *Schreibereien* beneath the county level could not be represented visually.

the county of Ilsfeld, a class I wine-producing area near the Neckar north of Stuttgart, exhibited the highest per capita exploitation (71.17), and Isny, in class IV down near Lake Constance, the lowest (only 3.60). Between these extremes, the distribution of exploitation figures was quite even, forming an elegant bell curve.

The principal visual impression conveyed by figure 12 is that of a clear and consistent decline within each set of variables graphed: by geographic location, *Kreis*, compensation class, form of land tenure, and form of marital property. High figures are observed, in other words, in precisely those types of district where one would expect intensive exploitation, and fall off progressively among districts increasingly less likely to be lucrative to the scribes. Thus Old Württemberg, a center of partible inheritance, intensive agricultural cultivation, and elaborate textual forms, bore a heavier burden than New, with mixed Old-New counties falling somewhere in between. When viewed by *Kreis*, it becomes even clearer that administrative exploitation varied in direct proportion to one's proximity to the old duchy's core lands: the nearer to Württemberg's historic heartland, the heavier the burden suffered. Hence the core Neckar region, followed by the neighboring Black Forest, exhibited high exploitation, while the newly annexed northwestern Jagst *Kreis*, trailed by the remotest counties down south, near the Danube, showed lower figures. Most notably, there is a steady and continuous drop-off from class I to class IV, a finding that confirms the government's hypotheses about the intensity of exploitation. The same holds true when one abstracts out only the practices of land tenure that formed the sociological basis for the four-class system: partible inheritance correlates strongly with high exploitation and decreases in regions of closed inheritance, declining still further in feudal territories. Finally, regions of separate marital property naturally created more legally mandated business, through compulsory estates inventories, than those in which property was held jointly, and subject to contractual renegotiation only at the insistence of the parties themselves.

Because it predicted the actual social conditions of exploitation so precisely, the compensation system worked remarkably well both fiscally and politically. The OVK observed that the tariff for class I—the core Old Württemberg—differed very little from previous estimates that had been made for the "better *Schreibereien* of the old lands" and expressed confidence that the same would hold true for the other classes. One can check this prediction by dividing the base tariff rate, 12–18 fl., by the actual per capita income generated, respectively, in each class of county, 22.78–43.49 fl. (from diagram 8 again). This reveals that scribes were effectively compensated at a rate ranging from 41% to 53% of their gross revenues, a proportion that squares remarkably well with the percentage of revenues that scribes already took home under the existing fee-for-service arrangement (38–51%, from diagram 5). Overall, the scribes' incomes declined by 22.45%, and no category of scribes suffered disproportionately from the compensation offered. Though some individuals fared well and others poorly as a result of this formula, no one group, when taken according to the political and sociological variables developed by the OVK, lost less than a fifth or much more than a quarter of its 1822 income.[50] This feat of financial balancing deserves special emphasis, since no necessary mathematical relation existed between actual incomes and calculated compensation. The OVK had simply *derived* a correlation between the two by a process of trial and error—one that was crucially informed by its sociographic investigations and incorporated into the four-class system. Thus the burden of compensation was distributed with a remarkable political deftness, so that no scribe could complain of discrimination on account of his geographic, social, or administrative location.

The OVK's achievement, in its compensation scheme, was based on the realization that sociography naturally complemented and reinforced reform edicts; social analysis enabled reformers to anticipate and adjust for the effects of their policies on civil society. Payment reform in particular, inasmuch as it opened a window on the sphere of local economy and society, proved the most effective instrument for disciplining the scribes. The OVK's methods for calculating the scribes' pensions resulted from a combination of educated guesswork about their daily official practices, pilot studies into the rural sociology of various counties, and, not least, a finely honed political instinct about what degree of financial incentive would be necessary to placate the scribes. In particular, the OVK's ability to defuse the formation of potential interest blocs among the scribes—whether based on common region, social geography, or other structural characteristics—prevented political groupings from coalescing around these same criteria. Precisely this type of shared disadvantage, years earlier and without the government's knowledge or understanding, had once inspired the Black Forest Cahier, after all. Combined with the other gains of Napoleonic policymaking, the OVK's painstaking research greatly increased the likelihood that no systematic resistance would emerge to the government's reform legislation—and it never did.

The disbursement of compensation incomes in 1823 left the OVK only one more task to complete its reforms and cement compliance with its enactments. Recall that their entire scheme had relied on the scribes' good conscience in reporting their incomes. Though the final four-class compensation method was mathematically independent of such figures, they nonetheless had provided the baseline for comparison throughout the calculation effort. OVK commissioners wanted to verify that their income benchmark had not been systematically inflated from the beginning, and then allowed to propagate through their calculations. Just as modern sociologists employ a variety of polling techniques to circumvent respondents' dishonesty and reluctance, government officials deviously employed a system of countervailing incentives that led scribes alternately to underestimate and overestimate their incomes. First they consulted the scribes' tax returns for the period 1821–25, which, like all tax returns, had a built-in incentive to minimize reported incomes. These they compared with the original income surveys of 1821, which had encouraged scribes to err on the high side in the hopes of maximizing future compensation. Whether any given scribe cheated on his income taxes or inflated his OVK survey income can never be known. Realizing this, commissioners arrived at an approximate version of the truth by averaging and adjusting the two figures. Discrepancies between taxable incomes and incomes used for compensation were quite high, ranging from 20–60% of the latter figure for most scribes.[51]

The government used these findings to discipline the scribes, complementing edict with enforcement in pragmatic recognition of its own limited powers of administrative fiat. OVK commissioners devoted a great deal of energy to auditing the scribes' income tax returns and then penalizing them with a diligence usually associated only with modern bureaucracies. Classic wrangling over itemized deductions for business expenses, like office supplies and travel on horseback, occupied their time. In 1825–26 several scribes were even required to submit formal explanations for discrepancies as low as 19 fl., whereas one honest soul, the *Schreiber* Ott in Horb, actually received a rebate for having overreported his income on his tax return.

A much less righteous or moralistic conception of official duty and its limits animated the government's thinking during the entire compensation and auditing process, particularly in contrast with the days of protocolled investigations. The state had begun to view its own officials as mere local notables, salaried and disciplined as bureaucrats but living out their lives in civil society. From the initial culling of their income surveys to the sociographic assessment of administrative exploitation to the verification of its own compensation reform, the OVK treated the local economy not as a creature of the state's command but as an autonomous entity governed by its own logic and laws. Information was extracted from this sphere on a need-to-know basis and then used to construct schematic models of institutions, like the *Schreiberei,* that were too complex and embedded in local life to be grasped in full detail. Its attitude upon obtaining such information was nothing if not modern, in the sense that, like most contemporary governments, it inculcated obedience through systems of incentives, reliance on self-policing, and spot-checking, not through paternalistic intervention. During the post-Napoleonic period, these corollary practices of sociography reflected a maturation of the state as a corps of bureaucratic officials. Bureaucratization did not mean simply elevating officials out of the "system of needs," as Hegel had seen it. Restyling the scribes as impartial agents of the state instead required attention precisely to the material and social conditions of their lives in civil society.

On account of the successful and far-reaching nature of the reform effort, the history of Württemberg scribal personnel dissolves into pure tedium after the 1820s. Notaries public in the young kingdom were no more controversial or corrupt or ambitious than notaries public anywhere in the modern world. The reform movement not only reflected the state's own disengagement from civil society, but also enforced an actual decline in the scribes' social position and career horizons. Through the 1820s, scribes and local officials became nothing if not solidly *bürgerlich* and well integrated with other town notables in terms of intermarriage, family structure, economic prospects, education, values, and lifestyle.[52] And by 1867, with the publication of a new handbook for Court Notaries on the costs of living in their assigned districts, the scribes' devolution into humble careerist functionaries was complete.[53] The most important outcome of the reform effort of the 1820s was that officials could no longer look to the state for succor and protection. Quite the opposite: many of them sought opportunity in civil society itself. The coda to this chapter shows how entrepreneurial rivals to the scribes cut into the scribes' former monopolies to pursue their own career paths—and did so independently.

KNOWLEDGE ENTREPRENEURS

The state's production of knowledge about civil society in the 1820s had as its mirror image a growing desire among the citizenry for better understanding of a government that had become more distant and detached. The legal reforms of 1817–21 had done away with the mechanisms of textual recourse granting access to the state under the scribes' tutelage. This facilitated the emergence of a new kind of advocate to shepherd citizens through their dealings with state authority. During the very years when the scribes were losing their grip on power, a number of ambitious entrepreneurs filled the breach they left behind by marketing their own expert knowledge to the populace. This group was dominated by ex-bureaucrats who had come to realize that their professional expertise and personal connections were valuable commodities in the post-Napoleonic world. Such "knowledge entrepreneurs" focused their energies on the state's petitioning apparatus. Under their influence, the same channels that Bolley and others had once used for their legalistic machinations became a forum through which to navigate bureaucratic red tape and obtain official dispensations for various types of independent economic activity. Official knowledge had begun to acquire a market value, which partly supplanted its previous political function.

The destruction of the scribes' functional monopolies had opened the formal space for this entrepreneurial activity to develop. Far from emerging exclusively from the 1817–22 reform legislation, however, this transformation was several decades in the making. Recall from the previous chapter that the Napoleonic annexations had provoked a flood of petitions from disgruntled citizens that an overtaxed government found itself forced to ignore. In response, the Württemberg state had enacted a wave of provisional edicts unburdening central authorities and shifting responsibility for handling citizen petitions to regional and local gatekeepers. Issued between 1807 and 1811, the new policies placed more trust in local officials to screen out frivolous grievances and relay only those of real significance to higher state organs.[54] Oral testimony was henceforth preferred to written protocolling except in extremely complex cases, and often a concise report drafted by the local *Oberamtmann* substituted for the ranting complaints that tended to be found in petitions drawn up by disgruntled citizens themselves.

These reforms aimed to prevent the irregularity, forgery, subornment, and ventriloquism that had been the stock-in-trade of the Old Württemberg scribes. A new emphasis was placed on the scribe's personal legal responsibility for the petitions he drafted. The comprehensive Notarial Ordinance of 1808 also prescribed a new set of standardized formalities to be observed by all officials—not just scribes—in drawing up documents based on citizen testimony.[55] It covered all day-to-day written instruments from wills and testaments to the certification of property transactions to marriage contracts. Among the provisions of the 1808 ordinance were the requirements that witnesses be mentally and physically sound, not blind, deaf, mute, or insane; that regular protocols be taken during all notarial proceedings, noting the day, hour, location, and names of all witnesses and other participants; and that transcripts be read back to the parties present for verification before being signed and sealed. Great emphasis was placed on the notary's duty to ensure that the parties to any written legal transaction understood their responsibilities and commitments.

These provisions constituted not so much innovations upon as clarifications of the government's existing policies. Implicit in its reasoning was the conviction that simple, honest grievances, presented cleanly and clearly, could be addressed with justice and swiftness. All else was the result of what it called *Klagewerk*—campaigns of complaint that stemmed more from troublemaking (and frequently penurious) local officials than the nominal complainants themselves. By the late 1810s, to stem the tide of random petitions still flowing into its chancelleries, the government devoted its (limited) resources to making examples of such campaigners. In 1818, for example, a poor Nagold schoolteacher was forced to pay a hefty penalty for improperly drafted petitions and a Stuttgart *Substitut* was actually jailed for three weeks for the same reason.[56]

While the reforms prescribed harsh penalties for those who attempted to circumvent these cumbersome channels and address the royal government directly, it would be unfair to accuse the government of illiberality. The Württemberg state remained quite open to citizens' voices during the post-Napoleonic period. One scribe from Crailsheim was even penalized for interpreting the laws too narrowly, having failed to transmit what the government found to be a perfectly legitimate supplication he had been asked to prepare.[57] In general, the government inclined to err on the side of mildness precisely because this was the philosophy that had underpinned the emancipatory *Schreiber* reform legislation of 1817: if citizens were to be entrusted with financial and other affairs once supervised by the scribes, they had to be given the leeway to make mistakes while learning their new responsibilities.[58] The state's aim was to streamline interactions with its subjects, not cut them off completely. It simply wanted to ensure that citizens did not take advantage of its indulgence. Allowing the various arms of government to do their respective jobs without fear of ad hoc interference provoked by petitions was entirely in keeping with the dignity of a *Rechtsstaat*. Thus, all the legal infrastructure was in place by 1810 for less monopolistic avenues of access to the state. This potential to widen the avenues of communication between government and society simply lay dormant until after the reform legislation had deprived the scribes of their power.

A more diffuse, but at the same time more decisive, contribution to the widening of social knowledge was a broad cultural movement in the 1820s for the democratization of official writing practice. This period witnessed an explosion in do-it-yourself handbooks for everyday people advising them how to wend their way through bureaucratic channels as well as dealings with their fellow citizens. Friedrich Bauer's *Introduction to the Management of Written Business for Civil Life,* for example, was written not only for officials but also schoolteachers, merchants, artisans, and "businessmen from all classes" wishing to improve their communications skills.[59] The manual was issued in several editions, each covering the various business forms and legal customs of a different region in Germany. It came complete with a series of boilerplate forms for handling occasions as diverse as drafting prenuptial agreements, welfare applications *(Armuthsatteste),* apartment leases, and IOUs; petitioning for widows' pensions; certifying real estate sales between private parties; settling boundary disputes between neighbors; and preparing powers of attorney, birth announcements, and business receipts. The book offered sage advice for those who "hesitate in uncertainty when writing and linking words" and who generally felt awkward in official situations. Simple, direct, on-the-point pleas were the most efficacious, it advised. Long-windedness, insincerity, and sycophantic flourishes (*"allerunterthänigst, devotest, demüthigst"*) were seldom appreciated. Good handwriting and solid visual presentation—text should always appear in a rectangle on the page and avoid "artistry" in layout—always inspired respect. Red seals (or black seals, but only in the case of condolence letters) should be applied with fine wax.

As part of an extensive genre of *Briefsteller,* guides to the proper drafting of both business and personal correspondence, works like Bauer's facilitated the shift from face-to-face collegiality to more impersonal networks of written communication accompanying the advent of civil society.[60] "In this way," Bauer's introduction counseled, "everyone is in the position to converse with a faraway person as if he were present." Exchanges became not only more impersonal but more directed to a specific end, a situation that required extreme delicacy to avoid brusqueness and offense. Moreover, the loosening of legal restrictions on the textual style of official documents meant that such formalities as terms of address ("Your Excellency," etc.) became all the more important as parts of an informal but equally elaborate etiquette.[61]

It was in this situation, finally, that well-positioned knowledge entrepreneurs could make themselves useful as advisors and consultants. They possessed precisely the practical knowledge and cultural literacy that anxious letter-writers and petitioners fearful of a remote state had occasion to draw upon. Composed largely of officials, whether still employed in various governmental capacities, recently let go, or long since retired, this group of individuals pressed the government for dispensations to allow them to draw up petitions for which the scribes had formerly been necessary.[62] Many of their pleas explicitly invoked the liberalizing legislation of the previous two decades. Dispensation requests came mainly from attorneys, schoolteachers, tax collectors, bookkeepers, jurists, and treasurers. Generally, those with some form of university education saw their requests rubber-stamped by the government. Dispensation pleas from those of humbler origin, however, were submitted to a more skeptical vetting. Uniformly, however, would-be consultants appealed to an ideology of good householding, according to which a well-fed official was a politically trustworthy and quiescent official. This was precisely the principle the OVK had adopted in compensating the scribes, which underlay its entire campaign to view officials as situated in civil society. Now petitioners turned this logic back upon the government to justify their petitions for new business. A great number of them had lost their positions during the bureaucratic reform wave of the 1820s and found retirement pensions insufficient to cover their domestic needs, with hungry mouths to feed at home. The vast majority were simply looking for a means to supplement their incomes with duties that could be performed by any educated person, but for which they possessed a special aptitude and ability.

A particularly interesting subset of these cases came from individuals who saw in the cultural and institutional climate of the 1820s the chance for a whole new career, and it was they who founded the precocious enterprises known as "commission bureaus" *(Commissions-Bureaux)*. Commission bureaus served the business needs of local merchants with designs on regional markets. They prepared translations and expert opinions, placed help-wanted ads in intelligence gazettes (see Chapter 8), navigated thickets of bureaucratic regulation, and mediated "private contacts that . . . customers cannot or do not wish to form," as one business prospectus put it.[63] The most elaborate prospectus for a commission bureau was submitted by the retired treasury official Carl Benjamin Nast in Ludwigsburg, north of Stuttgart.[64] Nast typified the downsized bureaucrat of the 1820s: well-connected, knowledgeable, and in the prime of life, but deprived of official employment in an era when educated men were overabundant and bureaucratic positions were less and less plentiful. Forced out of office by cutbacks in the tax collection administration, Nast found he needed extra money to supplement his pension and feed his five minor children. His petition to draw up supplications on his clients' behalf was granted in 1823, on the condition that he accept personal responsibility for his submissions to the government in accordance with the new legislation.

As motivation for his undertaking, Nast's petition cited "collected knowledge and rich experience" and "multifarious personal and written acquaintances acquired through previous journeys" as well as "the support of cultivated and educated men" he counted as friends. All these appeals were common formulas reflecting both the broad-based enthusiasm for the types of services men like Nast had to offer and the personal contacts and networks they could draw upon in order to make their ventures viable. Nast also cited as a precedent for his operation a consultancy founded in the previous year by another retired official, an accountant in Reutlingen.[65] The Reutlingen office had in turn been inspired by the example of a commission bureau in Mainz, itself originally founded to facilitate shipping between the left and right banks of the Rhine. In that city, the annexation of the left bank by Napoleonic France had created a wealth of new, formally international, commerce to which various new legal and bureaucratic regulations applied. The Mainz bureau was open from 8:00 to 12:00 in the morning and from 2:00 to 5:00 in the afternoon. Pro bono services were offered to poorer clients able to document their penury officially. Such altruism, albeit certainly motivated by a desire to please state officials, is striking for its appeal to the democratic potentials of modern civil society: everyone had business to perform, and everyone should enjoy the services of private consultants to do so. Besides being further evidence of the very collegiality that commission bureaus were intended to promote, this chain of connections establishes a direct link between Biedermeier Württemberg and the Napoleonic era.

Nast's prospectus for the Ludwigsburg commission bureau was even more ambitious than that of its grandfather institution in Mainz. It showcased all the ways in which officials like him intended to derive monetary gain from their administrative expertise. "This institution," he wrote, "is well suited for the times" and would perform the following functions:

1. all private business missions that [clients] do not wish or are unable to undertake for themselves;

2. the handling of petitions to the government, courts, city and village councils, insofar as these are not suited for the competence of attorneys;

3. the handling of correspondence and private matters both in domestic and foreign trade centers, not just in the German but also the French, Italian, and English languages, which also includes translations of letters, excerpts of legal documents and essays;

4. the management of private financial matters and the auditing and checking of [private finances];

5. expert opinions and written and oral advisories on trade matters and other matters arising in civil and commercial life.

That private consultancies flourished during the 1820s is, to say the least, a surprising finding for a period commonly thought to have wallowed in economic stagnation and backwardness. To be sure, they generated so little activity that none of the historical literature has even registered their presence, and even their archival traces remain thin. Despite their limited practical impact, however, the commission bureaus point to a deeper fascination with administrative knowledge as a vehicle of influence. The opportunity to create and exploit such knowledge had become available to a much wider range of groups after the fall of the scribes. The state's own bureaucrats comprised one such group, as we have seen in this chapter, and the citizenry itself—through various new species of local notables—another. The last two chapters of this book turn to the activities of those on both sides of the civic divide during the decades after the scribes' fall from power. Their collaboration created new knowledge about civil society and lay the basis for a renewed civic culture in nineteenth-century Württemberg.

7 Cataloging the Social World

Starting in the 1820s, the state's relationship with civil society was increasingly mediated by print. Because the reform of the *Schreiberei* deliberately curtailed handwritten exchange between them, the well-established technology of print could emerge as a natural alternative to the scribes' tutelage. The shift, it should be emphasized, was by no means automatic. As the OVK's sociographic methods showed, handwriting, still the quickest way to process information nimbly, played a vital role in an age otherwise dominated by print culture. Print enjoyed the unique advantage, however, of bringing information to the masses. For the state, it offered a compelling new means of addressing communities recently gathered into synthetic units of administrative and territorial convenience—the counties, or *Oberämter,* that replaced the cantons of the old duchy. For the citizenry, it made information with practical value regularly and anonymously available, in large quantities and without the assistance of intermediaries. After the scribes' fall, for local officials and bourgeois notables alike, it became possible to "read" civil society through print media taking sociographic, and in particular statistical, form.

The migration of sociographic techniques out of the bureaucratic chancelleries and into civil society catalyzed two new civic institutions taking printed form: statistical-topographical almanacs and intelligence gazettes. These are treated in the current chapter and in the next, respectively. Almanacs provided a comprehensive overview of each *Oberamt's* geography, economy, history, and population, while gazettes were county newspapers providing information of practical, and explicitly nonpolitical, import. Both media originated in the intellectual ferment of the German Enlightenment, whose encyclopedic imagination found a perfect outlet in the dissemination of practical knowledge on every conceivable aspect of social life. Both media made a relatively late appearance in Württemberg, having initially developed in more Enlightenment-friendly states in the 1700s. Both, however, spread rapidly and systematically in the kingdom, county by county, between the 1820s and the 1840s. The new print media not only sociographically represented but also materially propelled civil society's growth. At first, both almanacs and gazettes promoted state administrators' needs for quick and reliable data on the communities they served. Both media, however, evolved in a more popular direction, responding to a deeply diffused bourgeois enthusiasm for information and edification. Enveloping their producers and readers in novel practices of communication and association, they forged communities—imagined and concrete—among citizens, independently of the state.[1] Manifestations of a burgeoning supralocal civil society, they constituted the most significant change in Württemberg's civic landscape after the reform era. By popularizing the Enlightenment and bringing it to the villages, informational print media made encyclopedism a provincial and not merely a cosmopolitan passion.

The flourishing of a modern, Enlightened encyclopedism in the provincial counties of a post-Napoleonic kingdom belies our received image of Biedermeier Germany as a quaint, narrow world of philistines or *Spießbürger*, rooted in Romantic naturalism, hostile to intellectual abstractions, and ever-vigilant against the disruptive influence of a modernizing state.[2] Statistical-topographical almanacs and intelligence gazettes thrived instead on a peculiar cohabitation of modernity and traditionalism rooted in an unprecedented degree of cooperation between state officials and local citizens. The collaboration of these groups gave local color to the abstractions of the administrative mind even as it subjected provincials to bracing encounters with the more complex and anonymous social world taking shape around them.[3] The texts they produced animated the skeleton institutions of post-Napoleonic civil society with a vision of local and statewide identity to replace the cantonal patriotism so jealously guarded by the *Schreiber*. And whereas the scribes brought citizens into contact with the world around them through administrative, legal, and political texts, new civic leaders did so with statistical description and topographic depiction, practical information and didactic instruction. The individuals drawn to these projects, despite an extreme diversity in social background, straddled the realms of cosmopolitan and provincial society just as the scribes had, but now in a more informal way. Held together by cultural rather than administrative ties, local officials and bourgeois notables occupying the civic stratum vacated by the scribes began to cohere into a new leadership class.

STATISTICAL TOPOGRAPHY

Statistical science in its eighteenth-century incarnation stood at a drastic remove from the mind of the Biedermeier provincial. It instead reflected the concerns of the cameralist and the cosmopolitan. Enthusiasm for statistics, and especially for the subdiscipline of statistical topography, was a phenomenon of the Central European Enlightenment that affected many parts of Germany. In Württemberg, however, statistics only gained widespread popularity after Napoleon's invasions, and even then on account of its practical utility to the state, not for its potential to refurbish the sphere of civic life. Nonetheless, "Statistik," in its development over several decades, forged a path for encyclopedism to enter the nineteenth-century kingdom, bringing its multifarious objects of intellectual interest to bear on Württemberg's civic culture.

Unlike the modern-day numerical science, cameralist Statistik, literally a "science of the state," encompassed all the individual data bearing on its power and strength, including laws, ordinances, treaties, and other political information. It was less concerned with arithmetical tabulation than with the systematic collection of "noteworthy political facts" (staatsmerkwürdige Nachrichten). Gottfried Achenwall (1719–72), the Göttingen professor who popularized the term and its associated methods, emphasized the minute, mundane, day-to-day changes in law, manufacture, trade, finance, and the military underlying larger constitutional and political events. His approach allowed leading intellectuals to keep a running pulse on the state's powers. Achenwall's Universitätsstatistik, so called because of its intimate affiliation with seminars at universities like Göttingen and Halle (a Zeitungskolleg at the former met weekly to discuss statistical information in newspaper articles), anticipated the later bourgeois passion for practical knowledge but at this early date remained largely a concern of the academic elite.[4]

Over time, Statistik acquired a following outside the ivory tower and, in the process, accreted a variety of other subject matters. A variegated, almost hodgepodge discipline by the end of the Enlightenment, it truly encompassed an encyclopedic range of concerns. Achenwall's student August Ludwig Schlözer (1735–1809) introduced a livelier style and a thicker, more empirical description to his mentor's rather dry, but likewise qualitative techniques of intelligence gathering. Among his many substantive contributions, he made folklore and ethnology central to statistical method. By the 1780s, folklore (Volkskunde), originally an offshoot of statistics, had become a discipline in its own right.[5] Johann Peter Süßmilch (1707–67), the third titan of German *Statistik,* brought quantitative methods decisively into the fold in his influential treatise, *Divine Order in the Development of the Human Race, Based on its Birth, Death, and Propagation* (1741).[6] To call this text a theologically-inspired arithmetical demography does not clarify matters especially well. What it did was tabulate population statistics, drawing on Prussian administrative sources to discern a Providential role in the development of populations, a project some scholars have assimilated to the Foucauldian concerns of "biopolitics."[7]

It is an oversimplification to argue, as Ian Hacking has done, that the eighteenth century kept statistics under tight wraps whereas the nineteenth published with abandon. Publicity was in crucial respects the lifeblood even of early cameralist *Statistik.* Various cameralistic journals, such as Schlözer's influential *Staatsanzeigen* or Johann Peter Ludewig's *Dresdner Intelligenzblatt,* published statistical information as a basis for creative comparison and intellectual discussion among thinkers in the various German states.[8] As we will see in the chapter on intelligence gazettes, this symbiosis between statisticians as avid collectors of information and the press as a mouthpiece for it contributed to the development of the public sphere and the popularization of practical reason in Enlightenment Germany.

The proliferation of new knowledges, and the growth of an educated reading public eager both to generate and to consume them, led to an active cross-pollination between statistical and rival literary genres. The spate of statistical-topographical works that flourished starting in the 1780s marked the confluence of classical *Statistik* with the colorful ethnographic and geographical sensibility of late Enlightenment travel literature, newly focused on the German *Volk* as anthropological "other."[9] The products of this synthesis were, in intellectual conception, both pioneering and vague. A rash of "lexicons," "dictionaries," and "descriptions" prefacing their titles with concatenations like "geographic-statistical" or "historical-statistical-geographic-topographical," sometimes adding terms such as "technical," "hydrographical," or "orographical" for good measure, speaks to the infatuation with a new science, exciting and inchoate, whose coordinates could not entirely be pinned down. Each of these almanacs focused on a particular German (or sometimes other European) territory, gathered together as much data as could be had given the limited development of census-taking and other survey methods, and spiced up this technical presentation with copious commentaries on local customs and habits, all for the consumption of a national literary class.[10]

All this activity reflected a shift within the German intelligentsia from a state-centered elite whose statistical researches, for all their worldliness, retraced the hermeneutic circle of old-regime legal and political history, to a widely dispersed class of cosmopolitans taking a more fluid and flexible approach to the ascertainment of regional and national characteristics. Representative of the old school was Johann Jakob Moser, the staid Württemberg "anti-philosophe" who staked his literary reputation on painstaking reconstructions of constitutional law in the various German states. Though one of the most renowned and well-traveled statesmen of the late Holy Roman Empire, Moser never fully imbibed Enlightenment in its promiscuously encyclopedic modern forms.[11] Another statistical historian of this type was Christian Friedrich Sattler, the famed Württemberg state archivist who, doffing his hat to the new craze, had renamed his 1752 *Historical Description* of Württemberg a *Topographical History* by 1784. It was only a cosmetic change. While Sattler's history cataloged interesting tidbits from each of the old cantons (grouped according to their date of acquisition), the work, which at one point encompassed seventeen volumes, never overcame an exclusively high-political conception of topography, centering as it did on the various wars, contracts, and machinations whereby individual pieces of territory came into the dukes' possession.[12]

By contrast, Leopold Krug's *Topographical-Statistical-Geographical Dictionary of the Entire Prussian State* (1796–1803; reissued in the 1820s) ran only thirteen volumes (!), and reflected a more modern sensibility, anticipating the author's later concern with national productivity. Krug, a theologian trained at Halle who then leapt to amateur statistical topography, made his name in political economy, helping to popularize the ideas of Quesnay, Mirabeau, Steuart, and Smith in Germany.[13] His southern German counterpart Philipp Ludwig Heinrich Röder, another amateur, likewise cobbled together diverse statistical information while exhibiting less disciplinary focus than Krug. For his wide oeuvre, which included books on Swabia, Saxony, and even Italy, Röder employed a flexible style of anthropological fieldwork transportable from location to location and independent of local historiographical traditions for its findings. What he lacked in systematic presentation he made up for in ethnographic sensitivity—to dialect, material culture, and customary legal and religious usages.[14] This approach also stamped the work of Christian Heinrich Niemann, professor at Kiel, who similarly mixed together local statistics with natural and climatological description and analyses of communal constitutions, folk festivals and costumes, and food and housing customs.[15] Together, Krug, Röder, and Niemann speak to both the limitations and potential of statistical topography as it was practiced at the end of the Enlightenment, the field having exploded the boundaries of the old "science of state" but lacking institutional (state- or university-based) organization for its efforts.

Despite its powerful intellectual reorientation, statistical topography remained a movement whose roots in society remained as shallow as the German intelligentsia itself. Napoleon's conquests were thus able to prune back a great deal of its mental overgrowth, imposing a new regimentation on the statistical extravagance indulged by aficionados of the fin-de-siècle. Napoleon was both kind and unkind to the genre. His scramblings of territory put questions of topographical history literally on the map, but the censorious climate of his rule tamped down a formerly free-wheeling literary industry. Röder, to be sure, flourished from his base in Ulm, publishing two works dedicated to Württemberg's post-Napoleonic acquisitions (1804, 1812); his colleagues there produced topographies of Bavaria, Saxony, and the Rhenish lands.[16] Krug, having fought the censors throughout the 1790s, joined the Prussian administration and helped found its Statistical-Topographical Bureau, where he remained somewhat patronized and frustrated. In the main, however, the Napoleonic period witnessed a distinct lull in the statistical-topographical genre before it picked up again in the looser climate of the 1820s. The site of innovation had simply shifted, temporarily, out of the public sphere and into the state. As we saw in Chapter 6, administrative reform delivered a tremendous push to the refinement of quantitative—no longer exclusively qualitative—statistical methods in Germany. The cold calculation of the bureaucrat had elbowed the traveling amateur folklorist out of the spotlight.

The history of administrative statistics is relatively well-documented for France, Prussia, and other states.[17] Its development under Napoleon was all the more pronounced in Württemberg. Owing to the cameralism's weakness there, a rapid retooling within the bureaucracy was necessary to convert the duchy's creaking statistical apparatus into a streamlined numbers factory. A potentially promising source for systematic data had of course always been the *Schreiber*, with their stockbooks and land registries and piles of tax receipts. As early as 1610, Württemberg law enjoined them to keep a *Historiebuch* recording all noteworthy and significant events in their districts, and by 1736 they were prodded to submit lists of commodity prices and other local news items to the Stuttgart *Weekly Announcements*.[18] Not surprisingly, these injunctions failed miserably. Better hopes lay with the more tractable and better educated local pastors, who kept lists of souls, *Familienbücher*, and other information, suitable for tabulation, on baptisms, marriages, and deaths. Starting in 1787, pastors could receive a small pittance for their input. Crude attempts at census-taking, based on such sources, dated back to 1598, but only in 1757 did a ducal rescript order a semi-periodical counting of the population. This later, strikingly modern census acknowledged the key methodological distinction between legal inhabitants and mere residents of a place, required local church and secular officials to poll and physically visit families house by house, and made provisions for localities to share information on families who had recently moved.[19]

Still, the crucial turning point came only in 1805–7, when Württemberg abandoned its old *Generaltabellen* and undertook a comprehensive statistical overview of the new kingdom based on a 56-page questionnaire circulated to the various *Oberämter*, starting with New Württemberg. A host of new administrative requirements under Napoleon, having to do with taxation, the public debt, conscription and recruiting, and the need to track a population rendered mobile by the stress of war, underlay the levying of more systematic statistical data.[20] Bees, pigs, goats, stillborns, bastards, beggars, baptisms: all were counted in one form or another under the new regime. Numbers like these provided a snapshot of national productivity at a time when mustering national strength and integrating national resources were of the utmost importance. The sheer multiplicity of counted objects validated a postcorporative conception of society, broken down not politically or socially, according to the various geographic or occupational estates of the realm (as in Sattler's or Moser's histories), but analytically, according to its underlying demographic habits and economic activities. This imposed an entirely new grid of categorization on civil society, one born of administrative control and uniformity. Along with such instrumental factors, the cultural co-determinants of this shift were even wider. A veritable mania for tabular information seems to have set in within the bureaucracy: thus by the early 1800s we find for the county of Wildberg a list of dances and an index of dogs mustered for military service.[21]

Over time, the statistical imagination did settle into well-worn ruts of administrative practice. The classification of objects acquired a standard shape and narrower scope, so that by 1815 it had become routine for *Oberamtmänner* to submit yearly reports based on a strict ordering and categorization of material and human resources.[22] The tripartite hierarchy of these *Jahresberichte* moved from land to populations to administration, reflecting the cameralist conception of society as a progression from raw materials to human productive capacity to the power of the state. In a typical *Jahresbericht*, the value of all fields, houses, sheepfolds, cattle, commons, gardens, vineyards, and the like was calculated, followed by statistical breakdowns of the population by religion, sex, occupation, and "source of sustenance." Last came the organization of various departments and notes on the administration of public health and other police measures. Each form had scores of thin columns with plenty of space left for correcting, in red pencil, the inevitable arithmetic errors that crept in before the age of calculators. Recalcitrant officials who provided inaccurate or untimely information were sternly admonished.

The Napoleonic statistical tables bear a striking resemblance to the OVK income reports collected on the *Schreiber,* and in fact directly anticipated them. Both handwritten genres illustrate how the numerical imagination infiltrated state administrative practice after Napoleon. This development simultaneously distanced statistical science from the historic wellsprings of its popularity in the Enlightenment. Severed from the broader public of late eighteenth-century cameralist journals and topographical travel almanacs, a leaner, more systematic *Statistik* developed at this time, one that took a more instrumental approach toward the fiscal, military, and administrative management of populations under the pressure of war and rapid territorial change. It thus seemed a radical departure when the decision was taken to disseminate this information in print.

PATRIOTIC SCIENCE

In its more systematic incarnation under the state's aegis, statistical topography had graduated from the stuff of theoretical statecraft and Enlightened encyclopedism to the lifeblood of practical administrative science. In policy-makers' eyes, statistical information had acquired a tangible relevance to building "national" strength, which in the lexicon of contemporaries almost always referred to the Württemberg kingdom—and, crucially, not to the German *Volk*.[23] Only the return of statistics to the public sphere, however, could complete the project of assembling practical knowledge begun in the Napoleonic state. "Partiotic science" was the name this project acquired when it was applied, through print and publication, to the cultivation of modern citizenship practice. Promoters of the new project believed that statistical topography, despite its historic associations with an Enlightened elite, could be made appealing and useful to much broader segments of the population. In collaboration with other influential elements in the kingdom, these promoters made encyclopedism a truly civic pursuit for the first time in Württemberg.

The Württemberg Statistical-Topographical Bureau was the brainchild of Finance Minister Ferdinand A. H. Weckherlin. Weckherlin, who appeared briefly in Chapter 2, was the same man who had authored an influential late-eighteenth-century *Apologie* for the scribes. He had also penned a topographical description of Urach at about the same time.[24] The Bureau began its existence as an outgrowth of Weckherlin's finance ministry, to which it was formally subordinate. It had access to the ministry's holdings in addition to its own staff and resources, and close ties to various other offices in the fiscal administration. These included the Land Measurement Office *(Landesvermessungsamt)*, which completed geographical surveys and a comprehensive cadastral registry of the kingdom, as well as a special lithographic institute that drafted relief maps later accompanying the county almanacs as inserts. These maps, such as the one depicting the famous "fog caves" of Reutlingen, were coveted by collectors of the series, and signaled a new use for state cartography outside strictly military purposes.

The Statistical-Topographical Bureau's connection to the most historically secretive branches of state government signaled a new willingness to apply hard-won statistical expertise to public functions, and a new conception of the state-society partnership generally. As late as 1817 a special *Collegium* forming the Bureau's immediate predecessor had espoused a narrowly cameralistic approach to statistics, having been charged with assembling "the most perfect knowledge of the state's powers," not putting such knowledge in citizens' hands. By 1820–21, however, the royal decree ordering the Bureau's foundation envisioned it as providing "to every government official *and* every Württemberger a precise and comprehensive knowledge of the condition and circumstances of the country *(Vaterland)*." It also enjoined local preachers, doctors, and town councillors to provide any information and fill out any tabular forms the bureau might require, adding that aficionados of what was now called "*Vaterlandskunde*" were more than welcome to send in "observations and collected reports" voluntarily.[25]

The enterprise of *Vaterlandskunde*, which can be translated as "patriotic science," fulfilled a desire among the kingdom's elite for more active and open governmental participation in the sponsorship of the sciences. The idea of organizing the Bureau's work around a series of county almanacs, the *Oberamtsbeschreibungen*, came from Queen Katharina herself, the former Russian princess distinguished by her activism in cultural affairs, who was impressed by a topographical chronicle penned by Government Councillor and former *Oberamtmann* Kausler about his former county of Neuenbürg.[26] Kausler published his findings in 1819. He was in turn named co-director of the bureau, alongside Johann David Georg Memminger, a former student at the prestigious Tübinger *Stift* where Hegel had roomed with Hölderlin. Memminger, who had authored a survey of the Cannstatt region and a comprehensive *Description, or Geography and Statistics* of Württemberg, was already a well-known topographer and statistician. His appointment elevated him to the rank of Professor, and it was his personality, more than any other (including Kausler's), that stamped the Bureau's development in its first two decades.

It thus befell Memminger to articulate a philosophy to underpin *Vaterlandskunde* and the mission of the Württemberg Statistical-Topographical Bureau: "So that everyone will have a knowledge of his country." Memminger stressed even more clearly than the state's edicts the new, explicitly civic role the government meant to stake out in the post-Napoleonic period.[27] His vision finally brought statistics in its modern, arithmetical form out of the protected hothouse of state fiscal administration and into the public sphere. Declaring that a "new era" had been inaugurated with King Wilhelm's rule, Memminger proclaimed that the "most impartial openness" had taken the place of a "nervous secrecy" in the publishing of numbers and other information. He viewed the new publicity in updated ideological terms as well. Unlike the eighteenth-century scientists of state, Memminger regarded his discipline as serving the ends of state and citizenry simultaneously. *Statistik* did not merely measure the state's capacities, as a handmaiden of administration and political science, but actively unleashed the energies of civil society by making "knowledge of the fatherland" available to the people.

Memminger's openness contrasted with the situation in France, where the state's patronage of statistical science had only exacerbated its centralizing, bureaucratic, and secretive tendencies. There, the ideological association of statistics with Napoleon's dictatorship tainted the whole enterprise, from which the French failed to recover fully until the early 1830s.[28] Elsewhere, in Bavaria, state-sponsored statistical topography confined itself to tasks like the drafting of relief maps for the military; Prussian statistics similarly long remained a creature of the state's administration.[29] Württemberg, by contrast, profited from its latecomer status by introducing statistics in a climate already quite congenial to the ideology of "publicity." In the eyes of the modernizing progressives, whose hegemony replaced that of the Good Old Law traditionalists, the publication of statistical knowledge constituted but one key part of society's general emancipation; Memminger's vision, for this reason, commanded widespread assent.

What else had changed in wake of the Napoleonic interregnum? The reemergence of *Statistik* into the public sphere imparted some momentum to many of the Enlightenment projects that this period had seen co-opted and disrupted. Descriptive topography and historical folklore, which had responded only haltingly to the need for topographical understanding in a time of territorial flux, now turned, in Memminger's hands, squarely toward quantitative methods. Much more knowledge was available now, and this was seductive. Memminger clearly reveled in the mountains of sociographic data he inherited from the Finance Ministry. Only with the state's comprehensive cataloging and quantifying had it become feasible to undertake a general survey of "every object, every house, every highway and byway, every spring, and every creek" in the kingdom. Administrative consolidation in this sense was accompanied by a new emphasis on nation-building, to which the state would contribute. Memminger declared his wish that Württembergers (again, not Germans generally) become a *"Volk"* as a result of his efforts. Knowledge and information would increase the "insight" the common citizen could use to scrutinize "political conditions" in his country and replace "narrow local and private interest" with "a higher sense of citizenship." In this contention, Memminger's notions of national identity stood in direct opposition to the traditions of local patriotism so beloved by the Württembergers. There was more than a trace of the state reformer's impatience with local autonomy lurking in his favorable quota-tion of Weckherlin, that where patriotic instincts could not find a broad out-let beyond the horizons of the hometown community, "state administra-tion" had been deprived of its "most powerful support." To shape the identity of a state-bounded *Volk,* and not just catalog its movements, lent modern statistical topography a potentially more intrusive role than the patronizing, but somewhat ineffectual, Enlightenment publicists had been able to imagine.

True, Memminger clearly accorded a much greater role to the civic and patriotic, as opposed to the purely statist, purposes of statistics than his eigh-teenth-century predecessors. His rhetoric partook more freely of the slogans of "fatherland," "citizenship," and "civic ability" and ascribed more indepen-dence to civil society than had been possible, or desirable, for the cameralists. Like Friedrich List, Memminger invested great importance in civil freedoms for their own sake: they forwarded movement, undermined prejudice, and formed an indispensable basis of the modern constitutional state, not mere concessions of administrative convenience. Knowledge, for both men, liber-ated the individual: "Ensure that the citizen comes to know his rights and freedoms," Memminger wrote, "and the rest will take care of itself." But Memminger's political philosophy also shared the same blind spots as List's about the justification and boundaries of state power in civil society, weak-nesses that distanced them both from classical liberalism. Neither saw knowledge, and citizen empowerment, as placing limits on the state, but rather viewed them as adding to its capacities. The only common referent among "state," "citizen," and "knowledge" was a Württemberg *Vaterland* cleansed of the provincial's stubborn resistance toward modernity.[30]

Lest we overdraw the sinister Foucauldian implications of the statistical project, as a means by which to colonize citizens' minds with new knowledge and make them productive for the state, it helps to fix the scale of Memminger's ambitions firmly within the limiting context of his science. His *Description, or Geography and Statistics*, the first in a series of pan-Württemberg statistical handbooks he authored, modeled what "knowledge of the fatherland" meant on the ground.[31] A pioneering innovation over Sattler's and Röder's earlier treatments, it inspired the county almanacs that followed it. More than previous works, Memminger's book brought the knowledges of state and science together to assess, dissect, and measure the various elements of the *Vaterland*. It devoted large sections to administrative and constitutional arrangements and political history, on the one hand—forming what would today be called a *politische Landeskunde*[32]—and geological, botanical, and topographical measurements and descriptions, on the other. Its most striking departure from the earlier topographical literature is its highly quantified sociography, manifest in a fascination with imponderably large numbers. We learn, for instance, that there were 306,477 houses in the kingdom; that 964,685 *Morgen* of Württemberg's territory were covered by settlements, roads, and the like; and that the entire net worth of all enterprises, capital instruments, cattle, buildings, real estate, mills, mines, etc.—the so-called national worth, or *Nationalvermögen*—totaled 1,000,662,800 fl.[33]

When it came to translating this cameralist-inspired "measurement" of the fatherland into a full-blown statistical topography of the Württemberg *Volk*, Memminger was nevertheless back in familiar territory. The task of assembling a *Volk* out of the disparate peoples inhabiting the kingdom of Württemberg outstripped even the formidable capabilities of Memminger and his collaborators, which included (perhaps unhelpfully for this purpose) a mineralogist and a zoologist. He thus took shortcuts, painting his picture of the *Volk* in broad strokes. Memminger conceded there were no common "national qualities" to the Württemberger, "be they of the body or of the soul."[34] Where he did not rely upon stock stereotypes about the Swabians—that they had a way of chafing under authority despite remaining very loyal, that they were very diligent and reliable, or that they were very jocular and *gemütlich*, at least among their own kind—he gravitated to surer topics, like statistics on the confessional breakdown of the kingdom or the question of the Roman versus Germanic origins of the Swabian people. Foreign to the statistical-topographical mind, which analyzed more than it synthesized, was any coherent notion of ethnicity or conception of regional character, such as one finds in Herder or (in nascent form) in the folklorists.

Memminger's encyclopedic observations retain an eclectic, often derivative quality, betraying none of the Romantic's desire to distill a *Volksgeist* from the observation of a people. By situating ethnography alongside other sub-divisions of statistics, like geology or archeology, the topographical method relativized cultural difference. Ethnic peculiarity, when placed on a spectrum of natural, social, and political conditions, merely reflected the differing permutations and combinations of regional forms, much like landscape features themselves. One might even say that representing difference as a series of particular and discrete observations, and not in terms of competing historical-cultural identities, served a strategic purpose in constructing an integrated vision of the Württemberg *Volk*.

Where Memminger's work achieved unity was in its fundamentally Biedermeier outlook: here, too, the texture of his presentation conformed to the quaint, rolling landscape it was meant to depict. One sees this not so much in the traditional, patriotic account of Württemberg political history at the beginning of the work, which in literary form differs very little from Sattler's or Moser's treatments, but in the sections devoted to self-consciously modern disciplines, like botany, industry, and geography. Catalogs of plant and animal life, for example, gave Linnaean taxonomies and Latin names (in Roman font, alongside German ones in *Fraktur*) for various species, but enumerated in each case what specific valleys, water-ways, and patches of forest provided a home for these life forms. In his dedication to what Lisbet Koerner calls a "local modernity," Memminger in fact resembled Linnaeus himself.[35] Handy sketches on factories, mills, breweries, bookshops, and chemical plants similarly revealed a consciousness of place by providing precise detail on their location and activities, thus evoking industry's deep roots in particular regional settings. The lonely entrepreneur struggling to raise his factory above local repute was a Biedermeier stereotype upon whom works like the *Description* bestowed national recognition.[36] Finally, the short descriptions given on individual *Oberämter* rested more on anecdote than on systematic sociography, concentrating on things like noteworthy waterfalls and picturesque ruins in a way that would become even more pronounced in the county almanacs.

These scattered clues point to the ways in which modern statistics underwrote a cozy, rooted, naturalistic, yet increasingly nationalized sense of community, a generic sense of *Heimat* unattached to any particular locality or ethnic tradition. Acting less to dissolve local particularisms than to project them on a statewide scale, Memminger's science exploited the overlapping qualities of "community" and "society" in the Biedermeier imagination. It is important to view this less as a stylistic calculation than as an outgrowth of his scientific methods themselves. From this compact analysis it should be clear just how much Memminger's work was an act of collage, to the extent that he delegated the writing of some sections to other writers, and therefore counted on the reader to bring its elements together. If eighteenth-century statistical topography was a discipline in its infancy, nineteenth-century *Vaterlandskunde* was a teenage science, the frameworks governing its objects of knowledge much less interesting than the sheer generation of knowledge itself. Encyclopedic media had always had a quality of arbitrariness, a zeal to amass information and organize knowledge but not to codify or systematize it. They rested on public enthusiasm more than any program or discipline or method that could stand on its own, a fact that the systematizing efforts of later nineteenth-century *Wissenschaft* tend to obscure.

All this explains the somewhat ambiguous and incoherently theorized role Memminger ascribed to the "public" in his Listian liberalism. Memminger saw publicity not primarily as a political but as a *methodological* boon: a forum in which he could shape his science before an attentive and involved audience. He endorsed the citizenship aspects of publicity more as an afterthought, as part of a broad cultural movement that stirred his enthusiasm because of the particular stake he had in it. The Biedermeier public, in short, possessed a thicker texture and a tighter weave than its late Enlightenment forerunner, and its interest in, and contribution to, the encyclopedic endeavors of *Statistik* was what allowed Memminger to press forward in the development of a science still untested.

ENCYCLOPEDISM AS LOCAL PASSION

In order to appreciate the ways in which publicity subjected Memminger's project to broader ideological negotiation, notwithstanding its sponsorship by the state, we turn now to a more detailed examination of the field of local experts and amateurs whose efforts shaped the production and dissemination of patriotic science. Their participation shows how civil society took part, alongside the state, in cataloging the social world of post-Napoleonic Württemberg. The state's need for local knowledge at this time originated in the logistical necessities of producing county statistical almanacs, but soon became self-perpetuating on account of its tremendous popularity. Especially among provincials, who proved particularly receptive to the call for contributions to the almanacs, encyclopedism became not just a faculty of the imagination but a way of more tangibly cultivating one's involvement in far-flung social networks. Glimmers of "free association," in the sense that civic leaders of the old regime had lacked, reached the countryside by the 1820s.

Memminger's Bureau was but one institutional expression of the new passion for statistical topography. The Association for Patriotic Science *(Verein für Vaterlandskunde)* provided a scientific backbone to the statistical movement, its membership drawn by election from the elite of Württemberg scholarly life.[37] It included twelve regular members residing in Stuttgart and twelve corresponding members from other parts of the kingdom. A common arrangement, this structure combined the advantages of face-to-face presence and a widespread network of social contacts. Originally conceived as part of a Württemberg Academy of Sciences, which was to have had a general scientific mandate and royal sanction but which never got off the ground, the Association instead grew "from the bottom up" (according to Memminger) after King Wilhelm's coronation in 1817. It stood alongside similar Societies for agriculture, commerce, and trade that brought together notable personalities in various disciplines. Not surprisingly, professors and high-level bureaucrats (such as members of the *Regierungsrat*) predominated, along with a few doctors and a surprising number of theologians/pastors. The last group, as we shall see, proved especially important in the gathering of local statistics, for reasons having to do with the social geography of Enlightenment in Württemberg.

The members of the Association for Patriotic Science furnished expert opinions to the Statistical-Topographical Bureau and contributed heavily to the *Württemberg Yearbooks for Patriotic History, Geography, Statistics, and Topography*, which began publication in the early 1820s. The *Yearbooks* subsequently changed their name and eventually issued into a general regional history journal that remains the mouthpiece of historical *Landeskunde* in southwest Germany to this day.[38] The *Yearbooks* provided a forum in which scientists from a range of disciplines could bring their skills to bear on patriotic science. Their first volume contained studies on geology, mineralogy, and climate; tables of population statistics (which became a regular feature in subsequent years); and a historical piece on the Counts of Achalm in Urach and Pfullingen, authored by Weckherlin. Popular subjects in later years included archeological studies on Roman ruins and coins and old Germanic castles and fortresses; annual figures tabulated from the grain, cattle, and textile markets and the wine harvest in the fall; historical researches on commodity prices in the Middle Ages; "necrologies" or obituaries of famous Württembergers; reports on new factories for iron, glass, jewelry, and textiles and the invention of a "copy machine"; noteworthy meteorological events and natural catastrophes; news from the church, the university, administrative departments, medicine, charitable institutes, and bourgeois clubs *(Vereine)*; mini-topographies and natural histories of various noteworthy and scenic spots; and miscellaneous news and tabulated statistics on various administrative and judicial matters, like breakdowns on various violent crimes by *Kreis,* or the number of bankruptcies and testaments in the kingdom.

In comparison with the full-blown encyclopedism of the *Yearbooks,* the Association itself had only a slightly less motley composition. Corresponding to the various skeins of patriotic science generally, the Association divided itself into three divisions: the geographic, the political, and the historical.[39] Members could specialize at will in any or all of the three subdisciplines. Of special importance was the second category, the "political" division, concerned with "the condition of the population, trade, community life, state administration," and charitable, religious, and other institutions. Its objects of scrutiny corresponded in rough outline to Hegel's definition of civil society, which embraced the market, guild-like "corporations," and the lowest levels of administrative regulation and "police" in civil affairs. But the encyclopedic study of civil society did not remain the exclusive province of any particular subdiscipline. Public health and the "physical particularities of people and animals" counted as "geographic" subjects, while "historical" contributions had obvious relevance to the study of society. The fashioning of knowledge both *for* and *of* the *Volk*—Memminger's project for *Vaterlandskunde*—thus remained a fluid enterprise within the hazy institutional contours of statistical-topographical science.

This limitation was especially salient for the county almanacs, or *Oberamtsbeschreibungen,* which consumed the Statistical-Topographical Bureau's energies during its first decades. Unlike overviews such as Memminger's *Description,* county almanacs required more detailed information and a much deeper engagement with the statistical and historical sources on local life throughout the kingdom. The Bureau was thus perforce obligated to draw on external contributions from "dispersed friends of the fatherland" to complete its work in this area. Its methodological engagement with the public meant that the public's interests stamped the whole enterprise with a surprising thoroughness. Indeed, it is fitting that the publication history of the first series of county almanacs, 1824–86, should coincide so neatly with the period of bourgeois hegemony in the German hometowns.[40] True, as was noted earlier, the *Oberamtsbeschreibungen* originally served as administrative handbooks meant to provide a general overview of the economic, political, and physical conditions of a given county to *Oberamtmänner* and other state officials periodically rotated in and out. In this respect, they grew directly out of the sociographic abstraction of administrative practice pioneered during the Napoleonic period. Quickly, though, the county almanacs became a part of Württemberg's national cultural heritage, demanding a space on every learned person's shelf, celebrated to this day for their patriotic spirit, and continuing on in a series of late-twentieth-century *Kreisbeschreibungen* published by the Baden-Württemberg state government.[41]

Collectively, the *Oberamtsbeschreibungen* testify to a meeting of the minds between the Biedermeier provincial and the cosmopolitan statistician. They can be seen as a state-sponsored attempt to refashion a county *(Oberamt)* identity, based no longer on legal traditions and constitutional particularities but on the more abstract, generalizable methods of topographical observation and sociography. In short, they functioned as an ersatz for the corporative pride of the old *Städte und Ämter* for which the *Oberämter* were the post-Napoleonic continuations. The almanacs began publication in 1824 with a volume on Reutlingen, a former Imperial Free City and an enclave fully within Württemberg until its outright absorption in 1803.[42] Memminger himself edited the first fourteen installments and kept a diary of his observations; written in a rough, hasty hand, the document betrays a mix of scientific system and creative chaos in his work habits.[43] For the first twenty years of its existence, the series concentrated almost exclusively on the areas of Old Württemberg and Upper Swabia bordering on the Swabian Jura, a string of high hills running northeastward out of the Black Forest and along the path of the Danube. Aside from their considerable geological and topographical interest, which may have prompted Memminger to focus on the region, these areas were known for their dialect, remoteness, and economic underdevelopment. This was especially true in comparison with the free cities and prosperous principalities of the northeast or the closely knit Neckar valley heartland of the former duchy. The early county almanacs, for *Oberämter* like Münsingen, Ehingen, and Riedlingen, therefore introduced their subscribers to a picturesque backwater more in need of integration into the national territorial consciousness than any other of the kingdom.

Over time the Bureau developed an informal network of specialists and scientists encompassing a range of researchers (amateur and professional) whose fields the statistical-topographical genre embraced, including geologists, archeologists, land surveyors, folklorists, historians, foresters, and archivists.[44] The Bureau had the authority to grant honoraria for their contributions and to acquire scientific *Nachlässe* (literary bequests).[45] A second stratum, to some extent coterminous with the first but living in a less cosmopolitan milieu, consisted of local notables who generated more anecdotal, but often surprisingly thorough and well-researched work. A great many of these hobbyists undertook massive, lifelong efforts to chronicle their hometowns, acting on their own initiatives. Often hailing from old families, usually holding some form of municipal office, these individuals stood in a venerable tradition of municipal patriotism that added texture and color to the Bureau's findings. The almanac for Reutlingen, for example, drew on two eighteenth-century contributions to church history authored by a pair of father-and-son syndics, as well as two other chronicles dating as far back as 1603. Amateur local history was an avocation assiduously practiced even under difficult circumstances. Thus the Reutlingen almanac lists an 1805 *Attempt at a Description of the Town of Reutlingen* by Court Physician F. A. Memminger (relation to the Bureau's director unknown), whose complaint that "all sources" for his work "remained closed to him" speaks to the climate of secrecy and suspicion under Napoleon. The Bureau treated all these works with both respect and skepticism, labeling some as "unreliable" or "deficient in historical and statistical respects" and others as "very valuable," subordinating their findings in every case to the pretense of rigorous, scientific standards.[46]

The next lower stratum of contributors came from the village countryside. This group included pastors, doctors, and village councillors, who were specifically named as sources for information in the 1821 edict establishing the Statistical-Topographical Bureau. Such information included lists of local commodity prices, breakdowns on the types and functions of municipal buildings, reports on cattle or human epidemics, and various demographic data.[47] It counts among Memminger's most pathbreaking innovations that by drawing on these contributions, he broke with the musty, self-referential traditions of amateur local-patriotic history and sought to rebuild patriotic science from rawer, more impartial sources. Among the deficiencies in historical topography cited by nineteenth- and twentieth-century folklorists and statisticians was their quaint commemoration of favorite sons and bygone glories at the expense of more objective treatments. Memminger, by contrast, adopted a more detached attitude toward his materials, extracting bits of information from localities on a need-to-know basis. He solicited sources with particular questions in mind and plucked from the local, archival record the specific texts he needed: an extract from a baptismal registry here, a medieval *Urkunde* or certificate of village legal status there, a medical report from still another spot on the map.[48] Such texts were less overdetermined, lacking the same cultural thickness as documents drawn from the annals of municipal history, and consti-

tuted an open field for the finer and more systematic application of encyclopedic methods to specific historical and statistical problems.

None of this is to say that Memminger somehow worked in a vacuum
out in the countryside. Excitement about statistical topography and historical folklore had penetrated even down to the village level, where many
people happily contributed to these projects.[49] The high incidence of pastors
among local statistical contributors is in particular need of explanation.
Having constituted Württemberg's leading *cultural* element for centuries,
the clergy only came into its own as a *civic* group during this period. No
longer locked out of participation by the scribes, who had monopolized legal
and administrative channels of communication between government and
society, pastors now took advantage of the radically changed climate of the
reform era. They provide a window into the entire phenomenon of "patriotic knowledge" as a civic project bridging provincial and cosmopolitan societies. As noted earlier, pastors kept most of the village records, such as "lists
of souls" *(Seelentabellen)* and the *Kirchen-* and *Familienbücher,* with tables
of parishioners and marriages, that were not the responsibility of the
Schreiber. Together with secular officials, they were responsible for the collection of census data. Pastors' enthusiasm also had cultural roots: they
fashioned the village's cultural identity in much the same way that
Schreiber defined its legal and political status, composing sermons translating theological points and commentary on current events into an idiom
comprehensible to the everyday churchgoer. The clergy ranked among the
most educated members of their community; many trained in the theological faculty at Tübingen or at the *Stift* there. They were subject to a centralized and independent system of installment and promotion, as well as periodic visitations to ensure the quality of their work. No pastor was allowed
to serve in the village of his birth.[50]

All this led to a fruitful tension between cosmopolitan outlook and local
positioning, waiting to be activated by a propitious combination of historical circumstances. As a movement of locally-based Enlightenment, patriotic
science fit the bill ideally, resonating with Württemberg pastors who were
dispersed territorially and in need of outlets for their intellectual energy and
curiosity. One sees its clear influence in the writings of Friedrich August
Köhler (1768–1844), above all in his 1838 work on a village in Tübingen
county entitled *Nehren, Parish Village in the Steinlach Valley: Topography
and Chronicle.*[51] Köhler was a somewhat frustrated Tübingen graduate, a
preacher's son who, waiting to fill his father's shoes, assembled information
on Nehren as part of what proved to be an unending enthusiasm for chron-
icling. His *Nehren* is but one of a series of local monographs penned over a

long life, some of which were submitted to the Association for Patriotic Geography, and it stands as an exemplar of the village chronicle as a genre. Suffused with the concerns of material scarcity and the rhythms of the harvest, the text at the same time views village life through the prism of a minutely tabulating encyclopedic sensibility.

In addition to village records and a cache of documents he found neglected in a desk drawer at the *Bürgermeister's* office, Köhler based his chronicle on an earlier work by former *Schreiber* and city council member Johannes Conrad Bihner (1645–1724). Unlike Bihner's chronicle, which simply recorded events serially, as they happened, and which can be viewed as an uncomplicated extension of his local patriotism and official duties, Köhler's was the product of synthetic historical research, independently and "objectively" undertaken by an outsider. In the ways it grappled with the textual traces of village life in the past, Köhler's account is very encyclopedic: like Memminger he extracted bits of information for their utility and cobbled them together without eliciting any laws or general conclusions from them. Raw information sufficed to captivate his interest. The work is striking for its systematic attempt to reconstruct grain prices over time, correlating them with climatic and political factors like wars. To the statistical mind, there is perhaps no quicker avenue into the past and no more palpable way of gauging material standards of living historically.[52] Other passions of Köhler's came from the usual inventory of statistical topography, but reflect a more tragic sensibility than one typically finds amidst the buoyant optimism of the Enlightened encyclopedist. *Nehren's* pages list comets, eclipses, and other astronomical phenomena; hailstorms, hard winters, and similar weather events; famines, fires, cattle and human epidemics, and natural calamities like earthquakes; and wars and the burdensome taxes levied for their financing. A few murders are also included. It is difficult to know how to read this parade of disasters, either as the product of a sensibility resigned to the utter fragility of village sustenance, or as the Enlightenment's other, a picture of misery and deprivation to set against modern progress. Regardless, Köhler's work is patriotic science in a minor key, a Pietist-inflected collection of knowledge utterly typical of the paradoxical way Enlightenment was admixed with an older religiosity in Württemberg cultural life.[53] To the municipal patriotism of city fathers and the quaint naturalism of the amateur local scientist, both ingredients in the stew that was *Vaterlandskunde*, he added his own, unique brand of local color.

Thus, even in the village, the production of knowledge was conditioned by the public's participation. Far from fashioning a state-sponsored knowledge from the comfortable perch of a bureaucratic chancellery, Memminger acted more as a catalyst for a range of activities taking place spontaneously in the public arena. During the workups of the county almanacs, his office was in fact inundated with the products of individual toil and imagination. Historical chroniclers tended either to send in their materials, bequeath them to the Bureau upon their deaths, or offer up their collections for sale. This presented the Bureau with the methodological dilemma of whether to draw upon the unverified, sometimes unsound data these ad hoc contributors furnished, or simply exclude them as unscientific, as was reluctantly done for a collection on patriotic history the Bureau considered acquiring for the Urach county almanac.[54] Memminger and his collaborators made a pretense of subjecting such collections to strict criteria of methodological fitness, but in reality they were learning by doing. The mandate of the Bureau was so broadly defined and encompassed so many types of heterogeneous material that even the relatively segmented and discrete organization of its published products bespeaks, if nothing else, a heroic organization of paperwork. Its archives are a mass of information either painstakingly specific or impressionistically unsystematic. There is even some evidence to suggest that the Bureau extended its reach to some aspects of cultural policy (Kulturpflege), like the upkeep of monuments, as an internal discussion on financing improvements to the cloister church as Lorch attests. That historical preservation could stand alongside quantitative demography among the Bureau's charges testifies to the coexistence of nostalgic and progressive strains in its institutional culture, both peculiarly modern, both part of a very young science reshaping itself after Napoleon.

In conclusion, what counted as "patriotic science" in Württemberg was, during the entire first half of the nineteenth century, a matter of some vagueness, owing to the fluid boundaries between state and public, cosmopolitan and philistine, scientist and amateur, nation and locality. The Biedermeier world animating the otherwise inert and discrete findings of the county almanacs was a small, provincial one, but also thoroughly modern in accommodating a negative capability conjoining diverse types of knowledge in a single worldview. Only in the mind of the reader and the statistical contributor or author, who after all were drawn from the same notable circles, could the various and sometimes dissonant methods of statistical topography come together to paint a single picture. Only the widespread and generally diffused fascination with encyclopedic knowledge, in all the forms in which this was being created at the time, can account for the tremendous appeal that statistical-topographical compendia enjoyed during this period, for they can certainly make a dry and disappointing read today. And only the narrow, natural world in which the objects of such knowledge continued to exist gave the reader a framework, a living mental portrait, within which to situate the flora and fauna, the valleys and waterfalls, the monuments and famous personalities, the little industries and picturesque villages, the jagged legal boundaries and diverse customs and traditions, the palette of confessional, linguistic, and folkloric difference that form the stuff of patriotic science. Here, in the Biedermeier world, lay the true cosmopolitanism of the Romantic naturalism many find so regressive in post-Napoleonic German cultural life.

It hardly needs restating at this point that the jarring, almost risible notion of "Biedermeier statistics" reflects not the perversion of scientific reason by a nostalgic and reactionary provincialism but a very modern cultural attitude that trained the Enlightenment's encyclopedic gaze on local circumstances and conditions. This procedure underwrote new perceptions of society itself, outside the corporate order, which had erected procedural firewalls around the citizenry's participation in civil society. The genius of the Biedermeier, as reflected in the statistical-topographical genre, was to conflate the characteristics of "community" and "society" into a fungible, generic quaintness, and thereby to ease the hometownsman into encounters with modernity. The following chapter brings out even more clearly the practical consequences of this new identification with civil society. It shows how institutions and culture, the subjects of the previous two chapters, came together within the new order actually to found new networks of post-Napoleonic sociability.

8   The Intelligence Gazettes

If the effort to produce practical knowledge, begun in the state and negotiated with the public, culminated in the statistical almanacs, then the intelligence gazettes show how knowledge production created true markets for ideas and information. This surprisingly vigorous print medium flourished in provincial Württemberg between the 1820s and the 1840s, and, like the almanacs, brought local notables together with state officials under the banner of popular Enlightenment. More so than the almanacs, the intelligence gazettes depict a small-town world pulsating with entrepreneurship and treating information as the lifeblood of civic improvement. As local announcement bulletins, gazettes abstained from the cosmopolitan, critical, uncensored, rational discourse found in the classical public sphere. This, together with their status as semi-official organs dependent on government support, might suggest that they lacked emancipatory potential. Yet precisely in their mundane practicality, the gazettes traced new networks of social communication ushering both their readers and producers into civil society. They reveal, at the level of everyday practice, how German civil society emerged in a sphere of dynamism, partnership, and conflict at the interface between the state and local communities.

Typically, intelligence gazettes *(Intelligenzblätter)* consisted of three to six double-sided leaves, each seven or eight inches square, and resembled miniature newspapers. By 1800, Central Europe possessed 160 gazettes with a combined circulation of over 100,000 copies. If one reckons ten users per copy, a standard press historians' method, these collectively reached over one million readers.[1] In their original, eighteenth-century incarnation, gazettes supported the cameralist pedagogy of the so-called popular Enlightenment *(Volksaufklärung)*.[2] Although their content varied, they typically printed government laws and decrees, official announcements, notices of bankruptcies and property sales, classified advertisements, weather forecasts, commodity price tables, entertaining anecdotes and short stories, and didactic essays on agriculture, economics, science, natural history, and other subjects. Such information acted as a natural catalyst to economic development, at least in the eyes of the gazettes' promoters. Most of these promoters held some kind of official appointment, and gazettes themselves generally enjoyed direct state sponsorship. To Enlightened officials, they inculcated rational and utilitarian modes of thought in their readers, stressing the governance of personal conduct and the creation of productive citizens.

Between the 1770s and the 1840s, intelligence gazettes apprenticed a large segment of the German population in publicity, ultimately outgrowing the popular Enlightenment's paternalism. With an immediate connection to the world of material interests, gazettes instilled practices promoting civil society's independence. These included sociography, the ability to map one's position in the wider social world, and encyclopedism, a daily familiarization with cosmopolitan currents through print, both of which were significantly enhanced by the regular assimilation of practical information and exciting new discoveries. In Württemberg, more than fifty *Oberämter* founded their own gazettes in the 1820s and 1830s, spontaneously and without central coordination. Bringing together a diverse, activist class of local civic leaders, these enterprises organized a heretofore diffuse set of needs for information for the reading public. Subsequently, they developed in response to market forces, liberalizing trends in administration, changing reading habits, and the increasing sophistication of their local supporters. This evolution toward autonomy and political critique illustrates the emancipatory potential of free association in both its cognitive and social senses. Providing a nascent social formation with knowledge of itself, intelligence gazettes acted as a road map to civil society; and in turning to political agitation in 1848, they facilitated the emancipation of writing from the last vestiges of state interference.

POPULAR ENLIGHTENMENT

As with statistical topography, the flourishing of intelligence provision in post-reform Württemberg drew on cultural currents affecting many parts of Central Europe and reaching far back into the Enlightenment. The category of "intelligence" originated as a form of communicative practice spreading from England and France to Germany in the early eighteenth century. The term *Intelligenz* initially referred to services offered by

Das Intelligenzblatt erscheint jeden Dienstag. Preis 1 fl. 30 kr. für das Jahr, vierteljährig 24 kr. Einrückungsgebühr die Zeile 2 kr.

Intelligenzblatt

für die Oberamts-Bezirke

Schorndorf und Welzheim.

Mit Allerhöchster Genehmigung.

Gemeinnützige und zur Unterhaltung dienende Beiträge werden mit Dank angenommen.

Dienstag.   Nro. 15.   19. Mai 1835.

Amtliche Bekanntmachungen.

Welzheim, den 7. Mai 1835. Da in dem Oberamts-Bezirk hin und wieder Vergiftungen durch den Genuß sauer gewordener Würste vorkommen, so wird in Gemäßheit einer Entschließung der Königl. Regierung für den Jartkreis v. 10. April d. J. den Ortsvorstehern die beigefügte Belehrung über die Kennzeichen solcher Würste, welche der Gesundheit schädlich sind, unter der Weisung mitgetheilt, die aufgestellten Fleischschauer hievon gehörig zu unterrichten, und dieselben anzuhalten, daß sie sämmtliche Würste der Metzger und Wirthe wöchentlich genau untersuchen und das Ergebniß dem Schultheißenamt anzeigen.

Finden sich wirklich verdorbene Würste vor, so hat der betreffende Ortsvorstand sogleich solche in Beschlag zu nehmen uud hierüber der unterzeichneten Stelle Bericht zu erstatten.

K. Oberamt.
Scholl.

Mann erkennt die sauer gewordene oder sonst verdorbene Würste

1) schon äußerlich daran, daß sie sich schmierig und weicher, als sie seyn sollen, anfühlen;

2) noch mehr aber, wenn man sie aufschneidet und die Wurstmasse in der Mitte sehr schmierig und — bei geräucherten Würsten — auch heller gefärbt findet, als an der Außenseite;

3) ihr Geruch ist widrig säuerlich, eiterartig,

4) ihr Geschmack ranzig, d. h. sauer oder bitterlich sauer.

Hiebei wird bemerkt, daß der Verderbniß oder der Entwicklung des s. g. Wurstgifts vorzugsweise die Leber- Hirn- uud Blutwürste unterworfen sind, zumal solche, denen bei der Bereitung Milch oder Kesselbrühe beigesezt, und diejenigen, welche viel Fett enthalten, in dicke Gebärme gefüllt und geräuchert worden sind; auch ist es, da die oben erwähnten Kennzeichen nicht immer deutlich hervortreten, sehr rathsam, jede Wurst wegzuwerfen, wenn sie einen auch nur entfernt fremdartigen und verdächtigen Geruch und Geschmack zeigt, weil dieß schon den Anfang der Verderbniß andeutet.

Pfahlbron. In dem diesseitigen Staabs-Bezirk liegen folgende Pfleggelder zum Ausleihen zu 5 Prc. und 2 facher Versicherung parat.

1) Bei dem Pfleger alt Georg Friz in Vor-

Figure 14.   Two pages from the same issue of an intelligence gazette serving Schorndorf and Welzheim counties. Page 57 contains an official government warning on how to recognize and avoid spoiled sausages. Page 59 contains, among

Ausfertigung eines neuen Pfandscheins verursachen würde.

Mögen die Or obrigkeiten und Pfleger des hiesigen Bezirks mitwirken, durch dieses Mittel der Cedirung den Verkehr zu erleichtern, und die Gelder der Pflegbefohlenen gegen Pfandscheine unterzubringen.

Den 8. Mai 1835.

K. Oberamts-Gericht,
Arnold.

Schorndorf. [Gebäude-Verkauf] Der Verkauf nachstehender Gebäude hat die Genehmigung nicht erhalten, daher am Montag den 1ten Juni ihre Versteigerung wiederholt wird.

a) Ein 3 stockiges Gebäude, bisher die Wohnung des Kameral-Verwalters, an der Hauptstraße, und

b) Ein 4 stockiger Gefängnißthurm.

Indem die Liebhaber eingeladen werden, an gedachtem Tag Vormittags 10 Uhr auf dem Kanzleizimmer der unterzeichneten Stelle sich einzufinden, wird sich auf die Nummern 10. und 11. dieses Blatts bezogen, worin die Größe und der Gelaß dieser Gebäude bezeichnet ist.

Den 16. Mai 1835.

K. Kameral-Amt.

Privat-Anzeigen.

Schorndorf. Ich mache die ergebenste Anzeige, daß ich kürzlich von Stuttgart zurückgekehrt, und nun wieder Hüte in neuster Facon, und zu billigstem Preis fertige.

Auf vielseitiges Verlangen, erlernte ich zugleich das Kleidermachen, und empfehle mich auch in diesem Fach, in welchem ich, so wie in der Putzarbeit gründlichen Unterricht ertheile.

Friederike Gabler.

Schorndorf Unterzeichneter hat aus Auftrag 5 Stük schön gebleichte flächsene Leinwand in ungefähr 160 Ehlen zu verkaufen.

Carl Veil,
bei der Oberamtei.

Schorndorf. Stadtrath Krais hat 400 fl. Pflegschaftsgelder gegen gesetzliche Sicherheit auf einen oder mehrere Posten hinzuleihen.

Welzheim. Der Unterzeichnete ist von der Würtembergischen Hagelversicherungs-Gesellschaft als Anwalt für das Wiesenthal und den

Welzheimer Wald aufgestellt worden, und bittet er hiedurch die betreffenden Herrn Ortsvorsteher dieß gefälligst unter dem Anfügen bekannt machen zu wollen, daß von 100 fl. Werth an Früchten — 30 kr. und von 100 fl. Ertrag aus Weinbergen — 48 kr. gleich bei Aushändigung der Versicherungs-Urkunde zu bezahlen seyen, und daß die Anmeldungen zur Versicherung von jetzt an jeden Tag bei ihm gemacht werden können.

Den 4. Mai 1835.

Schulmeister Stähle.

In eine Oberamtsstadt des Donaukreises, wird ein junger Mensch, der Lust hätte, die Rothgerberei zu erlernen, unter billigen Bedingungen in die Lehre aufzunehmen gesucht. Auf gefällige Anfragen sagt das Nähere die

Redaction

Plüderwiesenhof. Unterzeichneter macht hiemit bekannt, daß er am Donnerstag den 21. Mai auf den Abbruch ein Haus 26' breit, und 32' lang ohne Bedeckung, verkauft, die etwaigen Liebhaber werden hiezu eingeladen.

Michael Vollmer.

Grunbach. [Geld auszuleihen.] Unterzeichneter hat aus einer Pflegschaft 2 bis 300 fl. und dann wieder 500 fl in einem oder mehreren Posten auszuleihen.

Dr. Wolff.

Miscellen.

Die Baumzucht.

[Schluß.]

Der Hausfreund sagte: „Adjunkt ihr seyd ein schlauer Gesell. Ihr denkt, wenn ich einen eigenen Baum hätte, so hätte ich auch einen eigenen Garten, oder Acker, wo der Baum darauf steht. Eine eigene Hausthüre wäre auch nicht zu verachten, aber mit einem Kühlein auf seinen vier Beinen könnet ihr übel dran seyn."

„Das ist's eben," sagte der Adjunkt, „so ein Baum frißt keinen Klee und keinen Haber. Nein er trinkt still wie ein Mutterkind den nährenden Saft der Erde, und saugt reines warmes

other things, a private advertisement from one Friederike Gabler, who, having recently returned from Stuttgart, now offers her services as a seamstress and haberdasher in response to popular demand.

semiprivate information clearinghouses often managed by moonlighting bureaucrats. "Intelligence offices" *(Intelligenzbüros)* and "address counters" *(Adreß-Comtoirs)* in large trading centers like Hamburg and Leipzig customarily dealt in goods and services for which demand could not be met by local commercial establishments. These included books, luxury items, medicines, and used housewares, all having a limited, irregular, or dispersed customer base, as well as lost and found, credit, and other commercial services.[3] Intelligence gazettes began as outgrowths of these enterprises, and thus, from the very beginning, concrete affiliations with the marketplace shaped the gazettes' history in the Germanies. Unlike the classic literary-political newspaper, which also had a business side, commercialism was the transparent purpose and practicality the ideological underpinning of what was called *Intelligenzwesen*. The latter term, an umbrella category for both the print medium and the bricks-and-mortar institution, points to the semantic overlap between "intelligence" as a mental construct and as a tangible, marketable commodity. *"Intelligenzien"* were the quanta of information that brought usefulness to the common reader, whether they were plucked from the printed page or obtained at an actual business establishment.

This immediate connection to the world of things made the *Intelligenzblatt* a uniquely potent medium. Gazettes excited the encyclopedic imagination precisely because their scope was mundane and practical.[4] Thus Justus Möser, the eighteenth-century publicist and administrator, pioneered a straightforward, pared-down aesthetic for his *Osnabrückische Intelligenzblätter*. He tailored scientific and instructive essays to local conditions, practical purposes, and unpretentious reading tastes. Frivolous, "satirical" articles he excised as irrelevant. And lest his format be perceived as dry or starkly utilitarian, Möser adopted layout innovations inspired by the example of German-American Intelligencers.[5] These featured easy-to-read, "immediately graspable" rubrics and formatting tricks, like large blocked letters and icons placed beside advertisements: saddled horses indicated those providing services, while filled purses signaled those offering credit. Such techniques, besides targeting the semiliterate, enhanced the accessibility of information. Intelligence gazettes' novelty as a print medium consisted in rendering their individual components easy to abstract, collect, and peruse, gathering together the objects of civil society encyclopedically. Reflecting a general move from "intensive" (mainly religious) to "extensive" practices of reading, the gazettes helped call forth what Roger Chartier terms a "freer, more casual, and more critical" way of reading, ideally suited to the processing of practical knowledge.[6]

Only relatively late in the eighteenth century did the gazettes acquire a predominantly official character. From the 1770s, German states increasingly provided them with financial support and inserted official decrees and announcements into their pages.[7] Acting as the medium's midwives, state officials loosened the gazettes' dependence on market forces, facilitating a much wider territorial coverage. The policy of *Intelligenzzwang,* or "compulsory intelligence," was among the crudest methods of state interference, by and large limited to Prussia.[8] It established regional monopolies on the publishing of both official and private announcements, and compelled certain public authorities to subscribe to and locally distribute intelligence gazettes. Most other states relied on the simple convenience of the new medium. Whether coercively or spontaneously, gazettes gradually displaced older, more irregular, and less efficient forms of publicity, including the posting of ordinances at town halls and public readings by town criers or, for more important decrees, from the pulpit. In bureaucrats' eyes, gazettes promised to bring regular, continual, and subtle, indirect reinforcement of state authority as a consequence of their form, a printed bulletin of public record.

State censors also constrained gazettes to develop in a circumscribed, ostensibly depoliticized space by distinguishing them from political and deliberative *(räsonnierende)* newspapers in the later nineteenth-century mold. Papers offering *Intelligenz* were subjected to much less surveillance and fewer taxes than those engaging in *Räsonnement. Intelligenz* was practical, useful, and earthbound, conveying only the information and habits of mind the productive citizen should have.[9] *Räsonnement* was abstract, reflective, and critical, with an irresponsible tendency to frivolity and, ultimately, politics. *Intelligenz* was just the form of deliberation state officials with a taste for popular Enlightenment wished to cultivate. *Räsonnement* was, at best, a potent instrument to be kept in the hands of a responsible educated elite and, at worst, a weapon that could be used to attack the state and its policies. *Räsonnement* was at home in the intimate society of the salons and the cosmopolitan discourse of the literary journal. *Intelligenz* belonged on the trader's ledger, near the craftsman's workbench, and in the bureaucrat's chambers.

Enlightened officials' broader vision for the gazettes was thus essentially cameralist, to harness local economic development under the aegis and watchful eye of a state institution. "Intelligence" was for them the handmaiden of *Statistik,* and, like its parent discipline, encompassed an encyclopedic range of data on the state, including laws, ordinances, treaties, and other political information.[10] Like statistics, *Intelligenzien* only took on a greater meaning when collected and studied. But while *Statistik* surveyed the whole, actively assigning each particularity its proper place from the vantage point of the intellectual, *Intelligenz* relied on the effects of passive accumulation of knowledge for limited purposes. In other words, intelligence enabled each citizen, in accordance with his particular needs, to adapt to currents of economy and society being analyzed and steered benevolently from above. Gerhard Petrat assimilates this project to the Foucauldian "work of ordering," a way of encouraging individual initiative alongside a new submission to the rules and regularities of the modern economy.[11] In this spirit, Petrat argues, an 1802 volume entitled *Intelligence Gazette Help for the Uneducated Private Man* taught readers how to draft, as well as interpret, classified advertisements:

> Simplicity and clarity result . . . from order, precision, and brevity or exactness, and therefore require the most practice and care. If your collected observations give you a general, albeit here and there also dark, idea of the whole, a continued attentiveness will clarify the individual parts little by little. . . . Their order on the paper will, indeed must, diverge perhaps entirely from the order *in your soul,* since the one is *your* conception and the other should be for others who have other needs, abilities, etc.[12]

The mixture of emancipatory and paternalistic attitudes in this passage reflected the confluence of rationalist pedagogy with absolutist state practice in the period of popular Enlightenment. Notionally, at least, this reinforced what contemporary German scholars call the "social disciplining" of the German population.[13]

Didactic essays, a popular feature of the late eighteenth century, constituted another rich field for the discursive construction of the disciplined, productive citizen. These essays concentrated directly on the pedagogy of the "common man," widening the scope of *Intelligenz* beyond commercial, legal, and statistical matters to encompass all spheres of life bearing on productive capacities, including agronomy, medicine and sanitation, householding, diet, natural science, and meteorology. Didactic essays employed the methods of reason and persuasion, personal experiential accounts *(Erfahrungsberichte)*, mockingly paternalistic warnings against peasant prejudices and superstitions, and the soothing authorial voice of the practical advice-giver—all in order to encourage readers to adopt new innovations and internalize new maxims of conduct.[14] One should not take these techniques at face value, of course. Resistances and unanticipated consequences often resulted when reason was marshaled too hastily into the service of state and economy. For example, while intelligence gazettes offered commentaries on new legal ordinances with reasoned justifications for state reforms, they also placed state authority implicitly in question when, as was common, such commentaries appeared alongside similar legislation drawn from other states. "Experiential accounts" similarly invited the resistance of those whose personal experience simply differed. One local official wrote to the *Lippisches Intelligenzblatt* complaining that he had met up with recalcitrance and obstinate adherence to traditional practices when, following an article he had read in the gazette, he tried to introduce new culinary applications for salt to the local peasantry.[15]

Such were the pitfalls in grafting so-called "learned matters" onto *Intelligenz,* with its ever-practical referents. Although cameralist officials intended intelligence provision to instill rational, obedient conduct and promote the health of populations and the growth of productive energies, their forays into *Räsonnement* produced ambiguous, unexpected results.[16] The encyclopedism of the Enlightenment, as a purely practical matter, could never be entirely divorced from its spirit of critique. Such critique in no way sprang from the immanent force of ideas, nor did it reflect the independence of a civil society as yet undeveloped in the late 1700s. Rather, the failure of popular Enlightenment to modernize and reform the ways of peasant society had much more to do with the limitations of the state's own vision and power. Only an event as threatening to the state as the Napoleonic conquests could therefore expose the true inefficacy of cameralist officials' disciplinary project.

REACHING THE CITIZENRY

Napoleon's conquests, by enlarging German states with new territories, made the conversion of new subjects into state citizens a pressing need. Providing the inhabitants of newly annexed regions with timely information on changes in laws, new commercial opportunities, and events and news from the wider world promised to fulfill this need quite conveniently. Intelligence provision during this time conformed, much more than before, to the practical goal of promoting sociography rather than to the vaguer proposition of enlightening the people. Flux and mobility in post-Napoleonic society gave intelligence a greater relevance to citizens attempting to visualize their place in new states, and gazettes responded, in much the same way that *Statistik* had, by turning squarely to matters of real-world import. To surmise that this reorientation automatically redounded to the benefit of the Napoleonic state would be mistaken, however. In Württemberg, to which we now return, the central government's sponsorship of intelligence gazettes foundered on the difficulties inherent in constructing a loyal, active, and informed citizenry. Their failure opened a significant new space where private initiatives could flourish.

Württemberg was extremely late to develop a network of *Intelligenz-*

blätter, owing to the Cotta family's longstanding, suffocating monopoly on intelligence provision. After abolishing their privileges between 1806 and 1808, the state began to officially recognize and sanction gazettes all over the kingdom. Of the ten gazettes existing in Württemberg in 1806, fully nine were published in its post-Napoleonic acquisitions, all but two of these in former Imperial Free Cities. Royal authorities, on taking possession of Württemberg's new territories, aimed to promote a greater uniformity among these enterprises and extend their coverage out from the urban centers and into the countryside. They also set guidelines standardizing gazettes' content to subjects such as police ordinances, troop quartering, searches for missing persons and deserters, warnings about swindles, lost and found articles, food and commodity prices, weather and epidemic observations, new discoveries, strange natural occurrences, and births and deaths.[17]

The trend in Württemberg was toward an increased reliance on *Intelligenzblätter* as replacements for oral publishing by town criers. This move was accompanied by a halting effort to make citizens legally responsible for the information—especially laws and ordinances—that they made known. While early initiatives to give intelligence a "perfectly binding power" on citizens failed, and traditional methods of publicizing information continued, the government nonetheless maintained that since "every inhabitant will have the opportunity to read [a gazette's] content himself, . . . that person who fails to do so will have only himself to blame for whatever disadvantages result."[18] Starting in the first two decades of the nineteenth century, state officials relied massively on the new medium to search for creditors in bankruptcy cases; publicize auctions, markets, fairs, and sales of forfeited property; inform subjects of new commercial and mercantile regulations; and make offers of public credit known. All this meant that individuals wishing to participate in property markets and commercial life ignored the latest intelligence at their peril. Alongside other encyclopedic media—the *Hauskalender,* for example, also subjected to government regulation at this time[19]—intelligence gazettes cultivated habits among citizens favoring rational market calculation on one hand, and adherence to state directives on the other.

The implicit appeal to citizens' self-interest marked a subtle but important shift from the paternalism of the popular Enlightenment: submitting intelligence gazettes to the laws of the market and the existing structure of economic incentives implicitly limited the state's power. Government efforts to centralize and coordinate the distribution of intelligence could thus founder for lack of effective marketing and packaging. Royal officials' only real attempt to found a statewide intelligence gazette, the *General*

Intelligence Gazette for New Württemberg, lasted only three years, from 1804 to 1806. Circulating exclusively in the kingdom's post-Napoleonic acquisitions, it was admittedly quite promising in conception. Providing "reliable news about the various arrangements, the culture, and the inner structure of the new [lands]," it explicitly served the agenda of territorial integration.[20] Substantive articles commended the practical scientific findings of (private) "learned men" to state "economists" in the trenches, touting the advantages of lightning rods, something called the "Papinian" cooking pot, and Pestalozzi's renowned pedagogical methods, for example.[21] Supporters of the *General Intelligence Gazette* thus envisioned social development as a partnership between government and leading inventors and intellectuals. This vision was belied, however, by the gazette's imperious tone and largely official content. It was targeted mainly at local officials, promoting such cameralistic goals as developing the commodity markets. New regulations to be implemented and new duties to be discharged dominated its pages, and no critical mass of inventive contributors could be located. Plagued by a failure to engage any public constituency, the paper attracted no more than a few hundred subscribers, among them very few private citizens, and collapsed financially as a result.[22]

The Württemberg administration soon abandoned the enterprise, shifting its attention to a series of official bulletins and handbooks confined to laws, decrees, and administrative announcements of a more general nature. The most important of these, the *Royal Württemberg State and Government Bulletin,* was the direct continuation of the *General Intelligence Gazette* and became the definitive repository of Württemberg legislation through the nineteenth century.[23] In addition, a yearly *Court and State Handbook* listed the kingdom's officials and the positions to which they were appointed, information first collected under the auspices of the Napoleonic statistical administration. Finally, a variety of legal compendia, privately authored but intended for state bureaucrats, served not only to codify police and other administrative regulations within the Württemberg territory, but also to facilitate the exchange of official information across the newly redrawn boundaries of the German states, especially Bavaria, Baden, and Prussia. All of these materials were intended as reference works and durable repositories of public record rather than up-to-date provisioners of intelligence. The famed publisher Cotta touted his officially-sanctioned court calendars as "lasting literary monuments" documenting the "historical, geographical, and statistical" glories of the new Württemberg kingdom for a foreign audience. In general, the state's retreat toward consolidating its own internal bureaucratic apparatus and bolstering its international reputation effectively severed mundane "intelligence" from the higher matters of state that *Statistik* had formerly encompassed. In keeping with its shift in policy focus, the central administration eventually lost all interest in publishing raw intelligence.[24]

It thus fell to private entrepreneurs to step into the breach, in the early 1800s. Private entrepreneurs were less constrained by the need to combine official content with practical information in their papers and further downplayed the disciplinary aspect of intelligence provision. Beset by local competition, publishers were continually conceiving new schemes to vault their papers into statewide recognition. Proposals for new national or superregional gazettes stressed their "civic utility" *(Gemeinnützigkeit)*, a term that updated the popular Enlightenment's emphasis on practical knowledge to reflect the new passion for state- and nation-building. The publisher C. F. Nast in Ludwigsburg identified a concrete role for private readers to contribute to this project. His proposed *General Announcer for the Kingdom of Württemberg* aimed to create a new statewide identity by "acquaint[ing] and bind[ing] the as yet still somewhat alien parts of Württemberg together":

> How much could such a newspaper . . . contribute to the topographical understanding of our blessed land . . . to the greater livelihood of its industry and trade . . . when insightful men have the place and *opportunity to collect reliable data and want to furnish their perceptions and discoveries* to [the paper].[25]

Other statewide intelligence endeavors likewise emphasized the national-economic advantages of networking and sharing information. Dr. Dingelmaier in Gmünd envisioned a series of papers offering "polytechnic" services to craftsmen and factory owners wanting to peddle their wares and inventions before the pan-Württemberg public. And an anonymous proposal for a statewide gazette promised to assemble "news [items] not merely of local but of a general interest . . . so that every reader can collect, reference, look over, and compare [these items] with one another." This publisher saw his subscribers and contributors as one and the same: a mercantile group exchanging practical tips and business suggestions among themselves.[26]

All these schemes failed: they are only preserved as proposals in the archives. Their efforts, however, modeled intelligence provision as a more participatory process, setting a precedent for later, more successful endeavors. What they had in common was a bid to cultivate sociographic reading practices: to enlist scattered local citizens in digesting and contributing intelligence items, to gather up and reprint useful information for widespread consumption, and thereby to extend community across large regions.

Regional and statewide papers suffered from an untimely overestimation, not of the supply but of the demand for such services. Their publishers misread the market at this level, which had little use for commodities or inventions still produced and circulated only locally. Rather, national readers were increasingly cosmopolitan and hungering for politics, entertainment, and criticism: *Räsonnement* in its pure form.[27]

THE MARKET FOR INFORMATION

Only on the local level did the intelligence gazettes find an audience in Württemberg and finally begin to stitch together networks of civil society. Out in the provinces, the disciplinary paradigm unsuccessfully promoted by the state finally dissipated in the face of rival conceptions of the medium's purpose. Locally, intelligence fulfilled social needs for practical information, not just an Enlightenment vision. To be sure, it took nearly two decades after the formal monopoly on intelligence gazettes had been abolished before even a partial coverage of Württemberg existed. But by the 1820s, gazettes had become the kingdom's dominant print medium, numbering fifty separate enterprises compared with only nineteen political papers and thirty-three of miscellaneous nonpolitical content. On the eve of the 1848 Revolution, fully fifty-seven of sixty-four counties across the kingdom possessed their own *Intelligenzblatt*.[28] Local gazettes appeared once or twice weekly with a print run of several hundred copies at a yearly subscription rate of 1–2 fl. Once a backwater of uneven development, untouched by the first wave of eighteenth-century gazettes, Württemberg now overtook its neighbors and rapidly acquired a systematic and uniform information network spanning the greater part of its territory.

All this occurred without central coordination or intent. County level intelligence gazettes arose from completely spontaneous collaboration among middling bureaucrats, town elders, enterprising guild printers, and, in many cases, crusading pastors and local civic and agricultural societies. These civic leaders converged with very different purposes in mind: streamlining administrative communication, promoting local markets, turning profits, providing instruction and entertainment, and generally introducing ordinary citizens to dealings outside their home villages. They owed their common interest purely to the integrative power of *Intelligenz* as an encyclopedic discourse: to a widespread, shared enthusiasm for practical knowledge, in all its multifarious forms, which enlisted them in the cause of intelligence provision. At no point did the Württemberg state itself undertake a centralized or systematic program to furnish its citizenry with local

Intelligenzblätter.[29] Especially after the Karlsbad decrees (1819) cracked down on press freedoms, the Württemberg Interior Ministry was content mostly to ignore the medium while it remained preoccupied with regulating, taxing, and censoring overtly political material. It would be wrong, however, to regard the vacuum thus created for local civic boosters merely as a product of state neglect. Intelligence gazettes instead flourished in a space intentionally carved out by bureaucratic reforms and aimed at emancipating county leaders from historic restrictions on their activities.

The reforms that put an end to the *Schreiberei* system had dismantled communication monopolies existing for hundreds of years in the old duchy and extended to Württemberg's new acquisitions after Napoleon. Until this time, the reproduction and dissemination of official announcements called "circulars" had fallen to the scribes. These circulars largely contained mundane information on auctions, bankruptcies, and government-mandated sales, but, as the mobilization surrounding the Black Forest Cahier showed, also recruited scribes into politically potent networks of information exchange and reciprocality. Heinrich Bolley's agitation in Waiblingen showed that these networks could extend to broader segments of the Württemberg population—particularly the residents of hinterland villages long isolated from the flow of communications in the cantonal seats. Both the Black Forest and Waiblingen incidents prove, however, that for all their progressive tendencies, scribes of the old regime were more concerned with pursuing reformist political agendas than with promoting economic growth or administrative rationalization. The deep-seated dualism between government and society, only overcome after the defeat of the *Altrechtler* in 1817–19, had ensured that scribes worked at cross purposes with ducal officials throughout the old regime. For this reason, repeated ducal exhortations that the scribes contribute intelligence items to the Stuttgart *Weekly Announcements* foundered for lack of interest.[30] The scribes' culture of collegiality, however vibrant it may have been, was simply alien to the encyclopedic sensibilities associated with *Intelligenz*.

The eighteenth-century information economy suffered less from any general backwardness, for it was quite robust in its own way, than from its severely restricted degree of publicity and conditions of access determined by one's proximity to the scribes. This liability constituted a unique hindrance to Württemberg's development of intelligence gazettes relative to other German states. All this rapidly changed in the 1820s. In the course of reforming the *Schreiberei* generally, state officials explicitly ordained that intelligence gazettes take over the scribes' monopoly on official circulars and announcements.[31] Thereafter followed the decade of the gazettes' greatest expansion in Württemberg.

The reforms favored two types of civic leaders who proved central in establishing intelligence gazettes: local officials and guild printers. The first group, consisting of royal superintendents *(Oberamtmänner)* and county councils (the refurbished *Amtsversammlungen)*, profited the most, politically, from the elimination of the scribes.[32] As middling state and local officials, they were concerned primarily with the economic development and smooth administrative operation of their districts. Intelligence gazettes appealed to them in both respects. The reliability and regularity of the new medium also promised to hasten the arrival of news in out-of-the-way places by undermining scribes' ability to hoard information in the county seats.[33] Financing arrangements in turn reinforced the dispersal of power. Sometimes, village offices covered their subscription costs by drawing on their own coffers and had their announcements inserted free of charge into the local gazette. In other cases, the county government footed the bill, ensuring full geographic coverage and unburdening localities of a significant expense. The county of Öhringen took this one step further. At the instigation of its councillors, the county contracted with the publisher Erbe to provide a bulk rate for ninety-eight copies of his *Intelligenzblatt*. This assured at least one copy for every village foreman in the county and secured civic leaders' "primary intent . . . [of] informing the public of all [official] arrangements."[34]

Such coverage by no means democratized the flow of news, but it vastly multiplied the circles in which intelligence traveled, reducing the social distance between those who occupied a privileged position in the information economy and those who did not. At a precise point, in the town hall where the village foreman had his office, distinctions became blurred between local officials who historically monopolized intelligence and a middle-class public now more able to use and consume information. There, and at places like the town pub, where subscriptions to gazettes were taken out, intelligence entered webs of local rumor, becoming a form of symbolic capital with which village and small-town notables jockeyed for position by keeping apprised of the latest news.[35] The shift toward a more negotiated relationship between officials and their public was made possible by the move from handwritten circulars to published intelligence accessible to all. As the government's *Main Report* on the *Schreiberei* system observed, the circular system had relied on the sporadic, discrete publication of "individual item[s], in [themselves] uninteresting"—except to those local notables, like the scribes, whose office had given them the means to exploit their knowledge. Now that such items were published together, regularly, all at one time, and in much greater quantities, broader segments of the population were likely to recognize their "important interest."[36] A cascade of news, it was thought, promoted a passively acquired familiarity with important events: a daily, spontaneous sociography engaged in by ordinary citizens. In this way, the rapid, periodic, comprehensive, impersonal distribution of information to even the smallest communities greatly increased the likelihood that matters of state and society would be viewed as matters of significant civic concern by the middle-class public.

Publishers, the second group of civic leaders, activated this theoretical potential and gave this public a more concrete shape. Their efforts catalyzed new practices of publicity and actively formed new markets for information. Seldom did they follow any explicit political agenda. Many were impoverished guild printers merely looking for a secure, government-guaranteed source of income. Leuze from Urach, for example, was a well-known public drunk, and Grözinger, of Reutlingen, was regarded as a "simple, poor printer who may not possess the necessary intellectual qualities [to print] deliberative [*räsonnierende*] articles."[37] Others, though they did preside over larger publishing empires, looked upon gazettes as sources of easy money to finance their more prestigious literary-intellectual publications. J. G. Ritter, every inch the businessman, fought for calendar and intelligence privileges in Ellwangen and Gmünd, but relied on county superintendent Milz to set up the Jagst region *Intelligenzblatt*. Evidently Ritter's collaboration with J. G. Pahl on the *Nationalchronik der Teutschen*, a regionally respected critical and political magazine, commanded more of his attention.[38]

None of this should detract from publishers' pivotal role. The source of innovation in the medium lay more in adjusting it to market conditions than in promoting a by now well-established ideology of popular Enlightenment. Simply by responding to market demand, publishers were forced to tailor the content of their papers to the popular fascination with civic utility and practical information. This prompted ad hoc changes of format to maximize readership, each relying on new permutations of substantive content and forging new pathways into civil society. The Hall guild printer Friedrich Haspel was one such experimenter. Submitting a series of prospectuses to local and regional censorship boards, he struggled for years to establish a solvent business in the publishing trade. An unusually diverse concatenation of intelligence items made up his proposed "Civic Polytechnic-Amusing Citizens' Journal for All Estates" of 1828. Besides announcements and advertisements, Haspel's proposed gazette included essays from the local Association for the Teaching and Improvement of the Trading and Commercial Estates. Even more interestingly, he intended to establish a "commission bureau" as an adjunct office to the gazette, reinforcing his claim to serve local business interests by providing them with valuable expertise and market information. Such services thrived where the traffic in commercial and social contacts had been emancipated from previous administrative monopolies. After casting about for several years, Haspel successfully contracted with the Gaildorf county council to publish his intelligence gazette in a modified form.[39]

What is noteworthy about such activity are the networks of alliances printers had to form in order to sell their product. They solicited contributions and/or financial support from a range of sources, including local agricultural improvement societies (the one in Gmünd was especially prolific); county superintendents who shepherded "improving" articles into their pet publications; charitable institutions and religious foundations; or local notables like preachers, factory owners, and agriculturalists. Publishers included notices and sometimes minutes of private agricultural, reading, social, and charitable associations and county fairs. They also acted as information clearinghouses for private citizens, whose advertisements for various products, services, and found items instructed readers to "inquire with the editors." The publisher Stahl offered "each businessman, professional, etc., the opportunity for a few *Kreuzer* to put his articles up for sale, which is of great utility for those who deliver excellent works that suffer from lack of demand because they are not known to the public."[40] In the cases of Rottweil and Esslingen, it appears that publishers spearheaded a market penetration of the countryside as a means of extending their audience.[41] In all these cases, experimentation with new forms of content provision capitalized on the new opportunities for institutional connections available in a rapidly expanding civil society: commission bureaus, agricultural societies, local governments, guilds, and foundations were but a few of their concrete manifestations. Again, not all these projects were successful, but the encyclopedism of their proposed contents denotes the space of possibilities in which publishers conceived of intelligence and offered it to their publics.

Over time this format ceased being coextensive with *Intelligenz* in its traditional sense, as frenetic market response ultimately ripped the gazettes from the state-policed confines of their medium. In the 1830s and 1840s, publishers fought bitterly with paternalistic superintendents who expunged articles they found impious. Regional censors objected to the ever-growing number of "merely entertaining" articles at the expense of practical, didactic essays. And interior ministry officials capriciously withheld permissions and demanded steep stamp taxes to print political news, even when it was simply reprinted out of precensored newspapers. These conflicts resulted from a more honest reckoning with the public, publishers having realized that the Enlightenment dream of teaching the *Volk* had been a bit too idealistic. For example, a publisher in Künzelsau who ran an "immoral" article depicting Luther in a bad light ran afoul of a "puritanical and pietistic" censor in the form of the county superintendent, who objected that "civic utility" had taken a back seat to entertainment. The author, a local preacher, had improperly depicted the devil as a "green hunter" in unholy alliance with a knight. This depiction was not judged a suitable representational device for "instructing the people." Dominikus Kistler, the publisher, replied that "the very nice idea that many readers have, that this *Kocher and Jagst Messenger* is an educational paper for these village inhabitants . . . is impractical. . . . These inhabitants neither read nor pay for the paper." They did not count among the "subscribers from the middle and educated class at whom the entertaining portion of my paper is directed."[42]

To the middle-class audience, the exclusion of politics, though constitutive of *Intelligenz* as a form of reason with purely practical referents, had grated from the very beginning. Some publishers complained of subscription cancellations on account of political censorship. Others grudgingly accepted the exclusion of political news upon founding their enterprises, only to sneak in such content later. By 1848, this tension flared into outright hostility, leading to at least one reprisal by a Sulz county superintendent infuriated by the local intelligence gazette's stray into "democratic" politics. He called it "one of the dirtiest" newspapers in Germany for indulging "cravings for revolution" and "liberati[ng] all passions," soon retracting all of its official business. In such cases it became clear that when politics was demanded "already in the first weeks" of a gazette's life, a mature, bourgeois market already existed, ready to engage in *Räsonnement*.[43] The paradox was that only government support had enabled the medium to take off: by maintaining full geographic coverage, keeping subscription costs low, ordering sample copies and making them publicly available at town halls, and serving the civic end of providing information of local scope and practical application. Ever since the gazettes' founding, in other words, only practical knowledge exclusive of politics embraced the whole spectrum of supporters, both private and official, necessary to sustain the new medium economically.

Nonetheless, in the decades leading up to 1848, the intelligence gazettes cultivated networks of local contacts sufficiently lucrative to support themselves financially. Only then did the supply of and demand for information become sufficiently intense to be useful. The local market for information was concentrated enough to appeal to common peasants and tradesmen taking out advertisements in intelligence gazettes, and at the same time, broad-based enough to generate economies of scale for the gazettes' owner-publishers. The 1830s and 1840s were thus marked by a clear privatization of the medium as the proportion of nonofficial content grew. In the *Öhringer Intelligenzblatt*, for example, the ratio of private to official nonstatistical column space increased from 1:8 in 1823–24 to 7:8 in 1835; in the same period, the number of insertions originating in the countryside grew from a quarter to over a third of all private ads.[44] Many private advertisements exhibited a distinctly entrepreneurial bent. Servant girls offered to clean house in columns previously filled with notices from wealthy book shop owners. December issues featured recommendations for Christmas presents. Craftsmen offered "recommendations" for their wares and "guaranteed quick and prompt delivery." Peasants made extra money on the side selling straw and timber.

At the root of the turn toward politics, entertainment, and critical content, then, was a market base secure enough to permit publishers to challenge old, resented limitations. Politics was only one interest among the many that the gazettes cultivated, but one whose potential to increase readership could not easily be ignored by publishers. The Raach brothers, for example, having unwittingly acquired an intelligence gazette without its attached official monopoly, found themselves forced to innovate. Their *Rems Valley Messenger* flourished in the 1840s, featuring political news, poetry, "charades," and private advertisements, while its competition, the officially sanctioned and increasingly boring *Amts- und Intelligenzblatt*, careened toward financial ruin.[45] The politicization of the intelligence gazettes was thus in no way inevitable but rather a patterned response to market forces. Much as public financing had artificially prolonged the life of the intelligence gazette—and promoted its associated social networks—so the increased willingness to found independent ventures now testified to publishers' possession of an alternative to *Intelligenz* as a road map for their precarious undertakings. This new road map was the classic nineteenth century newspaper, whose time had come in Württemberg by the 1850s.

· · · · ·

That *Intelligenz* ultimately issued into *Räsonnement* is a development with profound implications. It suggests a deep and historically novel link between evolving writing practices and civil society's emancipation from the state. A potent, independent "imagined community" was prefigured in the encyclopedic objects of knowledge populating the map of intelligence itself.[46] Private property sales, listed serially in the columns of intelligence gazettes, created an identity among households indefinitely replicated across the countryside. Commodity prices printed weekly showed one's own locality alongside others, gathering villages into regions of a scope intelligible to the common reader. A pair of advertisements for a single tobacco pipe, lost and found the same week by strangers on the road from Oberohrn to Waldenburg, testified to the power of *Intelligenzblätter* to render anonymous, chance interactions meaningful.[47] Such items inscribed a dense map of contacts and drew ever widening circles into a community whose participants had material interests in learning how to read this map. Without such a guide, these interests remained merely an inchoate "system of needs," in Hegel's words; without the interests, the notion of *Intelligenz* became a useless, empty construct. Taken together, however, the visual medium and the social networks it organized assembled an encyclopedic array of information into a weekly sociography of civil society.

The view of civil society reflected in the history of the intelligence gazettes is one that delves under the surface of institutions—newspapers, commodity markets, local governments, civic associations, business establishments (publishers, commission bureaus)—to access the repertoire of cognitive and social practices sustaining them. That this repertoire still incorporated many of the disciplinary and paternalistic biases inherited from the popular Enlightenment is undeniable. Access to and control over the gazettes' content was hardly democratic, but instead was structured by small-town market and political relationships favoring notable hegemony. Lurking beneath the continued institutional partnership between state and local notables, however, a seismic shift had occurred in the way citizenship was practiced in Biedermeier Württemberg. By bringing the Enlightenment's encyclopedic sensibility to bloom in community settings, and facilitating the practice of sociography among ever wider circles of the citizenry, the intelligence gazettes finally enabled "free association" to flourish as both cognitive and social practice. The panoply of their objects of knowledge corresponded to the variety in social background among their producers and consumers. The resultant forms of social communication reflected, and by 1848 even reshaped, the power of local citizens vis-à-vis the state. No accomplishment could more clearly illustrate the emancipation of writing and its role in founding civil society.

Conclusion

Practices of official writing vividly depict how bureaucratic power is applied, how citizenship is exercised within the state, and how civil society emerges from textual encounters between officials and citizens through a long learning process. This book has tracked changes in writing practice over a tumultuous period in Germany's history by examining four separate, yet interlocking, aspects of its civic culture. First, the quality of formality underlies actions and assumptions utterly fundamental to the rule of law in an ordered, civilized society, all centered on the ability to seize a text and derive from it a series of practical truths, interpersonal obligations, and standards of fairness and justice governing citizens' interactions with each other and with the state. Second, the circulation of texts sustains networks of collegiality crucial to the ability of both citizens and bureaucracies to associate freely, to participate in communicative action, and to reach common agreements and understandings, separately and in their mutual encounters. Third, sociography opens up a wide world of social practices to visual, textual understanding, enabling traditional face-to-face communities to be amalgamated into larger, more abstract, and ever more cosmopolitan civil societies. Finally, encyclopedism taps the very sources of intellectual creativity to breathe historically specific cultural meaning, derived from the European Enlightenment, into notions of progress, freedom, and modernity.

All four of these concepts denote crucial elements in the seamless web of cognitive and social practices undergirding civil society, and each retains its importance in the shift from the early modern to the modern world in Germany. Nonetheless, two broad shifts, from formality to sociography and from collegiality to encyclopedism, are discernible in the emancipation of writing from state power described in the pages above. Formality, the prime attribute of official texts ranging from contracts to protocols to mandates to petitions, is the artifact of a time when the state had an active hand in enforcing citizens' obligations through written texts, and when citizens in turn exploited this as a means to make their own wishes felt and interests known. Formality, of course, by no means disappeared with the advent of civil society. Yet it was soon complemented by sociography, precisely the faculty needed at a time when state and society had drawn apart, and each now had to read and interpret a more robust, free, and diverse social world—whether through dossiers and sociological surveys, on the state's side, or reference almanacs and intelligence gazettes, on the citizen's.

Collegiality, like formality, remains central to the practice of civil society; it is indeed the very mediator of civility informally, in daily life, as well as institutionally, in the voluntary association. Yet the collegiality found in a corporative society remained highly constrained by official procedures policed by the state. Not only does such a formalized collegiality fail to promote a truly free association among citizens, but it suffers amidst the continuous dissolution and reconstitution of social bonds characteristic of the modern epoch—and apparent in this book, in dramatic form, in Napoleon's rampage through Germany. In such contexts, new roadmaps become necessary to restore civic culture and a sense of community after traumatic reshufflings of territory and populations. Thus, beginning in the 1820s, Württemberg citizens no longer obtained their information exclusively from other people, in particular the scribes, but increasingly obtained it from printed sources, as repositories of useful knowledge. Citizens' ability to envision new prospects in a less mediated fashion is the hallmark of encyclopedism, whose objects of interest populate the brave new world of free association heralded by civil society's emancipation.

By focusing on the emancipation of writing from official tutelage, this book has reexamined the making of German civil society in the decades before and after Napoleon's invasions. It reverses what has come to be accepted as the standard narrative of civil society's emergence in Germany. This narrative views civil society as a project hatched in the voluntary associations and public sphere of the Enlightenment, implemented as a legal and infrastructural framework by the state's "reform from above," and then taken up by the German citizenry as a kind of gift (or curse) of freedom.[1] This book, by contrast, placed citizenship *first* and only then traced the development of state reform and popular Enlightenment. As Part 1 showed, citizenship practice was just as vibrant (if not more so) when state and society were indistinguishable, as it was when formal freedoms from state authority had been established. Part 2 demonstrated how the state had to reckon with its citizens even at the height of Napoleonic absolutism, and especially during the parliamentary and constitutional negotiations that produced reform from above. Only after this reform architecture was established could Enlightenment finally find a deep and lasting popular resonance—an argument to which the abortive attempts of the Black Forest Jacobins and Heinrich Bolley's constitutional fetishists constitute exceptions proving the rule. Thus it was the prior cooperation between state and citizenry that lay the foundations for civil society and Enlightenment culture, and not the other way around.

In some polemical formulations, civil society's origin in the state is thought to have hobbled the development of an independent culture of citizenship and condemned Germany to an authoritarian path. The 1848 revolution in particular is often seen as illustrating that a society which owed its freedoms to the state could never successfully rise up against it.[2] These arguments are obviated by the realization that citizenship practice was embedded in state formation from the beginning. This restores some historical contingency to the epoch of Germany's modernization during and after Napoleon. None of this is meant to deny the causal primacy of the state in all of the historical processes examined in the previous pages, and indeed in most German historiography generally. But at each level of my analysis I have shown how the powers the state conferred on writing eluded its grasp nonetheless. In communities, in parliament, in bureaucratic chancelleries, in political culture at large, the tutelage of intermediaries preserved the integrity of citizenship practices. And the plasticity of writing, the medium of their authority, ensured a broad social dispersal of their power after their fall from influence. Thus the *Schreiber* bequeathed even to their most vehement opponents a tradition of local activism and political involvement that outlasted their demise as a class of notables. All this affords a fundamentally new perspective on Germany's early-nineteenth-century transition to modernity after Napoleon. It demands a greater sensitivity to the abiding legacy and power of old-regime civic culture than has been common in past treatments, in which, amidst all the ruptures and disjunctures heralding modernity's advent in Germany, only the oppressive powers of the state are alleged to have continued unabated.

Embedding citizenship within state formation means that two movements in particular must be viewed as secondary to the development of civil society: nationalism and liberalism. Each of these movements posits that the source of political membership and civic identity lies outside the state and exists autonomously in either "culture" or "nature," respectively. It is therefore common to conceive of them as nurturing citizenship practices and social freedoms. But neither nationalism's faith in an underlying cultural unity and a common national patrimony, nor liberalism's vision of a prepolitical state of nature founded on natural law, individual rights, and spontaneous sociability proved relevant to the creation of civil society in Württemberg. Quite the opposite: the success of these ideologies in the pre-1848 period fed upon resources of civic activism established well before Napoleon. Both the "imagined communities" forming the modern nation and the framework of the public sphere and voluntary associations comprising liberalism's principal achievement derived from civil society rather than propelling its original creation.[3] Both arose only at the very end of the long historical process by which civil society was marked off from the state. By then, an entire tissue of practices, values, and institutions comprising the legacy of old-regime civic culture had been restitched. Woven and rewoven from thousands of daily negotiations over authority and achieving sporadic expression in mobilizations ranging from the Black Forest Jacobins to the turn against the Good Old Law to the politicization of the intelligence gazettes, this civic culture not only predated liberal and nationalist ideologies but gave them a home in which to flourish.[4]

This in no way diminishes the significance of these ideologies or their associated political movements in nineteenth-century German history. It is nonetheless important to distinguish their role in the construction of novel civic identities from the repertoire of prior citizenship practices on which they drew for support.[5] To put it sharply, contemporary historians focus too much on identity at the expense of practice—on who people *are* rather than what they *do*—which threatens to narrow the circle of social actors able to contribute to historical change.[6] Such an approach privileges those, like poets and thinkers, whose ideologies influence the cultural construction of identity, as well as those, like statesmen and policymakers, whose reforms establish the political frameworks in which questions of identity acquire tangible relevance. The tendency to focus exclusively on elites, ideology, and reform is especially seductive for a period dominated by towering figures like Goethe and Hegel, Napoleon and Metternich. Shifting the focus from questions of identity to questions of practice, however, promises to reintegrate the actions of everyday people into the analysis of power and thus of history itself.

This procedure yields two important lessons for the nineteenth century. First, with respect to nationalism, it corrects the common view of Germany's "age of liberation" as an epoch in which intellectuals conceived a *völkisch* Romanticism in reaction to cosmopolitan French invaders and then imparted their xenophobic sentiments to other strata of the population. The changes in civic practice described in this book in fact offer no evidence whatsoever that nationalist ideology contributed to the development of civil society: as late as the 1820s and 1830s, the "nation" and the "fatherland" unambiguously denoted the kingdom of Württemberg. At the very least, civic practice and national identity must be viewed as separable strains of political development whose contingent interaction gives subsequent German history its particular drama.[7] Second, with respect to liberalism, attention to practice complicates our view of how modern gender identity developed. An emergent scholarly consensus holds liberal legal reforms responsible for the marked intensification of patriarchy at the turn of the nineteenth century.[8] Thus in Württemberg, reforms of 1828 finally emancipated women to conduct official written business, but simultaneously enhanced husbands' control over their wives' property. As David Sabean has shown, however, the reforms' intent was not sexist but capitalist: to prevent women beset by bankruptcy from evading their creditors by taking refuge behind male protectors. Since the abolition of gender tutelage—supervised by Heinrich Bolley—occurred only two years after the dissolution of the *Schreiberei*, it must be seen as part of a broader effort to reconfigure the practices linking citizens with their families, their property, and the state after the end of the scribes' tutelage.[9]

Though more research is needed, a crucial point remains: civil society, while formed in the midst of ideological and legal exclusions—of class, nation, and gender identities—was not *founded* upon them. Fundamental, rather, are daily social practices, which may also be exclusionary but are not necessarily so. Modern civil society is in part defined by the unusual efficacy elite discourse acquires, as ideology and reform, to reshape social identities, but this should not obscure the fact that such discourse always develops in complex and contingent interaction with social practice.

For all these reasons, the citizen's encounter with the state must be regarded as the cardinal learning process by which civil society was formed. The benefits of this civic education far outlasted the state's dismantling of the textual formalities and official procedures once binding citizens so closely to their state. The emancipation of writing, to put it another way, by no means marked the end of old-regime civic culture, but instead propelled it into a new phase of creative reinterpretation in the age of voluntary association. Anyone who has attended the meetings of a local civic or fraternal organization can attest to the extreme seriousness with which rules of order and parliamentary procedure are taken by even the smallest and most intimate gatherings. The reading of minutes, the setting of agendas, the activities of recording and corresponding secretaries, the consultation of club archives for precedents, the extreme emphasis on proper bookkeeping and accounting—citizens learned many of these practices from their encounters with the state and then adapted and imitated them in their own dealings.[10] This was especially true of Germany, whose peculiar national fetish for formality helps explain one of the most noteworthy aspects of its nineteenth-century social landscape: *Vereinsmeierei*, the mania for associations, for which Germany is both famed and satirized.[11] There, the spread of gymnastic, choral, sharpshooting, and other forms of voluntary association was accompanied by strict statutes, elaborate rules of order, and national conventions. The state often acted as the midwife of such formalities in that it required local and national *Vereine* to register with the police and adhere to certain record-keeping procedures. But this just as surely reflects Germans' own historically acquired commitment to formality as a lubricant of civility.

If the old regime's culture of formality thus provided the seedbed for civil society to develop, then modernity, in the various guises denoted by the other three concepts, added a range of other civic practices to the voluntary association. Collegiality is of course the raison d'être of the voluntary association, and the craving for sociability it fulfills has long been recognized as an outgrowth of the Enlightenment. But only recently have scholars begun to appreciate that its institutional form derives from the state. In their mid-level organization, with subdivisions for every region, state, and locality, nineteenth-century voluntary associations of all sorts mimicked the federal structures—the political boundaries and administrative units—of the nation-states where they took root.[12] The voluntary association also performs sociography in many ways, all designed to facilitate communication, movement, and initiation, both of individual members and of affiliated associations in other locations. Published handbooks (on masonic rites, for example); local, regional, and national conventions; newsletters, correspondence networks, and letters of introduction accompanying out-of-town members from other branches; and ranks, grades, and titles all fulfill this function. Finally, the culture of voluntary association itself instantiates encyclopedism in the vast number and types of organizations to which it gives rise; these encompass every conceivable human interest and objective, and this circle continually expands as new needs are recognized and human endeavors imagined that require collective input and cooperation. The driving spirit behind all of their diverse undertakings is a commitment to progress, openness, and voluntarism, inherited directly from the Enlightenment's encyclopedic project.

All these observations suggest that while the voluntary association stands as the primary crystallized, institutional embodiment of civil society in the modern world, it is insufficient to approach its history with an exclusive focus on its outward, epiphenomenal manifestations. Civil society should rather be defined in terms of the underlying shifts in action, cognition, and imagination enabling citizens to socialize and communicate freely and independently of the state. These shifts are registered by changes in the civic landscape where citizens originally encountered the state, and where the sides of this divide began, over time, to draw apart. To be sure, a variety of other factors fed into civil society's development. Among these are the habits acquired in the market, which in classical social thought acts as a school for civility and accustoms everyday citizens to handling their affairs through regulations, record keeping, and formality. Nevertheless, it remains true that the distinctive characteristic of civil society as a peculiarly modern social order lies in imbuing private, voluntary, and otherwise completely informal interactions with an ethical quality normally associated with the laws and procedures of the state. In this way, notions of justice acquired by citizens in their interactions with the state were carried over into private life. This hybrid quality—half public, half private; half official, half informal—distinguishes the nineteenth-century voluntary association from the informal groupings found in every human society.

Thus the lesson remains that people can and do learn citizenship primarily by interacting with the state. It is easy to downplay the significance of these encounters in the contemporary age, when the very supremacy of civil society has authorized the belief that the state, at worst, actively thwarts civic freedom, and, at best, should confine itself to erecting an infrastructural framework where freedom can flourish. Such views, corresponding to the conservative and liberal philosophies respectively, are an inevitable by-product of civil society's emancipation, since a return to a fully integrated polity—with the state itself as the community of political participation—is, under present conditions, both undesirable and unattainable, at least on the level of nations. But in smaller, local civic communities as well as in global networks and organizations, engagement with the state provides a vital legacy, one that a purely informal, voluntary association of atomized citizens cannot offer. The history of official writing sheds light on the frameworks for action and imagination where citizenship in civil society first acquired this emancipatory potential.

Glossary

Altrechtler	Good Old Law partisan
Amt	cantonal hinterland (villages)
Amtsversammlung	cantonal assembly
Bildung	education, cultivation
Bürger	citizen
Bürgermeister	burgomasters (town fiscal officers)
Cahier	list of citizen grievances
Capitulation	scribe's official contract with his community
Ehrbarkeit	urban notability
gutes altes Recht	Good Old Law
Incipient	junior apprentice scribe
Landtag	estates assembly
Magistrat	city council (= *Bürgermeister, Gericht, und Rat)*
Nationalliste	bureaucratic personnel dossier
Oberamt	an *Oberamtmann's* office; after 1818, county (successor to *Stadt und Amt)*
Oberamtmann	superintendent; head ducal official in a canton
Schreiber	scribe
Schreiberei	a scribe's office; the institution in general
Schultheiß	village mayor
Skribent	apprentice scribe
Stadt und Amt	canton
Stadt, Amtsstadt	cantonal seat (city)
Stadt- und Amtsschreiber	head scribe in a canton *(Stadt und Amt)*

Stand	estate, corporation, status
Substitut	journeyman scribe (often prefixed *Stadt-* or *Amt-*)
Tübinger Vertrag	Tübingen Compact, Württemberg's constitution
Vielschreiberei	verbiage; red tape
Vollmacht	mandate; power of attorney

Note on currency: 1 Gulden (fl.) = 60 Kreuzer (kr.)

Abbreviations

parl.	parliamentary
Pol. Min.	Royal Capital City and Police Ministry
PrivC	Privy Council(lor) *(Geheimer Rat)*
Reg. Gov.	Regional government (post-Napoleonic *Kreisregierung)*
Sch.	*Schreiberei*
SCA	Section for Communal Administration
Schß.	*Schultheiß(en)*
Sect.	Napoleonic administrative sector *(Landvogtei)*
Stat. Ofc.	Statistical Office
Sub.	*Substitut*

Documents

§	legal paragraph or subsection
Cap.	*Capitulation* (service contract)
ch.	chapter *(Capitel* in *Commun-Ordnung)*
cop.	copy *(Copia)*
dft.	draft *(Concept)*
doc.	document
encl.	enclosure *(Beilage)*
exc.	excerpt *(Auszug)*
exhib.	exhibit *(Lit.)*
exp. opin.	expert opinion *(Gutachten)*
inc. rpt.	income report *(Einkommens-Fassion)*
mand.	mandate, power of attorney *(Vollmacht)*
NL	*Nationalliste*
ord.	ordinance *(Verordnung)*
pet.	petition *(Bittschrift, Petition, Memorial, Protestation, Eingabe, Supplikation, Beschwerde)*
prop.	proposal *(Entwurf)*
prot.	protocol *(Protokoll)*
resc.	rescript *(Rescript,* government enactment*)*
rpt.	report *(Relation)*
sec.	section *(Abschnitt* in *Commun-Ordnung)*

Document Collections

Bü	*Büschel* (file)
elec.	election investigation
inv.	other official investigation

Place Names

Back.	Backnang
Ellw.	Ellwangen
Heil.	Heilbronn
Kirch.	Kirchheim
Lud.	Ludwigsburg
Nag.	Nagold
Reut.	Reutlingen
Rott.	Rottweil
Schn.	Schorndorf
Stgt.	Stuttgart
Tüb.	Tübingen
Waib.	Waiblingen
Weil.	Weilheim
Wild.	Wildberg

COLLECTIONS

Commun-Ordnung	J. J. Moser, *Ordnung für die Communen in dem Herzogthum Württemberg* (with chapter, section, and paragraph numbers)
NWD	Walther Pfeilsticker, *Neues Württembergisches Dienerbuch* (with section numbers; all references are to volume 3)
Reg. Bl.	*Königlich-Württembergisches Staats- und Regierungsblatt* (with date and page numbers)
Verh.	*Verhandlungen . . . der Landstände des Königreichs Württemberg* (with date, section, and page numbers)

JOURNALS

AfS	*Archiv für Sozialgeschichte*
ASR	*American Sociological Review*
BdL	*Berichte zur deutschen Landeskunde*
CEH	*Central European History*
CSSH	*Comparative Studies in Society and History*
HJ	*Historical Journal*
HZ	*Historische Zeitschrift*
IASL	*Internationales Archiv für Sozialgeschichte der deutschen Literatur*

IRSH	International Review for Social History
JMH	Journal of Modern History
SH	Social History
SOWI	Sozialwissenschaftliche Informationen für Unterricht und Studium
WF	Württembergisch Franken
WVLG	Württembergische Vierteljahrshefte für Landesgeschichte
WW	Wirkendes Wort
ZHF	Zeitschrift für historische Forschung
ZWLG	Zeitschrift für württembergische Landesgeschichte

Notes

INTRODUCTION

1. On citizenship as practice, see Margaret Somers, "Citizenship and the Place of the Public Sphere: Law, Community, and Political Culture in the Transition to Democracy," *ASR* 58 (1993): 587–621; on citizenship as identity, Rogers Brubaker, *Citizenship and Nationhood in France and Germany* (Cambridge, Mass.: Harvard University Press, 1992).

2. The best guide to the discourse of civil society in Germany is Isabel Hull, *Sexuality, State, and Civil Society in Germany, 1700–1815* (Ithaca, N. Y.: Cornell University Press, 1996). The canonical philosophical treatment is that of G. W. F. Hegel (1770–1831), *Elements of the Philosophy of Right*, ed. Allen W. Wood (Cambridge, Eng.: Cambridge University Press, 1991 [1821]).

3. Most scholarship on German reform from above adopts a top-down, state-centered approach, concentrating on policymakers and intellectuals and neglecting the interaction between reformers and citizens under Napoleon. This tends to reinforce the view that the German state presided over a more or less passive population of "subjects." See note 5 in Chapter 1 and note 1 in Chapter 5 for references and the Conclusion for further discussion of this issue.

4. The literature on civil society is vast. See, in particular, Jean L. Cohen and Andrew Arato, *Civil Society and Political Theory* (Cambridge, Mass.: M. I. T. Press, 1992); John Keane, ed., *Civil Society and the State: New European Perspectives* (London: Verso, 1989); Frank Trentmann, ed., *Paradoxes of Civil Society: New Perspectives on Modern German and British History* (New York: Berghahn Books, 1999); John Ehrenberg, *Civil Society: The Critical History of an Idea* (New York: New York University Press, 1999).

5. Historians have been most influenced by Habermas's *Structural Transformation of the Public Sphere: An Inquiry into a Category of Bourgeois Society* (Cambridge, Mass.: M. I. T. Press, 1989 [1962]); but see also his *Theory of Communicative Action*, trans. Thomas McCarthy (Cambridge, Eng.: Polity Press, 1986).

6. Michel Foucault, *Power/Knowledge: Selected Interviews and Other*

Writings, 1972–1977, trans. Colin Gordon et al. (New York: Pantheon, 1980); an edited collection inspired by Foucault's work, Graham Burchell, Colin Gordon, and Peter Miller, eds., *The Foucault Effect: Studies in Governmentality* (London: Harvester Wheatsheaf, 1991), is particularly useful for the complex of problems treated in this book.

7. Robert Putnam, *Making Democracy Work: Civic Traditions in Modern Italy* (Princeton, N. J.: Princeton University Press, 1993) is a recent model for the study of civic regions and networks of local affiliation.

8. For Germany, see Mack Walker, *German Home Towns: Community, State, and General Estate 1648–1871* (Ithaca, N. Y.: Cornell University Press, 1971); and David Warren Sabean, *Power in the Blood: Popular Culture and Village Discourse in Early Modern Germany* (Cambridge, Eng.: Cambridge University Press, 1984).

9. Benedict Anderson, *Imagined Communities: Reflections on the Origin and Spread of Nationalism*, 2nd ed. (London: Verso, 1991), treats this theme in a number of creative ways.

10. This view of the state modifies and extends Weber's classic definition, which focuses more specifically on monopolies over legitimate violence. The hallmark of the modern state is its expansion of control from the methods of violence into the domain of the "social," and thus into many disparate practices of power. Modern citizenship may be defined as the brake on the state's potentially all-encompassing extension of influence.

11. I have been especially influenced by Pierre Bourdieu, *Outline of a Theory of Practice* (Cambridge, Eng.: Cambridge University Press, 1977); and Roberto Mangabeira Unger, *Politics: The Central Texts: Theory Against Fate* (London: Verso, 1997). My analysis differs from the pioneering studies of print culture by Roger Chartier and Robert Darnton as well as the anthropology of writing and literacy practiced by Jack Goody and Walter J. Ong.

12. Cf. Brinkley Messick, *The Calligraphic State: Textual Domination and History in a Muslim Society* (Berkeley: University of California Press, 1993), which emphasizes the role of formal writing in practices of domination rather than citizenship.

13. James C. Scott, *Seeing Like a State: How Certain Schemes to Improve the Human Condition Have Failed* (New Haven, Conn.: Yale University Press, 1998) focuses exclusively on pernicious uses by the modern state of what I call sociography. Christopher A. Bayly, *Empire and Information: Intelligence Gathering and Social Communication in India, 1780–1870* (Cambridge, Eng.: Cambridge University Press, 1996) is more attuned to negotiations on the ground, and sensitive to local actors and their appropriations.

14. See Robert Darnton, "Philosophers Trim the Tree of Knowledge: The Epistemological Strategy of the *Encyclopédie*," in *The Great Cat Massacre And Other Episodes in French Cultural History* (New York: Basic Books, 1984), 191–214; Daniel Roche, *France in the Enlightenment* (Cambridge, Mass.: Harvard University Press, 1998), 11–74, 608–640; and Richard R. Yeo, *Encyclopaedic Visions: Scientific Dictionaries and Enlightenment Culture* (Cambridge, Eng.: Cambridge University Press, 2001).

CHAPTER 1: THE CIVIC LANDSCAPE

1. On Württemberg's Protestant political culture, see Hermann Bausinger, "Zur politischen Kultur Baden-Württembergs," in *Baden-Württemberg: Eine politische Landeskunde,* ed. Hermann Bausinger and Theodor Eschenburg (Stuttgart: W. Kohlhammer, 1985), 13–38; and Laurence Dickey, *Hegel: Religion, Economics and the Politics of Spirit 1770–1807* (Cambridge, Eng.: Cambridge University Press, 1987). On its concomitant failure to count as an "Enlightenment-friendly" state, see Reinhart Siegert, "Zur Topograhie der Aufklärung in Deutschland 1789: Methodische Überlegungen an Hand der zeitgenössischen Presse," in *Französische Revolution und deutsche Öffentlichkeit,* ed. Holger Böning (München: K. G. Saur, 1992), 47–90, esp. 58, 80. Cf. Dieter Narr, *Studien zur Spätaufklärung im deutschen Südwesten* (Stuttgart: W. Kohlhammer, 1979), a heroic but ultimately unconvincing effort to reconcile Pietism and Enlightenment in Württemberg.

2. On late Enlightenment civic culture in Germany, see Hull, *Sexuality, State, and Civil Society;* James Schmidt, *What Is Enlightenment?: Eighteenth-Century Answers and Twentieth-Century Questions* (Berkeley: University of California Press, 1996); Richard van Dülmen, *Die Gesellschaft der Aufklärer: Zur bürgerlichen Emanzipation und aufklärerischen Kultur in Deutschland* (Frankfurt: Fischer Taschenbuch Verlag, 1986); Ulrich Im Hof, *Das gesellige Jahrhundert: Gesellschaft und Gesellschaften im Zeitalter der Aufklärung* (München: C. H. Beck, 1982); Hans Erich Bödecker and Ulrich Herrmann, eds., *Über den Prozeß der Aufklärung in Deutschland im 18. Jahrhundert: Personen, Institutionen und Medien* (Göttingen: Vandenhoeck & Ruprecht, 1987); Franklin Koptizsch, ed., *Aufklärung, Absolutismus und Bürgertum in Deutschland* (München: Nymphenburger Verlagshandlung, 1976); and Ulrich Herrmann, ed., *"Die Bildung des Bürgers": Die Formierung der bürgerlichen Gesellschaft und die Gebildeten im 18. Jahrhundert* (Weinheim: Beltz, 1989).

3. Long associated with the works of Peter Blickle and Winfried Schulze on the sixteenth and seventeenth centuries, the rehabilitation of early modern German civic culture (in both its legalistic and violent forms) was in the 1990s decisively extended to the eighteenth century and beyond. See in particular David Martin Luebke, *His Majesty's Rebels: Communities, Factions, and Rural Revolt in the Black Forest, 1725–1745* (Ithaca, N. Y.: Cornell University Press, 1997); Robert von Friedeburg, *Ländliche Gesellschaft und Obrigkeit: Gemeindeprotest und politische Mobilisierung im 18. und 19. Jahrhundert* (Göttingen: Vandenhoeck & Ruprecht, 1997); idem, "'Reiche', 'Geringe Leute' und 'Beambte': Landesherrschaft, dörfliche 'Factionen' und gemeindliche Partizipation 1648–1806," *ZHF* 23, no. 2 (1996): 219–65; Helmut Gabel, *Widerstand und Kooperation: Studien zur politischen Kultur rheinischer und maasländischer Kleinterritorien (1648–1794)* (Tübingen: Bibliotheca Academica, 1995); idem and Winfried Schulze, "Peasant Resistance and Politicization in Germany in the Eighteenth Century," in *The Transformation of Political Culture: England and Germany in the Late Eighteenth Century,* ed. Eckhart

Hellmuth (London: German Historical Institute/Oxford University Press, 1990), 119–48; Andreas Würgler, *Unruhen und Öffentlichkeit: Städtische und Ländliche Protestbewegungen im 18. Jahrhundert* (Tübingen: Bibliotheca Academica, 1995); and Peter Blickle, ed., *Gemeinde und Staat im Alten Europa, Beiheft 25 to HZ* (Munich: Oldenbourg, 1998).

4. Karl Wegert, "Contention with Civility: The State and Social Control in the German Southwest, 1760–1850," *HJ* 34, no. 2 (1991): 349–69.

5. The scribes' mediating role distinguished them from the high-echelon bureaucrat and the ambitious literary intellectual, to name the two most studied social types for this period. Emphasis on these groups has reinforced a top-down perspective in the historiography, which neglects interaction between elites and society. See, on both types, Hull, *Sexuality*. On bureaucrats, see Hans Rosenberg, *Bureaucracy, Aristocracy and Autocracy: The Prussian Experience 1660–1815* (Cambridge, Mass.: Harvard University Press, 1966); and Reinhart Koselleck, *Preussen zwischen Reform und Revolution: Allgemeines Landrecht, Verwaltung und soziale Bewegung von 1791 bis 1848* (Stuttgart: Klett-Cotta, 1967). Two studies that do emphasize official mediation are Walker, *German Home Towns;* and Alf Lüdtke, *"Gemeinwohl," Polizei, und "Festungspraxis": Staatliche Gewaltsamkeit und innere Verwaltung in Preußen, 1815–1850* (Göttingen: Vandenhoeck & Ruprecht, 1982). On literary intellectuals, see Hans Gerth, *Bürgerliche Intelligenz um 1800: Zur Soziologie des deutschen Frühliberalismus* (Göttingen: Vandenhoeck & Ruprecht, 1976 [1935]); Frederick C. Beiser, *Enlightenment, Revolution, and Romanticism: The Genesis of Modern German Political Thought, 1790–1800* (Cambridge, Mass.: Harvard University Press, 1992); and Klaus Epstein, *The Genesis of German Conservatism* (Princeton, N. J.,: Princeton University Press, 1966).

6. *Edinburgh Review* (Feb. 1818): 340–41.

7. On Württemberg parliamentarism, see Walter Grube, *Der Stuttgarter Landtag 1457–1957: Von den Landständen zum demokratischen Parlament* (Stuttgart: Ernst Klett, 1957), esp. 74–86.

8. Dickey, *Hegel*, 33–138.

9. On *Ehrbarkeit*, see Werner Gebhardt, *Bürgertum in Stuttgart: Beiträge zur "Ehrbarkeit" und zur Familie Autenrieth* (Neustadt an der Aisch: Degener, 1999); Martin Hasselhorn, *Der altwürttembergische Pfarrstand im 18. Jahrhundert* (Stuttgart: W. Kohlhammer, 1958); and for the point on dialect, Hans-Martin Decker-Hauff, "Die geistige Führungsschicht Württembergs," in *Beamtentum und Pfarrerstand 1400–1800*, ed. Günther Franz (Limpurg: C. A. Starke, 1972), 51–80; p. 57.

10. On the Württemberg state and estates, see James Vann, *The Making of a State: Württemberg 1593–1793* (Ithaca, N. Y.: Cornell University Press, 1984); Francis L. Carsten, *Princes and Parliaments in Germany from the Fifteenth to the Eighteenth Centuries* (Oxford: Oxford University Press, 1959); Peter H. Wilson, *War, State, and Society in Württemberg, 1677–1793* (Cambridge, Eng.: Cambridge University Press, 1995); Dickey, *Hegel;* and Grube, *Landtag.*

11. I call these officials "bureaucrats" in part because they possessed a series

of ideal-typical Weberian characteristics, and in part to distinguish them from local officials who by no means shared these traits. The former acted in accord with state, not narrowly ducal, interests; took a body of law, procedure, and precedent as a strict guide for their behavior; pursued career goals, not personal enrichment or particularist interests; were salaried and appointed as state servants; and were protected from arbitrary dismissal by official contracts *(Etats, Dienstverträge)*. Other aspects, such as the compartmentalization and hierarchical organization of functional tasks, were less strongly developed at this time. On this issue, see Vann, *Making of a State*, esp. 245; Friedrich Wintterlin, *Geschichte der Behördenorganisation in Württemberg* (Stuttgart: W. Kohlhammer, 1902), vol. 1, 11–31, 63–80, 104–107; also Wilhelm Bleek, *Von der Kameralausbildung zum Juristenprivileg: Studium, Prüfung und Ausbildung der höheren Beamten des allgemeinen Verwaltungsdienstes in Deutschland im 18. und 19. Jahrhundert* (Berlin: Colloquium Verlag, 1972); and Bernd Wunder, *Privilegierung und Disziplinierung: Die Entstehung des Berufsbeamtentums in Bayern und Württemberg 1780–1825* (München: Oldenbourg, 1978).

12. By treating the *Landtag* strictly on its own terms, as a decidedly non-modern "corporative" body, I mean to strenuously avoid the vexatious debate on whether premodern estates assemblies did or did not serve as the progenitors of modern, democratic parliamentarism in Germany. See Chapters 3 and 4 for more on this.

13. On Württemberg proto-industry, see Hans Medick, *Weben und Überleben in Laichingen 1650–1900:. Lokalgeschichte als Allgemeine Geschichte* (Göttingen: Vandenhoeck & Ruprecht, 1996); Sheilagh Ogilvie, *State Corporatism and Proto-Industry: The Württemberg Black Forest, 1580–1797* (Cambridge, Eng.: Cambridge University Press, 1997); and Walter Troeltsch, *Die Calwer Zeughandelskompagnie und ihre Arbeiter: Studien zur Gewerbe- und Sozialgeschichte Altwürttembergs* (Jena: G. Fischer, 1897).

14. Cf. Walker, *Home Towns*; see Medick, *Weben und Überleben* and Ogilvie, *State Corporatism*, on highland guilds supported by cameralist policy.

15. *Commun-Ordnung*, ch. 3, sec. 4, §8.

16. On gender equality, see immediately below; on gender inequality, see Chapter 2.

17. On property freedoms and land tenure see David Warren Sabean, *Property, Production, and Family in Neckarhausen, 1700–1870* (Cambridge, Eng.: Cambridge University Press, 1990); Wolfgang von Hippel, *Die Bauernbefreiung im Königreich Württemberg*, 2 vols. (Boppard am Rhein: Harald Boldt, 1977); Theodor Knapp, *Neue Beiträge zur Rechts- und Wirtschaftsgeschichte des württembergischen Bauernstandes*, 2 vols. (Tübingen: H. Laupp, 1919); idem, *Gesammelte Beiträge zur Rechts- und Wirtschaftsgeschichte vornehmlich des deutschen Bauerntums* (Tübingen: H. Laupp, 1902).

18. In Württemberg, as elsewhere, one should distinguish between de facto freeholdings still subject to seigneurial dues (through *Grundherrschaft*), and truly free land held outright by peasants, on which no dues were collected; these parcels continued to be subject to other levies and taxes (through *Gerichts-* and

Landesherrschaft), thus diminishing the importance of the distinction. In general, any property subject to the freedoms described above is and was considered peasant property *(Eigentum)*; see Hippel, *Bauernbefreiung* 1:99–105.

19. Sabean, *Property, Production, and Family*, 18, 183–207, 418–22; on partible inheritance *(Realteilung)*, see also Hippel, *Bauernbefreiung*, 63ff.

20. Over time, however, a shift toward intermarriage among notable elites did in fact give rise to such a class separation; this is a very important finding of David Warren Sabean, *Kinship in Neckarhausen, 1700–1870* (Cambridge, Eng.: Cambridge University Press, 1998).

21. Hippel, *Bauernbefreiung*, chart on p. 291, plus pp. 278–304 generally. Württemberg was a land of classical *Grundherrschaft*, lordship over the land, broadly typical of western Germany and the southwest particularly.

22. The alternative to this was to centralize powers territorially and subdivide them instead by function: the German answer to the separation of powers doctrine, which tended to promote bureaucratization rather than local self-government. This system was actually implemented in the Napoleonic period, though in a way that continued to respect local autonomy, as is discussed in Chapter 6. For comparative administrative history, see Walter Grube, *Vogteien, Ämter, Landkreise in der Geschichte Südwestdeutschlands* (Stuttgart: W. Kohlhammer, 1960).

23. Sabean, *Power in the Blood*, 20–27.

24. On Württemberg, see Hans Medick, "Von der Bürgerherrschaft zur Staatsbürgerlichen Gesellschaft: Württemberg zwischen Ancien régime und Vormärz," in *Bürgerliche Gesellschaft in Deutschland: Historische Einblicke, Fragen, Perspektiven*, ed. Lutz Niethammer (Frankfurt: Fischer Taschenbuch Verlag, 1990), 52–79; Helen P. Liebel, "The Bourgeoisie in Southwestern Germany, 1500–1789: A Rising Class?" *IRSH* 10, no. 2 (1965): 283–307. Current research on the *Bürgertum*, especially among the research associates of Lothar Gall, focuses more on urban patriciates and guilds than on small-town officeholders, but see the detailed prosopographical study by Stefan Brakensiek, *Fürstendiener, Staatsbeamte, Bürger: Amtsführung und Lebenswelt der Ortsbeamten in Niederhessischen Kleinstädten (1750–1830)* (Göttingen: Vandenhoeck & Ruprecht, 1999). A good review article on this subject is Jonathan Sperber, "*Bürger, Bürgertum, Bürgerlichkeit, Bürgerliche Gesellschaft:* Studies of the German (Upper) Middle Class and Its Sociocultural World," *JMH* 69 (June 1997): 271–97.

25. Sabean, *Kinship in Neckarhausen*, 37–62.

26. See Grube, *Vogteien*, 18–41 on the *Stadt und Amt* particularly; for specifics, *Commun-Ordnung*. Only a limited amount of the duchy's territory was exempt from cantonal organization; this included fourteen ecclesiastical districts *(Klosterämter)* and some private property held by the duke.

27. This had not always been the case. In former times this official, called a *Vogt* or *Stabsbeamter*, represented the canton in the Stuttgart *Landtag* and stood at the forefront of the countryside's efforts to assert its interests against the duke.

28. Johann Georg Bäuerlen, *Taschenbuch für angehende Wirtembergische Rechtsgelehrte und für Schreiber,* 2 vols. (Stuttgart: Johann Benedikt Mezler, 1793–94), 1793 vol., 92.

29. Sabean, *Power in the Blood,* 12–20 on local officials and institutions in Württemberg; also the *Commun-Ordnung;* on the workings of a magistracy in a single Württemberg city, see Rudolf Seigel, *Gericht und Rat in Tübingen: Von den Anfängen bis zur Einführung der Gemeindeverfassung 1818–1822* (Stuttgart: W. Kohlhammer, 1960).

30. Walter Grube, "Dorfgemeinde und Amtsversammlung in Altwürttemberg," *ZWLG* 13 (1954): 194–219. The competence and functions of the *Amtsversammlungen* were first codified in the 1758 *Commun-Ordnung.* See Chapter 4 for more.

31. Cantonal treasurers *(Amtspfleger),* physicians, and a variety of minor officials could and often did perform this function as well, but they were less important, with a less all-inclusive competence, than either superintendents or scribes.

32. Ecclesiastical territories headed by a prelate rather than an urban magistracy also employed only an *Amtsschreiber.*

33. The correlation between menial status and employment within smaller or dependent territories is illustrated by two examples from within Württemberg itself. So-called *Forstschreiber* and *Kammerschreiber* were employed, respectively, in the limited amount of forested territory and private ducal land exempt from cantonal organization. These scribes lacked the income, independence, and influence of the powerful *Stadt- und Amtsschreiber* and played no significant role in Württemberg political history.

34. Though the state reserved the right to confirm all cantonal elections, including for scribes, it rarely interfered unless a specific legal principle was violated.

35. See LT 9.4.2, Acta, der Stadt- und Amtsschreiber übermäsigen Schreibverdienst intendirende Schöpfung fixer Salrorium, documents and complaints from 1661–1738; and the lengthy case of Schreiber Schmid at Schorndorf discussed in Chapter 2.

36. Rudolf Magenau, *Wanderungen eines alten wirtembergischen Amtssubstituten aus einer Schreibstube in die andre, von ihm selbst beschrieben: Ein moralisches Erbauungsbuch für den wirtembergischen Schreiberstand* (Stuttgart: n.p., 1800), 6–7 for quotation; on cookbooks, LT 9.4.2, 1 Aug. 1780, letter to LT Cmte. from anonymous scribe; for other tales of household abuse, see Friedrich Bernritter, "Der Incipient eines Stadtschreibers schildert seine Behandlung," in *Wirtembergische Briefe* (Ulm: Stettin, 1840 [1786]), 116–20; and Friedrich Gutscher, *Bemerkungen und Vorschläge über das Schreiberei-Wesen im Wirtembergischen: Ein Beytrag zur Geschichte und Kultur dieses Landes* (n.p., 1792), 74.

37. General-Rescript of 13 Jan. 1739, cit. Gutscher, *Bemerkungen,* 67; also 70–71; repeated in the *Commun-Ordnung,* ch. 1, sec. 5, §14.

38. Certain neighboring cantons, like Urach and Münsingen, Besigheim and

Bietigheim, and Nagold and Wildberg, developed informal, reciprocal exchanges over the years. See *NWD* for these districts.

39. Balthasar Haug, *Das gelehrte Wirtemberg* (Hildesheim: Georg Olms, 1979 [1790]), 30–31, breaks this down as follows: of those employed, 153 served in ducal offices in Stuttgart, 20 on the *Landtag* staff, and 496 in cantonal and local positions; of those without permanent positions, 22 lived in Stuttgart, 286 were *Substituten* in the *Schreibereien*, and 227 worked in local ducal offices, chiefly the *Oberamteien*.

40. Thus its most famous geniuses went on to find fame and intellectual freedom elsewhere. G. W. F. Hegel, a native of Stuttgart, roomed with Schelling and Hölderlin at the Tübingen Theological Seminary, but gained his reputation in Jena and Berlin and later wrote about his native country with a kind of horrified distaste. See Gebhardt, *Bürgertum* (esp. on the *Familienstiftungen*); Hasselhorn, *Pfarrstand;* Dickey, *Hegel;* Sabean, *Power in the Blood;* Narr, *Spätaufklärung;* Hartmut Lehmann, *Pietismus und weltliche Ordnung in Württemberg vom 17. bis zum 20. Jahrhundert* (Stuttgart: W. Kohlhammer, 1969).

41. Ferdinand August Heinrich Weckherlin, *Apologie des wirttembergischen Schreiberstandes nebst einem Vorschlag zu seiner Vervollkommung* (Tübingen: Jacob Friedrich Heerbrandt, 1793), 90–91.

CHAPTER 2: THE TUTELAGE OF THE SCRIBES

1. Waib. assem. inv., #2, 28 Dec. 1794, Heinrich Bolley pet.

2. Schn. inv., 8 Sep. 1780, Entwurf einer Instruction, hereafter "Schn. Instruction," to which paragraph numbers refer.

3. The formal device of *Instruktion* was confined to the sole purpose of mandating parliamentary deputies (see Chapter 3). The Schorndorf Instruction was therefore annulled by ducal bureaucrats called upon to adjudicate its validity; ibid., 13 Oct. 1780, unsigned ducal judgment.

4. Medick, *Weben und Überleben,* 447–560, offers the most complete analysis of peasant literacy in its relation to Württemberg Pietism. Franz Quarthal is also engaged in a study of literacy in the German southwest; see his "Inventuren und Teilungen. Überlegungen zu Leseverhalten und Schreibfähigkeit" in the conference proceedings of the Arbeitskreis für Landes- und Ortsgeschichte, Hauptstaatsarchiv Stuttgart, 11 Nov. 1995. On schools, see Eugen Schmid, *Geschichte des Volksschulwesens in Altwürttemberg* (Stuttgart: W. Kohlhammer, 1926); also Rudolf Keck, *Geschichte der Mittleren Schule in Württemberg: Motive und Probleme ihrer Entwicklung von der Reformation bis zur Gegenwart unter besonderer Berücksichtigung von Stuttgart und Ulm* (Stuttgart: W. Kohlhammer, 1968).

5. Customarily, women were represented by their husband, but in cases of marital dispute, or when the woman was widowed or otherwise unattached, she could herself choose a separate *Kriegsvogt,* usually from among her relatives, to look out for her interests. Women retained full control over their property and

decisions, and the *Kriegsvogt* was legally limited to a consultative function. The term literally means "war steward," formally acknowledging the adversarial stance of the two parties to legal negotiation, including husbands and wives. On this institution, see Sabean, *Property, Production, and Family,* 208–18; and idem, "Allianzen und Listen: Die Geschlechtsvormundschaft im 18. und 19. Jahrhundert," in *Frauen in der Geschichte des Rechts: Von der Frühen Neuzeit bis zur Gegenwart,* ed. Ute Gerhard (Munich: C. H. Beck, 1997), 460–79.

6. *Commun-Ordnung,* ch. 1, sec. 8.

7. Walter Grube and Walter Bürkle, eds., *Das Archiv von Stadt und Amt Wildberg* (Stuttgart: W. Kohlhammer, 1952) is a catalog of a typical Schreiberei. On *Bücher* of various sorts, see 5–28, as well as *Commun-Ordnung,* ch. 3 and ch. 5, sec. 7; and Sabean, *Property, Production, and Family,* 70–87.

8. *Commun-Ordnung,* ch. 3, sec. 1, §§1–3.

9. Ibid., ch. 5, sec. 7, esp. §§8–9; also ch. 5, sec. 8, §§36–40 and passim.

10. Ibid., ch. 2, sec. 17 on mortgages and *Unterpfandsbücher* and *-zettel.*

11. Ibid., ch. 14, secs. 2–3 on *Rechnungs-Probe* and *-Abhör,* plus chs. 12–16 on *Rechnungswesen* and *Oekonomie* generally; see esp. ch. 14, sec. 2, §22 on the "Verlesung," where any individual, if competent in finance and politically influential enough to risk speaking up, could raise objections and correct errors in communal accounting. Also see Sabean, *Power in the Blood,* 19–20 on this institution.

12. Johann F. C. Weisser, *Das gesammte Rechnungs-Wesen: Zum Gebrauch für Wirtembergische Probatoren Substituten und Schreiber* (Stuttgart: Carl Eichele, 1802), iii–vi; also see Johann Georg Bäuerlen, *Lehrbuch sämtlicher Kameral- und Rechtswissenschaften, welche dem wirtembergischen Schreiber unentbehrlich sind* (Heilbronn: n.p., 1802). Others, including Friedrich List (on whom see Chapter 5, below) crusaded in frustration against the scribes' verbosity and inefficiency. Cf. Sabean, *Property, Production, and Family,* chs. 1–2, who argues instead that these records enhanced the state's ability to manage and control local "productive forces."

13. Philip T. Hoffman, Gilles Postel-Vinay, and Jean-Laurent Rosenthal, "Information and Economic History: How the Credit Market in Old Regime Paris Forces Us to Rethink the Transition to Capitalism," *American Historical Review* 104, no. 1 (Feb. 1999): 69–94, explores this theme in the related context of the French notarial class.

14. Weil. Sch. elec., 15 Oct. 1794, Salzer writing.

15. Wild. Sch. 5215, Stadtschreiber Diarium, 1802–4.

16. Schn. Instruction, §5, 22.

17. *Commun-Ordnung,* ch. 1, sec. 2, §2–3 on elections.

18. Schn. Instruction, §§14–15.

19. Sabean, *Property, Production, and Family,* 77; Schn. Instruction, §§12–13.

20. Wild. Sch. 5214, Formularbuch, ca. 1750s.

21. Ibid., pp. 38b–40, Contracta victalita.

22. Ibid., p. 64, Vergleich in Schwängerungssachen.

23. Sabean, *Property, Production, and Family,* 417–18 (for quotation), and

417n3 (for more examples); on the historicity of the person, see his *Power in the Blood*, 30–36.

24. Sabean, *Property, Production, and Family*, 71–72, 189–201; *Commun-Ordnung*, ch. 2, sec. 19.

25. Hildegard Mannheims, *Wie wird ein Inventar erstellt?: Rechtskommentare als Quelle der volkskundlichen Forschung* (Münster: F. Coppenrath, 1991), 28–54, 135ff., 242–45; also Angelika Bischoff-Luithlen, "Sprachschichten und Ausdrucksformen in altwürttembergischen Inventurakten," in *Ländliche Kulturformen im deutschen Südwesten: Festschrift für Heiner Heimberger*, ed. Peter Assion (Stuttgart: W. Kohlhammer, 1971), 107–22.

26. See Mannheims, *Inventar*; Philipp J. Späth, *Einleitung in das wirtembergische Inventur- und Teilungswesen* (Stuttgart: n.p., 1800).

27. *Commun-Ordnung*, ch. 2, sec. 19, §§18, 20, 22 on payment. Medick, *Weben und Überleben* and Sabean, *Property, Production, and Family* are two outstanding examples of microhistory based on careful reconstruction of Wurttemberg inventories.

28. *Commun-Ordnung*, ch. 2, sec. 19, §21; Sabean, *Property, Production, and Family*, 250–54 on *Loszettel*.

29. *Commun-Ordnung* ch. 2, sec. 19, §12 on the scribe's role during negotiations.

30. The proportion of those benefiting from nepotism ranged from 40% of scribes serving in the 1760s to 58% in the 1780s. In the 1750s, the decade of this case study, the number stood at 43% *(NWD)*.

31. Magenau, *Wanderungen eines alten wirtemberigschen Amtssubstituten aus einer Schreibstube in die andre*, 15–16.

32. Only 19% of scribes co-opted by this practice were the sons of scribes, versus 40% in the profession at large; more strikingly, only 9% came from their canton of service, as against 36% of all scribes *(NWD)*.

33. Wild. Sch. elec., 6 Oct. 1752.

34. Ibid., 18 Nov. 1752, dft. resc.

35. *Commun-Ordnung*, ch. 1, sec. 5, §2 on the scribe's *Capitulation;* also sec. 7; on deposits, which ranged as low as 100 and as high as 1000 fl., LT 9.4.2, Kaution-Formular; GovC inv. 8524, Schreiber Spannagel asks that his deposit be amortized.

36. Wild. Sch. elec., 11 Aug. 1753, dft. resc.; ibid., 9 Aug. 1753, rpt. from OA and Mag.

37. Scribes who inherited obligations to support their predecessors' families often reneged on them once comfortably installed in office. For denials of "Entschädigung," see *NWD* §2237; GovC inv. 8525, Regina Cuhorst case at Neuenbürg (1725); GovC inv. 8541, Senkeisen case at Weinsberg (1779).

38. Wild. Sch. elec., 12 Nov. 1752 for Wieland's letter.

39. Ibid., Grüb case, 21 Nov. 1796.

40. Weil. Sch. elec., 16 Jun. 1784 prot. on candidates, including Salzer, and election results.

41. Ibid., 15 Oct. 1794, Salzer writing.

42. Ibid., 6 Sep. 1784, inv. Klett rpt.; 5 Jun. 1784, Salzer application.

43. Weil. comm. inv. 487, #35, 7 Jan. 1789, OAM Zeller rpt. These cases *(Prozesse)* are from Kirch. Findbuch. For more on the various factions, see Weil. comm. inv. 486–93, Müller and Zeller invs.; GovC 629; and GovC inv. 2452.

44. Wintterlin, *Behördenorganisation,* 1:28–30, 76–80 on these policy organs. Also see diagram 1 above.

45. Sabean has made them the basis for his case-study approach in *Power in the Blood.*

46. Weil. comm. inv. 488, Gallus testimony from 1789; Salzer did in fact get married sometime before this testimony, perhaps to Finner's (now matured) daughter.

47. Weil. Sch. elec., 6 Oct. 1794, OA Kirch. prot. of Salzer on Gallus's charge of bribing the Mag.

48. Ibid., 11 Sep. 1793, prot. exc. from Johannes Sigel, with Gallus testimony as well, for more on the bribe; on the Gallus-Sigel connection, see 18 Oct. 1794 rpt. from comm. inv. Lempp; also Weil. comm. inv. 487, #35, 7 Jan. 1789 Zeller comm. rpt. on Sigel.

49. Weil. Sch. elec., 10 Sep. 1795, exp. opin. from GovC on Salzer-Bühler affair; 6 Oct. 1794, OAM prot. of Salzer.

50. Ernst Rheinwald, "Über 'Verehrungen' im alten Württemberg," *Württemberger Jahrbücher für Volkskunde* (1955): 17–48. It is not hard to imagine that such expressions of gratitude were hardly spontaneous, but rather a compulsory, ritualized part of community life. They were explicitly recognized as such by a state government on record as being opposed to the custom, but unable to punish it in practice. GovC inv. 6229, #3, 22 Dec. 1795, ducal decision on New Year's *Verehrung* at Altensteig; on its opposition, see *Commun-Ordnung,* 8; PrivC 2487, ords. on official gifts and *Accidentien,* 1773/1797.

51. Weil. Sch. elec., 15 Oct. 1794, Salzer pet.; Weil. comm. inv. 492, #6, 20 Oct. 1798, Salzer pet. for quotation.

52. Weil. comm. inv. 488, 25 May 1789, GovC decision on personal interview, including admonishments to friendship; 493, ad #70, 15 Dec. 1804, Tübingen law faculty exp. opin.

53. Weil. comm. inv. 492, #13, 21 Nov. 1798, Gentner accusation; #15, 22 Nov. 1798, Sendlinger and Gienger accusations, with quotation; #16, 29 Nov. 1798, encl. 2 of 26 Nov., Gallus and Mag. retort; also encl. 3, 24 Nov. 1798 on Bürger pet. in footnote below; #28, 28 Jun. 1800–23 Sep. 1801, OA inv. prot., on all these cases.

54. Ibid., #10, 25 Oct. 1798, original complaint from 70 Weilheim Bürger; also #11, 24 Nov. 1798, Schmidt and Franck complain about being duped by Gallus into signing a counter-complaint, and want to take their signatures back.

55. Ibid., #17, Lempp comm. rpt.; see also #29, 26 Sep. 1801, main rpt. from Lempp reviewing Salzer's writings summing up the ways they had been duped.

56. Weil. comm. inv. 491, Gallus Translocation, including his pet. of 1 Oct. 1795, a rare instance where Gallus himself writes; also 18 May 1795, Lempp

comm. rpt.; 492, #30 within #30a, 22 Oct. 1798, Gallus testimony; 493, #65, 28 May 1803, where Gallus speaks of the "aigentlich verwilderten Volck."

57. On the state's expansion generally, see Vann, *The Making of a State*. For Württemberg population statistics as well as useful reflections on the reliability of eighteenth-century census data, see Troeltsch, *Die Calwer Zeughandelskompagnie*, 394–430.

58. Schn. Sch. elec., encl. to #19c, 26 Jul. 1802, Gerichtsprot. Beutelsbach.

59. Ibid., #17, 29 Jun. 1802, OA rpt. on Schmid's son's election.

60. Ibid., #27, 27 Aug. 1802, Bilfinger pet.

61. Ibid., exhib. B to #17, 26 Jun. 1802, containing the Cap.; encl. to #6, 23 Feb. 1802, for an earlier version; #25, 27 Aug. 1802, OA rpt.

62. Ibid., exhib. E-L to #17, 22 Jun. 1802, the mands.; #24, 7 Aug. 1802, Wächter rpt. for the government's findings; these observations are echoed in #23, 3 Aug. 1802 and #31, 24 Sep. 1802, both rpts. from the central state Landrechnungs-Deputation.

63. Those becoming *Stadt- und Amtsschreiber* numbered 51% in the 1770s, 40% in the 1780s, and 25% in the 1790s; over these same decades, the rate of downward mobility climbed from 15% to 22% to 32%. Downward mobility refers to *Gerichtsschreiber, Unteramtmänner*, other low-level civil service posts, and city councils. These statistics were computed by cross-referencing a list of examined *Substituten* with NWD and Napoleonic personnel dossiers (see Chapter 5) to determine their fates. They thus do not account for the large additional number of dropouts. The list of *Substituten*, examined from 1723 to 1806, is found in Exam. comm. 16.

64. Haug, *Das gelehrte Wirtemberg*, 31.

65. GovC 635, Sub. marriages (1796–1802). This policy met with limited success, judging by the ducal government's repeated injunctions against the practice.

66. The percentage of scribes with legal training rose in each decade from the 1760s to the 1800s, increasing from 4.05% to 27.85%. Most of these were not the sons of scribes but were born outside the profession *(NWD)*. For the quotations, see respectively LT 9.4.2, Leidenschrift addressed to LT Cmte. by an anonymous *Schreiber*, 1 Aug. 1780; and anon., "Beobachtungen über die Gemeindecassen," *Schlettweins Archiv für den Menschen und Bürger* (1781): 89–242, here p. 186.

67. Grete Klingenstein, "Akademiker überschuss als soziales Problem im aufgeklärten Absolutismus," in *Bildung, Politik und Gesellschaft: Studien zur Geschichte des europäischen Bildungswesens vom 16. bis zum 20. Jahrhundert*, ed. Grete Klingenstein, Heinrich Lutz and Gerald Stourzh (München: R. Oldenbourg, 1978), 165–204, esp. p. 184; Anthony J. La Vopa, *Grace, Talent, and Merit: Poor Students, Clerical Careers, and Professional Ideology in Eighteenth-Century Germany* (Cambridge, Eng.: Cambridge University Press, 1988), 1–2, 19–57.

68. Wilhelm Ludwig Wekhrlin, "Über das Reich der Magister und Schreiber," *Das graue Ungeheuer* (1784): 294–309.

69. Bernritter's quotation, from *Wirtemberg: Pietismus, Schreiber, Schulen und Erziehung und Aufklärung überhaupt* (n.p., 1787), 58–59, appears in this more florid rendition in Ferdinand August Heinrich Weckherlin, *Apologie des wirttembergischen Schreiberstandes nebst einem Vorschlag zu seiner Vervollkommung* (Tübingen: Jacob Friedrich Heerbrandt, 1793), 16–18. Bernritter's book is often misattributed to Weckherlin, whose views on the scribes were diametrically opposed.

70. W. L. Wekhrlin, "Anselmus Rabiosus Reise durch Ober-Deutschland," in *Schriften* (Nendeln: KTO Press, 1978 [1778]), 1:105–6.

71. See F. A. Weckherlin, *Apologie*, 33; J. G. Bäuerlen, *Taschenbuch für angehende Wirtembergische Rechtsgelehrte und für Schreiber*, 1793 vol., 92–93 on these frictions.

72. Bernritter, "Der Incipient eines Stadtschreibers schildert seine Behandlung," , 116–20; also GovC inv. 621, 1/4 Feb. 1794, exp. opin. on "Kostgeldleichen."

73. Magenau, *Wanderungen*, 62–64; also Bernritter, *Wirtemberg*, 47–67.

74. Bleek, *Von der Kameralausbildung zum Juristenprivileg*, 61–82, 194ff.

75. Gutscher, *Bemerkungen*, 71, 73.

76. Bäuerlen, *Taschenbuch*, 1794 vol., 124.

77. F. A. Weckherlin, *Apologie*, 85–101 for all these quotations.

78. F. A. Weckherlin, *Magazin gemeinnütziger Aufsätze und Bemerkungen für württembergische Schreiber* (Stuttgart: Mezler, 1797f.), 6.

79. Weckherlin, *Apologie*, 102; Gutscher, *Bemerkungen*, 94 (respectively).

80. G. J. Roller, ed., "Vorstellungen der Substituten und Scribenten in dem grösten Theil der Oberämter des Landes an den Landschaftlichen verstärkten Ausschuß die Veredlung ihres Standes und die Verbesserung ihrer äussern Lage betreffend," in *Der Landtag in dem Herzogthum Würtemberg im Jahr 1797*, ed. E. G. Steeb (Tübingen and Stuttgart: Cotta, 1798), 1–48, p. 30 for the last two quotations.

81. Eberhard von Gemmingen-Bürg, "Meine Gedanken wegen der allzusehr zunehmenden Menge der Gelehrten und Schreiber," reprinted and discussed in Gutscher, *Bemerkungen*, 62–63.

82. LT 9.4.2, 3 Jan. 1797, Petition einiger Skribenten in Absicht auf die Anstellungen derselben nach dem Beispiel der Studenten der Theologie; see the earlier version dated 17 Dec. 1793 and the government replies of 1/4 Feb. 1794.

83. PrivC 2497, Vorschläge zur Verminderung des Andrangs jünger Leute aus dem gemeinen Stande zum Studieren und zur Schreiberei, exp. opins. and exchanges between PrivC and Duke dated 14 Feb. (including all quotations not attributed to Gemmingen), 8 Apr., and 24–27 Nov. 1788; also see Gemmingen-Bürg, "Meine Gedanken."

84. Most of these handbooks were themselves authored by scribes, such as Weckherlin's two-volume *Magazin*, with contributions from many authors, and Bäuerlen's *Taschenbuch* and *Lehrbuch*. The idea of a training institute for scribes ultimately came to fruition in the form of Tübingen's political science

faculty, which owed its inception to Friedrich List's proposal to reform the Schreiberstand (see Chapter 5).

85. Johann Georg Bäuerlen, *Versuch einer Anleitung zur Selbstbildung für wirtembergische Schreiber* (Stuttgart: Mezler, 1793), 6.

86. Roller, "Vorstellungen," 2, 30.

CHAPTER 3: THE BLACK FOREST CAHIER

1. Alexis de Tocqueville, *The Old Regime and the French Revolution*, trans. Stuart Gilbert (New York: Anchor, 1955 [1856]), viii.

2. Wild. Sch. 5377, Cahier (Zusammenstellung von Beschwerden) und Instruktion für den Landtagsdeputierten von Stadt und Amt Wildberg.

3. Grube and Bürkle, *Archiv*, xvii–xxiii.

4. See Barbara Vopelius-Holtzendorff, "Das Nagolder Cahier und seine Zeit. Beschwerdeschrift mit Instruktionen für den Abgeordneten zum württembergischen Landtag von 1797," *ZWLG* 37 (1978): 122–78, an excellent account; also Grube, *Landtag*, 453–54.

5. A contemporary account of the Nagold Vorlandtag is found in Philipp Christian von Normann and Johann Jakob Ostertag (hereafter: Normann-Ostertag), *Bemerkungen über den wirtembergischen Landtag von 1797–1799: Ein Beitrag zu Erläuterung der Wirtembergischen Geschichte und Verfassung* (n.p., 1800), 108–27.

6. Identification of the participants at the Vorlandtag is based on the signatories listed in the petitions cited in ftn. 8, by *NWD,* and from a list in Vopelius-Holtzendorff, "Cahier," 135–36.

7. On Hofacker, *NWD* §2652; GovC inv. 8524, folder dated 22 Nov. 1785, agreements regarding Wilhelm Friedrich and Johann Ludwig Hofacker. Hofacker should not be confused with the famous Swabian preacher of the same name, who lived a half-generation later.

8. LT 2.6, 15 Sep. 1796, mandated deputies to duke; 17 Sep. 1796, cop. rescs. from various cantons.

9. Wild. Sch. 5371, 14 Mar. 1797, Instruktion (Auftrag) from Wildberg to deputy Reichert.

10. Edmund Morgan, *Inventing the People: The Rise of Popular Sovereignty in England and America* (New York: W. W. Norton, 1988), 211–23.

11. Fritz Benzing, "Die Vertretung von 'Stadt und Amt' im altwürttembergischen Landtag" (Diss., Tübingen, 1924), 111ff. See also Rosi Fuhrmann, "Amtsbeschwerden, Landtagsgravamina und Supplikationen in Württemberg zwischen 1550 und 1629," in *Gemeinde und Staat im Alten Europa*, ed. Peter Blickle (Munich: R. Oldenbourg, 1997), 69–148.

12. LT 2.11, Legitimation der Landtagsmitglieder.

13. E.g., LT 2.6, ca. 1698, case of Stgt. Amt, denied its right to vote but conceded the option of submitting Gravamina "in place of instructions."

14. E.g., LT 2.12.2, 16 Mar. 1797 Ankunftszettel, Instruktion for Leonberg Bürgermeister Christian Friedrich Kochler; Benzing, "Stadt und Amt," 135–36.

15. LT 2.13.1, Subfasz. Markgröningen, docs. from Jan.–Feb. 1767; on Communicationsrecht, Benzing, "Stadt und Amt," 132–43.

16. Grube, "'Stadt und Amt' in altwürttembergischer Zeit," in *Nürtinger Heimatbuch*, ed. Hans Schwenkel (Würzburg: Kreisverband Nürtingen/Konrad Triltsch, 1953), 13–23, here 17 on the 1629 Landtagsabschied. These provisions were renewed in the *Commun-Ordnung*, ch. 2, sec. 3, §2.

17. Waib. Sch. elec., #32, 9 Jan. 1794, exp. opin. signed by Weckherlin, Elsässer, and others; this issue came up in the case of Waib. Schreiber Heinrich Bolley, who was suspected of an improper alliance with the OAM there. On this case, see the next chapter.

18. Benzing, "Stadt und Amt," 111ff., also 121ff. Though it is difficult to verify this conclusion, since the only centralized collection of cantonal mandates, in LT 9.41ff., was destroyed when the Landtag archive was bombed in the Second World War, the scattered examples discussed in this chapter and the next suggest that the scribes were at pains to conceal their direct influence in any case.

19. Only after word had leaked out of the Cahier's drafting did the state belatedly discover the document's existence. By then, though the duke did promulgate a ban on any organized discussion of political events outside parliament itself, the Nagold delegates had already adjourned and returned home. See Normann-Ostertag, *Bemerkungen*, 110–13.

20. Ludwig Timotheus Spittler, "Neben-Instruktion von der Stadt- und Amtsversammlung zu N. im Wirtembergischen, ihrem Landtagsdeputirten erteilt," discussed in Grube, *Landtag*, 456.

21. Wild. Sch. 5371, 9 June 1797, cantonal deps. from Neuenbürg and Herrenalb to Mag. Wildberg; 19 June 1797, An eine Hochlöbliche Landes-Versammlung (lists cantons involved).

22. See Vopelius-Holtzendorff, "Cahier," and Medick, "Von der Bürger-herrschaft zur Staatsbürgerlichen Gesellschaft, 67–68. This is a good place to note my departure from Vopelius-Holtzendorff regarding the social interests the Cahier represented. She argues for the participation of village *Amtsorte* in the drafting of the document, and a broad peasant constituency outside the elite of *Schreiber* and *Magistrat* leaders participating at the Nagold Vorlandtag. This is a view shared by Heinrich Scheel, *Süddeutsche Jakobiner: Klassenkämpfe und republikanische Bestrebungen im deutschen Süden Ende des 18. Jahrhunderts* (Berlin: Akademie-Verlag, 1962) and is especially seductive to those in search of a German Jacobin tradition. I see no evidence of this here, however, and indeed the subsequent history of *Stadt-Amt* and *Schreiber-Magistrat* relations in Nagold suggests the presence of fault lines beneath the façade of unanimity (see this chapter's final section). Evidence of *Amt* participation is powerfully in evidence elsewhere, however, and here, Vopelius-Holtzendorff, following Grube's seminal article, "Dorfgemeinde und Amtsversammlung in Altwürttemberg," makes excellent points. This entire dynamic forms the dominant subject of Chapter 4.

23. Wild. Sch. 5371, notes in last paper-wrapped folder in this Büschel.

24. Wild. Sch. 5371, 10 Sep. 1796, invitation from Nag. Mag.

25. HStAS L 6 Bü 2.31.1–2 Verkehr des Ausschusses (und Landtags) mit den Landständen. Rundschreiben: Mitteilung der Herr- und Landschaftlichen Verhandlungen, 1713ff.

26. Wild. Sch. 5309, 5336–48, 5351, 5363, 5371, 5380 (these cover the years 1627–1815).

27. Wild. Sch. 5371, 25 Dec. 1804, Amtsschreiber Lang at Maulbronn and Stadtschreiber Cuhorst at Liebenzell to Mag. and Schreiber Rieker at Wildberg; 26 Dec. 1804 to assems. at Calw and Wildberg from Mag. at Neuenbürg; 26 Jan. 1805, Amtsdeputation and Mag. Wildberg from Mag. Calw. At issue here were internal cantonal negotiations on ducal military appropriations. See also the sources cited in note 32, on wood prices.

28. LT 2.20.2, Eingriffe des Herzogs in die Landschaftliche Korrespondenz mit den Mandanten, 1797–1805, LT 2.31.3–4, Eingriffe Herzog Friedrichs in das Recht der freien Korrespondenz mit den Landständen, 1797–1805.

29. Wild. Sch. 5371, 27 May 1799 document signed at Herrenberg by scribes from Altensteig, Böblingen, Calw, Wildberg, and Sindelfingen. The presence of an *Oberamtmann* is atypical and worth comment. At this time, OAM Lang appears to have enjoyed good relations with the Stadtschreiber there, Hofacker, and to have enjoyed the trust of the other scribe more generally. See the final section on the souring of their collegiality and its implications for canton-state relations, however.

30. On these aspects of estates and cantonal business, and on the *Amtsversammlungen* generally, see especially Grube, *Vogteien, Ämter, Landkreise,* 13ff. See also David Warren Sabean, *Power in the Blood,* 193–94, who ties the collection and local-political negotiation over fiscal exploitation to the practice of *Herrschaft* and the local economy of information on the village level.

31. See Grube and Bürkle, *Archiv,* 11–14, 65 on general cantonal receipts *(Rechnungen),* 39–47 for military matters (mustering, quartering, fiscal levies, war taxes, etc.), and the documents in Wild. Sch. indexed there.

32. Wild. Sch. 5371, 19 Jun. 1797, Copia: An eine Hochlöbliche Landes-Versammlung gehorsamste Bitte der Staedt und Aemter Dornstett, Calw, Hirsau, Liebenzell, Merklingen, Neuenbürg, Herrenalb, Wildberg, Zavelstein, and signed by a group dominated by *Schreiber.*

33. See Robert von Friedeburg, " 'Reiche', 'Geringe Leute' und 'Beambte,' " 219–65, esp. 259–61.

34. Wild. Sch. 5312–13 (for the period of the 1760s), 5314 (seventeenth century).

35. Anderson, *Imagined Communities,* 52ff. Additionally, many scribes and/or their *Substituten* had themselves rotated among various *Schreibereien* in the Black Forest (*q.v. NWD* on the relevant districts).

36. Wild. Sch. 5315 (1810–1812), 15 Feb. 1812 document concerning Widmaier and Engel, and *passim,* with the sources cited above.

37. See Grube, *Landtag,* 409–24, 452–53 on the Black Forest's history of "refractory" behavior; also Vopelius-Holtzendorff, "Cahier," 135–36, as well as 157–58n79 for an analysis of the various Oberland cantons' wealth as measured

by tax receipts. Examples of more prosperous cantons might include Schorndorf, Urach, Kirchheim, and Göppingen.

38. LT 2.12.1–2, Ausschuß-Mitglieder, 1737–1804. Nagold itself appears only in 1798, riding a temporary wave of activism whose history is the subject of this chapter. For a confirming portrait of parliamentary oligarchy, based on similar sources plus fiscal records, see James Vann, *The Making of a State*, 179–82, 249, 249n82.

39. Johann Gottfried von Pahl, *Denkwürdigkeiten aus meinem Leben und aus meiner Zeit* (Tübingen: Ludwig Friedrich Fues, 1840), 113–14.

40. LT 2.12.1–2, Lokations- und Umfrags-Zettel of 1737, 1763, 1797 plus Ordnung der Städte und Ämter überhaupt.

41. LT 2.13.1–2, Gewaltübertragungen. See below on the significance of such transfers.

42. Wild. Sch. 5371, 14 Mar. 1797 Instruktion from Wildberg to Reichert, point V, 12.

43. See note 8 for the petitions, and for the duke's response, Normann-Ostertag, *Bemerkungen*, 112, reprinting the resc. of 17 Sep. 1796.

44. See J. G. A. Pocock, *The Machiavellian Moment: Florentine Political Thought and the Atlantic Republican Tradition* (Princeton, N. J.: Princeton University Press, 1975).

45. For this paragraph, see Scheel, *Süddeutsche Jakobiner*, chs. 5–6, Erwin Hölzle, *Das alte Recht und die Revolution: Eine politische Geschichte Württembergs in der Revolutionszeit 1789–1805* (München: R. Oldenbourg, 1931); and especially idem, "Altwürttemberg und die französische Revolution," *WVLG* NF 35 (1929): 272–86.

46. For a compact, detailed summary of political events, see Ewald Grothe, "Der württembergische Reformlandtag 1797–1799," *ZWLG* 48 (1989): 159–200. The best guide to the pamphlet campaign is Scheel, *Süddeutsche Jakobiner*, 293–352. The pamphlets themselves are under the title *Württembergische Landtagsschriften* (Stuttgart: n.p., 1796ff.).

47. Anon., "Der Konstitutionsfreund an die Landesversammlung," in *Württembergische Landtagsschriften*, vol. 3.

48. Heinrich Bolley, "Noch ein Beitrag zur Beantwortung der Frage: Wer kann zum württembergischen Landtag abgeordnet werden?" (1796) reprinted as no. 2 in *Württembergische Landtagsschriften*, vol. 5; see p. 7 of this essay for some of the writings to which he was reacting; also idem, "Bemerkungen über die Schrift: Über die Wahlfähigkeit zu der Stelle eines Landtagsdeputierten im Württembergischen" (1796), no 6 in vol. 6 of same, a response to Johann Christian Friedrich Rümmelin, "Ueber die Wahlfähigkeit zu der Stelle eines Landtags-Deputirten im Wirtenbergischen," itself occasioned by an earlier writing called "Gedanken über die Wahl der Abgeordneten zum Wirtenbergischen Landtag." Rümmelin in turn replied to both Bolley's pieces in "Antwort des Verfassers der Schrift: Ueber die Wahlfähigkeit zu der Stelle eines Landtags-Deputirten im Wirtenbergischen auf die dagegen erschienenen Bemerkungen von dem Verfasser der Schrift: Noch ein Beytrag zu Beantwortung der Frage:

Wer kann zum Wirtenbergischen Landtag abgeordnet werden?" (1797). Bolley's colleague in Waiblingen, Stadtschreiber Friedrich Ludwig Wilhelm Theuß, also contributed a piece, as did J. G. Pahl and an anonymous Württemberger whose pamphlet was published in Warsaw (!) in 1796. For complete references, see Scheel, *Süddeutsche Jakobiner,* 311–13.

49. Bolley, "Noch ein Beitrag," dated 22 Sep. 1796.

50. Ibid., 29–30.

51. Ludwig Hofacker, *Entwurf einer neuen landschaftlichen Ausschuß-verfassung* (Stuttgart: n.p., 1797).

52. Grothe, "Reformlandtag," 176, 185; Hölzle, "Altwürttemberg."

53. Nag. LT elec., 27 Mar. 1797, Hofacker exhib. to Landesversammlung. The phrase "aus dem Mittel des Magistrats" receives treatment below.

54. PrivC decree dated 20 Apr. 1797, discussing Hofacker's presentation, reprinted in Normann-Ostertag, *Bemerkungen,* 118–19.

55. Nag. LT elec., 27 Mar. 1797, LT asks PrivC for dispensation for Hofacker; 5 Apr. 1797, duke to LT declines; for the whole volley of proposals and counterproposals see Normann-Ostertag, *Bemerkungen;* Elias Gottfried Steeb, ed., *Der Landtag in dem Herzogthum Württemberg im Jahr 1797* (Tübingen and Stuttgart: Cotta, 1797–98); LT docs. of 4 Apr. 1797, Hofacker to PrivC; 20 Apr. 1797, PrivC to LT; 21 Apr. 1797, Hofacker to LT (expresses willingness to resign as "sacrifice for the country [Opfer fürs Vaterland])"; and 21 Apr. 1797, LT to duke; 26 Apr. 1797, GovC to LT; 29 Apr. 1797, Hofacker to LT; 2 May 1797, cop. LT to duke.

56. LT 2.12.2, 16 Mar. 1797 Gewaltübertragungen in Ankunfts-Zettel from Dornstetten, Freudenstadt, and Hornberg. Not to be confused with the Landschaftskonsulent, the most influential and highest-ranking staff member of the Landtag, Hofacker's position seems to have been an improvisation with a dubious formal status.

57. Normann-Ostertag, *Bemerkungen,* 118–19.

58. Rather the Gewalt simply named its possessor, according to Benzing, "Stadt und Amt," 116. Actual signature practices vary over time, and sometimes the Bürgermeister would sign them. See Alfred Rieger, "Die Entwicklung des württembergischen Kreisverbands" (Ph.D. diss., Tübingen, 1952), 13.

59. Waib. assem. inv., #1 exhib. F, 19 Sep. 1796, Waib. Actum signed by Mag. members.

60. Maulbronn LT elec., 1 Oct. 1796, dft. rpt. from LT Cmte. on Lang.

61. Steeb, *Landtag,* 1:49ff.

62. DukeLT 40, Auszug aus den oberamtlichen u[nterthänig]sten Anzeigen von der Wahl der neuen Landes Versammlungs Mitglieder, Apr. 1800.

63. Pahl, "Wohlgemeintes, in Vernunft und Schrift bestgegründetes, jedoch unmaßgebliches Gutachten über die Wahlfähigkeit eines Landtagsdeputirten in Württemberg; auf ausdrückliches Verlangen der ehrsamen Amtsversammlung zu Ypsilon . . . von Sebastian Käsbohrer" (1797), *Württembergische Landtags-schriften,* vol. 3, cited in Scheel, *Süddeutsche Jakobiner,* 313.

64. Bolley, "Noch ein Beitrag," 28–29.

65. LT 2.13.1, Gewaltübertragungen of 1763–70 for this item as well as this paragraph.

66. Benzing, "Stadt und Amt," 124–26.

67. LT 2.13.1, docs. of 17–23 May 1766 between *Landtagsassessor* and *Schreiber* Cuhorst at Liebenzell asking if it is necessary to appear "in person" and referring to a 13 Aug. 1763 gen. resc. on temporary attendance and substitution. Other documents in this file make it clear that the Landtag had to cajole and admonish poorer cantons to fulfill their patriotic duty.

68. Maulbronn LT elec., 1 Oct 1796, dft. from LT Cmte. regarding Lang's election.

69. LT 2.13.1–2, Gewaltübertragungen from eighteenth and nineteenth centuries, respectively, for these cantons. Additionally, Dornstetten and Liebenzell had become allied with Nagold and other Black Forest cantons and the former actually transferred its *Gewalt* to Hofacker when he became a *Privatkonsulent*.

70. DukeLT 40, 24 Apr. 1800, rpt. from OA Liebenzell.

71. Normann-Ostertag, *Bemerkungen*, 110–13.

72. Maulbronn LT elec., documents of Sep.–Oct. 1796, esp. 1 Oct. recommendation of Landschaftskonsulent to LT Cmte. that it recognize his election; for rest of paragraph, see also 17 Sep. report from OAM Kerner on Lang elec. and Lang's report of same day to GovC.

73. Sindelfingen LT elec., 3 Oct. 1796, exp. opin. dft. from LT Cmte., which also mentions suggestions by PrivC Uxküll and Hoffmann that Wagner have himself elected to the Sindelfingen Mag.; for the Landschaftskonsulent exp. opin., ibid., 1 Oct. 1796 characterizing scribes as "essential elements and members *[Glieder]* of the *Magistrate*" needing no special dispensations. See also Normann-Ostertag, *Bemerkungen*, 113–14, on public opinion; and Benzing, "Stadt und Amt," 67–69.

74. This move anticipates the common nineteenth-century pattern, in which small territories elected notable representatives who had perhaps never even visited their districts. Thus in Württemberg, the ecclesiastical territories around Tübingen became the favorites of professors wishing to enter politics. Perhaps sensing this threat, deputies from Wendlingen, Ebingen, Dornhan, and Murrhardt, all smaller and poorer cantons, objected to Steeb's election on the grounds that admitting well-heeled individuals like "law professors from Tübingen would drive out deputies from a lower *Stand*"; they thus realized that modern practices of representation could be just as neglectful of their rights as the ossified corporative system. See Normann-Ostertag, *Bemerkungen*, 116–17, 123–24 on this and the Steeb case in general.

75. Besides Steeb, several other non-*Schreiber* attempted to gain *Landtag* seats in 1797, including the Urach treasurer Scholl, his counterpart in Münsingen, and a doctor of law from Pflummern. See LT 2.6, documents on Christian Friedrich Scholl of 6 Feb. and 14 Mar. 1797; Normann-Ostertag, *Bemerkungen*, 110–13.

76. Nag. Sch. elec., 22 May 1797, OAM Lang to ducal gov. asks that Hofacker's *Ordnungswidrigkeiten* be investigated.

77. Ibid., 15 May 1797, pet. from Mag. Nag. to duke, explaining that it was custom and not "mistrust" against the OAM that prompted Hofacker to push the two BMs as *Urkunds-Personen*. Signed Günther, Schmidt, Sautter, Rauser, Fuchßstatt, and Eberhard.

78. Lang claimed no personal stake in the matter, merely expressing the wish to observe "the strictest legality" in all cantonal business; ibid., 18–22 May 1797, OA prot., concluding remarks. Given his own history there, and the numerous other opportunities there must have been to blow the whistle on Hofacker's many shady maneuvers, this seems entirely disingenuous. In Hofacker's absence, he had participated as late as 1799 alongside Black Forest *Stadtschreiber* in the informal network of information-sharing described earlier and brought no investigation to bear on the drafting of the Black Forest Cahier. The other incident mentioned in this paragraph involved a certain municipal shepherd named Kümmer, whose case came up at an illegal *Magistrat* meeting at burgomaster Schmidt's house where Lang was not present. See ibid., OA prot.

79. Ibid., OA prot., testimony of 20 May 1797 from Günther, Sautter, Rauser, Fuchßstatt, and Eberhard, who had signed the pet., for this whole paragraph.

80. Ibid., 15 Aug 1797, GovC rpt. describing election on 5 July under Krafft's supervision; 7 Aug. 1797 on confirmation by the *Chronik*.

81. DukeLT 40, 22 Apr. 1800, OAM Lang reporting for Nag.

82. Grube, *Landtag*, 473; for more details, see Hölzle, *Das alte Recht*.

83. DukeLT 39, Verdacht gegen Hofacker betr. Teilnahme an revolutionäre Machenschaften, part of Hauptbericht an den Kaiser, 10 Dec. 1801; ibid. 43–44, Hauptbericht der Untersuchungs-Kommission and Beilagen, including Originalschreiben von Hofacker an Baz in Wien vom 27 Dez. 1799.

84. Nag. assem. inv., 20 Nov. 1804, all Schß and deputies of the common *Amt* complain against the Nag. Mag.

85. Ibid., 14 Jan. 1805, OAM Lang sends Mag. explanation with various prot. exc.

86. Ibid., 17 Nov. 1804, assem. prot. exc.

87. Ibid., 20 Jun. 1805, gov. exp. opin.

88. Ibid., 6 Jul. 1805, Wächter rpt.

CHAPTER 4: CONSTITUTIONAL FETISHISM

1. Reg. Hist. Coll., Ludwig Hofackers Tagebuch, 1803–6, entry of 10 Jan. 1806, 174. Unfortunately, Hofacker's diary reveals little on his activities in Nagold and is concerned only with high politics. Also see Grube, *Landtag*, 485–86; Hölzle, *Das alte Recht*, 331–39.

2. Waib. pet. inv., 13 Jan. 1806, PrivC secretary Schott rpt., Weisser testimony.

3. This account is meant as a critique of Jürgen Habermas's model of participation in the public sphere. My interest in the sociology of political communication, especially of petitioning, also parallels David Zaret, *Origins of Demo-*

cratic Culture: Printing, Petitions, and the Public Sphere in Early-Modern England (Princeton, N. J., Princeton University Press, 2000), though I am less concerned than Zaret with print culture and its implications for Habermas's theory.

4. Sabean, *Power in the Blood*, 1. Sabean's account of the Beutelsbach incident, in some ways portraying a very different Bolley from the one depicted below, in other ways showing us the same arrogant, patronizing, Enlightened local official, is the subject of his sixth chapter.

5. On the Bolleys, see the personnel dossiers of: Heinrich Ernst Ferdinand Bolley, NL 1809 Lud.; Christian Friedrich Bolley, NL II 2658; NL 1809 Schn.; Carl Eberhard Bolley, NL 1809 Calw; also *NWD* §2661.

6. A *Kanzlei Advokat* was a chancery lawyer and a position frequently conferring upward mobility in the state's administrative and legal circles. See Waib. Sch. elec., exh. A to #25, 25 Nov. 1793, OAM Pistorius rpt. on Bolley's service under him.

7. Waib. Sch. elec., exhibs. *(Zeugnisse)* to #4 of 29 Mar. 1788, 20 Oct. 1793, and 4 Nov. 1793.

8. Ibid., #3, 12 Nov. 1793; to #4, 11 Nov. 1793; and #25, 14 Dec. 1793 for Mag. pets. On their nepotism, see encl. to #11, 17 Nov. 1793, Pistorius rpt.; for additional "connections," #37, 10 Feb. 1794, Mag.

9. This objection dropped away when, in a shakily written letter, she thankfully but inconveniently absolved the community of any responsibility for her welfare. Ibid., A to #10, 17 Nov. 1793; *NWD* §3021. Also see encl. to #11, 17 Nov. 1793, OAM Pistorius rpt., labeling the *Magistrat's* professed concern for Hagmaier's widow as disingenuous and self-interested.

10. Ibid., #25, 14 Dec. 1793, Mag.; #10, 18 Nov. 1793, Mag.; on the Pistorius-Mag. conflict, #23, 10 Nov. 1793, Schß. pet.; #40, 20 Feb. 1794, Georgii comm. rpt.; also GovC comm. inv. 1062, subfolder on BM Seeger and Sub. Weysser from 1792.

11. On friends and relatives, see Sabean, *Power in the Blood*, chs. 4–5. Here, the Mag. used the terms "Bluts Verwandtschaft" and "Bluts Freundschaft" and referred specifically to the ducal rescripts of 25 Jul. 1786 and 19 Mar. 1792, which prevented *Oberamtmänner* and *Stadt- und Amtsschreiber* in the same district from being (or becoming) related to one another. For the government's invalidation of the *Magistrat's* interpretation, #32, 9 Jan. 1794, exp. opin. See Waib. Sch. elec., #1, 7 Nov. 1793 for Pistorius's recusal; also #10, 18 Nov. 1793, Mag. alleges Pistorius distanced himself in order to push Bolley "that much more freely"; and exhib. A to #25, 25 Nov. 1793, in which Pistorius disclaims undue influence.

12. Waib. Sch. elec., #27, 16 Dec. 1793, Mag. "Spitzbube" was usually an insult women directed against men, especially their husbands; on such insults, see Sabean, *Property, Production, and Family*, 139–46, 325–27.

13. Waib. Sch. elec., #27, 16 Dec. 1793, Mag.; #25, 14 Dec. 1793, Mag.

14. Ibid., #32, 9 Jan. 1794, exp. opin.; #40, 20 Feb. 1794, Georgii comm. rpt.,

comment on OAM Pistorius's testimony; on the issue of "trust" see #25, 14 Dec. 1793, Mag.; #10, same.

15. Ibid., encl. to #23, 7 Dec. 1793 writing signed by eight Schß.

16. Ibid., #4, 12 Nov. 1793, OAM Roser (at Winn.) reports on deliberations of Waib. Gericht; also #3, 10, 25, 27 for Mag. arguments; #6, 31 for Schß arguments.

17. Ibid., #6, 14 Nov. 1793, Schß pets. (Vorstellungen); #23, 10 Nov. 1793, Schß.

18. Ibid., #25, 14 Dec. 1793, Mag.

19. Ibid., #7, 13 Nov. 1793, Waib. Gericht members Heinrich Knaus and Johann Georg Bunz Sr., as well as Johann Matthias Brodsag.

20. Ibid., to #31, n.d., Verzeichniß derjenigen Gerichtsverwandten, welche von dem Stadtmagistrat zu Waiblingen zur Stadtschreiberei Wahl werden gewält werden, which can be taken as an informal list of Franck's cronies. It is likely that younger members on the Rat were also allied with him.

21. Ibid., #40, 20 Feb. 1794, Georgii comm. rpt., protocolling of Keller on his 27 Dec. 1793 Exhib., including warnings of punishment against Keller. Cf. the "Promemoria" of 15 Feb. 1794, identified as such in #40, in which the Schß absolve Keller of responsibility, insisting that they are not so "dumb and ignorant" that they failed to understand to the petitions he drafted.

22. Ibid., #10, 18 Nov. 1793, Mag.

23. Ibid., #22, 6 Dec. 1793, BM Michael Luithard and Jacob Weiglen, along with councillors Jacob Luithard and Georg Jacob Luithard, protest the behavior of Schß. Schiller (who had sent Jacob Luithard away to Ludwigsburg on the occasion of some business for Jacob Fischer's widow) and express their support for candidate Cronmüller over Bolley, citing their rights under a 1725 General-Rescript. The accusations are repeated in Protestationen und Verwehrungen, B, 14 Feb. 1794, complaint from Luithard at Bittenfeld on the occasion of the new Vollmacht drafted there.

24. Ibid., #32, 9 Jan. 1794, exp. opin. signed Weckherlin, Elsässer, et al.; #33, 25 Jan. 1794 (with marginalia from 31 Jan.), exp. opin. signed Mandelsloh, Banger, Elsässer, Uxküll et al.; #34, 10 Feb. 1794, order from inv. Georgii to Schß. to meet their constituents and draft new mands.

25. Ibid., #10, 18 Nov. 1793 and #3, 12 Nov. 1793, Mag.; also encl. #16, 1 Dec. 1793, Mag. complaint; in #25, 14 Dec. 1793, the Mag. seems to reverse course, now petitioning for the right of instruction for their deputies.

26. Ibid., #35–36, 10 Feb. 1794, government order; #37, 10 Feb. 1794, Mag. complains against voting by lots, along the somewhat contorted logic that nepotism ("Familien Concatenation") in their midst would lead to overlapping votes from family members, effectively diluting their collective voice vis-à-vis the *Amt;* also #43, 23 Feb. 1794, Mag.; marginalia to #40, 27 Feb. 1794, on government reservations.

27. LT 2.6, 6 Feb. 1797, Duke to OA Urach, plus other documents on Urach.

28. Tub. assem. inv., especially docs. #5–7. The Tübingen case paralleled Waiblingen's experience very closely, with the cantonal *Amtsschreiber* arguing

for enhanced political rights for the village *Schultheißen* against a *Stadtschreiber* and a *Magistrat* wishing to restrict these rights.

29. Waib. Sch. elec., #8 (and attached exhib.), 18 Nov. 1793, OAM Pistorius on Sub. Schuster; #9, 17 Nov. 1793, Schuster seeks "righteous satisfaction" and restoration of his personal honor.

30. Ibid., #25, 14 Dec. 1793, Mag. pet. with its interpretation; #31, 27 Dec. 1793, Schß interpretation; see also #11, 18 Nov. 1793, OAM Roser sends in past Waib. prot. excerpts, concluding they are inconsistent and very "varied."

31. Ibid., encl. #11, 17 Nov. 1793, in which Pistorius resorts to this method and remarks on the difficulties of filtering out the opinions of "interested persons." It is conceivable that Franck's frictions with older *Magistrat* members may have derived from their inconvenient personal memories of past precedents that might have weakened his case. Pistorius mentions a case in which Franck pleads a lapse of memory regarding an election where he sat as secretary, only to have councillors Seeger and Knaus chime in with better recollections of the event, less congenial to Franck's purposes. Knaus, again, was one of those whom Franck attempted to have disqualified.

32. Recall that the government had aimed in this case to disrupt cantonal oligarchies simply by soliciting reports on their voting and deliberation practices. See also Back. assem. inv., used as an explicit precedent at Waiblingen.

33. Even the government mooted the proposal at one point that the *Stadt* electors be selected at large and by lot from the Waiblingen citizenry, though it ultimately backed away from this idea; see Waib. Sch. elec., marginalia to #40, 27 Feb. 1794, signed by various GovC members.

34. Ibid., #23, 10 Nov. 1793, Schß; and #31, 27 Dec. 1793, Schß.

35. Ibid., 18 Feb. 1794, Bittenfeld pet, enclosed within unnumbered 14 Mar. 1794 doc. from OAM Roser.

36. Ibid., #44b, 22 Feb. 1794, Pistorius rpt. plus docs. from Bittenfeld.

37. Ibid., encl. to #46, 6 Mar. 1794, Schß, possibly writing at Pistorius's instigation (this doc. was enclosed in #46, which he had penned).

38. Ibid., #43, 23 Feb. 1794, Mag. asks to elect its own *Stadtschreiber* and comments very favorably on Theuß and his qualifications; *NWD* §3020.

39. Waib. Sch. elec., 20 Feb. 1794, Georgii comm. rpt. on the origins of Theuß's proposal; marginalia to #40, 27 Feb. 1794, exp. opin., granting the *Schreiberei* division in recognition of Theuß's independent means and good character, and the substantial portion of *Amt* business (five-sevenths that of the whole *Schreiberei*) thereby left to Bolley; #52, 25 Mar. 1794, Georgii rpt. on the *Vergleich* concluded between *Stadt* and *Amt*.

40. Grube, "Dorfgemeinde und Amtsversammlung in Altwürttemberg" is the locus classicus of this argument; see also Alfred Rieger, "Die Entwicklung des württembergischen Kreisverbands" (Ph.D. diss., Tübingen, 1952), 33–40.

41. *Commun-Ordnung*, ch. 2, sec., 3, esp. §2 on attendance. The *Commun-Ordnung* prescribed an upper limit on *Stadt* delegates and mandated that each larger village send both its *Schultheiß* and a *Gericht* or *Rat* member, and that each smaller one send one of these officials. On the 1725 rescript, see below.

42. This observation echoes Mack Walker, *German Home Towns*, ch. 2, on guild constitutions. On a more technical level, it was the precise competence of cantonal standing committees, called *Amtsausschüsse*, that tended to vary from locality to locality in Württemberg. These developed over a longer time and in a more ad hoc fashion than the *Amtsversammlungen* themselves, a younger innovation whose roles were codified in the 1702 and 1758 communal ordinances. Another problem was that these ordinances often gave village delegates the right to attend without formally granting them the franchise or specifying how they were supposed to participate. See Grube, *Vogteien, Ämter, Landkreise*, 21–22; James Vann, *The Making of a State*, 239.

43. Waib. Sch. elec., #6, 14 Nov. 1794, Schß pet.

44. Ibid., 15 Sep. 1796, cop. to OA Waib. from PrivC.

45. Ibid., 13 Sep. 1796, Schß to duke; 14 Sep. 1796, Mag. to LT Cmte.

46. Bolley, "Noch ein Beitrag zur Beantwortung der Frage: Wer kann zum württembergischen Landtag abgeordnet werden?" (1796) reprinted as no. 2 in *Württembergische Landtagsschriften*, vol. 5. Despite its anonymous publication, there is universal agreement that Bolley authored the pamphlet. See Scheel, *Süddeutsche Jakobiner*, 311–14 and the card catalog at the Württembergische Landesbibliothek Stuttgart. Bolley later confessed authorship of a pamphlet bearing exactly this description, in Waib. pet. inv., 10 Jan. 1806, prot. rpt. p. 31 (answer to question 100).

47. Johann Gottfried von Pahl, *Denkwürdigkeiten aus meinem Leben und aus meiner Zeit* (Tübingen: Ludwig Friedrich Fues, 1840), 31. That Pahl is referring to "Noch ein Beitrag" and not some other writing is proven by the lengthy citation from Kant's "Answer to the Question: What is Enlightenment" that introduces Bolley's essay.

48. Bolley, "Noch ein Beitrag," 31.

49. Particularly in the 1730s, Duke Karl Eugen had often been able, through his superintendents, to personally intimidate city councilmen at cantonal assemblies. So-called *Unteramtmänner* installed in the 1760s performed a similar function in the countryside. Thereafter, parliament's resurgence shifted the source of initiative to the cantons themselves and increased their importance as bargaining chips between duke and estates. See Vann, *Making of a State*, 237–44, 278–79; Grube, "Dorfgemeinde und Amtsversammlung," 209–11.

50. Grube, "Dorfgemeinde und Amtsversammlung," 213–217; Back. assem. inv.; Tüb. assem. inv. esp. docs. #9–13 from 1771, also containing a collection of precedents and practices from other cantons.

51. Waib. LT elec., 15 Sep. 1796, cop. to OA Waib.; Waib. assem. inv., #1, 24 Oct. 1796, Pistorius to PrivC on latter's order of 15 Sep.; #1 exc. of 16–17 Sep.

52. Waib. assem. inv., #1, 24 Oct. 1796, OAM Pistorius to PrivC; *NWD* §1226.

53. "A deputy to the Landtag . . . must adhere literally to the given instruction and in cases of doubt or new circumstances fetch further instructions. One can easily see, then, that it is a matter of indifference who is named to be a deputy." Waib. assem. inv., #1 exhib. F, 19 Sep. 1796, Waib. Actum.

54. Ibid., #1 exhib. F, 19 Sep. 1796, p. 13R for the *Vergleich*; #3, 12 Dec. 1796, exp. opin. for commentary on its provisions.

55. On Nürtingen, Grube, "'Stadt und Amt' in altwürttembergischer Zeit," in *Nürtinger Heimatbuch*, ed. Hans Schwenkel (Würzburg: Kreisverband Nürtingen/Konrad Triltsch, 1953), 13–22, here 16–17; also Fritz Benzing, "Die Vertretung von 'Stadt und Amt' im altwürttembergischen Landtag" (Diss., Tübingen, 1924); generally, Vann, *Making of a State*, 239–44, 278ff.; Grube, "Dorfgemeinde und Amtsversammlung," 207–8, 213–19; Theodor Knapp, "Leibeigene Bauern auf den württembergischen Landtagen," *Jahrbücher für Nationalökonomie und Statistik* (1922): 531–32.

56. Waib. assem. inv., #1 O, exc. of 26 Sep. 1796, Bolley Protestation.

57. Ibid., #1 O, exc. of 14 Oct. 1794, prot. signed Schreiber Theuß, on OAM Pistorius's further negotiations with the Schß; #1, 24 Oct. 1796, OAM Pistorius asks PrivC to confirm his *Vergleich*.

58. For example, in cases of textual gaps and legal inconsistencies in the written record, witness testimonials from aged men could only complement and not supplant instructions, protocols, and compacts presumed to have a greater reliability. See above, text to note 31.

59. Waib. assem. inv., #3, 12 Dec. 1796, GovC Wächter's exp. opin.

60. General-Rescript in Betreff der Veranstaltung der Amtsversammlungen und der Beschlußnahme bei denselben, 31 Dec. 1725, reprinted in A. L. Reyscher, ed., *Vollständige historisch und kritisch bearbeitete Sammlung der württembergischen Gesetze* (Tübingen: Ludwig Friedrich Fues, 1843ff.), vol. 13, 1283–84. The 1725 rescript had been excluded from the 1758 *Commun-Ordnung* on account of the estates' resistance. It thus lay in abeyance until formally reactivated in later struggles such as these. See Grube, *Vogteien, Ämter, Landkreise*, 30–31.

61. Waib. assem. inv., #4, 12 Dec. 1796, GovC Wächter to OA Waib. In particular, government investigators took issue with the *Vergleich*'s third clause.

62. Indeed, as a practical matter, the village mandate recreated all those webs of informal scribal influence and formal corporative power familiar from the practice of political ventriloquism. Observing that "neither village councillors nor communes know the least little thing" about matters of cantonal importance, the 1725 General-Rescript enjoined the scribes, with their wide contacts over the countryside, to publicize any and all "points that may come into common deliberation" at cantonal assemblies. The spread of information was explicitly intended to counteract the same dynamic of influence at the center and marginalization of the periphery identified on a statewide level by the Black Forest Cahier, but now on the smaller scale of the cantons and their patronized villages.

63. Waib. assem. inv., #5, 16 Jan. 1797, dft. resc. to OAM Pistorius from GovC Wächter.

64. Waib. assem. prot., 5 Apr. 1800, with many of the same signatories from *Stadt und Amt*. The occasion seems to have concerned military conscription procedures and was referred to in Waib. pet. inv., 20 Mar. 1806, gov. rpt., Bolley

testimony, plus encl. A to p. 4b, in which Bolley, too, is said to have exerted pressure on the Amt delegates to assent to the new *Vergleich.*

65. Waib. Sch. elec., 15 Feb. 1794, note from Franck's doctor.

66. See Winfried Schulze, *Bäuerlicher Widerstand und feudale Herrschaft in der frühen Neuzeit,* vol. 6, *Neuzeit im Aufbau* (Stuttgart-Bad Cannstatt: frommann-holzboog, 1980); Helmut Gabel, *Widerstand und Kooperation: Studien zur politischen Kultur rheinischer und maasländischer Kleinterritorien (1648–1794)* (Tübingen: Bibliotheca Academica, 1995); Rosi Fuhrmann, Beat Kümin, and Andreas Würgler, "Supplizierende Gemeinden: Aspekte einer vergleichenden Quellenbetrachtung," in *Gemeinde und Staat im Alten Europa,* ed. Peter Blickle (Munich: R. Oldenbourg, 1997), 267–323.

67. Christopher Friedrich Baz, *Über das Petitionsrecht der württembergischen Landstände* (Stuttgart: n.p., 1797), 5–8; on his political activities and exiles, see Hölzle, *Altes Recht,* 263, 272, 276–85, 339, 339n3 and passim; also Scheel, *Süddeutsche Jakobiner,* 333–35; Grube, *Landtag,* passim.

68. Carsten, *Princes and Parliaments,* 430 on this connection.

69. Waib. pet. inv., 4 Jan. 1806, evidently the Mundum version (see below). The government later identified Bolley as the author who "naturally did not sign the petition" in Int. Min. 145, 22 Oct. 1815, exp. opin.. See also Waib. pet. inv., exhib. B. to Schott rpt., Theuß Concept.

70. Winn. pet. inv., encl. to #1, 27 Jan. 1805 for the Protestation itself.

71. Ibid., #6, 25 Feb. 1805, exp. opin., for quotations on authorship and responsibility; #5, 13 Feb. 1805, Pistorius comm. rpt. and encl. to #5, 8 Feb. 1805, the original prot. rpt., on the investigator's methods; and #7, 3 Mar. 1805, dft. resc. specifying punishments and resolving the case.

72. Waib. pet. inv., 13 Jan. 1806, Schott rpt.; 20 Mar. 1806, GovC rpt.

73. Ibid., 13 Jan. 1806, Schott rpt. and 10 Jan. 1806, prot. p. 31 to ques. 100 on Bolley's speechifying.

74. Ibid., exhib. A to Schott rpt., 11 Jan. 1806, Bolley's explanation; also prot. of 10 Jan. 1806, p. 11 on Bolley and Theuß exchanges.

75. Ibid., exhib. C to Schott rpt., 14 Jan. 1806, Weisser's written justification.

76. Ibid., 13 Jan. 1806, Schott rpt. prots., pp. 16, 18b-20, questions 32–33.

77. Ibid., 20 Mar. 1806, gov. rpt.

78. On Jacobinism, see Patrice Higonnet, *Goodness Beyond Virtue: Jacobins during the French Revolution* (Cambridge, Mass.: Harvard University Press, 1998); on civic republicanism, Pocock, *The Machiavellian Moment;* on Central European nationalism, Matthew Levinger, *Enlightened Nationalism: The Transformation of Prussian Political Culture, 1806–1848* (Oxford: Oxford University Press, 2000).

79. Dickey, *Hegel,* esp. chap. 3, can be read as an attempt to translate Pocock's *The Machiavellian Moment* onto Swabian soil.

80. Blickle, *Gemeinde und Staat im Alten Europa.*

CHAPTER 5: TRANSCENDING "TEXTUAL SERFDOM"

1. The best classic works on Napoleonic Germany are Reinhart Koselleck, *Preussen zwischen Reform und Revolution: Allgemeines Landrecht, Verwaltung und soziale Bewegung von 1791 bis 1848* (Stuttgart: Klett-Cotta, 1967); and Walker, *German Home Towns*. Hull, *Sexuality, State, and Civil Society* provides the best contemporary treatment. For guides to the voluminous literature on reform from above, see Paul Nolte, *Staatsbildung als Gesellschaftsreform: Politische Reformen in Preussen und den süddeutschen Staaten, 1800–1820* (Frankfurt: Campus, 1990); the bibliography of Bernd Sösemann, *Gemeingeist und Bürgersinn: Die preußischen Reformen* (Berlin: Duncker & Humblot, 1993), 281–320; and the works of Helmut Berding, Walter Demel, Elisabeth Fehrenbach, Barbara Vogel, and Eberhard Weis, some of which are reviewed in Otto Dann, "Deutschland unter französichem Einfluß," *AfS* 26 (1986): 416–28. In English, see T. C. W. Blanning, "The French Revolution and the Modernization of Germany," *CEH* 22, no. 2 (1989): 109–29. On Württemberg, see Manfred Hettling, *Reform ohne Revolution: Bürgertum, Bürokratie und kommunale Selbstverwaltung in Württemberg von 1800 bis 1850* (Göttingen: Vandenhoeck & Ruprecht, 1990); and Wolfgang von Hippel, *Die Bauernbefreiung im Königreich Württemberg*, vol. 1.

2. G. W. F. Hegel, "Beurteilung der in Druck erschienenen Verhandlungen in der Versammlung der Landstände des Königreichs Württemberg im Jahre 1815 u. 1816," in *Werke*, ed. E. Moldenhauer and K. M. Michel (Frankfurt: Suhrkamp, 1986 [1817]), vol. 4, 464–597, here p. 574.

3. Max Miller, *Die Organisation und Verwaltung von Neuwürttemberg unter Herzog und Kurfürst Friedrich*, serialized in *WVLG* 37 (1931): 112–76, 266–307; 39 (1933): 76–135, 232–92. See vol. 37, 159–76, esp. 173–74 on the quality of Friedrich's absolutism and despotic personality; also Paul Sauer, *Der schwäbsiche Zar: Friedrich, Württembergs erster König* (Stuttgart: Deutsche Verlags-Anstalt, 1984).

4. Erwin Hölzle, *Württemberg im Zeitalter Napoleons und der Deutschen Erhebung* (Stuttgart: W. Kohlhammer, 1937); Grube, *Vogteien, Ämter, Landkreise*; and Michael Holzmann, "Die Gliederung der Oberämter im Königreich Württemberg," *ZWLG* 38 (1979): 164–87 for the nuts and bolts of territorial reorganization.

5. One expert, throwing up his hands, chalked up scribal corruption to the "general conditions" of post-Napoleonic statemaking. See Int. Min. I 43, OA Künzelsau, Schreiber Schmid case, #111, 8 Mar. 1816, exp. opin.

6. Int. Min. I 36ff., Rubrik: Beamte, on Unteramteien, Stadt- und Amtsschreibereien; and archival Findbuch, 154–243 for these cases. Examples include Int. Min. I 43, OA Künzelsau, Schreiber Schmid (1816) and Int. Min. I 46, OA Mergentheim, Schreiber Dietrich (1812), both cases on exaggerated fees; Int. Min. I 43, OA Mergentheim, Schreiber Dietzsch at Weikersheim asks for compensation for loss of business; Rott. Sect. 237, for a conflict between OAM Burkardt and Schreiber Fischer at Rottweil (1804); also Sect. 71 Bü 65, on a con-

scription dispute at Rottweil (1810–11), plus Bü 64, 66, 68, 461; Sect. 75 Bü 182, 187, 200, 201, 203 (Laux's "beißender Hund"), 205, 210. See also SCA 941, Verhandlungen die Geschäfts Abtheilung zwischen den Central- u. Distrikts Stadt- und Amtsschreiber betrf., 1810–1814.

7. Miller, *Organisation und Verwaltung*, vol. 37, 156 for the term "organisationitis." There are no good works available on the Württemberg officialdom between 1806 and 1815; the best account is Wintterlin, *Behördenorganisation*, vol. 1, 184–94; Bernd Wunder, *Privilegierung und Disziplinierung: Die Entstehung des Berufsbeamtentums in Bayern und Württemberg 1780–1825* (München: Oldenbourg, 1978) skips over this period, since he is concerned only with the intra-administrative law on officials *(Beamtenrecht)*, which lay in an indeterminate state during the absolutist interregnum.

8. On the collection of the 1808 surveys, see *Reg. Bl.* 9 May 1808, 259–60; Cent. Org. Comm. 187–90, Einkommen der Stadtschreiber, 1807–12 for originals. For extensive treatment of the methodology and significance of the 1818 surveys, see the second section of the next chapter.

9. Sch. Comm. 281, Hauptbericht der Kommission zum Schreibereiwesen (1817), esp. §§14–24, 35–43; also see Hegel, "Beurteilung," 564–69.

10. Hegel, "Beurteilung," 570.

11. Gottfried Knapp, *Ueber das Württembergische Schreibereiwesen: Eine für die Ständeversammlung bestimmt gewesene Relation* (Tübingen: W. H. Schramm, 1817), 111–12 comments on these difficulties.

12. Decree of 16 May 1807, cited in Wintterlin, *Behördenorganisation*, vol. 1, 216; *Reg. Bl.* 22 Nov. 1824, 928–29 for the 1824 collection of Nationallisten.

13. The *Nationallisten* were entered into a large database for the purposes of analysis. They were collected by the government in two waves, in 1809 and 1824 (NL 1809 and NL 1824). Supplemental information was added from miscellaneous other personnel files, chiefly the *Nationallisten* of Ober- and Unteramt-*männer*, some of whom were present or former scribes, located in NL II 2657, 2658, 2660, 2661; and Jus. Min. 120. All this information was then correlated with New Württemberg appointment lists, which match particular individuals with particular (newly constructed) districts, in Int. Min III 1871, 1875–76; Int. Min. II 985–87, 1021–23; SCA 962. The *Staatshandbücher* available in the HStAS reading room were also consulted for this purpose. Finally, information from *NWD* was added in those instances where a scribe had served in the eighteenth century.

14. New appointeees are defined as those appointed in New Württemberg districts after 1803, and in Old Württemberg after 1807. Those whose dates are not given are assumed to be new appointees if and only if they served in New Württemberg. The candidate pool, though difficult to tabulate, probably encompassed several hundred officials, including both old-Württemberg *Schreiber* and various employed and un(der)employed officials from the new acquisitions. On the government's appointment process, see Int. Min. III 1871; SCA 962; and Int. Min. II 985, 987.

15. SCA 962, Wie dem Mangel an tüchtigen und hinlänglichen Substituten in den neuen Acquisitionen abgeholfen werden könne, prot. exc. of 12 Jan. 1810.

16. For example, sixteen scribes serving in New Württemberg are listed, in seeming paradox, as having been appointed before the kingdom took possession of their districts. These men were, in almost every case, old-Württemberg scribes by birth and training who had earlier found employment outside the old duchy. One may assume that in those districts where the government found a trustworthy scribe from the old duchy already in service, he was simply co-opted into his position and given a new title.

17. Specifically, 63.86% hailed from the old duchy. Note that this second group of *Nationallisten* runs past 1815, and through 1819, because the constitutional settlement and subsequent administrative reforms of the Schreiberei system were only in place by the latter year; the state's philosophy and room for maneuver in staffing the *Schreiberei* thus remained unchanged until then, before yielding to a new regime of exclusively provisional appointments between 1819 and 1826, the year the profession was abolished. It should be noted, moreover, that this sample only includes scribes still in service in 1824, the closest year for which a comprehensive series of *Nationallisten* is available. Those scribes who retired, died, or were fired between 1819 and 1824, and who were thus not a part of the 1824 group, do not constitute a statistically significant aberration.

18. Joachim Gerner, *Vorgeschichte und Entstehung der württembergischen Verfassung im Spiegel der Quellen (1815–1819)* (Stuttgart: W. Kohlhammer, 1989), 24–27, 80.

19. The new suffrage extended to all males over twenty-five years of age who derived at least 200 fl. in income from real property. This meant that anywhere from one to six percent of the total population actually voted in a typical district, or about 14.6% of all adult males of proper age in Württemberg. See Bernd Wunder, "Die Landtagswahlen von 1815 und 1819 in Württemberg: Landständische Repräsentation und Interessenvertretung," *WF* 58 (1974): 264–93, esp. 267.

20. Int. Min. II 986, 15 May 1807, Int. Min. to Graf v. Normann-Ehrenfels.

21. Wunder, "Landtagswahlen," 275–81 on this paragraph and for this interpretation; also Hartwig Brandt, *Parlamentarismus in Württemberg, 1819–1870: Anatomie eines deutschen Landtags* (Düsseldorf: Droste, 1987), 80.

22. Int. Min. II 3530, Verzeichnisse der gewählten Repräsentanten (copies A and B, 1815). Cf. Wunder, "Landtagswahlen," 269–74.

23. Wunder, "Landtagswahlen," 282. Many of those who stood for election outside their districts were officials of some sort barred from running in home districts.

24. *Verh.*, 26 Jun. 1815, sec. 8., 91–252; Heinrich Bolley and Schmid, eds., *Darstellung des Betragens der Württembergischen Landstände seit dem 15. März 1815: Mit erster Fortsetzung, enthaltend die Beschwerden des Landes* (n.p., 1815); see also Bolley's *Nachträge und Berichtigungen zu der Schrift: Worin bestand das alte Recht? Was schlugen die Landstände vor? Was bietet

der König an? (Stuttgart: n.p., 1817). The committee brought some of the most vocal and entrenched representatives of the *altes Recht* orthodoxy, including the *Schreiber* apologists Bolley and Gottfried Knapp, together with the two most prominent later critics of the profession, Georg Forstner von Dambenoy and Ludwig Griesinger, producing a very lukewarm indictment of the scribes. See Gerner, *Vorgeschichte*, 148n341 on the composition of the Grievances Committee, plus pp. 162–68 generally.

25. Gerner, *Vorgeschichte*, 209–12.

26. Int. Min. OA rpts., on countryside agitation, including part #4 on the meetings described below (Besigheim on 3 Sep. 1815, Metzingen on 20 Sep. 1815, Nagold on 1 Oct. 1815) with identification of their participants; part #3, reports from regional commissioners in the *Landvogteien*, 27 Aug.–5 Sep. 1815, including Kornwestheim assembly; also Gerner, *Vorgeschichte*, 219–36 for a detailed general account of this agitation.

27. Int. Min. I 141, part #5, Beschwerde der Ständeversammlung über Verfolgung gegen einige ihrer Mitglieder, 22 Oct. 1815 dft. to Int. Min. on assemblies of notables and *Amtsversammlungen* (including Leonberg case) and popular petitions (including Cammerer quotation); 6 Dec. 1815 exp. opin. on "disturbers of the peace," illegal petition drives, disallowed communications, and surveillance by OAM.

28. Int. Min. OA rpts., part #2, Berichte der Landvogtei- und Oberämter über die Stimmung des Volkes wegen Vertagung der Landstände Versammlung, 5 Aug. 1815 for the analysis in this section.

29. Ibid., rpt. of 27 Aug. 1815 from Landvogtei an der Jagst.

30. Ibid., OA rpts. from cities mentioned; also Gerner, *Vorgeschichte*, 214, 229 on festivals.

31. On the Ulm and Gamerschwang assemblies, see Int. Min. OA rpts., part #2, 28 Aug., 20 Sep., and 21 Sep. 1815.

32. Int. Min. II 3582, leaflet from Cannstatt, cited in Jonathan Rubinstein, "Society and Politics in the German Southwest, 1760–1819" (Ph.D. diss., Harvard University, 1969), 394ff.

33. Int. Min. OA rpts., part #5, exp. opin. of 6 Dec. 1815 (including quotations); part #4.

34. The scribes' role in the *altes Recht* mobilization has often been underestimated by historians, who attribute its success to the proud tradition of the Tübingen Compact. Such explanations fail to explain how "tradition" becomes woven into daily political practice and appeals to certain entrenched social interests; they also encounter great difficulty explaining why many New Württembergers threw their loyalties initially with the *Altrechtler*. Rehabilitating the scribes, who profited directly from the old constitution's continuation and exerted a statewide political influence within the kingdom's localities, addresses precisely these weaknesses in the standard account.

35. PrivC parl. pets. (Eingaben der Ständeversammlung) from 1815 and 1816.

36. Ibid. and *Verh.*, 22 Jan.–21 Oct. 1816, secs. 18–32 on these mobilizations.

The campaign was especially active in the localities of Horb, Spaichingen, Geislingen, Gmünd, and Mergentheim, districts that were scattered all over New Württemberg, with the northeast being slightly overrepresented.

37. *Verh.*, 6 Feb. 1816, sec. 18, 122–26, Beck for apologetic quotation; 24 Oct. 1816, sec. 32, 70–95, encls. 6 (Haack), and 5 (Reiter, for trusteeship quotation).

38. Ibid., 6 Feb. 1816, sec. 18, 126–31 for Kurz presentation; encl. of 22 Jan. 1816, sec. 18, 23–28, 35–36, 45–47 for Ott and Olnhausen side; PrivC parl. pets., Rep. OA Horb for Kurz pet. within Knapp pet., dated 23/26 Feb. 1816.

39. PrivC parl. pets., Nast remarks taken to protocol 19 Aug. 1816; *Verh.*, 29. Jan. 1816, sec. 18, 95–104, Gmünd pet.; *Verh.* 19. Aug. 1816, sec. 28b, 74, 81–83.

40. PrivC parl. pets., pet. of 3 Jan. 1816 from Schörzingen.

41. *Verh.*, 21/24. Oct. 1816, sec. 32, 47–54, 70–95 for Reiter presentation and responses.

42. PrivC parl. pets.; *Verh.* 9. Feb. 1816, sec. 19, 9–11, 26–36.

43. *Verh.*, 13 May 1815, sec. 5, 38, 57–59; 13 Jun. 1815, sec. 7, 8; 28 Jun. 1815, sec. 8, 43–48; 5 Dec. 1815, sec. 16, 68, 77–85; see his further remarks on 17 Jan. 1816, sec. 17, 131, 134–43; 22 Jan. 1816, sec. 18, 35–36, 45–47; 8 Feb. 1816, sec. 18, 144, 147ff. for this discussion.

44. Such was the view put forth by Eberhard Georgii, one of the Good Old Law party's most prominent intellectuals, in his *Anti-Leviathan oder über das Verhältnis der Moral zum äußeren Recht und zur Politik* (Göttingen: Vandenhoeck & Ruprecht, 1807), cited in Hölzle, *Württemberg*, 142; Beschwerden des Landes, *Verh.*, 26 Jun. 1815, sec. 8, 183; Albrecht List, *Der Kampf ums gute alte Recht (1815–1819) nach seiner ideen- und parteigeschichtlichen Seite* (Tübingen: J. C. B. Mohr, 1914), 27–28.

45. *Verh.*, 5 Dec. 1815, sec. 16, 77–85; for its methods, see the commission's final report, "Comité-Gutachten über die provisorischen Mittel zu Hebung der Gebrechen bei dem öffentlichen Schreibereiwesen," *Verh.*, 20 Nov. 1816, sec. 33 Unterbeilage 1 to Beilage 1, 101–13.

46. Gottfried Gabriel Knapp, *Schreibereiwesen*, 143, 181.

47. Ibid., 102 (emphasis added).

48. PrivC parl. pets., 18 Mar. 1817, pet. from scribes at Künzelsau.

49. This title was adapted from a massively popular handbook of folk Enlightenment; for this quotation, see *Noth- und Hilfsbüchlein für den Württembergischen Schreiberstand oder Etwas über die Frage: Was hat der Württembergische Schreiber in der gegenwärtigen kritischen Lage seines Standes zu thun* (Gmünd: Ritter, 1817), 22.

50. See the discussion of *Stand* in Chapter 2, above.

51. A. List, *Der Kampf ums gute alte Recht*, 65–68, also 68–78, 83–93; Carsten, *Princes and Parliaments*, 1–148.

52. Hegel, "Beurteilung," 557; also 465–66, 471, 504–8, 532, 535, 557ff., 570ff., more generally. On the place of this commentary in Hegel's work, see Terry P. Pinkard, *Hegel: A Biography* (Cambridge, Eng.: Cambridge University Press, 2000), 399–411.

53. Hans Lotheissen, "Der ständisch-korporative Gedanke, namentlich in der württembergischen Verfassungsgeschichte und den publizistischen Schriften Hegels und List's zur württembergischen Verfassungsreform" (Phil. diss., Gießen, 1928), esp. 63–78.

54. Hegel, "Beurteilung," 482–83 (emphasis added).

55. Compare Hegel's rhetoric, or Forstner's similarly organic imagery, with the mechanical imagery in this quotation, penned by the apologist Friedrich August Weckherlin: "Let us [scribes] . . . drive undaunted the wheel of the machine on which the great Creator has set us. . . . [But] let the wheel stand still for one day, and the entire machine threatens to break down," *Apologie des wirttembergischen Schreiberstandes nebst einem Vorschlag zu seiner Vervollkommung* (Tübingen: Jacob Friedrich Heerbrandt, 1793), vii–ix. This passage was often cited by the scribes' nineteenth-century defenders.

56. Hegel, "Beurteilung," 576 (including next quotation excerpt).

57. *Verh.*, June–July 1816, sec. 25, Beilage; Griesinger, "Gutachten über den Württembergischen Schreiberstand," *Württembergisches Archiv* (July–September 1816): I, 29–64; II, 99–152; III, 1–42; Beiheft I, 1–208; Ludwig Griesinger, *Das Schreiber-Institut in Württemberg in der Versammlung der Landstände des Königreichs Würtemberg* (n.p., 1816). On Griesinger, see Ernst Rheinwald's short biography in *Schwäbische Lebensbilder* 5 (1950): 118–27.

58. Good accounts of this are available in Gerner, *Vorgeschichte* and Hölzle, *Württemberg.* See also A. List, *Der Kampf ums gute alte Recht*, 83–93 on statist progressivism.

59. Griesinger, *Schreiber-Institut*, 164.

60. Ibid., 93–94.

61. See Brandt, *Parlamentarismus*, 67–73, 90–97, 496–99; Rudolf Vierhaus, "Liberalismus, Beamtenstand und konstitutionelles System," in *Liberalismus in der Gesellschaft des deutschen Vormärz*, ed. Wolfgang Schieder (Göttingen: Vandenhoeck & Ruprecht, 1983), 39–54; and Franz Mögle-Hofacker, *Zur Entwicklung des Parlamentarismus in Württemberg: Der "Parlamentarismus der Krone" unter König Wilhelm I.* (Stuttgart: W. Kohlhammer, 1981).

62. Friedrich List, "Vortrag eines Unbekannten über das Schreibereiwesen," *Verh.*, 6 Feb. 1816, sec. 18, Beilage Nr. 5, 113, 132–39; anonymously reprinted as a separate pamphlet under the title *Ein ächtes Mittel zur Vertilgung des Schreiberunfugs in Württemberg* (Frankfurt: Ferdinand Boselli, 1816); and reproduced in Paul Gehring, *Friedrich List: Jugend und Reifejahre 1789–1825* (Tübingen: J. C. B. Mohr, 1964), 384–90.

63. F. List, prologue to the "Komittee-Gutachten über die Schreiberfrage," *Allgemeine Zeitung*, 30 Nov. 1816, Außerordentliche Beylage Nr. 4; reprinted in Gehring, *List*, 391–98. Replies included Victor Keller, *Freimüthige Beleuchtung des Komitee-Gutachtens über die provisorischen Mittel zur Hebung der Gebrechen bei dem öffentlichen Schreibereiwesen* (n.p.: n.p., 1817); Johann Heinrich Zeller, *Auch einige Worte über das Schreibereiwesen in Würtemberg, mit besonderer Rücksicht auf die 4. außerordentliche Beilage zur allgemeinen Zeitung von 1816* (Stuttgart: Johann Friedrich Steinkopf, 1817); *Einige*

Bermerkungen über Nr. 4 der außerordentlichen Beilage zur allgemeinen Zeitung vom Jahre 1816: Von einem vieljährigen Routinier (n.p., 1816). Also see Gehring, *List*, 101–2, 121–22.

64. Gehring, *List*, 16–183 on List's early career. For the expert opinions, Int. Min. II 1000, Gedanken über die Nothwendigkeit einer Reform der den Oberämtern subordinierten Amtsstellen, insbesondere des Stadt- und Amtsschreiberey-Wesens: Von einem Geschäftsmanne (1814); Gutachten über das Stadt- und Amtsschreibereiwesen und die Ämterorganisation überhaupt (1815), discussed in Gehring, *List*, 81–85; and F. List, *Schriften, Reden, Briefe* (Berlin: Reimar Hobbing, 1932–34), vol. 9, 273–74.

65. Sch. Comm. 287, Akten der Kommission wegen des Schreibereiwesens, Subfasz. Beschuldigungen gegen den Actuar der Commission, Rechnungsrath List (1816–1817); on his bitterness, List letter to Robert Mohl, 1 Jan. 1846, *Schriften*, vol. 8, 775; for the quotation, Roman Szporluk, *Communism and Nationalism: Karl Marx versus Friedrich List* (Oxford: Oxford University Press, 1988), 114.

66. F. List, "Kritik des Verfassungsentwurfs der Württembergischen Ständeversammlung mit besonderer Rücksicht auf Herstellung der bürgerlichen Freiheit in den Gemeinden und Oberämtern" (1817) in *Schriften*, vol. 1, 205–83, here 205–9; "Über die Verfassung und Verwaltung der Korporationen," in *Schriften*, vol. 1, 308–16, 310 for quotation.

67. F. List, "Etwas über den Unfug in den Oberamteien Würtembergs," *Für und Wider: Eine politische Zeitschrift für Württemberg* IV (1817): 20–26; "Gedanken über die württembergische Staatsregierung," *Schriften*, vol. 1, 87–148, here 109–14, 127; "Vortrag eines Unbekannten" in Gehring, *List*, 387; "Kritik," 207, 219–23.

68. Karl Erich Born, *Geschichte der Wirtschaftswissenschaften an der Universität Tübingen 1817–1967* (Tübingen: J. C. B. Mohr/Paul Siebeck, 1967); Gehring, *List*, 163–261.

69. David Lindenfeld, *The Practical Imagination: The German Sciences of State in the Nineteenth Century* (Chicago: University of Chicago Press, 1997); Keith Tribe, "Cameralism and the Science of Government," *JMH* 56 (June 1984): 263–84; idem, "Friedrich List and the Critique of 'Cosmopolitical Economy,' " *Manchester School* 56 (1988): 17ff.; Albrecht Timm, "Von der Kameralistik zur Nationalökonomie," in *Festschrift Hermann Aubin*, ed. Otto Brunner (Wiesbaden: Franz Steiner, 1965), vol. 1, 358–74.

70. The view of List being critiqued here is strongly evident in Szporluk, *Communism and Nationalism*.

71. F. List, "Plan eines wissenschaftlichen Vereins für Beförderung der vaterländischen Nationalökonomie," *Schriften*, vol. 1, 338.

72. F. List, "Gedanken über die württembergischen Staatsregierung," 118; also Lotheissen, "Der ständisch-korporative Gedanke," 38–40.

73. A. List, *Der Kampf ums gute alte Recht*, 122–59 on List's monarchical republicanism; also F. List, "Reutlinger Petition," *Schriften*, vol. 1, 584; idem, "Gedanken über die württembergischen Staatsregierung," 127–28.

74. F. List, "Gedanken über die württembergischen Staatsregierung," 101–2, 127–28; also Gedanken über die Nothwendigkeit einer Reform (see note 64), in Gehring, List, 375.

75. F. List, "Vortrag," 384, 389–90; "Gedanken über die württembergischen Staatsregierung," 101–2.

76. Bolley wrote a pamphlet "Rede des Abgeordneten Bolley über die Frage: Ob der Abgeordnete List aus der Kammer auszutreten habe?"; see Gehring, List, on his expulsion from parliament.

CHAPTER 6: READING, WRITING, AND REFORM

1. As an example, see the trove of expert opinions and other government documents generated during the post-Napoleonic peasant emancipation in Württemberg, reproduced in Hippel, Bauernbefreiung, vol. 2.

2. The administrative sciences of cameralism and Polizeiwissenschaft, for example, arose in the eighteenth century. See Marc Raeff, The Well-Ordered Police State: Social and Institutional Change Through Law in the Germanies and Russia, 1600–1800 (New Haven, Conn.: Yale University Press, 1983); Hans Maier, Die ältere deutsche Staats- und Verwaltungslehre (Polizeiwissenschaft): Ein Beitrag zur Geschichte der politischen Wissenschaft in Deutschland, 2nd ed. (Munich: Deutscher Taschenbuch Verlag, 1980 [1966]); and Hull, Sexuality, State, and Civil Society, chs. 2–4.

3. Eingabe der Ständeversammlung wegen des Schreibereiwesens, Reg. Bl. 21/22 Nov. 1816, 391–92; Kommission zur Untersuchung der Gebrechen des Schreibereiwesens, ibid., 11 Dec. 1816, 392–95; Jus. Min. 280, #3, 2/9 Dec. 1816, Kann das Schreiber-Institut nach dem Beispiele anderer deutscher Staaten ganz aufgehoben werden? (including quotation). The other two commissions were the Ämter-Organisations-Kommission (ÄOK), established 5 May 1818; and the Organisations-Vollziehungs-Kommission (OVK), existing in several incarnations between 1817 and 1828. The OVK's activities are described in the second section. The best sources on this activity are Wintterlin, Behördenorganisation, vol. 2, 3–28, 183–290; and Hettling, Reform ohne Revolution, 43–51, 96–102.

4. Jus. Min. 280, #2, 2/9 Dec. 1816, parliamentary proposal for collaborative work; #19, 8 Mar./11 Apr. 1817, response from gov. Sch. comm. to PrivC rejecting the offer.

5. Sch. Comm. 281, Hauptbericht der Kommission zum Schreibereiwesen (Jul.–Aug. 1817).

6. Royal ord., Verfügungen in Schreiberei-Sachen betr., Reg. Bl. 20 Aug. 1817, 413–15; ibid., 5 Sep. 1817, 441–42; Royal ord., weitere Verfügungen in Ansehung des Schreiberei-Wesens betr., 10 Sep. 1817, 456–59. For earlier reforms, Vorschrift, die Inventur- und Theilungskosten betr., ibid., 24 Jan. 1815, 25–27; also simplifications of official style (Schreibart), ibid., 24 Jun. 1816, 408; Sch. Comm. 282, Revision der Inventur- und Theilungskosten (1810–16).

7. A royal ord. of 11 Apr. 1810 brought the scribes' districts into closer conformity with those of the Oberämter as a means of ensuring a more precise

overlap of administrative functions. See Alfred Rieger, "Die Entwicklung des württembergischen Kreisverbands" (Ph.D. diss., Tübingen, 1952), 47ff., 53ff.

8. Koselleck, *Preußen zwischen Reform und Revolution*, 238ff., 262ff.

9. Sch. Comm. 287 Subfasz.: Beschuldigungen gegen den Actuar der Commission, Rechnungsrath List, #s 44, 46, 47, 49, 51, 55, 56, 67, 71, 78.

10. Organisations-Edikt, *Reg. Bl.* 31 Dec. 1818 [printed in 1819 volume], 28ff., produced by the ÄOK; also see Wintterlin, *Behördenorganisation*, vol. 2, 193–94, 203–6; and idem, "Die rechtsgeschichtlichen Grundlagen des Rechts-staats in Württemberg," *WVLG* 38 (1932): 318–41 on the doctrine of Gewaltenteilung.

11. Notariats-Ordnung, *Reg. Bl.* 25 Oct. 1808, 561–567; also *Reg. Bl.* 12 May 1807, 125–26 on Memorialien and Bittschriften (both discussed below). On the creation of the so-called Kommunrechnungsrevisoren, see Wintterlin, *Behördenorganisation*, vol. 1, 217–18; also *Reg. Bl.* 17 Apr. 1811, 177; 7 Dec. 1812, 618. For the ordinances creating new *Gerichtsschreiber*, *Reg. Bl.* 6/10 Feb. 1809, 77; 20/28 Jul. 1809, 317–19; on *Amtsschreibereien*, 11 Apr. 1810, 125.

12. Hettling, *Reform ohne Revolution*, 43–47; Wintterlin, *Behörden-organisation*, vol. 2, 213–30.

13. As Chapter 2 noted, eighteenth-century cameralist policy on the scribes had been sharply limited in its efficacy. By contrast, post-Napoleonic government created new ministries for justice, finance, interior affairs, and the like, in addition to empowering commissions, like those charged with *Schreiber* reform, holding front-line responsibility for the drafting of government policies.

14. Cab. I 88, "Oberamts-Verfassung" (with Schmidlin), "Verwaltung der Stiftungen" (same), "Gerichtsverfassung" (with Huber), "Notariatsordnung" (with Schmidlin), "Über die Stadt- und Amtsschreibereien," "Über die Gerichtsorganisation," "Ideen zur Organisation der Gerichte," all 1818.

15. Wintterlin, *Behördenorganisation*, vol. 2, 208, 267–68.

16. Ibid., 205–8.

17. Heinrich Bolley, *Entwurf einer Amtsintruktion für die Gerichtsnotarien im Königreich Württemberg* (Stuttgart: n.p., 1821); Wintterlin, *Behörden-organisation*, vol. 2, 246, 255–62.

18. Notariats-Edikt, *Reg. Bl.* 29 Aug. 1819, 561ff. According to the edict's provisions, *Gerichtsnotare* would still be primarily responsible for noncon-tentious litigation *(freiwillige Gerichtsbarkeit)* but could be hired on an ad hoc basis by communities for administrative business if no one else could do the job.

19. Wintterlin, *Behördenorganisation*, vol. 2, 256, 318.

20. Landtags-Abschied, *Reg. Bl.* 30 Jun. 1821, 469–89; this principle is also reflected in a resc. of 16 Jun. 1821; see Wintterlin, *Behördenorganisation*, vol. 2, 273–81.

21. See Int. Min. III 2163, #16, 28 Aug. 1820, for Neckarsulm Amtsschreiber John's complaint against several communities in his district for outsourcing his business. See elsewhere in this file, as well as OVK I files on Erledigung von Stadt- und Amtsschreibereien, 1819–1826, for dispensations granted to the scribes for performance of various sorts of business in subsequent years.

22. Verwaltungsedikt, *Reg. Bl.* 1 Mar. 1822, 131ff.

23. A. Zeller, "Über die Entwicklung württembergischer Verwaltungsein-richtungen," *Zeitschrift für die gesamte Staatswissenschaft* 54 (1898): 441–66, esp. 456 on Verwaltungsaktuare.

24. Sch. Comm. 285 for early complaints; Int. Min. III 2163, die Vorstellung mehrerer Stadt- und Amtsschreiber wegen Schmälerung ihres Einkommens for later ones (1819–22), including Bolley's assertion of his own *Dienst-Vertrags-Rechte* on 28 Nov. 1817, followed by irritated replies from the Jus. Min. and the King himself, 25 and 29 Nov. (respectively). Also OVK I for still later complaints.

25. See Wunder, *Privilegierung und Disziplinierung*, 321 and passim on the *Beamtenrecht*.

26. The edicts of 1817–21 had largely sidestepped the issue for this reason but did at least establish a framework for payment reform. The 1818 Organiza-tional Edict, following the 1817 Main Report, provided that *Gerichtsnotare* (but not yet *Schreiber*) be paid in large part from public treasuries, envisaged the con-version of fee-for-service payment into fixed yearly incomes, and outlawed the taking of gifts/bribes. It also promised monetary compensation for those who would lose their jobs and/or income. Negotiations surrounding the Parlia-mentary Agreement provided that *Gerichtsnotare* be paid from county trea-suries, but after 1826 they would draw their incomes from the state treasury.

27. *Reg. Bl.* 18 Mar. 1812, 137–38 on actuaries and *Substituten;* Wintterlin, *Behördenorganisation*, vol. 2, 258, 261, 307–12; see also Int. Min. II 988. Cf. Wunder, *Privilegierung und Disziplinierung*, 307–10 on the *Dienstpragmatik* of 1821, reserving the full benefits of state service to the highest officials.

28. Exam. comm. 5, Examinations-Tabelle (1806–1812); ibid., 13–165, indi-vidual Verzeichnisse and Prüfungen, 1806–1816; SCA 969; Exam. comm. 3 for exam questions in 1813.

29. Royal ord., die Auflösung der Stadt- und Amtsschreibereien betr., *Reg. Bl.* 17 Apr. 1826, 211–18; see also the edicts of 21 Mar. 1826, 24 May 1826, and 26 May 1826 on the naming of *Gerichtsnotare*. Fifty-two scribes were eased out of service and replaced usually by receipt auditors or other mere functionaries; sixty-two were retained in their old districts in these new positions; and a final forty-five were transferred to new districts; on this, see *Reg. Bl.* 29 Mar. 1826, 176–86.

30. *Denkschrift eines Stadtschreibers in Württemberg über den ihm zugedachten Amtsmanns-Wechsel* (Esslingen: J. G. Helfferich, 1818).

31. The concepts of material and symbolic capital, together with the notion of their interconvertibility, derive from Bourdieu, *Outline of a Theory of Practice*, 171–82.

32. See Jane Caplan, "The Imaginary Universality of Particular Interests: The 'Tradition' of the Civil Service in German History," *SH* 4 (1979): 299–317 for a critique of this line of thought.

33. Cab. I 84, 6 Sep. 1826, pensions *(Ergänzungs-Gehalte)* of individual *Gerichtsnotare*. *Gerichtsnotare* were otherwise paid on a four-tiered salary

schedule indexed to population size and ranging from 600 to 1000 fl., substantially below what scribes tended to make.

34. Organisations-Vollziehungs-Kommission.

35. OVK I, 2 Oct. 1821, instruction for collection of income information; Cab. I 84, for Einkommens-Erklärungen and Entschädigung, 1822–34; OVK inc. rpts. for scribes' Dienst-Einkommens-Berechnungen, based on templates found in Sch. Comm. 286, on Pensionirung und Entschädigungs-Ansprüche der Stadt- und Amtsschreiber, 1821–26.

36. The Neckar and Black Forest *Kreise* were predominantly composed of Old Württemberg districts and the Jagst and Danube of New Württemberg districts, though there was substantial overlap in every case. The Black Forest *Kreis* was located west-southwest of Stuttgart; the Neckar slightly to the north, covering roughly the present-day metropolitan region; the Jagst in the northwest, on the Hohenlohe plains, and the Danube between Lake Constance and the Swabian Alb, up through Ulm.

37. Jus. Min. 93, chart on OA incomes (1822).

38. To put it another way, this amount was roughly the price of a nineteen-pound bag of barley. For price and wage data (from 1820–21), see Wolfgang von Hippel, "Bevölkerungsentwicklung und Wirtschaftsstruktur im Königreich Württemberg 1815/65. Überlegungen zum Pauperismusproblem in Südwestdeutschland," in *Soziale Bewegung und politische Verfassung: Beiträge zur Geschichte der modernen Welt*, ed. Ulrich Engelhardt, Volker Sellin and Horst Stuke (Stuttgart: Ernst Klett, 1976), 270–371, tables 21 on p. 335, 24 on p. 343.

39. Between 1808 and 1822, the gap between Old and New Württemberg incomes narrowed from 31% of the latter to only 2%: on average, scribes in the old duchy were now no longer significantly richer than their counterparts in the annexed regions. This convergence can partly be attributed to a 13% across-the-board decline in average incomes since 1817, one which, however, was concomitantly greater in New Württemberg than in Old (17% vs. 10%). These statistics are based on figures from the income surveys.

40. OVK II, rpt. of 8 Jun. 1823.

41. Sch. Comm. 283, Vergleichende Uebersicht der Verdienst Taxen und Sporteln von verschiedenen Geschäften der Bezirks-Staats-Verwaltungs Behörden.

42. Ibid., Bemerkungen über den Aufwand in verschiedenen Staats-Verwaltungs-Zweigen, welcher nach den vorliegenden Akten in vormals Preußisch-Bairischen, Hohenlohischen, Ritterschaftlichen [usw.] Gebiets-Teilen statt gefunden hat.

43. Regions where marital property was held jointly by husband and wife spent more on contracts than those where such property was held separately (4.61 fl. versus 3.61 fl. per 100 inhabitants). Source: OVK II, Übersicht des Einkommens der Stadt- und Amtsschreiber von Ehe-Verträge, Kauf-Briefen, Testamenten, Memorialien, Schuld-Verschreibungen, Geburts-Briefen, Bürger-Rechts-Verzichten, Auszügen, Abschriften, Beglaubigungen (1823).

44. Those scribes with only provisional appointments were excluded from

compensation and thus the classification scheme itself; besides, they were already being paid at a much lower rate.

45. These data are drawn from Reutlingen, a mixed-use region; see J. G. D. Memminger, ed., *Beschreibung des Oberamts Reutlingen: Mit einer Karte des Oberamts, zwey lithographischen Blättern und Tabellen,* (Stuttgart and Tübingen: J. G. Cotta, 1824), 53.

46. OVK II, rpt. on collection of income information dated 8 Jun. 1823.

47. Hippel, *Bauernbefreiung,* 64n20 on the connections between viniculture and partible inheritance; 58–78 on patterns of land tenure and agricultural practices in the kingdom of Württemberg generally.

48. In many of these regions, the practice of primogeniture was legally encouraged but in the final analysis remained a choice for individual families. The resultant regularity of inheritance patterns was another social fact unearthed by the government's probing beneath mere law and ordinance.

49. See note 44. This close correspondence merely indicates that the *Schreibereien* eligible for compensation were a representative sample, no more or less exploitative as a group than *Schreibereien* generally.

50. The percentages of income lost all fall roughly within the same range, 20–25%, for each category graphed in diagram 8. The source of these data is OVK II, General-Übersicht der Einkommens-Fassionen der Stadt- und Amts-schreiber und der ihnen auszusetzenden Entschädigungs-Summen, prob. 1823, which tabulates reported income and overall compensation plus overall loss by class. It was augmented with data from the sources for diagram 8, providing population sizes for each category, so that averages could be computed.

51. OVK II, Subfasz. F6a, die Steuer Fassionen der Stadt- und Amtsschreiber und ihre Differenz mit den Diensteinkommens Berechnungen von 1821, esp. tables #5 ad 3 and #6 used to compare reported 1821 incomes, compensation incomes, and reported taxable incomes from 1821 to 1825.

52. Heinz Bühler, *Das beamtete Bürgertum in Göppingen und sein soziales Verhalten 1815–1848* (Göppingen: Stadtarchiv Göppingen, 1976), documents these trends in a core Old Württemberg city.

53. Carl Schaffert, *Beschreibung der Gerichts- und Amts-Notariate des Königreichs Württemberg* (Biberach: n.p., 1867).

54. *Reg. Bl.* 12 May 1807, 125–26; 31 Mar. 1810, 101; 26 Jan. 1811, 57; 1 Jun. 1811, 262 on *Memorialien, Suppliken, Bittschriften, unmittelbare Eingaben;* see also Jus. Min. 7, Subfasz. 38 on direct pets. *(unmittelbarer Bittschriften),* 1808–1812; Ellw. Sect. 153, Abfassung und Versendung von Suppliken, Berichten, Beiberichten und Exhibiten in Klagsachen (1806) for early cases.

55. Notariats-Ordnung, *Reg. Bl.* 5 Nov. 1808, 561–67, improved upon in legislation of 1826 and 1834, on which see *Reg. Bl.* 29 Jun. 1826, 321; 7 Apr. 1834, 327–33.

56. Int. Min. III 2164, 23 Jun. 1818, case of Johann Wolfgang Melchinger; Lud. Reg. Gov. I 1035, 30 Sep. 1818, case of Christian Friedrich Ledermann.

57. NL 1824, Karl Ludwig Becher.

58. Jus. Min. 7, #2, 3 Jan. 1822, Int. Min. rpt. to Jus. Min.; #20, 15 Sep. 1821, PrivC to Jus. Min.

59. Friedrich Bauer, *Anleitung zur schriftlichen Geschäftsführung für das bürgerliche Leben* (Stuttgart: J. G. Munder, 1830).

60. On *Briefsteller,* see Dieter Cherubim, Georg Objartel, and Isa Schikorsky, "'Geprägte Form, die lebend sich entwickelt': Beobachtungen zu institutionsbezogenen Texten des 19. Jahrhunderts," *WW* 37, no. 2 (1987): 144–76.

61. Ibid., 156, 158.

62. Petitions for *Memorial-Schreiben* and *Bittschrift-Stellen* privileges are collected in Int. Min. III 2164–2165 and commented upon by the government there and in Jus. Min. 7.

63. Lud. Reg. Gov. III 6833, ad #4, undated printed plan of Allgemeines Geschäfts- und Kommissions Bureau in Mainz.

64. Ibid., #1–6, 20 Nov. 1821, first Nast pet. to Neckar dist. gov., plus encl. docs. and granting of the privilege on 7 Jul. 1822; Int. Min. III 2164, 29 Jan. 1822, second Nast pet. to Neckar dist. gov.; Jus. Min. 7, #9, 12 May 1823, Int. Min. to Jus. Min. on Nast case.

65. Int. Min. III 2164, 6 Nov. 1822, Reut., Bitte des in dem Quiescentenstand versezten Cammer Assessor Scheffold allhier um die Erlaubniß ein allgemeines Geschäfts und Commissions Bureau errichten zu dürfen.

CHAPTER 7: CATALOGING THE SOCIAL WORLD

1. See Anderson, *Imagined Communities.*

2. Cf. Walker, *German Home Towns,* ch. 10 on the Biedermeier.

3. Similar arguments have been advanced by Silvana Patriarca, *Numbers and Nationhood: Writing Statistics in Nineteenth-Century Italy* (Cambridge, Eng.: Cambridge University Press, 1996); and Rita Krueger, "From Empire to Nation: The Aristocracy and the Formation of Modern Society in Bohemia, 1770–1848" (Ph.D. diss., Harvard University, 1997), ch. 3.

4. See Vincenz John, *Geschichte der Statistik: Ein quellenmässiges Handbuch für den akademischen Gebrauch wie für den Selbstunterricht* (Stuttgart: Enke, 1884), which is good on the academic disputes surrounding the "Göttinger Schule"; for more on the *Zeitungskolleg* and *Universitätsstatistik,* W. Schöne, *Zeitungswesen und Statistik: Eine Untersuchung über den Einfluss der periodischen Presse auf die Entstehung und Entwicklung der staatswissenschaftlichen Literatur, speziell der Statistik* (Jena: Gustav Fischer, 1924), 70–75, 84–97. Also the useful collection by Mohammed Rassem and Justin Stagl, eds., *Statistik und Staatsbeschreibung in der Neuzeit* (Paderborn: Ferdinand Schöningh, 1980).

5. On Schlözer, see Justin Stagl, "August Ludwig Schlözers Entwurf einer 'Volkskunde' oder 'Ethnographie' seit 1772," *Ethnologische Zeitschrift* 2 (1974): 73–91; and John, *Geschichte der Statistik,* 98–113; on *Volkskunde* and its connections to *Statistik,* Helmut Möller, "Aus den Anfängen der Volkskunde als Wissenschaft. A: Volkskunde, Statistik, Völkerkunde 1787," *Zeitschrift für*

Volkskunde 60 (1964): 218–33; and the provocative, though spotty, essay by Uli Linke, "Folklore, Anthropology, and the Government of Social Life," *CSSH* 32, no. 1 (Jan. 1990): 117–48.

6. J. P. Süßmilch, *Die gottliche Ordnung in der Veränderung des menschlichen Geschlechts, aus der Geburt, dem Tode, und der Fortpflanzung desselben erwiesen* (Berlin: n.p., 1741).

7. Ian Hacking, *The Taming of Chance* (Cambridge, Eng.: Cambridge University Press, 1990), 20–23. Thus medical topography, in the hands of such authors as Johann Peter Franck, constituted a well-developed subgenre of German *Statistik*.

8. This is the innovative argument of W. Schöne, *Zeitungswesen und Statistik*, 69–97; cf. Hacking, *Taming*, 20; on the importance of *"Räsonnement"* to folklore and statistics, Dieter Narr and Hermann Bausinger, "Aus den Anfängen der Volkskunde als Wissenschaft" (1964), in Narr, *Studien zur Spätaufklärung*, 279–86, here 282–83.

9. Wolfgang Griep, "Reiseliteratur im späten 18. Jahrhundert," in Rolf Grimminger, ed., *Hansers Sozialgeschichte der deutschen Literatur vom 16. Jahrhundert bis zur Gegenwart* (München, Wien: Carl Hanser, 1980), vol. 3, 739–64; see also vol. 4, 781–89. For famous examples of the genre, Wilhelm Ludwig Wekhrlin, "Anselm Rabiosus Reise durch Ober-Deutschland," in *Schriften* (Nendeln: KTO Press, 1978 [1778]), vol. 1; Friedrich Nicolai, *Beschreibung einer Reise durch Deutschland und die Schweiz im Jahre 1781: Nebst Bemerkungen über Gelehrsamkeit, Industrie, Religion und Sitten* (Berlin: n.p., 1783–96).

10. For genre classics, see the works cited below by Röder and Krug and (for example) Johann Wolfgang Melchinger, *Geographisches statistisch-topographisches Lexikon von Baiern: Oder vollständige alphabetische Beschreibung aller im ganzen baiernschen Kreis liegenden Städte, Klöster, Schlösser, Dörfer, Höfe, Berge, Thäler, Flüsse, Seen* (Ulm: n.p., 1796–1802); more creative titles included the anonymous *Neueste geographisch-statistisch-technisch-topographische Beschreibung des preußischen Schlesiens* (Glogau: n.p., n.d.) and *Siebenburgisches geographisch-topographisch-statistisch-hydrographisch- und orographisches Lexikon* (Wien: n.p., n.d.). Territories, big and small, represented by the genre included Württemberg, Bavaria, Prussia, Baden, Saxony, Lusatia, Silesia, the Rhineland, Altenburg, Magdeburg, Siebenburg, Erfurt, Dresden, Great Britain, Italy, and Egypt.

11. Mack Walker, *Johann Jakob Moser and the Holy Roman Empire of the German Nation* (Chapel Hill: University of North Carolina Press, 1981), 283–95 and passim.

12. Christian Friedrich Sattler, *Historische Beschreibung des Herzogtums Würtemberg und aller desselben Städte, Clöster und darzu gehörigen Aemter, nach deren ehmaligen Besitzern, Schicksalen undsowohl historischen, als Natur-Merkwürdigkeiten* (Stuttgart and Esslingen: J. N. Stoll and G. Mäntlern, 1752); idem., *Geschichte des Herzogtums Württemberg unter der Regierung der Herzoge* (Tübingen: n.p., 1769–83); idem., *Christian Friedrich Sattlers*

Topographische Geschichte des Herzogthums Würtemberg (Stuttgart: n.p., 1784). See also the collection on Johann Christoph Schmidlin, in HStAS J 8, for similar "patriotic" history endeavors.

13. Leopold Krug, *Topographisch-statistisch-geographisches Wörterbuch der sämmtlichen preussischen Staaten oder Beschreibung aller Provinzen, Kreise, Distrikte, Städte in den preussischen Staaten* (Halle: n.p., 1796–1803); on Krug, see Hacking, *Taming*, 29–33; Meitzel, "Krug, Leopold" in *Handwörterbuch der Staatswissenschaften* (Jena: Gustav Fischer, 1923–29), 4th ed., vol. 6, 91–92; *Neue Deutsche Biographie* (Berlin: Duncker & Humblot, 1953), vol. 13, 113.

14. Philipp Ludwig Hermann Röder, *Geographie und Statistik Wirtembergs* (Laybach am Krain/Ulm: n.p., 1787–1804); idem, *Geographisches-statistisch-topographisches Lexikon von Schwaben* (Ulm: Stettin, 1791–92); idem, *Reisen durch das südliche Teutschland* (Leipzig: G. L. Crusius and F. C. Walliser, 1789–91); also Hermann Bausinger, "Philipp Ludwig Hermann Röders 'Geographie und Statistik Wirtembergs,' " *BdL* 31 (1963): 447–60.

15. Christian Heinrich Niemann, "Skize zur Beschreibung eines Landdistrikts," *Schleswig-Holsteinische Vaterlandskunde* 1 (1802): 9–52; Ingeborg Weber-Kellerman, *Deutsche Volkskunde: Zwischen Germanistik und Sozialwissenschaften* (Stuttgart: J. B. Metzler, 1969), 5; John, *Geschichte der Statistik*, also treats Niemann.

16. P. L. H. Röder, *Neu-Wirtemberg oder geographische und statistische Beschreibung der durch die Entschädigung etc. an Wirtemberg gekommenen neuen Ländern, Städte, Klöster, Ortschaften etc.* (Ulm: n.p., 1804); idem, *Neueste Kunde von dem Königreiche Württemberg: Mit Charten u. Kupfern* (Weimar: Landes-Industrie-Comptoir, 1812).

17. Stuart Woolf, "Towards the History of the Origins of Statistics: France, 1789–1815," in *State and Statistics in France, 1789–1815*, ed. Jean-Claude Perrot and Stuart Woolf (Chur, Switz.: Harwood Academic Publishers, 1984), 81–194; Marie-Noëlle Bourguet, *Déchiffrer la France: La statistique départmentale à l'époque napoléonienne* (Paris: Editions des archives contemporaines, 1988); Richard Boeckh, *Die geschichtliche Entwicklung der amtlichen Statistik des preussischen Staates* (Berlin: n.p., 1863).

18. J. G. D. Memminger, "Neue, die Vaterlandeskunde fördernde, Anstalten," *Württembergische Jahrbücher für vaterländische Geschichte, Geographie, Statistik und Topographie* 1 (1822): 1–32, here 18 on the *Landrecht;* Hermann Remppis, "Die württembergischen Intelligenzblätter von 1736–1849" (Diss., Stuttgart, 1922), 13, 31, 38–39.

19. For this section, see the two thorough articles of Meinrad Schaab, "Die Anfänge einer Landesstatistik im Herzogtum Württemberg, in den Badischen Markgrafschaften und in der Kurpfalz," *ZWLG* 26 (1967): 89–112, and "Die Herausbildung einer Bevölkerungsstatistik in Württemberg und Baden während der ersten Hälfte des 19. Jahrhunderts," *ZWLG* 30 (1971): 164–200.

20. Wild. Sch. 7034–36, materials on the statistische Übersicht des

Kurfürstentums Württemberg (1804–7); and Schaab, "Herausbildung einer Bevölkerungsstatistik."

21. Wild. Sch. 7037–38, Verzeichnisse of 1807 and 1811 respectively.

22. Int. Min. III 2223, preparation of Jahres- and Verwaltungsberichte, 1814–15; Schaab, "Herausbildung einer Bevölkerungsstatistik," 171, 177–80.

23. On the irrelevance of nationalism to the development of civil society in Württemberg, see the Conclusion.

24. Ferdinand A. H. Weckherlin, *Achalm und Mezingen unter Urach: Ein Beytrag zur Topographie und Statistik von Würtemberg* (Tübingen: Ludwig Fues, 1790).

25. Italics added. On the Bureau's founding see *Reg. Bl.* 1820, 635 and 1821, 155–56; on its early development, Helmut Kluge, "Die amtliche Landesbeschreibung in Württemberg bis zum Ende des 19. Jahrhunderts," *BdL* (1957): 77–92; and "Die amtliche Statistik in Württemberg und Baden von 1820 bis 1945," in Statistisches Landesamt Baden-Württemberg, *150 Jahre amtliche Statistik in Baden-Württemberg* (Stuttgart: J. Fink, 1970), 34–44; on the Collegium, Memminger, "Neue Anstalten," 29.

26. Peter Goessler, "Die württembergische Oberamtsbeschreibung: Ein Beitrag zur Geschichte der Landeskunde," *BdL* 3 (1943): 136–45, here 138–39; the county-by-county model was also certainly inspired by the example of French departmental statistics; see Bourguet, *Déchiffrer la France.*

27. See Memminger, "Neue Anstalten" for this section.

28. Woolf, "Towards the History of the Origins of Statistics," 81–194, here 93, 156, 168.

29. Bavaria, following the French model, established a Statistical Bureau in 1801; see Kluge, "Amtliche Landesbeschreibung," 83–84. Prussia followed in 1805; see Hacking, *Taming,* 30.

30. This interpretation represents, mutatis mutandis, the current historiographical understanding of state-sponsored statistical endeavors; see Stuart Woolf, "Statistics and the Modern State," *CSSH* 31, no. 3 (Jul. 1989): 588–604, esp. 599, 602–3.

31. J. G. D. von Memminger, *Beschreibung oder Geographie und Statistik, nebst einer Übersicht der Geschichte von Württemberg* (Stuttgart and Tübingen: J. G. Cotta, 1820). The book was later reissued under the more direct auspices of the Bureau as *Beschreibung von Württemberg: Herausgegeben vom Königlich statistisch-topographischen Bureau* (Stuttgart: J. G. Cotta, 1841).

32. Hermann Bausinger and Theodor Eschenburg, eds., *Baden-Württemberg: Eine politische Landeskunde* (Stuttgart: W. Kohlhammer, 1985), produced under the auspices of the Landeszentrale für politische Bildung.

33. Memminger, *Beschreibung,* 273, 293, 362, and passim.

34. Ibid., 249–62.

35. See her *Linnaeus: Nature and Nation* (Cambridge, Mass.: Harvard University Press, 1999).

36. On all this, ibid., 328ff., 475, and section on "Landbau." On Biedermeier entrepreneurialism, see the description of Carl Deffner of Esslingen in

Wolfgang Kaschuba and Carola Lipp, *1848—Provinz und Revolution: Kultureller Wandel und soziale Bewegung im Königreich Württemberg* (Tübingen: Tübinger Vereinigung für Volkskunde, 1979), 56–91.

37. *Reg. Bl.* 1821, 203–4; Memminger, "Neue Anstalten," 23ff.; Stat. Ofc. G1, Verein für Vaterlandskunde, Statuten and other materials; *150 Jahre amtliche Statistik.*

38. The *Würtembergische Jahrbücher für vaterländische Geschichte, Geographie, Statistik und Topographie,* started in 1822, continued the *Würtembergisches Jahrbuch,* started in 1818, which had a similar content. Subsequent continuators were the *Württembergische Vierteljahrshefte für Landesgeschichte (WVLG) and the Zeitschrift für württembergische Landesgeschichte (ZWLG).*

39. Stat. Ofc. G1, §12 of the Verein's statutes.

40. Dates for the second and third series, 1893–1930 and 1953–present, are similarly perfect fits within the various epochs of German social and political history. Up-to-date publication histories are given in Eugen Reinhard, "Oberamtsbeschreibungen und Kreisbeschreibungen: 175 Jahre amtliche Landesforschung im deutschen Südwesten," in *Regionalforschung in der Landesverwaltung,* ed. Eugen Reinhard (Stuttgart: W. Kohlhammer, 1995), 89–112.

41. See the retrospective on the first series, Königlich Statistisch-Topographisches Bureau, "Uebersicht über die 64 Oberamtsbeschreibungen," in *Oberamtsbeschreibung Ellwangen* (Stuttgart: W. Kohlhammer, 1886), x–xii.

42. J. G. D. Memminger, *Beschreibung des Oberamts Reutlingen.*

43. Stat. Ofc. S 9, Memminger's Notizen über die Reise durch das Oberamt Reutlingen.

44. Goeßler, "Die württembergische Oberamtsbeschreibung," 137–38.

45. Stat. Ofc. G 8, Erwerb wissenschaftlicher Nachlässe.

46. *Beschreibung des Oberamts Reutlingen,* 79–80; cf. HStAS J 9, Sammlung Prälat Schmid, 1756–1827, on municipal history in the Swabian *Kreis.*

47. Stat. Ofc. S 2–12, passim.

48. Stat. Ofc. S 9, exc. from aus Urkundenrepertorien within Memminger's notes; S 10, historische Materialien zu Einzelfragen, for example, exc. from baptismal registry in Pfullingen from Pfarrer Meyer in 1692.

49. See, in addition to Köhler (below), HStAS J 10, Sammlung Schöttle, 1819–84, from a local pastor, on the Oberämter of Neresheim and Riedlingen, and the sources cited in note 48.

50. Hasselhorn, *Der altwürttembergische Pfarrstand* is the standard prosopographical work; see also Martin Leube, *Das Tübinger Stift 1750–1950* (Stuttgart: J. F. Steinkopf, 1954).

51. Friedrich August Köhler, *Nehren: Eine Dorfchronik,* ed. Carola Lipp, Wolfgang Kaschuba, and Eckart Frahm (Tübingen: Tübinger Vereinigung für Volkskunde, 1981 [1838]). The edition gives copious details on Köhler's life and information on Bihner as well (see below).

52. Commentary by Wolfgang Kaschuba, in *Nehren,* 173.

53. Narr, *Studien zur Spätaufklärung,* despite focusing on intellectuals and theologians, paints a broad and convincing portrait of Pietist Enlightenment in all its rich contradictions.

54. Cab. II 1970, Statistisch-topographisches Büro 1821–83 on this case, the Klosterkirche at Lorch, and the general mix of Kulturpflege and Landesgeschichte in which the Bureau engaged; also Stat. Ofc. G 8, S 2–12. Reg. Hist. Coll. contains scores of bequests from amateur and independent local historians, many of which ended up in the Statistical-Topographical Bureau.

CHAPTER 8: THE INTELLIGENCE GAZETTES

1. Friedrich Huneke, *Die "Lippischen Intelligenzblätter" (Lemgo, 1767– 1799): Lektüre und gesellschaftliche Erfahrung* (Bielefeld: Verlag für Regionalgeschichte, 1989), 49, 196.

2. See Jürgen Voss, "Der Gemeine Mann und die Volksaufklärung im späten 18. Jahrhundert," in *Vom Elend der Handarbeit: Probleme historischer Unterschichtenforschung,* ed. Hans Mommsen and Winfried Schulze (Stuttgart: Klett-Cotta, 1981), 208–33; Jonathan Knudsen, "On Enlightenment for the Common Man," in *What Is Enlightenment? Eighteenth-Century Answers and Twentieth Century Questions,* ed. James Schmidt (Berkeley: University of California Press, 1996), 270–90; Holger Böning, "Mündliche und publizistische Formen der politischen Volksaufklärung," in *Presse und Geschichte II: Neue Beiträge zur historischen Kommunikationsforschung,* ed. E. Blühm and H. Gebhardt (München: K. G. Saur, 1987), 259–85; Holger Böning and Reinhart Siegert, eds., *Volksaufklärung: Biobibliographisches Handbuch zur Popularisierung aufklärerischen Denkens im deutschen Sprachraum von den Anfängen bis 1850* (Stuttgart-Bad Cannstatt: Frommann-Holzboog, 1990); Wolfgang Ruppert, "Volksaufklärung im späten 18. Jahrhundert," in *Hansers Sozialgeschichte der deutschen Literatur vom 16. Jahrhundert bis zur Gegenwart,* ed. Rolf Grimminger (Munich: Hanser, 1980), 341–61.

3. Hubert Max, "Intelligenzblatt—Intelligenzwesen," in *Handbuch der Zeitungswissenschaft,* ed. Walther Heide (Leipzig: K. W. Hiersemann, 1940), 1806–45, here 1806–11; Schöne, *Zeitungswesen und Statistik,* 75–80.

4. Gerhardt Petrat, "Das Intelligenzblatt—eine Forschungslücke," in *Presse und Geschichte II: Neue Beiträge zur historischen Kommunikationsforschung,* ed. E. Blühm and H. Gebhardt (Munich: K. G. Saur, 1987), 207–31, here 210–2.

5. Justus Möser, "Etwas zur Verbesserung der Intelligenzblätter" (1775), in *Sämtliche Werke* (Oldenburg: Gerhard Stalling, 1943), vol. 4, 153–55; "Anmerkung wegen dieser Intelligenz-Blätter" (1767), ibid., vol. 8, 109–10.

6. Roger Chartier, *The Cultural Origins of the French Revolution,* trans. Lydia Cochrane (Durham, N. C.: Duke University Press, 1991), 90.

7. Huneke, *Die Lippischen Intelligenzblätter,* 86–88, 192, table 1.

8. Thomas Kempf, *Aufklärung als Disziplinierung: Studien zum Diskurs des Wissens in Intelligenzblättern und gelehrten Beilagen der zweiten Hälfte des 18. Jahrhunderts* (München: Iudicium, 1991), 106–9.

9. That the word *Intelligenz* also referred in this period to the intelligentsia is an infelicitous coincidence, since intelligence gazettes targeted a much broader, humbler audience.

10. Schöne, *Zeitungswesen und Statistik*, 70–75, 78–79, 85–86, 90–97.

11. Petrat, *"Intelligenzblatt,"* passim.

12. *Die Intelligenzblätterkunde für den nicht unterrichteten Privatmann* (Weimar and Berlin: n.p., 1802), 21–22, cited in Petrat, "Intelligenzblatt," 218 (emphasis in original).

13. The "social disciplinary" perspective dominates the current scholarship on the *Intelligenzblätter*, which focuses mainly on its late-eighteenth-century incarnation. See Holger Böning, "Das Intelligenzblatt als Medium praktischer Aufklärung: Ein Beitrag zur Geschichte der gemeinnützig-ökonomischen Presse in Deutschland von 1768 bis 1780," *IASL* 12 (1987): 107–34; idem, "Zeitungen für das 'Volk': Ein Beitrag zur Entstehung periodischer Schriften für einfache Leser und zur Politisierung der deutschen Öffentlichkeit nach der Französichen Revolution," in *Französische Revolution und deutsche Öffentlichkeit*, ed. Holger Böning (München: K. G. Saur, 1992), 467–526; and the works of Huneke, Kempf, and Petrat already cited. More generally, see Martin Dinges, "The Reception of M. Foucault's Ideas on Social Discipline in German Historiography," in *Reassessing Foucault*, ed. C. Jones and R. Porter (London: Routledge, 1993), 181–211.

14. Huneke, *Die Lippischen Intelligenzblätter*, 88ff.

15. Ibid., 96, 107ff. for this anecdote.

16. In a similar vein, Andreas Gestrich, *Absolutismus und Öffentlichkeit: Politische Kommunikation in Deutschland zu Beginn des 18. Jahrhunderts* (Göttingen: Vandenhoeck & Ruprecht, 1994) emphasizes the importance—and limitations—of publicity to the legitimation of the absolutist state.

17. *Reg. Bl.* 4 Jun. 1808, 273–76 (§9 of Censur-Ordnung); Ellw. Sect. 106, message to all *Oberämter*, 14 Dec. 1803 (on standardization); Hermann Remppis, "Die württembergischen Intelligenzblätter von 1736–1849" (Ph.D. diss., Stuttgart, 1922), 61–65. On pre-Napoleonic information media in Württemberg, particularly the Stuttgart *Wöchentliche Anzeigen*, see Werner Gebhardt, *Burgertum in Stuttgart: Beitrage Zur "Ehrbarkeit" und Zur Familie Autenrieth* (Neustadt an der Aisch: Degener, 1999), 165–208.

18. Int. Min. III 2163, Subfasz: Ein Intelligenzblatt, welches die Oberamtl. Ausschreiben in den geeigneten Fällen ersetzen soll, exp. opin. of 25 Sep. 1817; Pol. Min. 462, Ober-Censur-Collegium, 24 Jul. 1811; also 2 Nov. 1810; Pol. Min. 468 rpt. of 19 Sep. 1812.

19. *Hauskalender* were calendars for peasants, containing harvest dates and religious holidays, astronomical information and statistics on the seasons, and illustrations and miscellaneous practical advice. For Württemberg, see Ellw. Sect. 105, Herausgabe von Hauskalendern für Neuwürttemberg, Jul. 1803–Jan. 1806; in general, Gerhardt Petrat, *Einem besseren Dasein zu Diensten: Die Spur der Aufklärung im Medium Kalender zwischen 1700 und 1919* (München: K. G. Saur, 1991).

20. Ellw. Sect. 106, message to all *Oberämter*, 14 Dec. 1803 and 13 Mar. 1804.

21. *Allgemeines Intelligenzblatt für Neuwürttemberg* (1804): 77, 148, 188, 343; (1806): 59, 106.

22. Rott. Sect. II 76, Ritter cover letter of 29 Dec. 1803; ibid., announcement of the intelligence gazette, Ellw., 23 Dec. 1803; also see Remppis, "Die württembergischen Intelligenzblätter," 59–60.

23. By systematizing the publication of government enactments for the first time, the *Königlich-Württembergisches Staats- und Regierungsblatt* (abbreviated as *Reg. Bl.* in this book) also marked a significant improvement over state practices of the late-eighteenth century. Thus, as late as the 1790s, cameralist police ordinances on the *Schreiber* had been published only in learned periodicals and privately compiled compendia.

24. See the *Schwäbische Chronik* and the various *Hof- und Staatshandbücher;* also Int. Min. III 4872, 31 Mar. 1810, Cotta's proposal for a *Hof- und Staats-Calender;* on law compendia *(Gesetzesammlungen)*, Int. Min. III 6639, Gesuche um Genehmigung zur Herausgabe von Werken über Gesetze und Verordnungen; also A. L. Reyscher, *Vollständige, historisch und kritisch bearbeitete Sammlung der württembergischen Gesetze* (Tübingen: Ludwig Friedrich Fues, 1843ff.).

25. Int. Min III 4940, Nast proposal dated 1 Nov. 1818 (emphasis added).

26. On Dingelmaier, Ellw. Reg. Gov. 1424, announcement dated Oct. 1825; cf. Int. Min. III 4893, prop. of 6 Nov. 1823; also Int. Min. III 4884, announcement, 15 Dec. 1821.

27. See Daniel Moran, *Toward the Century of Words: Johann Cotta and the Politics of the Public Realm in Germany, 1795–1832* (Berkeley: University of California Press, 1990).

28. Int. Min. III 4718, Verzeichnisse sämtlicher in Württemberg erscheinender Zeitblätter for 1826/38 and 1838/48; Remppis, "Die württembergischen Intelligenzblätter," 44–60, 98–108. The counties of Aalen, Brackenheim, Neckarsulm, Neresheim, Tettnang, Weinsberg, and Wiblingen lacked intelligence gazettes. All these districts were in New Württemberg, and intriguingly, all, with the exceptions of Aalen and Weinsberg, were located on Württemberg's borders, suggesting a close link between intelligence provision and membership in spontaneous networks of statewide community.

29. A proposal to revive a statewide gazette like the defunct *Allgemeines Intelligenzblatt*, this time combining official announcements and circulars with political and literary articles, never got off the ground. See note 18 and Sch. Comm. 281, Hauptbericht der Kommission zum Schreibereiwesen (hereafter: Hauptbericht), §§8, 13–17.

30. Remppis, "Die württembergischen Intelligenzblätter," 13, 31, 34; *Wöchentliche Anzeigen* (Stuttgart), no. 1, 17 Dec. 1736.

31. Hauptbericht; Int. Min. III 2163, Intelligenzblatt proposal.

32. For the case of a *Schreiber* balking about loss of business, see Ellw. Reg. Gov. 6243, OA Gerabronn to Jagst reg. gov., 12 Dec. 1825.

33. See, for example, Cens. Coll. 468, rpt. of 19 Sep. 1812; Rott. Sect. II 76, announcement for Landvogtei Rott., 23 Dec. 1803; Int. Min III 4881, announcement for *Süddeutsche Courier* of 29 Dec. 1819.

34. Ellw. Reg. Gov. 6243, OA Öhringen rpt., 10 Dec. 1821, and assem. prot. exc., 15 Sep. 1821, §4.

35. Sabine Kienitz, *Sexualität, Macht und Moral: Prostitution und Geschlechterbeziehungen Anfang des 19. Jahrhunderts in Württemberg* (Berlin: Akademie-Verlag, 1995), 132–96 treats rumor networks extensively.

36. Hauptbericht (emphasis added).

37. Int. Min. III 4905, printer Bühler appeal to Int. Min., 5 Apr. 1830; Int. Min. III 4718, OA Reut. to same, 27 Dec. 1823.

38. Pol. Min. 462; Ellw. Reg. Gov. 6243, Ritter prop. of 5 Nov. 1818 and passim.

39. On Haspel, Ellw. Reg. Gov. 1424, prop. and rpt. dated 3–4 Nov. 1828 for OA Hall, 5 Nov. 1829 for OA Gaildorf.

40. Ellw. Reg. Gov. 1425, Stahl prospectus of 5 Apr. 1824.

41. New Württ. Gov. 975, prospectus for the *Eßlinger Anzeigen für den Bürger und Landmann,* Jul. 1803; Rott. Sect. II 76, announcement for Rott., 23 Dec. 1803.

42. Ellw. Reg. Gov. 1424, OAverweser Häberle and publisher Kistler at Künzelsau, exchanges of Jan./Feb. 1837.

43. Int. Min. III 4895, Schnitzer prop. for Wangen, 10 Jul. 1825; Ellw. Reg. Gov. 1425, Stahl request to OA Gmünd, 24 Mar. 1831; Reut. Reg. Gov. 2908, OA Sulz rpt., 7 Nov. 1849.

44. These and other items from this paragraph are drawn from a sample of the *Öhringer Intelligenzblatt* in 1806/12, 1823/4, and 1835.

45. Ellw. Reg. Gov. 1425, docs. on Raach, Keller, and Dillenius at Gmünd, 1833/44.

46. This terminology and argument are inspired by Anderson, *Imagined Communities,* 9–36.

47. *Öhringer Intelligenzblatt,* 28 Jul. 1835, 358f.

CONCLUSION

1. See esp. Hull, *Sexuality, State, and Civil Society;* and Barbara Vogel, "'Revolution von oben': Der deutsche Weg in die bürgerliche Gesellschaft?" *SOWI* 8 (1979): 67–74.

2. The notion of a flawed citizenship marks the two major monographs spanning the period between the old regime and the 1848 revolution in Germany, Koselleck, *Preußen zwischen Reform und Revolution* and Walker, *German Home Towns.* For a revisionist interpretation emphasizing the *success* of civic order in Württemberg, whose 1819 constitution lasted until 1918, see Hettling, *Reform ohne Revolution.*

3. On nationalism, see Anderson, *Imagined Communities;* and, on Germany specifically, Levinger, *Enlightened Nationalism.* On early German liberalism,

James Sheehan, *German Liberalism in the Nineteenth Century* (Chicago: University of Chicago Press, 1978; and Dieter Langewiesche, *Liberalismus in Deutschland* (Frankfurt: Suhrkamp, 1988).

4. Two examples are the salience of regional parliaments (such as Württemberg's) as incubators of liberal nationalism and the legacy of popular Jacobinism as providing a ready-made political culture for the 1848 Revolution. See Jonathan Sperber, *Rhineland Radicals: The Democratic Movement and the Revolution of 1848–1849* (Princeton, N. J.: Princeton University Press, 1993); Kaschuba and Lipp, *1848—Provinz und Revolution;* idem, "Revolutionskultur 1848: Einige (volkskundliche) Anmerkungen zu den Erfahrungsräumen und Aktionsformen antifeudaler Volksbewegung in Württemberg," *ZWLG* 39 (1980): 141–65.

5. Brubaker, *Citizenship and Nationhood* connects the discourse of nationhood to citizenship as an identity; Dagmar Herzog, *Intimacy and Exclusion: Religious Politics in Pre-Revolutionary Baden* (Princeton, N. J.: Princeton University Press, 1996) in some ways performs a similar analysis on liberalism.

6. In James Sheehan's hands, the search for a German national identity becomes the master narrative for the entire time period treated in this book. See his magisterial *German History 1770–1866* (Oxford: Clarendon Press, 1989), together with his more programmatic statement, "What is German History? Reflections on the Role of the *Nation* in German History and Historiography," *JMH* 53 (1981): 1–23.

7. On German civic culture in the later nineteenth century, see Margaret Anderson, *Practicing Democracy: Elections and Political Culture in Imperial Germany* (Princeton, N. J.: Princeton University Press, 2000).

8. Hull, *Sexuality;* Herzog, *Intimacy;* Marion W. Gray, *Productive Men, Reproductive Women: The Agrarian Household and the Emergence of Separate Spheres in the German Enlightenment* (New York: Berghahn, 2000).

9. Bolley himself would also have brought men under stricter individual legal responsibility had it been politically feasible to do so. That his remarks on gender tutelage occur in a treatise on mortgage law running over 1,000 pages illustrates the importance of context. See David Sabean, "Allianzen und Listen: Die Geschlechtsvormundschaft im 18. und 19. Jahrhundert," in *Frauen in der Geschichte des Rechts: Von der Frühen Neuzeit bis zur Gegenwart,* ed. Ute Gerhard (Munich: C. H. Beck, 1997), 460–79, esp. 475–76.

10. Freemasonry, the archetypical form of voluntary association in civil society, provides an excellent illustration of this point. In Margaret Jacob's words, "in eighteenth-century masonic sociability . . . we find a consuming identification with laws and regulations that will ensure order and good government." The lodge constitution illustrates that the culture of civil society was primarily textual in nature, deriving its cardinal values from writing. While it stood as but one element in a masonic culture dominated by any number of ceremonial trappings and visual representations (cinder blocks, robes, compasses, etc.) it is this text to which masons return as the ultimate source of their fraternity's moral authority. See Margaret Jacob, *Living the Enlightenment: Freemasonry and*

Politics in Eighteenth-Century Europe (Oxford: Oxford University Press, 1991), 49 and passim.

11. See Otto Dann,, ed., *Vereinswesen und bürgerliche Gesellschaft in Deutschland* (München: R. Oldenbourg, 1984); Carola Lipp, "Verein als politisches Handlungsmuster: Das Beispiel des württembergischen Vereinswesens von 1800 bis zur Revolution 1848–1849," in *Sociabilité et société bourgeoise en Allemagne et en Suisse 1750–1850*, ed. Etienne François (Paris: Editions Recherche sur les Civilisations, 1986), 275–98; Wolfgang Kaschuba and Carola Lipp, "Zur Organisation des bürgerlichen Optimismus. Regionale Formierungsprozesse des Bürgertums im Vormärz und in der Revolution 1848," *SOWI* 8 (1979): 74–82.

12. This observation derives from Theda Skocpol's analysis of voluntary associations in the United States, "How Americans Became Civic," in Theda Skocpol and Morris P. Fiorina, eds., *Civic Engagement in American Democracy* (Washington, D. C.: Brookings Institution Press, 1999), 27–80, here pp. 47–49.

Sources

I have relied on descriptive abbreviations in the source notes to indicate the specific documents on which my interpretations are based, since the customary citation format can be very obscure to nonspecialists. The guide below is intended for readers wishing to track down particular archival references. It is also designed to help the nonspecialist appreciate the archives' structure, as well as my own approach to researching in them.

Customary Citation Format

In the Württemberg state archives, "signatures" for document collections appear in this form:

[HStAS or StAL] [Call letter and number] Bü [*Büschel* number]
A *Büschel* is a file, usually string-bound and up to three inches thick, containing anywhere from one to several hundred individual documents. Each *Büschel* bears an archivally-assigned title listed in the appropriate catalog index *(Findbuch)* at HStAS or StAL. These titles are only given in the notes when they are necessary to identify specific files uniquely or when they are essential to interpretation and contextualization.

Archive Organization

The call letters and numbers below are taken directly from the categorization scheme of the Württemberg state archives. German rubrics have been translated into English and new abbreviations assigned. In the notes, the numbers following these abbreviations refer to *Büschel.*

The chart below takes the following form:

Call #   Description   Abbreviation

Hauptstaatsarchiv Stuttgart (HStAS)

A Old Württemberg archive, pre-1806

11	Ducal cabinet on the *Landschaft* (*Landtag*)	DukeLT
202	Privy Council	PrivC (pre-1806)
211	Government Council: General	GovC
213	Government Council: Specific	GovC inv.
214	Government Council: Commissions	GovC comm. inv.
234	Lawyer and *Schreiber* examination commission	Exam. comm. (pre-1806)
364 L	*Stadt und Amt* Kirchheim	Kirch.
573	Stadt- und Amtsschreiberei Wildberg	Wild. Sch.

E Central and intermediate authorities, 1806/1817–1945

7	Royal Cabinet: General state administration	Cab. I
14	Royal Cabinet II	Cab. II
31	Privy Council	PrivC (post-1806)
141	Interior Ministry I	Int. Min. I
143	Interior Ministry II	Int. Min. II
146/1	Interior Ministry III, Part 1	Int. Min. III (Bü 2500+)
146/2	Interior Ministry III, Part 2	Int. Min. III (Bü 1–2499)
301	Justice Ministry	Jus. Min.

J Collections

1	General collections on regional history	Reg. Hist. Coll.

L *Landtag* archive

6	Materials registry	LT

Staatsarchiv Ludwigsburg (StAL)

D Authorities of the transitional period, 1803–17

1	New Württemberg Government (*Oberlandesregierung* Ellwangen)	New Württ. Gov.
5 I	Ellwangen administrative sector (*Landvogtei*)	Ellw. Sect.
6 I	Heilbronn administrative sector	Heil. Sect.
7 I	Rottweil administrative sector	Rott. Sect.
21	Central Organization Commission	Cent. Org. Comm.
23–28	Organization Commissions	Org. Comm.
49	Section for Communal Administration	SCA
52	Royal Capital City and Police Ministry	Pol. Min.
54	Supreme Censor Collegium	Cens. Coll.

54a	Lawyer and *Schreiber* examination commission	Exam.comm. (post–1803)
71–82	Other administrative sectors	Sect. (w/ call #, Bü #)

E Supreme and intermediate authorities, 1806/1817–1945

173 I	Regional government Ludwigsburg: General	Lud. Reg. Gov. I
173 III	Regional government Ludwigsburg: Specific	Lud. Reg. Gov. III
175 I	Regional government Ellwangen	Ellw. Reg. Gov.
177 I	Regional government Reutlingen: Administration	Reut. Reg. Gov.
179 II	Regional government Ulm: Administration	Ulm Reg. Gov.
181	Organization Implementation Commission (*Organisations-Vollziehungs-Kommission,* pre-1821 incarnation)	Pre-OVK
258 VI	Countrywide Statistical Office	Stat. Ofc.

F Subordinate administrative authorities, 1806-ca. 1945

210 II	Waiblingen cantonal assembly protocols	Waib. assem. prot.

Source Groupings

These cases pertain to specific scribes and/or cantons and are grouped according to patterns that emerge in canton after canton. The groupings were devised by the author and should *not* be considered artifacts of the archives' own organization. Other, miscellaneous or incidental, documents referred to in the notes (such as interdepartmental policy memos) are not indexed here.

The chart below takes the following form:

Scribe/(Canton)	Archival signature	Years covered	Abbreviation

Scribes and community life in the late Enlightenment

Complete Stadt- und Amtsschreiberei archive

(Wildberg)	HStAS A 573	pre-1806	Wild. Sch. (w/ Bü #)

Contested scribes' elections to the *Schreiberei*

C. E. Salzer	HStAS A 213 Bü 8513	1784–94	Weil. Sch. elec.
V. I. Hofacker	HStAS A 213 Bü 8524	1797	Nag. Sch. elec.
H. E. F. Bolley	HStAS A 214 Bü 1062	1793–94	Waib. Sch. elec.
G. V. E. Schmid	HStAS A 213 Bü 8532	1800–2	Schn. Sch. elec.
K. C. Grüb	HStAS A 213 Bü 8543	1752	Wild. Sch. elec.

Contested scribes' elections to the *Landtag*

L. F. Lang	HStAS L 6 Bü 2.6	1796	Maulbronn LT elec.
J. L. Hofacker	HStAS L 6 Bü 2.6	1796–97	Nag. LT elec.
N. F. Wagner	HStAS L 6 Bü 2.6	1796	Sindelfingen LT elec.
H. E. F. Bolley	HStAS L 6 Bü 2.6	1796	Waib. LT elec.

Scribal misconduct: Official abuse

C. G. Schmid	HStAS A 213 Bü 8532	1780	Schn. inv.
C. E. Salzer	HStAS A 211 Bü 629	1793–94	Weil. inv. I
C. E. Salzer	HStAS A 213 Bü 2452	1784–85	Weil. inv. II
C. E. Salzer	HStAS A 214 Bü 486–93	1780–1805	Weil. comm. inv. (Bü #)

Scribal misconduct: Disloyal petitions

F. L. Theuß	HStAS A 213 Bü 6511	1805–6	Waib. pet. inv.
F. C. Schmid	HStAS A 213 Bü 6509	1805	Winn. pet. inv.

Cantonal assembly struggles

(Backnang)	HStAS A 213 Bü 2159	1786–87	Back. assem. inv.
(Nagold)	HStAS A 213 Bü 6508	1804–5	Nag. assem. inv.
(Tübingen)	HStAS A 213 Bü 2895	1771	Tüb. assem. inv.
(Waiblingen)	HStAS A 213 Bü 3001	1796–97	Waib. assem. inv.

Government sources on the post-Napoleonic scribes

Dossiers (*Nationallisten*)

(all)	HStAS E 141 Bd. 228	1809	NL 1809
(all)	HStAS E 301 Bü 93–94	1824	NL 1824
(all)	HStAS E 146/1 Bü 2637–63	1807–46	NL II (w/ Bü)

Income reports (*Einkommens-Fassionen*)

(all)	HStAS E 301 Bü 107–18	1808–22	OVK inc. rpts.

Reform commissions

n/a	HStAS E 31 Bü 280–93	1816–17	Sch. Comm. (w/ Bü #)
n/a	HStAS E 31 Bü 332–48	1818–19	ÄOK (w/ Bü #)
n/a	HStAS E 301 Bü 96	1819–26	OVK I
n/a	HStAS E 301 Bü 106	1821–23	OVK II

Anti- or post-scribal activity in civil society

Parliamentary agitation of 1815–1816

(all)	HStAS E 141 Bd. 145	1815	Int. Min. OA rpts.
(all)	HStAS E 31 Bü 294–95	1815–16	PrivC parl. pets.

Commission bureaus and petitioning services

(various)	HStAS E 146/2 Bü 2164–65	1819–67	Int. Min. III 2164–5
Ludwigsburg	StAL E 173 III Bü 6833		Lud. Reg. Gov. III 6833

Intelligence gazette prospectuses

Esslingen	StAL D 1 Bü 975 975	1805	New Württ. Gov.
(various)	StAL D 5 I Bü 106–7	1803–4	Ellw. Sect. 106–7
New Württ.	StAL D 7 I Part II Bü 76	1803–4	Rott. Sect. II 76
(various)	StAL D 52 Bü 451–72	1806–14	Pol. Min. 451–72
(various)	StAL E 175 I Bü 1424–25, 6243–45	1818–49	Ellw. Reg. Gov.
(various)	StAL E 177 I Bü 2908	1848–49	Reut. Reg. Gov. 2908
(various)	HStAS E 146/1 Bü 4718–962	1806–53	Int. Min. III 4718–962

PUBLISHED MATERIALS

Bauer, Friedrich. *Anleitung zur schriftlichen Geschäftsführung für das bürgerliche Leben.* Stuttgart: J. G. Munder, 1830.

Bäuerlen, Johann Georg. *Lehrbuch sämtlicher Kameral- und Rechtswissenschaften, welche dem wirtembergischen Schreiber unentbehrlich sind.* Heilbronn: n.p., 1802.

———. *Taschenbuch für angehende Wirtembergische Rechtsgelehrte und für Schreiber.* Stuttgart: Johann Benedikt Metzler, 1793–94.

———. *Versuch einer Anleitung zur Selbstbildung für wirtembergische Schreiber.* Stuttgart: Metzler, 1793.

Baz, Christopher Friedrich. *Über das Petitionsrecht der württembergischen Landstände.* N.p., 1797.

"Beobachtungen über die Gemeindecassen, und über die für die Gemeinden arbeitenden Scribenten, nebst Vorschlägen zu heilsamen Reformen in Einrichtung und Verwaltung der ersten und Ausbildung und Anstellung der letzten." *Schlettweins Archiv für den Menschen und Bürger* (1781): 89–242.

[Bernritter, Friedrich]. *Wirtemberg: Pietismus, Schreiber, Schulen und Erziehung und Aufklärung überhaupt.* N.p., 1787.

———. "Der Incipient eines Stadtschreibers schildert seine Behandlung." In *Wirtembergische Briefe.* Ulm: Stettin, 1840 [1786]. 116–120.

"Beschwerden des Landes." *Verh.* 8. Abt. (26 Jun. 1815): 91–252.

Bolley, Heinrich Ernst Ferdinand. *Bemerkungen über die Schrift: Über die Wahl-fähigkeit zu der Stelle eines Landtagsdeputierten im Württembergischen.* N.p., 1796.

―――. *Das Wichtigste von den Rechten und Verbindlichkeiten Wirtem-bergischer Bürger in ihren öffentlichen und Privatverhältnissen: Ein Auszug aus den wirtembergischen Gesetzen zum Gebrauch jedes Bürgers und besonders der Ortsvorsteher bestimmt.* Tübingen: J. G. Cotta, 1801.

―――. *Drey und dreyssig Aufsätze und Testamente, Erbschafts- und andere Theilungen, besonders Theilungs-Rechnungen, Gantungen und verwandte Rechts-Geschäfte, für Rechtsgelehrte und Schreiber.* Stuttgart: Löflund, 1808.

―――. *Eingabe des Amtsschreibers Bolley zu Waiblingen bei dem Königlichen Ober-Justizkollegium wegen der neuen Verordnungen das Schreibereiwesen betr. vom 23. Okt. 1817 Mit einem Vorwort und Anhang.* N.p., 1817.

―――. *Entwurf einer Amtsinstruktion für die Gerichtsnotarien im Königreich Württemberg.* Stuttgart: n.p., 1821.

―――. *Nachträge und Berichtigungen zu der Schrift: Worin bestand das alte Recht? Was schlugen die Landstände vor? Was bietet der König an?* Stuttgart: n.p., 1817.

[―――]. "Noch ein Beitrag zur Beantwortung zu der Frage: Wer kann zum württembergischen Landtag abgeordnet werden?" In *Württembergische Landtagsschriften.* Stuttgart: n.p., 1796.

―――, ed. *Darstellung des Betragens der Württembergischen Landstände seit dem 15. März 1815; mit erster Fortsetzung, enthaltend die Beschwerden des Landes.* N.p.: n.p., 1815.

Christlieb, Wilhelm Christian. *Theoretisch-praktisches Handbuch für Beamte, Ortsvorsteher, Gemeinde- und Stiftungsräte, auch Bürgerausschüsse.* Min-kenkringen: n.p., 1823.

Denkschrift eines Stadtschreibers in Württemberg über den ihm zugedachten Amtsmanns-Wechsel. Esslingen: J. G. Helfferich, 1818.

Einige Bermerkungen über Nr. 4 der außerordentlichen Beilage zur allge-meinen Zeitung vom Jahre 1816: Von einem vieljährigen Routinier. N.p., 1816.

Einige Vorschläge wie die aus Advokaten und Schreibern bestehende grosse Anzahl von Candidaten mit Bedienstungen nach und nach versorgt, auch jeder Herzogliche Diener nach Verdienst bezahlt werden könnte? N.p., 1797.

Etwas zum Abschiede: Am Sarge des Württembergischen Schreiberstandes. Scherz und Ernst. Mit Beziehung auf das patriotische Journal von und für Württemberg. Gmünd: Ritter, 1817.

Frick, Clem. *Kurze Darstellung der nach der neuesten Staatsorganisation des Königreichs Württemberg bei Appellationen und Provocationen geseztlich zu beobachtenden Formalien und Fatalien.* Tübingen: n.p., 1808.

Fromme Wünsche und Hoffnungen der Württembergischen Advokaten. N.p., 1797.

"Gedanken eines ehemaligen Schreiberei-Verwandten wegen Abhülfe der

Beschwerden über den Schreiber-Unfug." *Für und Wider: Eine politische Zeitschrift für Württemberg* 3 (1814): 162–71.

Geisheimer, Friedrich C. L. *Über die zweckmäßige Haltung der Vogtruggerichte in Württemberg.* Stuttgart: n.p., 1814.

Gemmingen-Burg, Eberhard. "Meine Gedanken aus Gelegenheit des von Serenissimo gnädigst erforderten Gutachtens wegen der allzusehr zunehmenden Menge von Gelehrten und Schreibern." *Strasburgisches politisches Journal* 2 (March 1792): 321–32.

Georgii, Eberhardt Friedrich. *Anti-Leviathan oder über das Verhältnis der Moral zum äußeren Recht und zur Politik.* Göttingen: Vandenhoeck & Ruprecht, 1807.

Griesinger, Ludwig. *Das Schreiber-Institut in Württemberg in der Versammlung der Landstände des Königreichs Würtemberg.* N.p., 1816.

———. "Gutachten über den Württembergischen Schreiberstand." *Württembergisches Archiv* (July–September 1816): vol. 1, 29–64; vol. 2, 99–152; vol. 3, 1–42; Beiheft vol. 1, 1–208.

Gutscher, Friedrich. *Bemerkungen und Vorschläge über das Schreiberei-Wesen im Wirtembergischen: Ein Beytrag zur Geschichte und Kultur dieses Landes.* N.p., 1792.

Haug, Balthasar. *Das gelehrte Wirtemberg.* Hildesheim: Georg Olms, 1979 [1790].

Hegel, G. W. F. *Elements of the Philosophy of Right.* Edited by Allen W. Wood. Cambridge, Eng.: Cambridge University Press, 1991.

———. "Beurteilung der in Druck erschienenen Verhandlungen in der Versammlung der Landstände des Königreichs Württemberg im Jahre 1815 u. 1816." In *Werke.* Edited by E. Moldenhauer and K. M. Michel. Frankfurt: Suhrkamp, 1986 [1817]. Vol. 4, 464–597.

Her, Maximilian. *Kurze Anleitung zu Inventuren nach den neuesten Verordnungen und jetzigen Gewohnheiten.* Reutlingen: J. J. Mäcken, 1818.

Hoch, August. *Der württembergische Schreiber und seine Vorbereitung zum Examen.* Tübingen: Schramm, 1810.

———. *Über die Lehre von Revision der Inventuren und Teilungen.* Tübingen: n.p., 1809.

Hochstetter, Friedrich Ludwig. *Anleitung für angehende wirtembergische Stadt- und Amtsschreiberei-Scribenten zu Inventur- und Theilungs- auch Steuer-Geschäften.* Stuttgart: Johann Benedict Metzler, 1782.

———. *Anleitung zu Inventur-, Theilungs- und Steuergeschäften für wirtembergische Schreiberei-Verwandte.* Stuttgart: n.p., 1780.

Hofacker, Ludwig. *Entwurf einer neuen landschaftlichen Ausschußverfassung.* Stuttgart: n.p., 1797.

Die Intelligenzblätterkunde für den nicht unterrichteten Privatmann. Weimar: n.p., 1802.

Kapff, Johann Friedrich Melchior, ed. *Sammlung im Herzogthum Wirtemberg einzeln ergangener Verordnungen.* Tübingen: J. G. Cotta, 1800.

Keller, Victor Gustav David. *Freimüthige Beleuchtung des Komitee-Gutachtens über die provisorischen Mittel zur Hebung der Gebrechen bei dem* öffentlichen Schreibereiwesen dd. 20. Nov. 1816 und des im. 4. außerordentlichen Blatt der allgemeinen Zeitung dazu erschienenen Prologs. N.p., 1817.

"Klage der Juristen, Kameralisten, und Schreiber des Herzogthums Württemberg über Verletzung der Landes-Verfassung in Betreff der Dienst-Ersezungen, als über eine Reihe der grössten Beschwerden, welche auch zugleich sie insbesondere betrifft 5.–8.1790." In Miszellen aus der wirtembergischen Geschichte, edited by K. Pfaff. N.p., 1790 [1824]. 111–16.

Knapp, Gottfried Gabriel. Neueste Organisation des Königreichs Württemberg. Stuttgart and Tübingen: Cotta, 1817.

———. Ueber das Württembergische Schreibereiwesen: Eine für die Ständeversammlung bestimmt gewesene Relation. Tübingen: W. H. Schramm, 1817.

———, ed. Repertorium über die Königlich württembergische Gesetzgebung von den Jahren 1797 bis 1809. Tübingen: n.p., 1810.

Köhler, Friedrich August. Nehren: Eine Dorfchronik. Edited by Carola Lipp, Wolfgang Kaschuba, and Eckart Frahm. Tübingen: Tübinger Vereinigung für Volkskunde, 1981 [1838].

Königlich Statistisch-Topographisches Bureau. "Uebersicht über die 64 Oberamtsbeschreibungen." In Oberamtsbeschreibung Ellwangen. Stuttgart: W. Kohlhammer, 1886. X–xii.

———, ed. Württembergische Jahrbücher für vaterländische Geschichte, Geographie, Statistik und Topographie. Stuttgart and Tübingen: n.p., 1819–21.

Königlich-Württembergisches Staats- und Regierungsblatt. Stuttgart: August Friedrich Macklor, 1807–9. (Reg. Bl.)

Krug, Leopold. Topographisch-statistisch-geographisches Wörterbuch der sämmtlichen preussischen Staaten oder Beschreibung aller Provinzen, Kreise, Distrikte, Städte in den preussischen Staaten. Halle: n.p., 1796–1803.

Kur[t]z, C. F. H. Abhandlung[en] über das württembergische Schreibereifach und andere damit verwandte Gegenstände. Gmünd: n.p., 1817.

List, Friedrich. Ein ächtes Mittel zur Vertilgung des Schreiberunfugs in Württemberg. Frankfurt: Ferdinand Boselli, 1816.

———. Schriften, Reden, Briefe. Berlin: Reimar Hobbing, 1932–34.

———. "Der Kampf um die württembergische Verfassung" (1817). In Schriften, Reden, Briefe. Vol. 1, 462–85.

———. "Etwas über den Unfug in den Oberamteien Würtembergs." Für und Wider: Eine politische Zeitschrift für Württemberg 4 (1817): 20–26.

———. "Gedanken über die württembergische Staatsregierung" (1816). In Schriften, Reden, Briefe. Vol. 1, 87–148.

———. "Kritik des Verfassungsentwurfs der Württembergischen Ständeversammlung mit besonderer Rücksicht auf Herstellung der bürgerlichen Freiheit in den Gemeinden und Oberämtern" (1817). In Schriften, Reden, Briefe. Vol. 1, 205–283.

———. "Plan eines wissenschaftlichen Vereins für Beförderung der vaterländischen Nationalökonomie" (1816). In *Schriften, Reden, Briefe*. Vol. 1, 338–40.

———. "Reutlinger Petition" (1821). In *Schriften, Reden, Briefe*. Vol. 1, 684–88.

———. "Über die Verfassung und Verwaltung der Korporationen" (1818). In *Schriften, Reden, Briefe*. Vol. 1, 308–16.

———. Untitled prologue to the "Komittee-Gutachten über die Schreiberfrage." *Allgemeine Zeitung*, 1816. *Außerordentliche Beylage*, no. 4.

Magenau, Rudolf Friedrich Heinrich. *Wanderungen eines alten wirtembergischen Amtssubstituten aus einer Schreibstube in die andre, von ihm selbst beschrieben: Ein moralisches Erbauungsbuch für den wirtembergischen Schreiberstand*. Stuttgart: n.p., 1800.

Melchinger, Johann Wolfgang. *Geographisches statistisch-topographisches Lexikon von Baiern: Oder vollständige alphabetische Beschreibung aller im ganzen baiernschen Kreis liegenden Städte, Klöster, Schlösser, Dörfer, Höfe, Berge, Thäler, Flüsse, Seen mit deren Ursprung*. Ulm: n.p., 1796–1802.

Memminger, J. G. D., ed. *Beschreibung des Oberamts Reutlingen: Mit einer Karte des Oberamts, zwey lithographischen Blättern und Tabellen*. Stuttgart and Tübingen: J. G. Cotta, 1824.

———. *Beschreibung oder Geographie und Statistik, nebst einer Übersicht der Geschichte von Württemberg*. Stuttgart and Tübingen: J. G. Cotta, 1820.

———. "Neue, die Vaterlandeskunde fördernde, Anstalten." *Württembergische Jahrbücher für vaterländische Geschichte, Geographie, Statistik und Topographie* 1 (1822): 1–32.

———, ed. *Beschreibung von Württemberg: Herausgegeben vom Königlich statistisch-topographischen Bureau*. Stuttgart: J. G. Cotta, 1841.

Moser, Johann Jakob, ed. *Ordnung für die Communen auch deren Vorsteher und Bediente in dem Herzogthum Würtemberg*. Ludwigsburg: n.p., 1758. *(Commun-Ordnung)*

Möser, Justus. "Anmerkung wegen dieser Intelligenz-Blätter." In *Sämtliche Werke*. Oldenbourg: Gerhard Stalling, 1955–56 [1767]. 109–10.

———. "Avertissement wegen der osnabrückischen Intelligenz-Blätter." In *Sämtliche Werke*. Oldenbourg: Gerhard Stalling, 1955–56 [1767]. 127–29.

———. "Etwas zur Verbesserung der Intelligenzblätter." In *Sämtliche Werke*. Oldenbourg: Gerhard Stalling, 1943 [1775]. 153–55.

Mühlreiter. *Mühlreiters arithmetische Hülfstafeln für Cameralbeamte und Privat-Oekonomen, oder Zeit- und Mühe ersparende Resultaten-Tabellen bey allerley Geld-Einnahme und Ausgabe-Berechnungen zum öffentlichen und Privat-Gebrauch: Für öffentliche Rendanten, Rechnungs-Revisoren, Schreiber, Gewerbs- Handels- und Handwerksleute, so wie überhaupt für Hausväter, Hausmütter und Dienstboten brauchbar*. Gmünd: n.p., 1808.

Nicolai, Friedrich. *Beschreibung einer Reise durch Deutschland und die Schweiz im Jahre 1781: Nebst Bemerkungen über Gelehrsamkeit, Industrie, Religion und Sitten*. Berlin und Stettin: n.p., 1783–96.

Noch einige Bemerkungen über die Versorgung der Advokaten und Schreiber in Würtemberg. N.p., 1797.

Normann, Philipp Christian von, and Johann Jakob Ostertag. *Bemerkungen über den wirtembergischen Landtag von 1797–1799: Ein Beitrag zu Erläuterung der Wirtembergischen Geschichte und Verfassung.* N.p., 1800.

Noth- und Hilfsbüchlein für den Württembergischen Schreiberstand oder Etwas über die Frage: Was hat der Württembergische Schreiber in der gegenwärtigen kritischen Lage seines Standes zu thun. Gmünd: Ritter, 1817.

Pahl, Johann Gottfried von. *Denkwürdigkeiten aus meinem Leben und aus meiner Zeit.* Tübingen: Ludwig Friedrich Fues, 1840.

Pfeilsticker, Walther. *Neues Württembergisches Dienerbuch.* 3 vols. Stuttgart: J. G. Cotta Nachfolger, 1957–1974. (*NWD*)

Reyscher, A. L., ed. *Vollständige, historisch, und kritisch bearbeitete Sammlung der württembergischen Gesetze.* Tübingen: Ludwig Friedrich Fues, 1843–45.

Reyscher, Friedrich Christoph Ludwig. *Alphabetisches Handbuch der Amts-Praxis königlich-württembergischer Cameralbeamten in einem Auszuge der dahin einschlagenden Gesetze und Ordnungen.* Stuttgart: J. H. Kutscher, 1806.

Röder, Philipp Ludwig Hermann. *Geographie und Statistik Wirtembergs.* Laybach am Krain/Ulm: n.p., 1787–1804.

———. *Geographisches-statistisch-topographisches Lexikon von Schwaben.* Ulm: Stettin, 1791–92.

———. *Neueste Kunde von dem Königreiche Würtemberg: Mit Charten u. Kupfern.* Weimar: Landes-Industrie-Comptoir, 1812.

———. *Neu-Wirtemberg oder geographische und statistische Beschreibung der durch die Entschädigung etc. an Wirtemberg gekommenen neuen Ländern, Städte, Klöster, Ortschaften etc.* Ulm: n.p., 1804.

———. *Reisen durch das südliche Teutschland.* Leipzig: G. L. Crusius and F. C. Walliser, 1789–91.

Roller, G. J, ed. "Vorstellungen der Substituten und Scribenten in dem größten Theil der Oberämter des Landes an den Landschaftlichen verstärkten Ausschuß die Veredlung ihres Standes und die Verbesserung ihrer äussern Lage betreffend." In *Der Landtag in dem Herzogthum Würtemberg im Jahr 1797*, edited by E. G. Steeb. Tübingen and Stuttgart: Cotta, 1798. 1–48.

Röslin, Adam Israel. *Abhandlung von Inventuren und Abtheilungen, auch andern dahin einschlagenden Materien.* Stuttgart: n.p., 1760.

Ruthardt. *Über das Würtembergische Theilungs- u Inventurwesen nebst Untersuchungen über die Berechnung des Pflichtteils etc.* Frankfurt and Leipzig: n.p., 1790.

Sattler, Christian Friedrich. *Christian Friedrich Sattlers Topographische Geschichte des Herzogthums Würtemberg.* Stuttgart: n.p., 1784.

———. *Geschichte des Herzogtums Württemberg unter der Regierung der Herzoge.* Tübingen: n.p., 1769–83.

———. *Historische Beschreibung des Herzogtums Würtemberg und aller desselben Städte, Clöster und darzu gehörigen Aemter, nach deren ehmaligen Besitzern, Schicksalen und sowohl historischen, als Natur-Merkwürdigkeiten.* Stuttgart and Esslingen: J. N. Stoll and G. Mäntlern, 1752.

Schwarzkopf, Joachim von. *Ueber politische und gelehrte Zeitungen, Meßrelationen, Intelligenzblätter und über Flugschriften zu Frankfurt am Mayn.* Frankfurt: n.p., 1802.

———. *Ueber politische Zeitungen und Intelligenzblätter in Sachsen, Thüringen, Hessen und einigen angränzenden Gebieten.* Gotha: n.p., 1802.

———. "Uebersicht der sämmtlichen Intelligenz- und Nachrichtenblätter in Deutschland." *Neues Hannöverisches Magazin* (1801): 961–80.

Späth, Philipp J. *Bemerkungen über das wirtembergische Inventur- und Teilungswesen in Hinsicht auf Zubringens-Inventarien und Teilungs-Rezeß.* Stuttgart: n.p., 1802.

———. *Einleitung in das wirtembergische Inventur- und Teilungswesen.* Stuttgart: n.p., 1800.

Steeb, Elias Gottfried, ed. *Der Landtag in dem Herzogthum Würtemberg im Jahr 1797.* Tübingen and Stuttgart: Cotta, 1797–98.

Süßmilch, Johann Peter. *Die gottliche Ordnung in der Veränderung des menschlichen Geschlechts, aus der Geburt, dem Tode, und der Fortpflanzung desselben erwiesen.* Berlin: n.p., 1741.

Über die Bedienstung der Advokaten und Schreiber in Württemberg. N.p., 1797.

"Über die württembergischen Schreiber und ein zu ihrem Behufe angelegtes Journal." *Allgemeiner Cameral-Correspondent* 67–68 (1813).

"Ueber die bisherigen Verhältnisse der Schreibereiverwandten und der Staats- und Rechtsgelehrten in Württemberg." *Patriotisches Journal von und für Württemberg* 23 (7 May 1818): 353–63.

"Verdienstjahre des württembergischen Schreiberstandes, ihre Ungenügsamkeit und die Mittel, wie dieser abgeholfen werden könne." *Patriotisches Journal von und für Württemberg* 1, no. 8 (23 Nov. 1817): 123–25.

Verhandlungen in der Versammlung der Landstände des Königreichs Württemberg. (Verh.)

Wagner. *Offene Erklärung über einen in einer a.o. Beilage zur Allg. Ztg. erschienenen Aufsatz, Stuttgart 30. Nov. 1816 und über ein ständisches Comité-Gutachten vom 22. Nov. 1816.* N.p., 1816.

Weckherlin, Ferdinand August Heinrich. *Achalm und Mezingen unter Urach: Ein Beytrag zur Topographie und Statistik von Würtemberg.* Tübingen: Ludwig Fues, 1790.

———. *Apologie des wirttembergischen Schreiberstandes nebst einem Vorschlag zu seiner Vervollkommung.* Tübingen: Jacob Friedrich Heerbrandt, 1793.

———, ed. *Magazin gemeinnütziger Aufsätze und Bemerkungen für württembergische Schreiber.* Stuttgart: Metzler, 1797–98.

Weisser, Johann Friedrich Christoph. *Das gesammte Rechnungs-Wesen: Zum Gebrauch für Wirtembergische Probatoren Substituten und Schreiber.* Stuttgart: Carl Eichele, 1802.

Wekhrlin, Wilhelm Ludwig. *Geographie und Statistik Würtembergs.* Laibach in Krain: n.p., 1787.

————. "Anselmus Rabiosus Reise durch Ober-Deutschland." In *Schriften*. Nendeln: KTO Press, 1978 [1778]. Vol. 1.

————. "Über das Reich der Magister und Schreiber." *Das graue Ungeheuer* (1784): 294–309.

Württembergische Landtagsschriften. Stuttgart: n.p., 1796–98.

Zeller, Johann Heinrich. *Auch einige Worte über das Schreibereiwesen in Würtemberg, mit besonderer Rücksicht auf die 4. außerordentliche Beilage zur allgemeinen Zeitung von 1816*. Stuttgart: Johann Friedrich Steinkopf, 1817.

SELECTED SCHOLARLY LITERATURE

Here, rather than simply replicating citations from the notes, I have listed the works that have influenced my thinking and guided my research the most.

Anderson, Benedict. *Imagined Communities: Reflections on the Origin and Spread of Nationalism*. London: Verso, 1991.

Bausinger, Hermann. "Zur politischen Kultur Baden-Württembergs." In *Baden-Württemberg: Eine politische Landeskunde*. Edited by Hermann Bausinger and Theodor Eschenburg. Stuttgart: W. Kohlhammer, 1985. 13–38.

Bayly, Christopher. *Empire and Information: Intelligence Gathering and Social Communication in India, 1780–1870*. Cambridge, Eng.: Cambridge University Press, 1996.

Benzing, Fritz. "Die Vertretung von 'Stadt und Amt' im altwürttembergischen Landtag." Diss., Tübingen, 1924.

Berding, Helmut, ed. *Napoleonische Herrschaft und Modernisierung*. Göttingen: Vandenhoeck & Ruprecht, 1980.

————, Etienne François, and Hans-Peter Ullmann, eds. *Deutschland und Frankreich im Zeitalter der Französischen Revolution*. Frankfurt: Suhrkamp, 1989.

———— and Hans-Peter Ullmann, eds. *Deutschland zwischen Revolution und Restauration*. Königstein/Ts.: Athenäum/Droste, 1981.

Blanning, T. C. W. "The French Revolution and the Modernization of Germany." *CEH* 22, no. 2 (1989): 109–29.

Bleek, Wilhelm. *Von der Kameralausbildung zum Juristenprivileg: Studium, Prüfung und Ausbildung der höheren Beamten des allgemeinen Verwaltungsdienstes in Deutschland im 18. und 19. Jahrhundert*. Berlin: Colloquium Verlag, 1972.

Blickle, Peter. *Landschaften im Alten Reich: Die staatliche Funktion des Gemeinen Mannes in Oberdeutschland*. Munich: C. H. Beck, 1973.

————. *Obedient Germans? A Rebuttal: A New View of German History*. Translated by Thomas A. Brady. Charlottesville: University of Virginia Press, 1997.

————, ed. *Resistance, Representation, and Community.* Oxford: Clarendon Press, 1997.

Bödecker, Hans Erich and Ulrich Herrmann, eds. *Über den Prozeß der Aufklärung in Deutschland im 18. Jahrhundert. Personen, Institutionen und Medien.* Göttingen: Vandenhoeck & Ruprecht, 1987.

Böning, Holger. "Das Intelligenzblatt als Medium praktischer Aufklärung: Ein Beitrag zur Geschichte der gemeinnützig-ökonomischen Presse in Deutschland von 1768 bis 1780." *IASL* 12 (1987): 107–34.

————. "Mündliche und publizistische Formen der politischen Volks-aufklärung." In *Presse und Geschichte II: Neue Beiträge zur historischen Kommunikationsforschung.* Edited by E. Blühm and H. Gebhardt. Munich: K. G. Saur, 1987. 259–85.

————. "Zeitungen für das 'Volk.' Ein Beitrag zur Entstehung periodischer Schriften für einfache Leser und zur Politisierung der deutschen Öffentlichkeit nach der Französichen Revolution." In *Französiche Revolution und deutsche Öffentlichkeit.* Edited by Holger Böning. Munich: K. G. Saur, 1992. 467–526.

Bourdieu, Pierre. *Outline of a Theory of Practice.* Translated by Richard Nice. Cambridge, Eng.: Cambridge University Press, 1977 [1972].

Brandt, Hartwig. *Parlamentarismus in Württemberg, 1819–1870: Anatomie eines deutschen Landtags.* Düsseldorf: Droste, 1987.

————. "Gesellschaft, Parlament und Regierung in Württemberg 1830–1840." In *Gesellschaft, Parlament und Regierung: Zur Geschichte des Parlamentarismus in Deutschland.* Edited by Gerhard A Ritter. Düsseldorf: Droste Verlag, 1974. 101–18.

Breuilly, John. "State-building, Modernization, and Liberalism from the Late Eighteenth Century to Unification: German Peculiarities." *European History Quarterly* 22 (April 1992): 257–84.

Brubaker, Rogers. *Citizenship and Nationhood in France and Germany.* Cambridge, Mass.: Harvard University Press, 1992.

Bruns, Alfred, ed. *Die Amtssprache: Verdeutschung von Fremdwörtern bei Gerichts- und Verwaltungsbehörden in der Bearbeitung von Karl Burns.* Münster: Westfälisches Landesamt für Archivpflege, 1980.

Burchell, Graham, Colin Gordon, and Peter Miller, eds. *The Foucault Effect: Studies in Governmentality.* London: Harvester Wheatsheaf, 1991.

Calhoun, Craig, ed. *Habermas and the Public Sphere.* Cambridge, Mass.: M. I. T. Press, 1992.

Caplan, Jane. "The Imaginary Universality of Particular Interests: The 'Tradition' of the Civil Service in German History." *SH* 4 (1979): 299–317.

Carsten, Francis L. *Princes and Parliaments in Germany from the Fifteenth to the Eighteenth Centuries.* Oxford: Oxford University Press, 1959.

Chartier, Roger. *The Cultural Origins of the French Revolution.* Durham, N. C.: Duke University Press, 1991.

Cherubim, Dieter, Georg Objartel, and Isa Schikorsky. "'Geprägte Form, die lebend sich entwickelt': Beobachtungen zu institutionsbezogenen Texten des 19. Jahrhunderts." *WW* 37, no. 2 (1987): 144–76.

Cohen, Jean L. and Andrew Arato. *Civil Society and Political Theory*. Cambridge, Mass.: M. I. T. Press, 1992.

Conze, Werner, ed.. *Staat und Gesellschaft im deutschen Vormärz 1815–1848*. Stuttgart: Ernst Klett, 1962.

Dann, Otto. "Deutschland unter französischem Einfluß." *AfS* 26 (1986): 416–28.

———, ed. *Vereinswesen und bürgerliche Gesellschaft in Deutschland*. Munich: R. Oldenbourg, 1984.

Dickey, Laurence. *Hegel: Religion, Economics and the Politics of Spirit 1770–1807*. Cambridge, Eng.: Cambridge University Press, 1987.

Dülmen, Richard van. *Die Gesellschaft der Aufklärer: Zur bürgerlichen Emanzipation und aufklärerischen Kultur in Deutschland*. Frankfurt: Fischer Taschenbuch Verlag, 1986.

Ehrenberg, John. *Civil Society: The Critical History of an Idea*. New York: New York University Press, 1999.

Epstein, Klaus. *The Genesis of German Conservatism*. Princeton, N. J.: Princeton University Press, 1966.

Fehrenbach, Elisabeth. "Verfassungs- und sozialpolitische Reformen und Reformprojekte in Deutschland unter dem Einfluss des napoleonischen Frankreichs." *HZ* 228 (1979): 288–316.

Foucault, Michel. *Power/Knowledge: Selected Interviews and Other Writings, 1972–1977*. Translated by Colin Gordon et al. New York: Pantheon, 1980.

———. "Governmentality." In *The Foucault Effect*. Edited by Graham Burchell, Colin Gordon, and Peter Miller. Chicago: University of Chicago Press, 1991 [1979]. 87–104.

Friedeburg, Robert von. "'Reiche,' 'Geringe Leute' und 'Beambte': Landesherrschaft, dörfliche 'Factionen' und gemeindliche Partizipation 1648–1806." *ZHF* 23, no. 2 (1996): 219–65.

Gall, Lothar. *Bürgertum in Deutschland*. Berlin: Siedler, 1989.

———. "Liberalismus und 'bürgerliche Gesellschaft': Zu Charakter und Entwicklung der liberalen Bewegung in Deutschland." *HZ* 220 (1975): 324–56.

Garber, Jörn. *Spätabsolutismus und bürgerliche Gesellschaft: Studien zur deutschen Staats- und Gesellschaftstheorie im Übergang zur Moderne*. Frankfurt: Keip, 1992.

Gehring, Paul. *Friedrich List: Jugend und Reifejahre 1789–1825*. Tübingen: J. C. B. Mohr, 1964.

Gerner, Joachim. *Vorgeschichte und Entstehung der württembergischen Verfassung im Spiegel der Quellen (1815–1819)*. Stuttgart: W. Kohlhammer, 1989.

Gerth, Hans. *Bürgerliche Intelligenz um 1800: Zur Soziologie des deutschen Frühliberalismus*. Göttingen: Vandenhoeck & Ruprecht, 1976 [1935].

Gestrich, Andreas. *Absolutismus und Öffentlichkeit: Politische Kommunikation in Deutschland zu Beginn des 18. Jahrhunderts*. Göttingen: Vandenhoeck & Ruprecht, 1994.

Goody, Jack. *The Logic of Writing and the Organization of Society.* Cambridge, Eng.: Cambridge University Press, 1986.

Grimminger, Rolf, ed. *Hansers Sozialgeschichte der deutschen Literatur vom 16. Jahrhundert bis zur Gegenwart.* Munich, Wien: Carl Hanser, 1980.

Grube, Walter. *Der Stuttgarter Landtag 1457–1957: Von den Landständen zum demokratischen Parlament.* Stuttgart: Ernst Klett, 1957.

———. *Vogteien, Ämter, Landkreise in der Geschichte Südwestdeutschlands.* Stuttgart: W. Kohlhammer, 1960.

———. "Dorfgemeinde und Amtsversammlung in Altwürttemberg." *ZWLG* 13 (1954): 194–219.

——— and Walter Bürkle, eds. *Das Archiv von Stadt und Amt Wildberg.* Stuttgart: W. Kohlhammer, 1952.

Habermas, Jürgen. *Structural Transformation of the Public Sphere: An Inquiry into a Category of Bourgeois Society.* Translated by Thomas McCarthy. Cambridge, Mass.: M. I. T. Press, 1989 [1962].

Hacking, Ian. *The Taming of Chance.* Cambridge, Eng.: Cambridge University Press, 1990.

Hasselhorn, Martin. *Der altwürttembergische Pfarrstand im 18. Jahrhundert.* Stuttgart: W. Kohlhammer, 1958.

Hettling, Manfred. *Reform ohne Revolution: Bürgertum, Bürokratie und kommunale Selbstverwaltung in Württemberg von 1800 bis 1850.* Göttingen: Vandenhoeck & Ruprecht, 1990.

Heyd, Wilhelm, ed. *Bibliographie der württembergischen Geschichte.* Stuttgart: W. Kohlhammer, 1895ff.

Hippel, Wolfgang von. *Die Bauernbefreiung im Königreich Württemberg.* 2 vols. Boppard am Rhein: Harald Boldt, 1977.

Hölzle, Erwin. *Das alte Recht und die Revolution: Eine politische Geschichte Württembergs in der Revolutionszeit 1789–1805.* Munich: R. Oldenbourg, 1931.

———. *Württemberg im Zeitalter Napoleons und der deutschen Erhebung.* Stuttgart: W. Kohlhammer, 1937.

Hull, Isabel. *Sexuality, State, and Civil Society in Germany, 1700–1815.* Ithaca, N. Y.: Cornell University Press, 1996.

Huneke, Friedrich. *Die "Lippischen Intelligenzblätter" (Lemgo 1767–1799): Lektüre und gesellschaftliche Erfahrung.* Bielefeld: Verlag für Regionalgeschichte, 1989.

John, Vincenz. *Geschichte der Statistik: Ein quellenmässiges Handbuch für den akademischen Gebrauch wie für den Selbstunterricht.* Stuttgart: Enke, 1884.

Kaschuba, Wolfgang. "Aufbruch in die Moderne: Volkskultur und Sozialdisziplinierung im napoleonischen Württemberg." In *Volkskultur zwischen feudaler und bürgerlicher Gesellschaft: Zur Geschichte eines Begriffs und seiner gesellschaftlichen Wirklichkeit.* Frankfurt/Main: Campus, 1988. 73–126.

Kaschuba, Wolfgang, and Carola Lipp. *1848—Provinz und Revolution: Kultureller Wandel und soziale Bewegung im Königreich Württemberg.* Tübingen: Tübinger Vereinigung für Volkskunde, 1979.

————. "Revolutionskultur 1848: Einige (volkskundliche) Anmerkungen zu den Erfahrungsräumen und Aktionsformen antifeudaler Volksbewegung in Württemberg." *ZWLG* 39 (1980): 141–65.

————. "Zur Organisation des bürgerlichen Optimismus: Regionale Formierungsprozesse des Bürgertums im Vormärz und in der Revolution 1848." *SOWI* 8 (1979): 74–82.

Keane, John, ed. *Civil Society and the State: New European Perspectives.* London: Verso, 1989.

Kempf, Thomas. *Aufklärung als Disziplinierung: Studien zum Diskurs des Wissens in Intelligenzblättern und gelehrten Beilagen der zweiten Hälfte des 18. Jahrhunderts.* Munich: Iudicium, 1991.

Kienitz, Sabine. *Sexualität, Macht und Moral: Prostitution und Geschlechterbeziehungen Anfang des 19. Jahrhunderts in Württemberg.* Berlin: Akademie-Verlag, 1995.

Klingenstein, Grete. "Akademikerüberschuss als soziales Problem im aufgeklärten Absolutismus." In *Bildung, Politik und Gesellschaft: Studien zur Geschichte des europäischen Bildungswesens vom 16. bis zum 20. Jahrhundert.* Edited by Grete Klingenstein, Heinrich Lutz, and Gerald Stourzh. Munich: R. Oldenbourg, 1978. 165–204.

Knapp, Theodor. *Gesammelte Beiträge zur Rechts- und Wirtschaftsgeschichte vornehmlich des deutschen Bauerntums.* Tübingen: H. Laupp, 1902.

————. *Neue Beiträge zur Rechts- und Wirtschaftsgeschichte des württembergischen Bauernstandes.* Tübingen: H. Laupp, 1919.

Knemeyer, Franz Ludwig. *Regierungs- und Verwaltungsreformen in Deutschland zu Beginn des 19. Jahrhunderts.* Köln: Grote, 1970.

Knudsen, Jonathan. "On Enlightenment for the Common Man." In *What is Enlightenment? Eighteenth-Century Answers and Twentieth-Century Questions.* Edited by James Schmidt. Berkeley: University of California Press, 1996. 270–90.

Koerner, Lisbet. *Linnaeus: Nature and Nation.* Cambridge, Mass.: Harvard University Press, 1999.

Koptizsch, Franklin, ed. *Aufklärung, Absolutismus und Bürgertum in Deutschland.* Munich: Nymphenburger Verlagshandlung, 1976.

Koselleck, Reinhart. *Preußen zwischen Reform und Revolution: Allgemeines Landrecht, Verwaltung und soziale Bewegung von 1791 bis 1848.* Stuttgart: Klett-Cotta, 1967.

Krueger, Rita. "From Empire to Nation: the Aristocracy and the Formation of Modern Society in Bohemia, 1770–1848." Ph.D. diss., Harvard University, 1997.

LaVopa, Anthony J. *Grace, Talent, and Merit: Poor Students, Clerical Careers, and Professional Ideology in Eighteenth-Century Germany.* Cambridge, Eng.: Cambridge University Press, 1988.

Lehmann, Hartmut. *Pietismus und weltliche Ordnung in Württemberg vom 17. bis zum 20. Jahrhundert.* Stuttgart: W. Kohlhammer, 1969.

Liebel, Helen P. "The Bourgeoisie in Southwestern Germany, 1500–1789: A Rising Class?" *IRSH* 10, no. 2 (1965): 283–307.

Linke, Uli. "Folklore, Anthropology, and the Government of Social Life." *CSSH* 32, no. 1 (January 1990): 117–48.

Lipp, Carola. "Verein als politisches Handlungsmuster. Das Beispiel des württembergischen Vereinswesens von 1800 bis zur Revolution 1848–1849." In *Sociabilité et société bourgeoise en Allemagne et en Suisse 1750–1850*. Edited by Etienne François. Paris: Editions Recherche sur les Civilisations, 1986. 275–98.

List, Albrecht. *Der Kampf ums gute alte Recht (1815–1819) nach seiner ideen- und parteigeschichtlichen Seite*. Tübingen: J. C. B. Mohr, 1914.

Lotheissen, Hans. "Der ständisch-korporative Gedanke, namentlich in der württembergischen Verfassungsgeschichte und den publizistischen Schriften Hegels und List's zur württembergischen Verfassungsreform." Phil. diss., Gießen, 1928.

Lüdtke, Alf. *"Gemeinwohl," Polizei, und "Festungspraxis": Staatliche Gewaltsamkeit und innere Verwaltung in Preußen, 1815–1850*. Göttingen: Vandenhoeck & Ruprecht, 1982.

Luebke, David Martin. *His Majesty's Rebels: Communities, Factions, and Rural Revolt in the Black Forest, 1725–1745*. Ithaca, N. Y.: Cornell University Press, 1997.

Maier, Hans. *Die ältere deutsche Staats- und Verwaltungslehre (Polizeiwissenschaft): Ein Beitrag zur Geschichte der politischen Wissenschaft in Deutschland*. Munich: Deutscher Taschenbuch Verlag, 1980 [1966].

Mannheims, Hildegard. *Wie wird ein Inventar erstellt? Rechtskommentare als Quelle der volkskundlichen Forschung*. Münster: F. Coppenrath, 1991.

Medick, Hans. *Weben und Überleben in Laichingen 1650–1900. Lokalgeschichte als Allgemeine Geschichte*. Göttingen: Vandenhoeck & Ruprecht, 1996.

———. "Von der Bürgerherrschaft zur staatsbürgerlichen Gesellschaft. Württemberg zwischen Ancien régime und Vormärz." In *Bürgerliche Gesellschaft in Deutschland: Historische Einblicke, Fragen, Perspektiven*. Edited by Lutz Niethammer. Frankfurt: Fischer Taschenbuch Verlag, 1990. 52–79.

Melton, James van Horn. "The Emergence of 'Society' in 18th and 19th Century Germany." In *Language, History, and Class*. Edited by Penelope J. Corfield. Oxford: Blackwell, 1991. 131–49.

Messick, Brinkley. *The Calligraphic State: Textual Domination and History in a Muslim Society*. Berkeley: University of California Press, 1993.

Morgan, Edmund. *Inventing the People: The Rise of Popular Sovereignty in England and America*. New York: W. W. Norton, 1988.

Narr, Dieter. *Studien zur Spätaufklärung im deutschen Südwesten*. Stuttgart: W. Kohlhammer, 1979.

Oestreich, Gerhard. "Zur Vorgeschichte des Parlamentarismus: Ständische Verfassung, landständische Verfassung, und landschaftliche Verfassung." *ZHF* 6, no. 1 (1979): 63–80.

Petrat, Gerhardt. *Einem besseren Dasein zu Diensten: Die Spur der Aufklärung im Medium Kalender zwischen 1700 und 1919*. Munich: K. G. Saur, 1991.

———. "Das Intelligenzblatt—eine Forschungslücke." In *Presse und Geschichte II: Neue Beiträge zur historischen Kommunikationsforschung.* Edited by E. Blühm and H. Gebhardt. Munich: K. G. Saur, 1987. 207–31.

Pocock, J. G. A. *The Machiavellian Moment: Florentine Political Thought and the Atlantic Republican Tradition.* Princeton, N. J.: Princeton University Press, 1975.

Press, Volker. "Der württembergische Landtag im Zeitalter des Umbruchs 1770–1830." *ZWLG* 42 (1983): 255–81.

———. "Herrschaft, Landschaft und 'Gemeiner Mann' in Oberdeutschland vom 15. bis zum frühen 19. Jahrhundert." *Zeitschrift für Geschichte des Oberrheins* 123 (1975): 169–214.

———. "Landstände des 18. und Parlamente des 19. Jahrhunderts." In *Deutschland zwischen Revolution und Restauration.* Edited by Helmut Berding and Hans-Peter Ullmann. Königstein/Ts.: Athenäum, 1981. 133–57.

Putnam, Robert. *Making Democracy Work: Civic Traditions in Modern Italy.* Princeton, N. J.: Princeton University Press, 1993.

Rassem, Mohammed, and Justin Stagl, eds. *Statistik und Staatsbeschreibung in der Neuzeit.* Paderborn: Ferdinand Schöningh, 1980.

Remppis, Hermann. "Die württembergischen Intelligenzblätter von 1736–1849." Diss., Stuttgart, 1922.

Rieger, Alfred. "Die Entwicklung des württembergischen Kreisverbands." Ph.D. diss., Tübingen, 1952.

Rosenberg, Hans. *Bureaucracy, Aristocracy and Autocracy: The Prussian Experience 1660–1815.* Cambridge, Mass.: Harvard University Press, 1966.

Sabean, David Warren. *Power in the Blood: Popular Culture and Village Discourse in Early Modern Germany.* Cambridge, Eng.: Cambridge University Press, 1984.

———. *Property, Production, and Family in Neckarhausen, 1700–1870.* Cambridge, Eng.: Cambridge University Press, 1990.

———. "Allianzen und Listen: Die Geschlechtsvormundschaft im 18. und 19. Jahrhundert." In *Frauen in der Geschichte des Rechts: Von der frühen Neuzeit bis zur Gegenwart.* Edited by Ute Gerhard. Munich: C. H. Beck, 1997. 460–79.

Scheel, Heinrich. *Süddeutsche Jakobiner: Klassenkämpfe und republikanische Bestrebungen im deutschen Süden Ende des 18. Jahrhunderts.* Berlin: Akademie-Verlag, 1962.

Schöne, W. *Zeitungswesen und Statistik: Eine Untersuchung über den Einfluss der periodischen Presse auf die Entstehung und Entwicklung der staatswissenschaftlichen Literatur, speziell der Statistik.* Jena: Gustav Fischer, 1924.

Schulze, Winfried. *Bäuerlicher Widerstand und feudale Herrschaft in der frühen Neuzeit.* Stuttgart-Bad Cannstatt: Frommann-Holzboog, 1980.

———. "Die veränderte Bedeutung sozialer Konflikte im 16. und 17. Jahrhundert." In *Europäische Bauernrevolten der frühen Neuzeit.* Edited by Winfried Schulze. Frankfurt: Suhrkamp, 1982. 276–308.

———. "Herrschaft und Widerstand in der Sicht des 'gemeinen Mannes' im

16./17. Jahrhundert." In *Vom Elend der Handarbeit: Probleme historischer Unterschichtenforschung.* Edited by Hans Mommsen and Winfried Schulze. Stuttgart: Klett-Cotta, 1981. 182–97.

Scott, James. *Seeing Like a State: How Certain Schemes to Improve the Human Condition Have Failed.* New Haven, Conn.: Yale University Press, 1998.

Siegert, Reinhart. "Zur Topograhie der Aufklärung in Deutschland 1789: Methodische Überlegungen an Hand der zeitgenössischen Presse." In *Französiche Revolution und deutsche Öffentlichkeit.* Edited by Holger Böning. Munich: K. G. Saur, 1992. 47–90.

Somers, Margaret. "Citizenship and the Place of the Public Sphere: Law, Community, and Political Culture in the Transition to Democracy." *ASR* 58 (1993): 587–621.

Theil, Bernhard, Franz Quarthal, and Christel Köhle-Hezinger. "Neue Wege der Landes- und Ortsgeschichte II: Inventuren und Teilungen." Arbeitskreis für Landes- und Ortsgeschichte im Verband der württembergischen Geschichts- und Altertumsvereine, Stuttgart, 11 November 1995.

Trentmann, Frank, ed. *Paradoxes of Civil Society: New Perspectives on Modern German and British History.* New York: Berghahn Books, 1999.

Tribe, Keith. "Cameralism and the Science of Government." *JMH* 56 (June 1984): 263–84.

Troeltsch, Walter. *Die Calwer Zeughandelskompagnie und ihre Arbeiter: Studien zur Gewerbe- und Sozialgeschichte Altwürttembergs.* Jena: G. Fischer, 1897.

Uhland, Robert. *Geschichte der hohen Karlsschule in Stuttgart.* Stuttgart: W. Kohlhammer, 1953.

Unger, Roberto Mangabeira. *Politics: The Central Texts: Theory Against Fate.* London: Verso, 1997.

Vann, James Allen. *The Making of a State: Württemberg 1593–1793.* Ithaca, N. Y.: Cornell University Press, 1984.

Vierhaus, Rudolf. *Deutschland im 18. Jahrhundert. Politische Verfassung, soziales Gefüge, geistige Bewegungen.* Göttingen: Vandenhoeck & Ruprecht, 1987

———. "Liberalismus, Beamtenstand und konstitutionelles System." In *Liberalismus in der Gesellschaft des deutschen Vormärz.* Edited by Wolfgang Schieder. Göttingen: Vandenhoeck & Ruprecht, 1983. 39–54.

———. "Politisches Bewußtsein in Deutschland vor 1789." In *Deutschland zwischen Revolution und Restauration.* Edited by Helmut Berding and Hans-Peter Ullmann. Königstein/Ts.: Athenäum, 1981. 161–83.

———. "Ständewesen und Staatsverwaltung in Deutschland im späteren 18. Jahrhundert." In *Deutschland im 18. Jahrhundert: Politische Verfassung, soziales Gefüge, geistige Bewegungen.* Göttingen: Vandenhoeck & Ruprecht, 1987. 33–49.

Vogel, Barbara. "'Revolution von oben': Der deutsche Weg in die bürgerliche Gesellschaft?" *SOWI* 8 (1979): 67–74.

Vopelius-Holtzendorff, Barbara. "Das Nagolder Cahier und seine Zeit:

Beschwerdeschrift mit Instruktionen für den Abgeordneten zum württembergischen Landtag von 1797." *ZWLG* 37 (1978): 122–78.

Voss, Jürgen. "Der Gemeine Mann und die Volksaufklärung im späten 18. Jahrhundert." In *Vom Elend der Handarbeit: Probleme historischer Unterschichtenforschung.* Edited by Hans Mommsen and Winfried Schulze. Stuttgart: Klett-Cotta, 1981. 208–33.

Walker, Mack. *German Home Towns: Community, State, and General Estate 1648–1871.* Ithaca, N. Y.: Cornell University Press, 1971.

———. *Johann Jakob Moser and the Holy Roman Empire of the German Nation.* Chapel Hill: University of North Carolina Press, 1981.

———. "Rights and Functions: The Social Categories of Eighteenth-Century German Jurists and Cameralists." *JMH* 50 (June 1978): 234–51.

Warner, Michael. *Letters of the Republic: Publication and the Public Sphere in Eighteenth Century America.* Cambridge, Mass.: Harvard University Press, 1990.

Wegert, Karl. "Contention with Civility: The State and Social Control in the German Southwest, 1760–1850." *HJ* 34, no. 2 (1991): 349–69.

Weis, Eberhard. "Kontinuität und Diskontinuität zwischen den Ständen des 18. Jahrhunderts und den frühkonstitutionellen Parlamenten." *Parliaments, Estates, and Representation* 4, no. 1 (1984): 51–65.

Wilson, Peter H. *War, State, and Society in Württemberg, 1677–1793.* Cambridge, Eng.: Cambridge University Press, 1995.

Wintterlin, Friedrich. *Geschichte der Behördenorganisation in Württemberg.* Stuttgart: W. Kohlhammer, 1902.

———. "Beamtentum und Verfassung im Herzogthum Württemberg." *WVLG* NF 32 (1925–26): 1–20.

———. "Die altwürttembergische Verfassung am Ende des 18. Jahrhunderts." *WVLG* NF 23 (1914): 195–210.

———. "Die rechtsgeschichtlichen Grundlagen des Rechtsstaats in Württemberg." *WVLG* 38 (1932): 318–41.

Woolf, Stuart. "Statistics and the Modern State." *CSSH* 31, no. 3 (July 1989): 588–604.

———. "Towards the History of the Origins of Statistics: France, 1789–1815." In *State and Statistics in France, 1789–1815,* edited by Jean-Claude Perrot and Stuart Woolf, 81–194. Chur, Switz.: Harwood Academic Publishers, 1984.

Wunder, Bernd. *Privilegierung und Disziplinierung: Die Entstehung des Berufsbeamtentums in Bayern und Württemberg 1780–1825.* Munich: Oldenbourg, 1978.

———. "Die Landtagswahlen von 1815 und 1819 in Württemberg: Landständische Repräsentation und Interessenvertretung." *WF* 58 (1974): 264–93.

Wunder, Heide. *Die bäuerliche Gemeinde in Deutschland.* Göttingen: Vandenhoeck & Ruprecht, 1986.

Württembergischer Geschichts- und Altertumsverein, ed. *Herzog Karl Eugen von Württemberg und seine Zeit.* Esslingen: Paul Neff (Max Schreiber), 1907–9.

Württembergisches Landesmuseum Stuttgart. *Baden und Württemberg im Zeitalter Napoleons.* 3 vols. Stuttgart: Cantz, 1987.

Index

STUDIES ON THE HISTORY OF SOCIETY AND CULTURE

Victoria E. Bonnell and Lynn Hunt, Editors

Compositor:	BookMatters, Berkeley
Text:	10/13 Aldus
Display:	Aldus
Printer and Binder:	Thomson-Shore, Inc.